Communications
in Computer and Information Science   1088

Commenced Publication in 2007
Founding and Former Series Editors:
Phoebe Chen, Alfredo Cuzzocrea, Xiaoyong Du, Orhun Kara, Ting Liu,
Krishna M. Sivalingam, Dominik Ślęzak, Takashi Washio, and Xiaokang Yang

T0211745

More information about this series at http://www.springer.com/series/7899

Constantine Stephanidis · Margherita Antona (Eds.)

HCI International 2019 – Late Breaking Posters

21st HCI International Conference, HCII 2019
Orlando, FL, USA, July 26–31, 2019
Proceedings

Editors
Constantine Stephanidis
University of Crete
and Foundation for Research
and Technology – Hellas (FORTH)
Heraklion, Crete, Greece

Margherita Antona
Foundation for Research
and Technology – Hellas (FORTH)
Heraklion, Crete, Greece

ISSN 1865-0929 ISSN 1865-0937 (electronic)
Communications in Computer and Information Science
ISBN 978-3-030-30711-0 ISBN 978-3-030-30712-7 (eBook)
https://doi.org/10.1007/978-3-030-30712-7

This Springer imprint is published by the registered company Springer Nature Switzerland AG
The registered company address is: Gewerbestrasse 11, 6330 Cham, Switzerland

Foreword

The 21st International Conference on Human-Computer Interaction, HCI International 2019, was held in Orlando, FL, USA, during July 26–31, 2019. The event incorporated the 18 thematic areas and affiliated conferences listed on the following page.

This year the HCI International (HCII) conference introduced the additional option of "late-breaking work." This applies both for papers and posters with the corresponding volumes of the proceedings published after the conference. A total of 5,029 individuals from academia, research institutes, industry, and governmental agencies from 73 countries submitted contributions, and 1,274 papers and 209 posters were included in the pre-conference proceedings. In addition, 46 papers and 56 posters were included in the post-conference proceedings. These contributions address the latest research and development efforts and highlight the human aspects of design and use of computing systems. The contributions thoroughly cover the entire field of human-computer interaction, addressing major advances in knowledge and effective use of computers in a variety of application areas.

The volumes constituting the full set of the pre-conference and post-conference proceedings are listed in the following pages.

I would like to thank the program board chairs and the members of the program boards of all thematic areas and affiliated conferences for their contribution to the highest scientific quality and the overall success of the HCI International 2019 conference.

This conference would not have been possible without the continuous and unwavering support and advice of the founder, Conference General Chair Emeritus and Conference Scientific Advisor Prof. Gavriel Salvendy. For his outstanding efforts, I would like to express my appreciation to the communications chair and editor of *HCI International News*, Dr. Abbas Moallem.

July 2019   Constantine Stephanidis

HCI International 2019 Thematic Areas and Affiliated Conferences

Thematic areas:

- HCI 2019: Human-Computer Interaction
- HIMI 2019: Human Interface and the Management of Information

Affiliated conferences:

- EPCE 2019: 16th International Conference on Engineering Psychology and Cognitive Ergonomics
- UAHCI 2019: 13th International Conference on Universal Access in Human-Computer Interaction
- VAMR 2019: 11th International Conference on Virtual, Augmented and Mixed Reality
- CCD 2019: 11th International Conference on Cross-Cultural Design
- SCSM 2019: 11th International Conference on Social Computing and Social Media
- AC 2019: 13th International Conference on Augmented Cognition
- DHM 2019: 10th International Conference on Digital Human Modeling and Applications in Health, Safety, Ergonomics and Risk Management
- DUXU 2019: 8th International Conference on Design, User Experience, and Usability
- DAPI 2019: 7th International Conference on Distributed, Ambient and Pervasive Interactions
- HCIBGO 2019: 6th International Conference on HCI in Business, Government and Organizations
- LCT 2019: 6th International Conference on Learning and Collaboration Technologies
- ITAP 2019: 5th International Conference on Human Aspects of IT for the Aged Population
- HCI-CPT 2019: First International Conference on HCI for Cybersecurity, Privacy and Trust
- HCI-Games 2019: First International Conference on HCI in Games
- MobiTAS 2019: First International Conference on HCI in Mobility, Transport, and Automotive Systems
- AIS 2019: First International Conference on Adaptive Instructional Systems

Conference Proceedings Volumes Full List

Pre-conference Proceedings Volumes

1. LNCS 11566, Human-Computer Interaction: Perspectives on Design (Part I), edited by Masaaki Kurosu
2. LNCS 11567, Human-Computer Interaction: Recognition and Interaction Technologies (Part II), edited by Masaaki Kurosu
3. LNCS 11568, Human-Computer Interaction: Design Practice in Contemporary Societies (Part III), edited by Masaaki Kurosu
4. LNCS 11569, Human Interface and the Management of Information: Visual Information and Knowledge Management (Part I), edited by Sakae Yamamoto and Hirohiko Mori
5. LNCS 11570, Human Interface and the Management of Information: Information in Intelligent Systems (Part II), edited by Sakae Yamamoto and Hirohiko Mori
6. LNAI 11571, Engineering Psychology and Cognitive Ergonomics, edited by Don Harris
7. LNCS 11572, Universal Access in Human-Computer Interaction: Theory, Methods and Tools (Part I), edited by Margherita Antona and Constantine Stephanidis
8. LNCS 11573, Universal Access in Human-Computer Interaction: Multimodality and Assistive Environments (Part II), edited by Margherita Antona and Constantine Stephanidis
9. LNCS 11574, Virtual, Augmented and Mixed Reality: Multimodal Interaction (Part I), edited by Jessie Y. C. Chen and Gino Fragomeni
10. LNCS 11575, Virtual, Augmented and Mixed Reality: Applications and Case Studies (Part II), edited by Jessie Y. C. Chen and Gino Fragomeni
11. LNCS 11576, Cross-Cultural Design: Methods, Tools and User Experience (Part I), edited by P. L. Patrick Rau
12. LNCS 11577, Cross-Cultural Design: Culture and Society (Part II), edited by P. L. Patrick Rau
13. LNCS 11578, Social Computing and Social Media: Design, Human Behavior and Analytics (Part I), edited by Gabriele Meiselwitz
14. LNCS 11579, Social Computing and Social Media: Communication and Social Communities (Part II), edited by Gabriele Meiselwitz
15. LNAI 11580, Augmented Cognition, edited by Dylan D. Schmorrow and Cali M. Fidopiastis
16. LNCS 11581, Digital Human Modeling and Applications in Health, Safety, Ergonomics and Risk Management: Human Body and Motion (Part I), edited by Vincent G. Duffy

34. CCIS 1033, HCI International 2019 - Posters (Part II), edited by Constantine Stephanidis
35. CCIS 1034, HCI International 2019 - Posters (Part III), edited by Constantine Stephanidis

Post-conference Proceedings

36. LNCS 11786, HCI International 2019 – Late Breaking Papers, edited by Constantine Stephanidis
37. CCIS 1088, HCI International 2019 – Late Breaking Posters, edited by Constantine Stephanidis and Margherita Antona

http://2019.hci.international/proceedings

HCI International 2019 (HCII 2019)

The full list with the Program Board Chairs and the members of the Program Boards of all thematic areas and affiliated conferences is available online at:

http://www.hci.international/board-members-2019.php

HCI International 2020

The 22nd International Conference on Human-Computer Interaction, HCI International 2020, will be held jointly with the affiliated conferences in Copenhagen, Denmark, at the Bella Center Copenhagen, July 19–24, 2020. It will cover a broad spectrum of themes related to HCI, including theoretical issues, methods, tools, processes, and case studies in HCI design, as well as novel interaction techniques, interfaces, and applications. The proceedings will be published by Springer. More information will be available on the conference website: http://2020.hci.international/.

General Chair
Prof. Constantine Stephanidis
University of Crete and ICS-FORTH
Heraklion, Crete, Greece
E-mail: general_chair@hcii2020.org

http://2020.hci.international/

Contents

Cognitive Issues in HCI

Accessibility and Universal Access

Learning and Games

HCI in Health and Rehabilitation

HCI in Business and Society

Big Data, Machine Learning and Visual Analytics

User Studies

Interaction Design

Design Considerations for Developing
a Mobile Storytelling Game Application

Duck-Ki Ahn[1], Yun-Gyung Cheong[2], and Byung-Chull Bae[1(✉)]

[1] School of Games, Hongik University, Sejong, South Korea
{dkahn927,byuc}@hongik.ac.kr
[2] College of Software, Sungkyunkwan University, Suwon, South Korea
aimecca@skku.edu

Abstract. In this paper we explore design issues in developing a mobile storytelling game application for young children. As a prototype, we have developed a digital story-reading game application based on Aesop's fable titled "The lion and the mouse". The prototype features chapter-divided storytelling sequences, mini games including quizzes and puzzles, player interaction, and voice recording. These features are designed and implemented based on the concept of Lazzaro's four keys to fun.

Keywords: Storytelling game · Mobile application · Four keys to fun

1 Introduction and Backgrounds

Game is different from narrative by nature. While combining narrative structure (such as character development and drama) with game design (e.g., interactivity and player's agency) is challenging and debatable [2], various suggestions and clarifications have been made to represent or explain narrativity in games. For example, Aarseth proposed four common aspects between narrative structure and game design - world, objects, agents, and events [1]. In this paper we explore game design issues in developing a mobile storytelling game application for young children.

Emotion is a key factor both in game design [6] and narrative understanding [4]. Lazzaro [3] suggested the concept of four keys that are related to invoking emotions in playing games: (1) the internal experience key for controlling the player's mental state (e.g., escaping from boredom); (2) the challenge and strategy key for hard fun; (3) the immersion key for easy fun (e.g., exploring game environments); (4) the social experience key for playing with other players. Our proposed game design is mainly based on these four keys to fun.

We developed a prototype digital story-reading game application based on Aesop's fable titled "The lion and the mouse". The prototype features chapter-divided storytelling sequences, mini games including quizzes and puzzles, player interaction, and voice recording, based on the concept of Lazzaro's 4 keys to fun.

© Springer Nature Switzerland AG 2019
C. Stephanidis and M. Antona (Eds.): HCII 2019, CCIS 1088, pp. 3–8, 2019.
https://doi.org/10.1007/978-3-030-30712-7_1

2   Design and Implementation

We consider four design factors in our mobile storytelling game app - narrative sequences, interaction, mini-games (such as quizzes and puzzles), and socialization, which are based on the concept of the 4 keys to fun.

2.1   Chapter-Divided Narrative Sequences for Easy Fun

Curiosity is a crucial emotion in game design. Curious players will keep exploring the game world, eager to see what will happen next. Curiosity is associated with the immersion key and easy fun by providing *ambiguity*, *incompleteness*, and *detail* [3].

For the immersion key, we consider two narrative constraints in game design - local and global. While the former applies locally to a part of narrative, the latter applies to the whole storytelling structure.

First, in this paper, we define a term 'local constraint' as having an effect on the "pace" of the narrative: Using simple heuristics, key scenes that are related to emotions such as suspense are depicted in slow-motion or close-up with more details. Figure 1 shows an example of the image sequences that are rendered in detail with close ups such that the young players can digest the story with easy fun in immersion, maintaining their curiosity and tension about what will happen next.

Next, as a global constraint, we design a chapter-divided storytelling structure to attract the young player's attention through curiosity. This storytelling structure allows the player to comfortably follow the unfolding story, wondering how the story will run in the next chapter. In our prototype app, the only action a first-time player can take while playing a chapter is to pause. If the player chooses to play the chapter again, he or she will be given other control options (such as skipping and fast-forwarding), to the extent that they feel in control of the story progression.

Fig. 1. Examples of narrative sequences with detailed close-ups

The proposed game application consists of 11 chapters in total, as seen in Fig. 2, where the full story is divided into 4 sections mainly based on Preytag's dramatic arc [3] - exposition (Chaps. 1–3), development or rising actions (Chaps. 4–6), climax (Chaps. 7–10), and denouement (Chap. 11). Each chapter is maximum 20 s long with at least two main characters, in order to maintain the tension of narrative. The player, who plays a chapter for the first time, cannot move on to the next chapter unless the reward option is unlocked, which is presented only after completing the current chapter.

Fig. 2. Divided chapters based on Preytag's Pyramid structure

2.2   Interaction Design for Serious Fun

Giving the player a sense of agency without harming the story progression is critical in the design of a storytelling game. Player's sense of agency can be obtained through "compelling interactions" using visual or auditory feedback, which is associated with the internal experience key and serious fun [3].

Limited interactions with audio-visual feedback were included, particularly associated with emotional expressions or behaviors such as being surprised, yawning, crying, etc. The key interactive scenes are drawn differently from the previous chapters to prevent the players from feeling bored with repeated stimuli. Figure 3 shows two examples of visual feedback with sound effects, focusing on emotional interactions.

Fig. 3. Interaction examples with audio-visual feedbacks

2.3   Mini-Games (Quizzes and Puzzles) for Hard Fun

Hard fun refers to a type of fun associated with challenge and strategy [3]. For the players who like challenges, we designed some mini games containing quizzes and puzzles.

In both quizzes and puzzles, the story characters (i.e., the lion and the mouse) play the role of teachers with two opposite types of empathic expressions - happy-for and sad-for [5]. Happy-for expressions are displayed for correct answers with excited voice, animation effects (e.g., fireworks), and appropriately-chosen complimentary remarks (e.g., "Good job!", "Awesome!", "Great work!"); sad-for expressions appear for wrong answers and give encouraging remarks (e.g., Try again!) (See Fig. 4).

Quizzes are currently designed to have two difficulty levels - normal and hard, mostly depending on the player's age. For instance, questions on weather and movement are aimed for children age 5–8; questions associated with animal's behaviors or story conclusion are designed for children more than 8 years old. In addition to the internal reward (such as compliments) for the correct answers, we are also designing external rewards (such as collecting virtual coins and using them for customizing) to further motivate the players.

For the puzzles, players are engaged to drag-and-drop 9 pieces of jig-saw card images to the right window on the screen (See the image sequences below in Fig. 4). Images on the right side are selected to represent key scenes of the corresponding chapter, which are designed to help the player remember important scenes of each chapter.

Fig. 4. Mini-game examples with empathic expressions of a story character (above: quiz example; below: puzzle example)

2.4   Socialization for People Fun

One of the key reasons for playing games is to have social experiences with other players through competition, cooperation, etc., which is associated with people fun [3].

When the players complete all 11 chapters, they are rewarded by being able to unlock the Rec (recording) button on the main page. With this voice-recording feature, players can record their own voices (or the voices of friends or parents) and then play them in the main voice streaming in each chapter. The duration of each dialog is approximately 10 s, and the player can maximize the fun of social experience through cooperation and (possibly) competition (Fig. 5).

Fig. 5. Screenshots of voice-recording feature

3 Conclusion and Future Work

In this paper we introduced our mobile story-reading game app that is designed to incorporate the four types of fun - easy, serious, hard, and social. We implemented chapter-divided narrative sequences, interactions with audio-visual feedback, mini games with quizzes/puzzles, and voice-recording feature for each type of fun.

While our prototype app is mainly aimed at helping young children learn English as a second language, we were not able to consider any pedagogical standards or criteria due to time constraints. We intend to include them in the next version (e.g., design of quiz questionnaire with different levels according to children's cognitive development).

Another further study will adopt gamificaiton for educational purposes to increase the player's motivation. After completing the adoption of gamificaiton, we plan to conduct a pilot study to investigate the effects of gamification elements and player experiences with various age groups.

Acknowledgement. This work was supported by Basic Science Research Program through the National Research Foundation of Korea (NRF) funded by the Ministry of Science and ICT (2017R1A2B4010499). This research was also supported in part by Basic Science Research Program through the National Research Foundation of Korea (NRF) funded by the Ministry of Education (2016R1D1A1B03933002).

References

1. Aarseth, E.: A narrative theory of games. In: Proceedings of the International Conference on the Foundations of Digital Games, FDG 2012, pp. 129–133. ACM, New York (2012). http://doi.acm.org/10.1145/2282338.2282365
2. Jenkins, H.: Game Design as Narrative Architecture. The MIT Press, Cambridge (2004)
3. Lazzaro, N.: Why we play games: four keys to more emotion without story. In: Game Developers Conference, March 2004. http://xeodesign.com/xeodesign_whyweplaygames.pdf
4. Oatley, K.: A taxonomy of the emotions of literary response and a theory of identification in fictional narrative. Poetics **23**(1–2), 53–74 (1995)
5. Ortony, A., Clore, G., Collins, A.: The Cognitive Structure of Emotions. Cambridge University Press, Cambridge (1990)
6. Yannakakis, G.N., Karpouzis, K., Paiva, A., Hudlicka, E.: Emotion in games. In: D'Mello, S., Graesser, A., Schuller, B., Martin, J.-C. (eds.) ACII 2011. LNCS, vol. 6975, pp. 497–497. Springer, Heidelberg (2011). https://doi.org/10.1007/978-3-642-24571-8_62

Co-creation in the Localization of Interactive Systems Designed for Communicating Science to the Public: An Experience Report

Lama Alluwaymi[1(✉)], Lama Alrashed[1], Hailah Alqaffary[1],
Lamia Alabdulkarim[2], Nouf Alaloula[2], Rasha Alruwaili[3],
Amal Alabdulkarim[1], Lamees Alsuhaibani[1], and Areej Al-Wabil[1]

[1] Center for Earth and Space Science, King Abdulaziz City for Science
and Technology (KACST), Riyadh, Saudi Arabia
{lalluwaymi,lrashed,halqaffary,abalabdulkarim,
lalsuhaibani,aalwabil}@kacst.edu.sa
[2] College of Computer and Information Sciences,
Al-Imam Muhammad Ibn Saud Islamic University (IMSIU),
Riyadh, Saudi Arabia
{lmabdulkarim,nmaloula}@imamu.edu.sa
[3] Riyadh, Saudi Arabia

Abstract. This study describes the design iteration in the localization process of Nasa's Eyes on the Earth which was aligned with co-creation. The paper provides insights from an experience report on project-based learning (PBL) conducted in the context of a collegiate course for Human-Computer Interaction (HCI). We will highlight how co-creation and collaborative work on an existing real-world project was aligned with increased levels of students' engagement and markedly improved interaction design in prototypes. The implications of the co-creation and design shift for the education of designers and researchers in HCI will be discussed.

Keywords: Co-creation · Human-computer interaction · Project-based learning

1 Introduction

Recent advances in design research have led to a paradigm shift from a user-centered approach to co-designing with target user populations. These shifts have changed the roles of the designer(s), the researcher(s), and the users in co-creation contexts. The importance of co-creation is to connect with, work with, and enable individuals to generate thoughts and to make ideas cooperatively [1]. In co-creation contexts, designers have been moving progressively closer to the target user populations by engaging with them early in the design process. This is particularly evident in systems design for a diverse group of users such as web platforms designed for communicating science to the public. As a consequence of these changes in the design practice and in the changes in the meaning and value of systems designed for scientific communication for the public, we present an experience report on design methods for the localization of NASA's Eyes on Earth for Arabic-speaking populations.

© Springer Nature Switzerland AG 2019
C. Stephanidis and M. Antona (Eds.): HCII 2019, CCIS 1088, pp. 9–15, 2019.
https://doi.org/10.1007/978-3-030-30712-7_2

The paper provides insights from an experience report on project-based learning (PBL) conducted in the context of a collegiate course for Human-Computer Interaction (HCI) at the College of Computer and Information Sciences (CCIS) in Al-Imam Muhammad Ibn Saud Islamic University (IMSIU). The objectives of the HCI course are to apply HCI principles to practical problems and to develop an understanding of universal design in technical systems. PBL models have been applied in HCI education contexts [2] to improve the students' engagement by increasing the degree of interest in learning HCI principles. The key contributions in this particular experience report are design methods for introducing students to iterative prototyping in an ongoing real-world project in collaboration with researchers in an R&D center [3]. The students were undergraduate students who enrolled in an HCI course. They were divided into groups to complete the HCI project in collaboration with researchers at the Center of Excellence for Earth and Space Science at King Abdulaziz City for Science and Technology (KACST), which aims to create a localized prototype of NASA's Eyes on the Earth. Each student contributed to the success of the HCI project as they complete their tasks.

Due to the lack of sources that emphasize the importance of co-creation and collaboration between the designers and the users in the education field, this study empirically explores and highlights how co-creation and collaborative work on an existing real-world project was aligned with increased levels of students' engagement and markedly improved interaction design in prototypes.

The remainder of this paper is structured as follows. In Sect. 2, we describe the design process and how the co-creation is applied in HCI. Section 3 gives a general description of the methodology. In Sect. 4, we discuss the findings of the study based on the information gathered as a result of the methodology. We conclude in Sect. 5 with a summary of insights.

2   Co-creation in the Design Process

Co-creation is an interaction between two or more entities (i.e. designers, students, users, communities) to jointly integrate their respective resources to produce a mutually valued outcome. As co-creation is originally a concept from business literature, most literature describes the interaction between the organizations and the user. However, in the education context, the interaction could be between the researcher and the student [4, 5].

Through co-creation, the involvement of students, lecturers, and researchers into the design process is a powerful means to guarantee the fulfillment of requirements towards functionality, usability, and other factors. Moreover, students' differing knowledge can jointly interact with the researchers to further create more integrated and preferred outcomes [5].

In this particular case, co-creation has been applied in the design process of the localization of NASA's Eyes on Earth for Arabic-speaking populations. A cohort of students enrolled in an HCI course was tasked with prototyping the mobile and web versions of the platform in collaboration with an R&D center leading the localization effort in the region. Students focused on the need to adapt the designs more and more to the human 'end-user' (e.g. the consumer, student, or teacher) and to the specific context of use or ecology of the localized version of the platform. The student, who has played the role of the designer, has been moving closer to the researcher, who has played the role of the user, throughout the design process. Within this paper, the effects of co-creation approach will be analyzed through the use of survey and focus group methods.

3 Methodology

The HCI course is an elective level course at the Department of Computer Science at IMSIU. It is provided to the students in their senior year after they have several programming and systems design and development courses. The objectives of the HCI course are to apply HCI principles to practical problems and to develop an understanding of universal design in technical systems. The course lectures concentrate on design and theory. Lectures are synchronized with the students' implementation of a real-world project to enhance the classroom learning experience in an introductory HCI course.

A semester-long project was given to the students in the HCI course. The IMSIU lecturers taught the course in two consecutive semesters. Group A and Group B represent the first and the second semesters respectively. In both semesters, the project was a team-based project, each team consisted of 3–4 students. The students applied classroom knowledge in analysis, design, implementation and evaluation on their own projects. Students were required to design and conduct a research investigation about the topic of the project. Project phases were released in four phases, each phase built on the other after receiving feedback from lecturers. The difference between group A and B will be explained below.

Group A worked on the localization of NASA's Eyes on Earth, which is "an interactive computer application that displays the current and future locations of NASA's Earth-observing fleet of satellites and visualizes the data they collect from the Earth in near real-time or from data archives. Thus, it allows users to monitor Earth's vital signs, for example, global surface temperature, sea level, and carbon dioxide concentration. It also allows exploration of the latest Earth events such as sandstorms, wildfires, and hurricanes through geo-located satellite images" [6]. Students were required to develop a localized prototype of NASA's Eyes on the Earth web application or the mobile version 'Earth now'. Moreover, each student had the option of choosing their tools to develop the prototype. The project was as a collaboration between IMSIU and KACST. During the early stages of the project, a workshop was conducted by the researchers at KACST to showcase the wireframes and mockups of the platform, and to help the students in the requirements elicitation process. Moreover, a prize was offered to the winning teams at the end of the course.

On the other hand, group B worked on the Localization of an English website. The project was a typical undergraduate semester-long project. The students were required to develop an Arabic UIs for an English website. Unlike group A, group B project was not in collaboration with an independent entity. Additionally, no monetarily prizes were promised. However, the lecturers explained the project and encouraged the students to do their best, and the project carried the same grade weight as in the previous semester and the same four-phases design process.

3.1 Survey Approach

A survey was distributed at the end of the semester with the intent to solicit students' feelings and attitude towards the course's project. Surveys were distributed and collected electronically via email and anonymity was protected and that was made clear to the students. All surveys were collected after the course's final grades were made available to the students. Hence, no relation with grades can be made which hopefully encourages honest responses. Survey questions were:

1. I was interested in the HCI project more than usual for other courses' projects.
2. I felt enthusiastic about the HCI project more than previous courses' projects.
3. I cared about the results of my HCI project regardless of the grade I get.
4. I felt interested in the results of my HCI project even after the semester ended.
5. I enjoyed being a part of the HCI project.

All questions were required to submit the survey; all were in the form of statements expressing feelings regarding aspects of the project followed by a 5-point scale ranging from 0, representing a strong disagreement with the statement, to 4 representing a strong agreement. The Survey was in Arabic, the mother tongue of all students who took the course.

3.2 Focus Group Approach

This study is also supported by a focus group discussion, which was done by the researchers at KACST on the IMSIU's students. Focus group is a qualitative research method that provides information and an in-depth understanding of feelings that people have about certain topics or concepts. Generally, it consists of 3–9 participants for each group, with a moderator and a moderator assistant. Hughes and DuMont (1993: 776) characterize focus groups as group interviews: "Focus groups are in-depth group interviews employing relatively homogenous groups to provide information around topics specified by the researchers" [7].

During the focus group discussion, researchers adopted the roles of a moderator and an assistant moderator. Each researcher performed a specific role to ensure a smooth progression of the discussion. The moderator is someone who asks questions, takes the lead in the discussion, and creates a comfortable environment for the participants. The assistant moderator role includes observing participants' interactions, taking comprehensive notes and recording the discussion. Seven questions were asked for participants during the focus group discussions:

1. Do you prefer working in a team or individually?
2. Do you prefer working on a fictional project or a real-world project?
3. How familiar are you with King Abdulaziz City for Science and Technology?
4. How did you feel while working on the project?
5. What encouraged you to do this project?
6. What do you think are the pros and cons of this project?
7. How likely would you be to complete the project afterwards?

In this study, the focus group discussion was conducted with two groups. The first group consisted of 3 students from Group A, similarly the second group consisted of 3 students from Group B. Additionally, both discussion groups are homogeneous, the participants share similar characteristics such as gender, age range, and social class background, to permit cross-group comparability. After the focus group discussion, the audiotape was transcripted, and a large amount of data was produced, the data have been chunked into smaller units, and coded by the researcher, these codes are grouped into categories to help the researchers find common themes of the discussion [8].

4   Results and Discussion

4.1   Survey Results

A total of 23 students completed the survey, with 14 respondents from Group A and 9 respondents from Group B. For Group A, a large majority of the students' answers were positive especially in questions 3 and 5 (see Sect. 3.1), almost all of the students strongly agreed with the statements. The responses are indicative of the students' enjoyment in doing the project. The answers of Group B were mostly varied. In question 3, 65% percent of the students strongly agreed with the statement. In contrast, question 4 showed that 55% of the students strongly disagreed with the statement. As a comparison of both groups' answers to question 4, we found that the answers were somewhat contradictory. We believe this is caused by the students' engagement in a "real-world project" versus a "fictional project".

Overall, responses indicated that the majority of students in Group A were more engaged and satisfied with their learning experiences in compared to the students in Group B. Furthermore, the lecturers noted that students' energy in Group A was more vibrant, more attention was given to the project details and definitely more questions were asked. Group A students frequented lecturers' offices more often, asked more questions and showed more interest. Moreover, most of them showed signs of a boost in moral evident in their demeanor in class in general. In contrast, Group B students did not show any abnormalities, they were in comparison more aloof and indifferent toward the project.

4.2   Focus Group Results

The analysis of the focus group discussions revealed four overarching themes, these themes is discussed below:

- **Positivity:** Students in Group A addressed positively the benefits of working in a real-world and team-based project. They were satisfied with the clear project requirements gathered from the researchers. The students used positive words while describing the project such as wonderful, creativity, and innovation. In Group B, students reported positively about the benefits of working in a team-based project. Moreover, they used positive words while describing the project such as impressive.
- **Opportunity:** Students in Group A worked in collaboration with researchers at KACST to improve the interaction design of the localized prototypes. In Group B,

students contributed to the enrichment of Arabic content on the internet through the localization of the English website. Students in both groups gained experience in the designing field which satisfied their current and future interests.

- **Negativity:** Students in Group B preferred to work on a fictional-project rather than working on a real-world project.
- **Challenges:** Students in Group A discussed a range of challenges that impeded their ability to do better such as the need of proper communication with researchers to suggest domain-specific tools, and the tight deadlines for submissions. In Group B, students had no communication with the entity who is responsible for the English website. Also, it was difficult for them to handle tight deadlines for submission.

5   Conclusion

In this study, we presented how co-creation and collaborative work on an existing real-world project was aligned with increased levels of students' engagement and satisfaction with their learning experiences. These approaches have shown a very positive effect on both students and lecturers of the course. The results of the focus groups and the survey adequately validate our hypothesis: a course taught using real-world and co-designed project is as or more educationally effective and enjoyable than a traditional lecture-based course. The findings would benefit HCI educators on how to create an effective collaborative learning environment with a project-based learning approach.

Acknowledgments.   Authors wish to thank the students and lecturers of the Human-Computer Interaction course at IMSIU. This study was supported by a grant awarded to the Center of Excellence for Earth and Space Science at the King Abdulaziz City for Science and Technology (KACST).

References

1. Bertini, P.: Co-Creation: Designing With the User, For the User (2014)
2. El Kamoun, N., Bousmah, M., Aqqal, A.: Virtual environment online for the project-based learning session. Cyber J. Multidiscip. J. Sci. Technol. J. Sel. Areas Softw. Eng. (JSSE) (2011)
3. Alsuhaibani, L., Alabdulkarim, A., Hussey, K., Al-Wabil, A.: UX design in the localization and internationalization of NASA's eyes on the earth. In: Karwowski, W., Ahram, T. (eds.) IHSI 2018. AISC, vol. 722, pp. 402–407. Springer, Cham (2018). https://doi.org/10.1007/978-3-319-73888-8_62
4. Dollinger, M.: Technology for the scalability of co-creation with students. In: ASCILITE 2018: Open Oceans: Learning without Borders, pp. 346–349 (2018)
5. Dollinger, M., Lodge, J., Coates, H.: Co-creation in higher education: towards a conceptual model. J. Mark. High. Educ. **28**(2), 210–231 (2018)
6. Data Visualization Project. http://ce2s2.kacst.edu.sa/projects/data-visualization.html. Accessed 29 Mar 2019

7. Hughes, D., DuMont, K.: Using focus groups to facilitate culturally anchored research. Am. J. Community Psychol. **21**(6), 775–806 (1993)
8. Onwuegbuzie, A.J., Dickinson, W.B., Leech, N.L., Zoran, A.G.: A qualitative framework for collecting and analyzing data in focus group research. Int. J. Qual. Methods **8**, 1–21 (2009)

Themes Validation Tool

Everlandio Fernandes[(✉)], Rodrigo Correia, Adriano Gil, Juliana Postal,
and Mikhail R. Gadelha

Sidia Institute of Science and Technology, Manaus, Brazil
{everlandio.fernandes,rod.correia,a.gil,j.postal,
mikhail.gadelha}@sidia.com
https://www.sidia.org.br/en/home/

Abstract. When themes for smartphones are created, several elements can be customized. They are usually colorful and with artistic drawings in the background. One of the main challenges in creating themes is the validation of the color contrast between the fore- and background elements, so people with visual impairments can perceive the difference between them. Human validation of low visibility issues requires a lot of effort and can generate undesirable bias. Thus, an automated bias-free system is necessary for validation of smartphone themes. In this context, we propose the use of a machine learning technique known as automatic object detection to identify and classify elements with contrast issues. We used a dataset of 1,500 artificially generated Android OS homescreens to train a Faster-RCNN, each screen with at least ten elements (icons) and a balanced distribution between four levels of contrast. Our tool obtained high performance when detecting objects and high accuracy when classifying them.

Keywords: Themes evaluation · Human computer interaction ·
Faster RCNN · Machine learning

1 Introduction

Users tend to customize the interfaces of their computer systems to provide a personal sense of identity, e.g., a wallpaper with their family photo or a soccer team theme. In particular in smartphones, several elements can be customized when designing a new theme such as wallpapers, widgets, icon packs, sounds, etc. Usually they are colorful and with artistic designs in the background. When designers develop a new theme, this should be sent to a theme store to be marketed, where they go through a series of validations.

One of the main challenges during the approval of smartphone themes is the validation of the color contrast between their elements fore- and background. This is required to comply with the "Web Content Accessibility Guidelines" (WCAG) 2.0 recommendations [1], which covers a wide range of suggestions to make Web content more accessible. In particular, item 1.4.3 of the WCAG 2.0 defines the recommended contrast ratio between elements, so that it can be perceived by people with moderately low vision impairments.

© Springer Nature Switzerland AG 2019
C. Stephanidis and M. Antona (Eds.): HCII 2019, CCIS 1088, pp. 16–22, 2019.
https://doi.org/10.1007/978-3-030-30712-7_3

Human validation of low visibility issues requires huge efforts since hundreds of operating system screens need to be validated. Furthermore, an unwanted human bias on what is low contrast will be introduced in the validation. In this context, the benefit of an automated validation system for smartphone themes is twofold: it reduces the number of designers submitting faulty themes and helps the store validator not approve a theme that has a contrast problem.

To solve this problem, we propose the use of a machine learning technique known as automatic object detection. It handles the task of detecting instances of semantic objects in digital images and videos. The automatic detection of objects in images has improved drastically in recent years with the advent of deep learning techniques. One of the most popular object-detection algorithms is Faster-RCNN, which is the basis for many derived networks. Due to its high precision, speed and simplicity, we have selected this architecture to develop our automatic theme validation tool.

We trained our tool using an artificial data set of 1,500 screenshots of the Android OS home screen. The home screens contain at least ten objects (icons) and a balanced distribution between 4 (four) levels of contrast concerning the background: very low, low, regular, and high. Our tool achieved high performance, detecting objects, and high accuracy when classifying them, reaching a mean Average Precision (mAp) of 79,91%.

2   Faster RCNN

Object detection, one of the most fundamental and challenging problems of computer vision, seeks to locate object instances from a large number of predefined categories in natural images; given an image or a frame of a video, the automatic object detection aims to obtain:

- a list of bounding boxes.
- a label assigned to each bounding box.
- a probability for each label and bounding box.

Faster RCNN [2] is an architecture for object detection in images originally presented in Twenty-ninth Conference on Neural Information Processing Systems - NIPS 2015. It is one of the most popular object detection architectures using Convolutional Neural Networks (CNN) [3] to extract features from images and videos.

The neurons of the convolutional layers function as the filters of the classic image processing, i.e., an array of values representing a particular pattern that must be searched in the image. The filter traverses the entire image searching its pattern; the filter is fired when the pattern is detected. Activating all the filters on a layer produces the activation map, also known as a feature map [4].

The feature map of one layer serves as input to the next layer, increasing the level of abstraction of the patterns sought. Usually, they begin with edge patterns in the first layer, followed by more complex patterns in deeper layers,

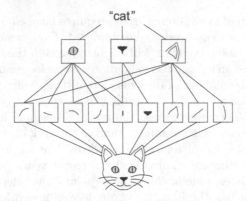

Fig. 1. Edges combine into local objects such as eyes or ears, which combine into high-level concepts such as "cat". Image reproduced from [5]

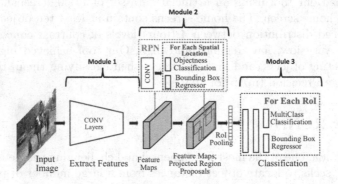

Fig. 2. Faster RCNN. Image reproduced from [6]

e.g., a cat's eye is identified in the intermediate layers while the cat's face is identified in a deeper layer, as shown in Fig. 1, reproduced from [5].

The architecture of the Faster RCNN, as shown in Fig. 2, consists of three modules. The input images are represented as tensors height × width × channels (multidimensional arrays), which are passed by a CNN to produce feature maps. These feature maps are consumed by a Region Proposal Network (RPN) [2]. RPN uses the feature maps to find a predefined number of regions which are highly likely to contain objects. Finally, the classification module uses the features extracted by the CNN, and the bounding boxes with relevant objects produced by the RPN to classify the image, and to predict the offset values for the bounding boxes.

3   Related Work

Nguyen et al. [7] propose a method to infer UI elements hierarchy in screenshots of mobile application screens and to generate working computer code. Authors use border detection techniques like Canny Edges [8] and Edges Dilatation to identify elements of interest in the given screenshots, find their contours, compute their bounding boxes, and use heuristics to estimate which UI component are each one based on its features. Mozgovoy et al. [9] address the challenge of hand-drawn user interface elements detection to improve GUI tests automation, and use mobile games as case of study. The experiments consisted of using several image pattern matching algorithms to compare their precision in recognizing elements of interest, and to suggest which algorithm should be used to analyse a given game screen with its particular features. Chen et al. [10] present a method that generates a GUI skeleton code from UI design images. Differently from [7], however, neural networks are used identify the visual elements in the UI images. The authors use Convolutional Neural Networks (CNN) [3] to learn features from images and a Recurrent Neural Network (RCNN) [11] to infer spatial layouts, which are used to produce GUI skeleton code. Similar to these works, our tool is aimed to find visual elements in a screenshot, but we are mainly interested in classify the elements' contrast ratio. Similar to Chen et al. [10], we use a neural network to identify and classify the elements but we are using the Faster RCNN instead.

4   Experiments

In this section, we describe the methodology used to build and train our tool. First, we describe how the dataset of Android OS Home screens was generated in Sect. 4.1, followed by the description of the parameters and configurations used by the Faster RCNN in Sect. 4.2.

4.1   Dataset

In order to have a very diversified dataset of Android OS home screen, we decided on artificially generation of images instead of an extensive and laborious manual screenshot gathering. Each synthetic image simulates a screenshot from Home Screens of Android OS. We picked a resolution of 1440×2960, which is used in last flagship smartphones, Samsung S9.

We are targetting only Home screens because of the high variance of its user interface (UI) elements, i.e, its background image, icons, labels exhibit a higher intraclass difference.

Our synthetic-based dataset generation algorithm generates a screenshot from a set of overlayed images: the full-screen wallpaper, the applications icons, and the application labels. This implementation is written in python and makes use of OpenCV [12] to read and blend the set of overlayed images. Furthermore, we induce 4-level contrast errors by hue shifting icon images to white colors, and ensuring that their luminance channel are proportional to background luminance. A greater proportional difference means a high contrast while a low difference means low contrast. Figure 3 shows an example of a generated home screen.

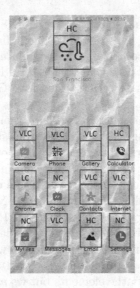

Fig. 3. Example of a synthetic home screen with icons at different levels of contrast and their labels as classified by our tool. Tags: Very Low Contrast (VLC), Low Contrast (LC), Normal Contrast (NC), and High Contrast (HC).

4.2   Faster RCNN

We used the configuration of the Faster RCNN[1] as suggest by the authors in the paper where it was first presented [2], except for the neural network that generates the feature maps: where the authors use a pre-trained VGG16 [13], we use a ResNet [14] trained from scratch for our problem.

Currently, ResNet architectures have replaced VGG as primary networks to extract features in many situations. The main advantages of ResNet over VGG is that it facilitates the training of deep models with the use of residual connections and batch normalization features not presented in the VGG architecture. Furthermore, ResNet is larger then VGG, so it has more ability to learn what is needed.

For the training, we defined the quantity of 100 epochs, each with 100 cycles. The training took place on a GeForce GTX 1080 GPU installed on a desktop device running Windows 10 Enterprise 64-bit, and had training time of approximately 26 h.

5   Results

As previously stated, we used the 1500 artificially generated screen shots to train our theme validation tool. We create the images with a balanced number of icons

---

[1] Keras implementation of Faster R-CNN. Available on https://github.com/yhenon/keras-frcnn/.

in 4 levels of contrast and with their respective markings (bounding boxes). The training was performed with 100 epochs, each with 100 cycles. After the training, we generated a new dataset of 300 screen shots to perform the tool tests. The images were generated with the same characteristics of the training images, in number of objects and contrast levels.

As evaluation metric, we have used mean Average Precision (mAP) [15]. This metric performs an acceptable balance between the errors of the detected bounding boxes and the classification of the object present in each bounding box. Then it is widely used in works related to object detection in images.

Our tool achieved a mAP of 79.91% in the test set. The Average Precision for very low contrast icons was 81.14%, 71.00% for low contrast icons, 73.62% for normal contrast and 93.87% for high contrast icons. This result indicates that our tool has high performance for identifying and classifying objects from low to high contrast.

6 Conclusion and Future Works

In this paper, we presented our tool for validation of smartphone themes based on a machine learning technique known as object detection. This tool was used to validate the visual problems of contrast between elements of new themes. Our tool uses Faster RCNN method to locate icons in screenshots of the Android OS Home screen, and classifies them into one of the four (4) pre-defined contrast level categories (very low, low, regular, and high). We plan to extend our tool so that it also identifies contrast problems in texts and videos that are part of customization on themes for smartphones.

References

1. Web content accessibility guidelines (WCAG) 2.0. web, December 2008
2. Ren, S., He, K., Girshick, R.B., Sun, J.: Faster R-CNN: towards real-time object detection with region proposal networks. In: NIPS, pp. 91–99 (2015)
3. Krizhevsky, A., Sutskever, I., Hinton, G.E.: Imagenet classification with deep convolutional neural networks. In Pereira, F., Burges, C.J.C., Bottou, L., Weinberger, K.Q. (eds.) Advances in Neural Information Processing Systems 25, pp. 1097–1105. Curran Associates, Inc. (2012)
4. Mueller, J.P., Massaron, L.: Machine Learning for Dummies, 1st edn. For Dummies (2016)
5. Chollet, F.: Deep Learning with Python, 1st edn. Manning Publications Co., Greenwich (2017)
6. Liu, L., et al.: Deep learning for generic object detection: a survey. CoRR abs/1809.02165 (2018)
7. Nguyen, T.A., Csallner, C.: Reverse engineering mobile application user interfaces with REMAUI (T). In: 2015 30th IEEE/ACM International Conference on Automated Software Engineering (ASE), pp. 248–259. IEEE (2015)
8. Canny, J.F.: Finding edges and lines in images. Technical report, Massachusetts Inst of Tech Cambridge Artificial Intelligence Lab (1983)

9. Mozgovoy, M., Pyshkin, E.: Using image recognition for testing hand-drawn graphic user interfaces. In: 11th International Conference on Mobile Ubiquitous Computing, Systems, Services and Technologies (UBICOMM 2017) (2017)
10. Chen, C., Su, T., Meng, G., Xing, Z., Liu, Y.: From UI design image to GUI skeleton: a neural machine translator to bootstrap mobile GUI implementation. In: Proceedings of the 40th International Conference on Software Engineering, pp. 665–676. ACM (2018)
11. Liang, M., Hu, X.: Recurrent convolutional neural network for object recognition. In: The IEEE Conference on Computer Vision and Pattern Recognition (CVPR), June 2015
12. Bradski, G.: The OpenCV library. Dr. Dobb's J. Softw. Tools **25**, 120–125 (2000)
13. Simonyan, K., Zisserman, A.: Very deep convolutional networks for large-scale image recognition. In: International Conference on Learning Representations (2015)
14. He, K., Zhang, X., Ren, S., Sun, J.: Deep residual learning for image recognition. In: 2016 IEEE Conference on Computer Vision and Pattern Recognition (CVPR), pp. 770–778 (2016)
15. Liu, L., Özsu, M.T. (eds.): Mean Average Precision, pp. 1703–1703. Springer, Boston (2009). https://doi.org/10.1007/978-0-387-39940-9

Designing a Bulletin Board-Type Art Game for the Collection and Resolution of Conflict

Hyun-Jee Kim and Byung-Chull Bae[✉]

School of Games, Hongik University, 2639 Sejong-ro, Sejong, South Korea
{luluhyunjee,byuc}@hongik.ac.kr

Abstract. In this paper, we present a new type of bulletin board game designed for the collection and resolution of various types of conflict or personal concerns that can occur in organizations or groups. Particularly, we focus on visualization of conflicts that students may encounter in schools. In the proposed bulletin board game, individual problems and suggested solutions form a set of clusters consisting of cards with images and texts. We exemplify three aspects that the players can choose when attaching a card for clustering - shape, color, and typeface. We envisage that our game design can promote players' interactions, and contribute to inducing positive aspects of games, as well as visualizing the players' problems through design.

Keywords: Bulletin board game · Conflict · Gestalt psychology

1 Introduction

Conflict is social by nature and it is everywhere in our everyday lives. Conflict, as a social phenomenon, can be broadly defined as "a process which begins when one party perceives that another has frustrated, or is about to frustrate, some concern of his" [9]. In general, conflict and attempts to its resolution entail both a negative side (e.g., stress and negative affect) and a positive side (e.g., mental health and social adjustment) [5].

In this paper, we present a new type of bulletin board game designed for the collection and resolution of various types of conflict or personal concerns that can occur in organizations or groups. Particularly, we focus on visualization of conflicts that students may face in schools.

The main contribution of this paper is threefold. First, we suggest an outline of a 2D interactive game platform to provide a virtual or online space where multiple users can share their concerns or conflict situations through iconic image cards. Second, we provide an approach to visualize the collected conflicts and (attempts to their) resolutions, particularly based on Gestalt theory by arranging the bulletin board in a symmetrical balance. Finally, we provide a platform where all the game participants can present both problems that they may have and

© Springer Nature Switzerland AG 2019
C. Stephanidis and M. Antona (Eds.): HCII 2019, CCIS 1088, pp. 23–29, 2019.
https://doi.org/10.1007/978-3-030-30712-7_4

solutions for any problem that others have posted, such that participants can empathize with each other, finding ways to view their lives and their problems from a different or more positive perspective.

2   Related Work and Background

2.1   Conflict Resolution in Games and Narrative

Serious games refer to "any piece of software that merges a non-entertaining purpose (serious) with a video game structure (game)", which cover a wide range of domains including education, sciences, military, politics, etc. [3]. In terms of conflict, a number of serious games and studies have been proposed. For example, Fearnot! [1] deals with bullying, a type of conflict that can occur in elementary schools, with a purpose of evoking the player's empathy towards the victims. Another video game Quandary[1] focuses on decision making, especially in ethically conflicted situations. Village Voices [2] also teaches how to handle conflicts by playing a collaborative video game, targeting young children age 9–12.

Conflict is also a key factor in narrative, as building-up and maintaining tension is important for a reader to continue reading the whole story. Here, tension can be either inter-personal (e.g., a conflict between protagonist and antagonist) or intra-personal (e.g., a protagonist's inner conflicts). In Façade [7], the player continuously encounters high tension situations related with conflicts of two non-player characters. Ware and his colleagues also employed the concept of conflict for narrative generation using narrative planning techniques [11].

2.2   Gestalt Psychology

Gestalt psychology states that "a whole is not simply the sum of its parts, but a synergistic whole effect" and embraces various domains and disciplines including art and design [8]. In our proposed bulletin board game, we focus on visual perception according to the principles of Gestalt psychology; the players of the bulletin board game may not be aware of the whole but will recognize it at the end of the game.

We design a bulletin board game by selecting and integrating several laws of Gestalt psychology: proximity, similarity, closure, continuity, and past experience principle [10]. To represent conflicts that can possibly occur in a specific social relationship at school (e.g., between students and faculties/staffs, among students themselves), we create iconic image cards with different shapes, colors, and typefaces that are parts of a whole as Gestalt. At first, the bulletin board may appear rather chaotic with the different icons attached. But at the end of the game, the cards are classified by the law of grouping (See Figs. 3 and 4).

---

[1] https://www.quandarygame.org/.

3 Design Procedure and Exemplification

3.1 Design Procedure

Our study includes a three-phase development pipeline. The first phase is a conflict-collection stage where real conflict cases that students experience are collected and categorized into several clusters under common topics (e.g., grades, relationship, etc.).

In the second phase, based on the categorized clusters, we design a 2D bulletin board game with a number of iconic image cards using different shapes, symbols, and typefaces.

Finally, players can decorate the bulletin boards by choosing appropriate image cards. Players can pick a triangle image card with a certain conflict situation written on it. If they cannot find a particular conflict among the pre-designed triangle card, they can write down their concerns or conflicts in text. The players' texts are automatically attached to the bulletin board as a new triangle image card. Other players can provide possible solutions to a particular conflict. The possible solutions are presented in round image cards. Like the players who posted their conflicts, the other players can select pre-defined round image cards with possible solutions to a problem or present their own solutions using square post-its. (See Fig. 1).

Fig. 1. Exemplified visualization of conflicts and resolution in the proposed bulletin board-type game.

3.2   Exemplification

In the proposed bulletin board game, players can communicate concurrently with each other in real time. Individual problems, posted by the crowd of players, form a set of clusters consisting of cards with iconic images representing different problems. We present three aspects for the cards that the players can choose when clustering - shape, color, and typeface.

We first focus on *geometrical shape*, such as triangle and circle that are emphasized in the Bauhaus [4]. Each shape can represent a player's emotional state (e.g., triangular shape for conflict, round shape for resolution).

As the second facet, we define *color* as a subjective factor as was the case with the use of color by Claude Monet. At this stage, colors chosen by the players may have different meanings depending on the ethnic cultures of the players.

Lastly, players can choose different *typefaces* to best describe their conflicts. In our design, the typefaces used are calligraphy and graffiti style. We posit that graffiti font (e.g., bubble font, old and new school style) and calligraphy typefaces(e.g., italic font, script style) can give different impressions - either friendly or aggressive. The two typefaces can also symbolize the young generation's ideals of freedom and peace, with their informal, emotional appeal and be representative of the times. Figure 2 shows some exemplifications of ideas and methods for visualization.

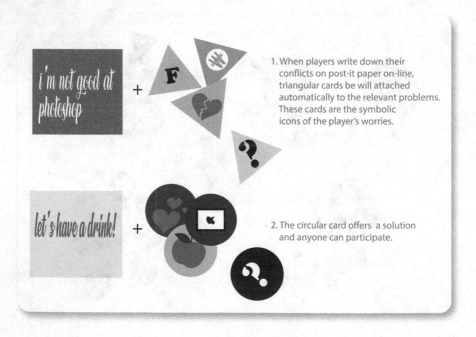

1. When players write down their conflicts on post-it paper on-line, triangular cards be will attached automatically to the relevant problems. These cards are the symbolic icons of the player's worries.

2. The circular card offers a solution and anyone can participate.

Fig. 2. Visualization idea using square post-its and iconic images with different shapes (triangle-shaped cards for conflicts or concerns; round-shaped cards for possible solutions).

At the end of the game, the players who posted their conflicts can identify all the solution cards that are attached to the posted conflicts. They can accept or reject the provided solutions. Currently we designed two solution signs using the well-known peace symbol and a Möbius strip as an infinity symbol. No matter what the problem is, if the player's problem is solved, it will show the peace symbol (Fig. 3). For the players who have not resolved their problems, they will have all their cards arranged in the shape of a Möbius strip in achromatic colors (Fig. 4). It symbolizes that the players will eventually come back to the game to resolve his or her conflict and try to escape the endless Möbius strip.

Fig. 3. An exemplified visualization of collected image cards on the bulletin board game based on Gestalt psychology.

3.3   Discussion

It might be questionable whether the proposed bulletin board game can be called a *game*, as there are no explicitly specified goals or competitions for winning in this game. We expect, however, the players' emotional states can be altered by playing this game from negative (e.g., discomfort or anxiety, anger, etc.) to positive (e.g., comfort or relaxation, cheerfulness, etc). In this regard, we consider our game as a kind of art game with '*serious fun*' or '*altered states*' [6].

The main purpose of our game is to promote voluntary participation of the players as a hidden helper. Our game is a healing game, and thus does not have any form of attack or defense in it. In this game, any player can be an unknown helper and encourage other participants to solve the presented problems together. The players acting as hidden helpers can receive an intrinsic reward through this process.

The game prototype is currently under development through Unity[2] game engine with two different versions - one with Android platform for smartphone and tablet devices; the other with Web-based platform for any Web browser.

Fig. 4. An exemplified visualization of collected image cards at the final stage without any solutions.

4   Conclusion and Future Work

In this paper we proposed a bulletin board-type board game where the players (e.g., students) can communicate with each other by attaching either predesigned cards or writing down their concerns on post-its.

We envisage that our game design can promote players' interactions, and contribute to inducing positive aspects of games, as well as visualizing the players' problems through design. As a follow up, we plan to conduct a pilot study focusing on the investigation of the relations between game design and the possible alteration of the player's emotional state.

---

[2] https://unity.com/.

Acknowledgement. This work was supported by Basic Science Research Program through the National Research Foundation of Korea (NRF) funded by the Ministry of Science and ICT (2017R1A2B4010499).

References

1. Aylett, R.S., Louchart, S., Dias, J., Paiva, A., Vala, M.: FearNot! – an experiment in emergent narrative. In: Panayiotopoulos, T., Gratch, J., Aylett, R., Ballin, D., Olivier, P., Rist, T. (eds.) IVA 2005. LNCS (LNAI), vol. 3661, pp. 305–316. Springer, Heidelberg (2005). https://doi.org/10.1007/11550617_26
2. Cheong, Y.-G., Khaled, R., Holmgård, C., Yannakakis, G.N.: Serious games for teaching conflict resolution: modeling conflict dynamics. In: D'Errico, F., Poggi, I., Vinciarelli, A., Vincze, L. (eds.) Conflict and Multimodal Communication. CSS, pp. 449–475. Springer, Cham (2015). https://doi.org/10.1007/978-3-319-14081-0_21
3. Djaouti, D., Alvarez, J., Jessel, J.P.: Classifying serious games: the G/P/S model. In: Felicia, P. (ed.) Handbook of Research on Improving Learning and Motivation through Educational Games, chap. 6, pp. 118–136. IGI Global
4. Dreksler, N., Spence, C.: A critical analysis of colour–shape correspondences: examining the replicability of colour–shape associations. i-Perception **10**(2) (2019). https://doi.org/10.1177/2041669519834042
5. Laursen, B., Hafen, C.: Future directions in the study of close relationships: conflict is bad (except when it's not). Soc. Dev. **19**, 858–872 (2010)
6. Lazzaro, N.: Why we play games: four keys to more emotion without story. In: Game Developers Conference, March 2004
7. Mateas, M., Stern, A.: Façade: an experiment in building a fully-realized interactive drama, April 2003
8. Behrens, R.R.: Art, design and gestalt theory. Leonardo **31**(4), 299–303 (1998)
9. Thomas, K.W.: Conflict and conflict management: reflections and update. J. Organ. Behav. **13**(3), 265–274 (1992)
10. Todorovic, D.: Gestalt principles. Scholarpedia **3**(12), 5345 (2008). Revision #91314
11. Ware, S.G., Young, R.M., Harrison, B., Roberts, D.L.: A computational model of plan-based narrative conflict at the fabula level. IEEE Trans. Comput. Intell. AI Games **6**(3), 271–288 (2014)

Babel VR: Multimodal Virtual Reality Environment for Shelf Browsing and Book Discovery

Jonatan Lemos$^{(\boxtimes)}$ and Ed Finn

Arizona State University, Tempe, AZ 85281, USA
{jlemoszu, edfinn}@asu.edu

Abstract. This paper presents the results of the development of a system called Babel VR, part of a work-in-progress research project aimed at obtaining insights into how a multimodal virtual reality environment can enhance shelf browsing and the discovery of books that exist in a physical library. Babel VR provides a virtual browsing experience of library items which display bibliographic attributes such as title, author, topic and location in a library, aided by the use of voice commands. The representation of physical library shelves enables the possibility of having some affordances of physical browsing within a virtual environment, while at the same time providing readers with a browsing experience enhanced by multimodal features such as the use of voice commands for searching and browsing.

Keywords: Multimodal environment · Virtual reality library · Book discovery

1 Introduction

When readers visit libraries to browse through bookshelves, they are exposed to a physical experience which enables the possibility of finding items by way of serendipitous encounters [33]. Studies have found that more than half of library visitors when browsing shelves find items that are around the items they are searching for [25], exposing them to the discovery of new materials. However, physical libraries face situations where sometimes their collections cannot be browsed physically [3], making it necessary to consider novel ways to keep providing support for such experiences of browsing and discovery.

One of the main features of physical library stacks is that they have a clearly defined sorting order. Commonly, materials are found sorted by thematic areas, which makes it easy for readers to discover similar items, but in most occasions, it is the only way in which these items are arranged. This is in contrast to digital libraries, which have advantages such as giving readers the possibility of rearranging collections based on their interests [19]. By having items in a digital space, library stacks could be rearranged by bibliographic attributes, without losing some physical features that the browsing experience affords, such as providing spatially mediated and contextualized access to the neighbors of a particular book.

© Springer Nature Switzerland AG 2019
C. Stephanidis and M. Antona (Eds.): HCII 2019, CCIS 1088, pp. 30–38, 2019.
https://doi.org/10.1007/978-3-030-30712-7_5

The advent of virtual reality (VR) technology has made possible the implementation of virtual spaces for a myriad of applications, among these book access in libraries [16]. Given that VR brings the possibility of allowing its users to experience environments that cannot be easily recreated in the physical world, this project sets out to explore the implications of browsing and searching in library shelves using multimodal features within a virtual environment. Since browsing through library bookshelves already involves navigating through physical as well as informational space, and can be a somewhat confusing activity, some design guidelines to support book encounters while browsing digital shelves have been proposed [35] and taken into consideration for this project.

Given that the affordances of different input modalities within virtual environments have been previously analyzed [27], and that recently speech has been identified as an effective mechanism for searching within virtual environments [4], voice commands were implemented to enhance the browsing and searching experience within the environment. This project also draws design cues from the understanding of the behavior of readers when they browse physical shelves [26], and attempts to apply them in a virtual reality context.

2   Related Work

Several approaches to the digital representation of library collections have recently been implemented. Among them are Stacklife [17], which is a representation of an infinite stack of books from the Harvard Library collection, and Virtual Bookshelf from ExLibris [14], used to present library items based on their physical shelf representations. In the past, other digital visualization tools such as libViewer [30] have been used to display different book metadata attributes in virtual environments. The Search Wall [13] is also an approach aimed at kids that uses tangible elements to interact with digital items on a projected screen. Other projects aimed at encouraging book discovery are Bookfish [29], which is a web application that lets children find books based on their preferences, and Whichbook [28], which lets readers choose between several combinations of categories to discover books that fit their choices.

One of the most similar approaches to this project is the Blended Shelf [23], which is an interface that uses 3D visualization to enable readers to browse a physical collection of books from a library, using the browsing strategies they are already familiar with. This proposal differentiates itself from such projects because it is a fully immersive environment in which readers use different interaction mechanisms, VR controllers and voice commands, to perform queries. Another similar approach is the Digital Bookshelf [2] which makes use of projections and motion sensors to display book collections allowing the readers to browse through them. Other approaches have used desktop and mobile applications to visualize physical shelve contents [21], but miss the multimodal interaction possibilities that a virtual space affords.

The use of immersive environments for libraries has also been widely explored. In one of the earliest studies, Das Neves and Fox [11] evaluated the behavior of users while searching in a VR library and found that clustering techniques helped in the discovery of items within collection topics, and that presenting books in the original physical order from the library is as effective as presenting them reorganized based on queries; however, in the latter case there is less reader movement when browsing, making the task shorter. The metaphors in a three-dimensional space that can be used to arrange books on virtual spaces have also been explored [9], along with the ways in which book browsing and reading are carried out within a virtual environment [10]. Three-dimensional virtual spaces have also been used to display library document data on collaborative interfaces [7], as well as to present digital book collections using immersive hemispherical displays [1]. Also game-like approaches have been used to present library data in three-dimensional settings [8].

The use of voice commands in virtual environments has also been explored, along with the design issues for the integration of speech processing in virtual environments [24]. The voice interaction modality has been previously used to support simulations of the design and maintenance of systems and assemblies in virtual reality [36], and recent approaches have also used speech recognition to aid in maintenance tasks in what are called virtual maintenance simulations, resulting in smoother interactions with the system they are implemented in [18]. The use of voice commands has also been useful for interacting in virtual environments and facilitating room layout tasks [22]. The latter study pointed out that some of the limitations of voice interaction have to do with the fact that users have to be instructed in the commands that are needed to interact with the system beforehand, possibly generating a high cognitive load.

Although there have been few approaches that use immersive virtual environments for library data exploration [1, 8, 11], most do not use enhanced interfaces for browsing. Given that the use of voice interfaces in virtual environments has not been applied for data browsing and searching, this project seeks to investigate how virtual shelf exploration and book discovery in virtual reality can both be enhanced by the implementation of voice commands within a virtual environment.

3   Babel VR

In the Library of Babel short story [6], Argentinian writer Jorge Luis Borges presented a library setting that was made of a labyrinth of hexagonal rooms that librarians traversed endlessly. This fictional library was meant to contain all of the books that had been or will ever be written. The metaphor is powerful today because in the digital age access to materials appears to be unbounded. Thus the design of this project is based on the concept of library shelves that can be browsed in the same endless manner, and becomes a design fiction exercise inspired by Borges' infinite library. Here we attempt to create a virtual space where readers can access a seemingly endless catalog of books within the comforting finitude of a single room filled with shelves.

One of the goals of Babel VR is to recreate the experience of shelf exploration in a virtual space and find out what it means to browse and search within an environment, in this case through a representation of a library room. According to Bates, browsing implies exploring a visual field, selecting an object from the field, examining it, and acquiring or abandoning it [5]. Thus when readers enter the Babel VR room to initiate the browsing and discovery experience, they encounter virtual stacks which are populated with MAchine-Readable Cataloging (MARC) records from an actual physical library. To enhance the shelf browsing and search experience voice recognition features have been implemented into the system. In the room, readers can also load portions of the catalog onto the shelves and search the stacks by bibliographic attributes such as title, author, topic and location, using voice commands.

3.1   VR Interaction Design

The interaction design cues for Babel VR build on McKay et al's analysis of the physical act of browsing library shelves [26], using five of the seven guidelines they proposed to design the system as follows:

- **Display a large range of books for browsing:** currently the system displays portions of 300 books distributed in 6 shelves from a 10,000 book record sample, which can be traversed with the help of voice commands.
- **Enable multiple points of access to the collection:** this feature is reflected mainly in the search functionality where books appear shelved together after a keyword search has been performed, as well as the ability to "pick up" titles using VR controllers.
- **Support zooming capability:** as the main setup of the environment is a library aisle, readers can walk freely through the room and move close or away from the shelves.
- **Seamless transitions:** readers can freely grab books from the shelves to display their records, and they can put the virtual books back on the shelves.
- **Access to book information:** data from the MARC records of the books that are selected is displayed in one of the walls of the virtual environment. This data contains fields such as title, author, topic and location in the physical library.

The two design recommendations that were not considered were the use of place marking, given that there are search features, and the use of visual alternatives during book triage, because there is no non-bibliographic data from the books such as covers or blurbs to individuate books on our virtual shelves.

Figure 1 shows the main interaction flow that readers can follow in the system. First, they have the option to register their email outside of the virtual environment to be able to send to themselves the book records they find interesting. Once in the virtual room they can walk freely around the aisle which contains six shelves with 50 books each. Then with the aid of a VR controller they can grab books from the shelves. Once they have grabbed a book the can see its record information displayed in one of the walls of the room. Each record contains four fields: title, author, topic and location. If readers are interested in the book record, they can send its information to their email just by using a voice command and without interrupting their book browsing activity.

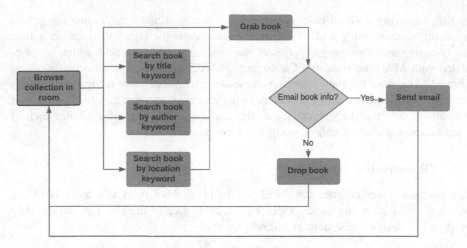

Fig. 1. Babel VR interaction flow diagram

If readers are not interested in the book they are inspecting, they can put it back on the shelf or just drop it into the floor (do not try this in physical libraries). Other voice commands that are available in the system are the search commands, where by saying either 'title', 'author' or 'location' plus a desired search keyword, readers can query the loaded collection and the resulting books along with their records will be stacked onto the shelves.

The voice commands that are currently implemented in the system are: the "Next" command, which is used to load sequential sections of the library catalog into the stacks; the "Title" + keyword, "Author" + keyword and "Location" + keyword commands, which allow for searching using keywords that are present in the Title, Author or Location fields from the book records; and the "Send" voice command, which enables readers to send the chosen book record to their email so that they can request the found item from the library at a later time.

One of the drawbacks of voice keyword search is that readers would have to memorize each of the voice commands; that is why they were implemented as single word commands. There can also be errors in speech command recognition due to word pronunciation or noise in the environment [15].

The virtual shelves were designed to resemble the size of typical physical shelves and are laid out in an aisle distribution setup to resemble the way books are arranged in a physical library, to provide a setting which readers are already familiar with. Readers start the virtual experience in the middle of the aisle which has a preloaded section of books from a set of MARC records that are extracted from a collection of books from a real library (Fig. 2). Then they can proceed to interact with the system using voice commands to load content in the shelves and by searching using commands and keywords in the defined bibliographic categories of title, author, topic or location, and by grabbing individual books using the VR controllers, or just "pointing" at them with the controllers.

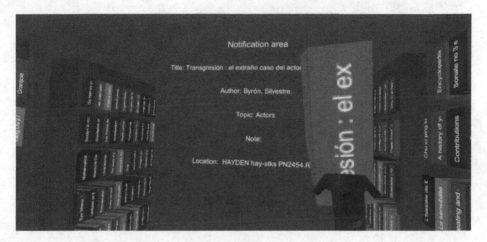

Fig. 2. A library visitor holding a book in Babel VR

3.2 System Architecture

The software architecture of Babel VR is divided into four main parts (Fig. 3). First, the Babel VR client, which loads the virtual reality environment which displays portions of the library catalog data into book representations contained in virtual shelves. The virtual environment was developed using the personal free edition of the Unity game engine [34], and the HTC Vive virtual reality system runs with the help of the SteamVR software [32]. The second element is a Google Cloud-based server where the data from the book records is stored in JSON files which have been generated from actual MARC records. The server uses the Deployd API [12], which runs on a Node.JS server, and is a web interface that provides the library data feeding mechanism, database search functionalities and email client interaction. The third component is the speech to text service from IBM Watson [20] that provides speech recognition functionality for the voice commands through their API. Finally, the fourth component which handles the email sending functionality is SparkPost [31], which provides a service to manage the sending of the book records from the virtual environment to user email accounts.

The data that is currently being used to populate the virtual library environment is a sample of 10,000 book records extracted from XML MARC records from the Arizona State University (ASU) library catalog.

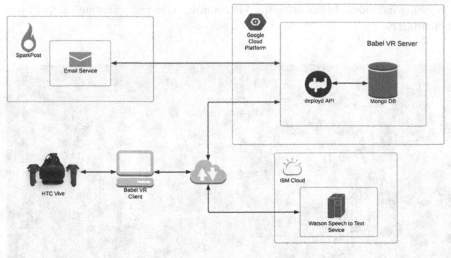

Fig. 3. Babel VR system architecture

4   Conclusion and Future Work

This paper presented the Babel VR system, which aims to provide an interface within a virtual environment for readers to browse virtual book shelves and create a space enabling serendipitous encounters with new materials. In the virtual environment readers have the possibility of performing shelf browsing the same way they do it on a physical library but with the added advantage of using voice commands to traverse and search within the stacks, and virtual controllers to access record information from the virtual books.

The main contribution of this project is to provide a virtual reality environment to display book records from an actual library, where readers can browse and search as part of a seamless immersive experience. The foreseen impact of this work is that it could be applied in cases where users wish to browse a library collection remotely because it is not physically accessible or is not stored in stacks at all [3]. Moreover, this work aims to enhance book discoverability in libraries by providing voice-based search commands.

Based on prior findings of visitor browsing behavior in real-world library settings, [26], we intend to conduct a qualitative field study to observe how readers behave within the virtual environment and to evaluate the implemented interaction mechanisms, focusing on voice commands for browsing and searching as well as VR controls for interacting with the virtual books. For the study, a portion of the catalog from the ASU library, which holds a subset of more than 5 million records, will be chosen. After the first study has been carried out, a quantitative study will be performed to compare the actual physical shelf browsing experience with the virtual reality experience, where readers will be provided with the same shelf browsing and searching tasks.

For every reader that tries the system, several metrics related to browsing behavior will be registered, such as the number of books they grab from the shelves, the number of books they drop or put back, and the number of records they choose to send to email.

In regard to search behavior, the metrics that will be recorded are number of book searches by title, author or location.

In the future, the act of reading, sampling, and skimming books within the Babel VR virtual environment will be analyzed as well, by extending the virtual library metaphor to allow readers to open the books they grab from the shelves and read from their pages.

References

1. Almeida, R., Cubaud, P., Dupire, J., Natkin, S., Topol, A.: Experiments towards 3D immersive interaction for digital libraries. In: Pan, Z., Aylett, R., Diener, H., Jin, X., Göbel, S., Li, L. (eds.) Edutainment 2006. LNCS, vol. 3942, pp. 1348–1357. Springer, Heidelberg (2006). https://doi.org/10.1007/11736639_168
2. Aslan, I., Murer, M., Primessnig, F., Moser, C., Tscheligi, M.: The digital bookshelf: decorating with collections of digital books. In: Proceedings of the 2013 ACM Conference on Pervasive and Ubiquitous Computing Adjunct Publication, pp. 777–784. ACM (2013)
3. ASU Library, Books are moving out of Hayden Library. https://lib.asu.edu/librarychannel/books-are-moving-out-hayden-library. Accessed 28 Mar 2019
4. Badam, S.K., Srinivasan, A., Elmqvist, N., Stasko, J.: Affordances of input modalities for visual data exploration in immersive environments. In: 2nd Workshop on Immersive Analytics (2017)
5. Bates, M.J.: What is browsing-really? A model drawing from behavioural science research (2007)
6. Borges, J.L.: The Library of Babel. Collected fictions (1998)
7. Börner, K., Feng, Y., McMahon, T.: Collaborative visual interfaces to digital libraries. In: Proceedings of the 2nd ACM/IEEE-CS Joint Conference on Digital Libraries, pp. 279–280. ACM (2002)
8. Christoffel, M., Schmitt, B.: Accessing libraries as easy as a game. In: Börner, K., Chen, C. (eds.) Visual Interfaces to Digital Libraries. LNCS, vol. 2539, pp. 25–38. Springer, Heidelberg (2002). https://doi.org/10.1007/3-540-36222-3_3
9. Cubaud, P., Stokowski, P., Topol, A.: 3D metaphors to access a digitalized library. In: Virtual Reality International Conference 2002, Laval, France (2002)
10. Cubaud, P., Stokowski, P., Topol, A.: Binding browsing and reading activities in a 3D digital library. In: Proceedings of the 2nd ACM/IEEE-CS Joint Conference on Digital Libraries, pp. 281–282. ACM (2002)
11. Das Neves, F.A., Fox, E.A.: A study of user behavior in an immersive virtual environment for digital libraries. In: Proceedings of the Fifth ACM Conference on Digital Libraries, pp. 103–111. ACM (2000)
12. Deployd. The simplest way to build and API. http://deployd.com. Accessed 28 Mar 2019
13. Detken, K., Martinez, C., Schrader, A.: The search wall: tangible information searching for children in public libraries. In: Proceedings of the 3rd International Conference on Tangible and Embedded Interaction, pp. 289–296. ACM (2009)
14. Ex Libris. The Virtual Bookshelf. https://www.exlibrisgroup.com/the-virtual-bookshelf. Accessed 28 Mar 2019
15. Ferracani, A., Faustino, M., Giannini, G.X., Landucci, L., Del Bimbo, A.: Natural experiences in museums through virtual reality and voice commands. In: Proceedings of the 2017 ACM on Multimedia Conference, pp. 1233–1234. ACM (2017)
16. Hahn, J.F.: Virtual Reality Library Environments. American Library Association, Chicago (2017)

17. Harvard University. Stacklife. http://stacklife.harvard.edu. Accessed 28 Mar 2019
18. He, Z., Lv, C., Peng, D., Yu, D.: A speech recognition-based interaction approach applying to immersive virtual maintenance simulation. In: 2017 Second International Conference on Reliability Systems Engineering (ICRSE), pp. 1–5. IEEE (2017)
19. Hinze, A., McKay, D., Vanderschantz, N., Timpany, C., Cunningham, S.J.: Book selection behavior in the physical library: implications for ebook collections. In: Proceedings of the 12th ACM/IEEE-CS Joint Conference on Digital Libraries, pp. 305–314. ACM (2012)
20. IBM. Watson Speech to Text. https://www.ibm.com/watson/services/speech-to-text. Accessed 28 Mar 2019
21. Jervis, M., Masoodian, M.: Visualization of physical library shelves to facilitate collection management and retrieval. In: Proceedings of the 5th ACM SIGCHI Symposium on Engineering Interactive Computing Systems, pp. 133–138. ACM (2013)
22. Kefi, M., Hoang, T.N., Richard, P., Verhulst, E.: An evaluation of multimodal interaction techniques for 3D layout constraint solver in a desktop-based virtual environment. Virtual Reality **22**, 1–13 (2018)
23. Kleiner, E., Rädle, R., Reiterer, H.: Blended shelf: reality-based presentation and exploration of library collections. In: CHI'13 Extended Abstracts on Human Factors in Computing Systems, pp. 577–582. ACM (2013)
24. Kranzlmüller, D., Reitinger, B., Hackl, I., Volkert, J.: Voice controlled virtual reality and its perspectives for everyday life. Itg Fachbericht **168**, 101–108 (2001)
25. McKay, D., Smith, W., Chang, S.: Lend me some sugar: borrowing rates of neighbouring books as evidence for browsing. In: 2014 IEEE/ACM Joint Conference on Digital Libraries (JCDL), pp. 145–154. IEEE (2014)
26. McKay, D., Chang, S., Smith, W.: Manoeuvres in the dark: design implications of the physical mechanics of library shelf browsing. In: Proceedings of the 2017 Conference on Conference Human Information Interaction and Retrieval, pp. 47–56. ACM (2017)
27. Miner, N.E.: Using voice input and audio feedback to enhance the reality of a virtual experience (No. SAND–94-0670C; CONF-9406136–1). Sandia National Labs., Albuquerque, NM (United States) (1994)
28. Opening the Book. Whichbook. https://www.whichbook.net. Accessed 28 Mar 2019
29. Pearce, J., Chang, S.: Exploration without keywords: the bookfish case. In: Proceedings of the 26th Australian Computer-Human Interaction Conference on Designing Futures: The Future of Design, pp. 176–179. ACM (2014)
30. Rauber, A., Bina, H.: A metaphor graphics based representation of digital libraries on the world wide web: using the libviewer to make metadata visible. In: Proceedings of the Tenth International Workshop on Database and Expert Systems Applications, pp. 286–290. IEEE (1999)
31. SparkPost. SparkPost: Email Delivery Service for Developers and Enterprises. https://www.sparkpost.com. Accessed 28 Mar 2019
32. Steam. SteamVR. https://store.steampowered.com/steamvr. Accessed 28 Mar 2019
33. Thudt, A., Hinrichs, U., Carpendale, S.: The bohemian bookshelf: supporting serendipitous book discoveries through information visualization. In: Proceedings of the SIGCHI Conference on Human Factors in Computing Systems, pp. 1461–1470. ACM (2012)
34. Unity. Unity Personal. https://store.unity.com/products/unity-personal. Accessed 28 Mar 2019
35. Waugh, S., McKay, D., Makri, S.: 'Too much serendipity': the tension between information seeking and encountering at the library shelves. In: Proceedings of the 2017 Conference on Conference Human Information Interaction and Retrieval, pp. 277–280. ACM (2017)
36. Zhao, W., Madhavan, V.: Virtual assembly operations with grasp and verbal interaction. In: Proceedings of the 2006 ACM International Conference on Virtual Reality Continuum and Its Applications, pp. 245–254. ACM (2006)

Cross-Cultural User Design: Divergences in Chinese and Western Human Computer Interface Interaction

Marcus Liljenberg[1], Kathy Tian[2(✉)], and Mike Yao[2]

[1] Lunds University, Lund, Sweden
[2] University of Illinois at Urbana-Champaign, Champaign-Urbana, IL, USA
kathyt2@illinois.edu

Abstract. In this paper, the authors examine how cultural background informs human-computer-interactions, particularly as pertaining to user experience (UX) and user interface design (UI). Prior studies suggest that East Asians are more likely to process information holistically while Westerners tend to engage with visual stimuli analytically. It is believed that such differences in information processing may inform web design and user experience as well. In this research, the authors took inspiration from a news site from China (i.e., QQ.com), reflective of holistic thinking, and a Western-based news site (i.e., BBC.com), representing analytical thinking, to investigate how the design of these pages would affect the perceived user experience. We find that both Chinese and Western participants found the design of the BBC site to be more aesthetically appealing. However, Chinese participants exhibited greater ease of navigation relative to Western participants on the QQ-inspired site.

Keywords: Cross-culture · User experience ·
Holistic and analytical processing

1 Introduction

As globalization and technological innovations continue to support the rise of multinational corporations, it has become increasingly pressing for business to cater to a worldwide audience. Particularly, websites from these companies must be both navigable and easily comprehensible to individuals across cultures to cater to global audiences. Interestingly, however, according to the authors' knowledge, few studies have explored how individuals from different cultural backgrounds may process information differently and, thus, interact with websites distinctively. In this study, the researchers explore how cross-cultural differences influence user experience and interface interactions across cultural environments.

Specifically, the researchers investigate how individuals from China, who tend to process information holistically, differ from Westerners, who tend to process content analytically, in navigating two news sites. To examine distinctions in navigation patterns, two interactive websites were built reflecting Western (i.e., BBC.com) and Eastern (i.e., QQ.com) designs. Further, participants were subject to tests measuring

© Springer Nature Switzerland AG 2019
C. Stephanidis and M. Antona (Eds.): HCII 2019, CCIS 1088, pp. 39–45, 2019.
https://doi.org/10.1007/978-3-030-30712-7_6

response times to search queries in addition to surveys measuring their evaluations to the sites. Specifically, we had participants respond to questions gauging their self-reported perceptions of the news sites.

2 Literature Review

There currently exits and extensive body of research on holistic versus analytical information processing, particularly in the cross-cultural literature. Prior studies have found that individuals from different cultures tend to process visual stimuli distinctively. In particular, the influence of culture on information processing appears most relevant when considering how Easterners (e.g., Chinese, Japanese, etc.) and Westerners (e.g., American, Swedish, etc.) perceive information differently [2]. Specifically, research suggests Westerners, who tend to be individualists, interpret content analytically while Easterners, who tend to hold collectivists values, generally process information holistically [3]. The difference between Western analytical thinking and Eastern holistic thinking is that holistic thinking emphasizes the interconnectedness of perceptual stimuli, while analytical thinking involves the interpretation of objects independently (e.g., in isolation of surrounding cues) [1].

It is believed that Easterners are able to synthesize and consider more pieces of information relative to their Western counterparts. For example, in eye-tracking studies, East Asians tended to scan through an entire image, bouncing between focal and background objects. Conversely, eye-tracking heat maps indicate that Western subjects did the opposite; instead of taking account of all the objects in an image, Westerners tended to gaze extensively at focal objects. As such, Westerners were able to recall more details surrounding central objects, while Easterners made saccades between various information cues. As such, holistic processing "involves an orientation to the context or fields as a whole" [4] whereas analytical processing "involves a detachment of the object from its context, a tendency to focus on attributes of the object" [1]. These findings suggest that Eastern collectivists (e.g., Chinese, Korean, Japanese people), will be more likely take in more information content than Westerners. Additionally, they may be more inclined to incorporate non-central cues for information processing. Conversely, it is suggested that Western analytical thinkers may prefer to focus on fewer objects and may tend to use only central information.

2.1 F-Shaped Pattern

The F-shaped pattern refers to findings made in a study on user eye movements [7]. This pattern has been dubbed the "F-shaped pattern" since prior research suggests that users typically scan pages starting with a horizontal movement, usually across the upper part of the content area. Users then tend to read across in a second horizontal movement further down on the page that typically spans a shorter area. Finally, users scan the content's left side in a vertical movement. When measuring users' eye gazing as a heat map, this creates a pattern that resembles an F. Web developers, either consciously or unconsciously, often design their websites according to this pattern. The F-shaped pattern is not an absolute law and several other scanning patterns exist, but the F-shaped pattern remains the most prevalent in Western cultures [8]. If a developer designs a page without knowledge about this pattern, they risk putting important information in places where users might miss it.

3 Methodology

The aim of the investigation phase is to obtain a more nuanced understanding regarding the differences in perception and navigation of Western versus Chinese websites. This information facilitated the decision-making process concerning which features to keep, which features need to be analyzed, and what usability metrics should be implemented in the study. As an initial step, Chinese websites, along with their Western equivalents, were identified and curated. After obtaining a corpus of websites from China and Western countries (e.g., United Kingdom), the key design differences between these respective sites were documented. Once the primary design variances were explored, this information was used to decide which design patterns should be tested in the study. Finally, the specific metrics to measure the results of these different designs were concluded. In reviewing the websites, it was evident that Chinese pages differed significantly from Western counterparts. The differences between sites extended from the look and feel to the UX design. A few of China's most popular browsing sites were then analyzed and compared to similar Western counterparts to further investigate these design variations.

BBC is a very popular Western new site. The design of the site follows similar trends, in terms of information design and density, of other Western news media sites. The layout of various landing pages in the BBC appear to closely follow the F-shaped pattern. Each news section has a large news figure in the top left corner and two rows. Simply looking at the large picture and the first row then glazing down to the next news section would have the users quite naturally follow the F-shaped pattern. The site itself is quite information sparse with large images taking most of the space. Without hovering over any content on a standard computer screen, there are roughly 48 clickable elements [10].

QQ is one of the most visited media websites in China [11, 12]. QQ, like many other Chinese websites, does not focus on one thing but has multiple functions. Some of the functions that QQ supports are instant messaging, online games, music, shopping, microblogging, news, movies, group chat software, and etc. On the QQ homepage, users are greeted by the site's news page, which is highly information dense. Without hoovering over any content on a standard computer screen, there are roughly 147 clickable elements. One element that is notably common on Chinese websites, including QQ, is the menu bar design. On the QQ page, the menu bar contains two rows with a total of 40 clickable options. This format of menus is typical in China and is shared by multiple other Chinese sites (e.g., Sina, Taobao).

4 Analysis

For the purposes of this research two interfaces were created, with one following a Western design (e.g., similar to BBC) and the other one using a Chinese layout (e.g., similar to QQ). Both these sites were translated to both English and Chinese. The translation process was iterative and two bilingual researchers performed the meaning translations. The goal of implementing these interfaces were to explore how fluidly users from different cultural backgrounds can navigate sites containing high information density (i.e., copious amounts of images and texts). Both interfaces contain roughly equivalent levels of material and clickable elements; the primary difference is that the Western site became longer (due to translations), forcing users to scroll down the page. Additionally, some of the information were mapped in sub-menus using natural mapping for the Western site [5].

Conversely, the Chinese inspired site provided most of the material directly on the screen for users to view without any nested menus. The interfaces, cable of measuring what actions users take in responding to certain tasks, was developed given the feedback from these prototypes. Main measurements that were used are task-success, time-on-task and a modified System usability scale [9]. Research from Nisbett and Miyamoto [1] suggest perception differs in Western and Eastern cultures. Dong and Lee [13] further indicate that this perception difference holds true in the case of people observing websites. Specifically, users using analytical processing follow the F-shaped pattern when browsing sites [7]. Holistic thinkers, conversely, do not follow the F-shaped pattern when browsing through a website [13]. In light of these past studies, it will be interesting to explore how these perception differences will influence users' abilities to navigate and perceive web pages.

To investigate this question, we select elements both in accordance to the F-shaped pattern and elements outside of this pattern. By testing the performance on analytical and holistic thinkers, an indication of the differences and how well people follow the F-shaped pattern when looking for specific elements will be derived. The test was unsupervised, as a larger test audience was necessary in order to obtain significant results. To measure variations in perception, tests for the sites BBC and QQ were created. On these pages, participants were requested to find elements following an F-shaped pattern and elements that not following this pattern.

Results on time differences and survey responses were stored in a database for significance testing. The corpus of collected data were applied to statistical significance analyses of differences between groups. Our findings indicate that (1) there is a significant difference between how Chinese and Western users process information ($t = -3.1606$, $p < 0.05$), (2) Westerners are more reliant on the F-shaped pattern than Easterners ($t = -3.1606$, $p < 0.05$), and (3) Chinese individuals are comfortable with Western pages ($t = 5.3301$, $p < 0.05$), suggesting that a universal interface can be deployed cross-culturally. This study offers contributions both to theoretical understandings of cross-cultural user experience as well as industry practitioners. Findings from this study suggest that culture significantly influences information processing which subsequently effects how users evaluate and navigate websites

5 Discussion

The aim of this research was to examine (1) how differences in interface design may be due to differences in information processing styles or simply trends, (2) how do different processing styles in Western (analytical) versus Chinese (holistic) users affect performance on different interfaces, and (3) if one global interface should be created or if web designers should focus on creating separate user interfaces for different cultures. Concerning the question of how interface design may be due to different information processing styles or trends, my research suggests that a mix of both factors have contributed to the different web designs from China and its western counterparts. Specifically, Chinese users preferred the Western based design over the Chinese one, according to self-reports (M = 4.11 for QQ and M = 5.04 for BBC).

Interestingly, this suggests that perhaps the reason why Chinese news sites tend to be more information dense may simply be due to a trend in web design rather than fundamental perception differences. For instance, Chinese users performed as well as English users navigating both the BBC site (t = −0.49, p > 0.05) and QQ site (t = 0.42, p > 0.05) indicating that there is no significant difference between the two groups. Regarding the question of how information processing styles (analytical versus holistic) would affect user performance on different interfaces, the findings suggest that information processing style does significantly influence performance. Unsurprisingly, the research indicated that English, or analytical-thinking, users who used the BBC site were much quicker at finding important objects within the F-shaped pattern compared to outside of it (t = 2.8479, p < 0.05). On average, these participants took 12 s longer outside the F-shaped pattern compared to within. This is congruent with the existing literature on UX, in which eye tracking studies suggest Western users tend to scan through a website using an F-shaped pattern.

However, it was surprising to find that Chinese users were actually also able to answer questions more quickly when questions were within the F-shaped pattern versus outside (t = 5.3301, p < 0.05). It appears that for both Chinese and English users of the BBC site, objects that fell within the F-pattern were easier to find that those outside. However, the effect size was significantly larger for English users, with a 12 s difference inside and outside the F-pattern, than for Chinese users, who only had a 4 s difference. Overall, it appears that a Western based design seems easily navigable for both Eastern and Western users. The F-shape appears to increase performance for both groups. The main difference, however, is that English users were significantly better within the F-pattern (taking 12 s less) than outside, whereas Chinese users only saw a slight improvement (taking only 4 s less within the F-shape).

On the effects of information processing and website navigability, the results suggest that English speakers using the QQ site were quicker inside the F-shaped pattern than outside of the pattern (t = −3.1606, p < 0.05), with a 3 s difference. For Chinese users on the QQ site, conversely, they were marginally slower inside the F-pattern (using 22.6 s) than outside (22.4 s) the pattern (t = −5.907, p 0.05), English users were still slightly more dependent on the F-pattern, like the findings form the BBC site. Interestingly, however, according the questionnaire self-reports, it appeared that Chinese users found both the QQ and BBC websites to be similarly likeable

(M = 4.11 for QQ vs. M = 5.04 for BBC) and did not seem to be overwhelmed by the information density of the QQ site (M = 2.8 on the question "I felt overwhelmed using this site"). For the English users, however, self-reports indicated that they were highly uncomfortable with the layout of the page, finding the information overwhelming. They had an average of 4.23 from 1 to 5 on the question "I felt overwhelmed using this site". Western users also tended to give higher ratings for BBC than QQ (M = 4.46 for BBC vs. M = 2.28 for QQ).

Taken together, these results suggest that information processing does influence how users interact with different interfaces. It appears that while Western users can use a Chinese designed site, they find the experience to be extremely unpleasant (M = 2.28 for QQ). Conversely, the findings indicate that Chinese users found both sites similarly likeable (M = 4.11 for QQ vs. M = 5.04 for BBC). Furthermore, English users were more reliant on the F-shaped pattern than Chinese users, which is in-line with existing research on user perception. Concerning the question of whether or not one global interface should be created or if web designs should be tailored to different cultures, these results suggest that one global interface can be deployed to maximize efficiency. Chinese users found BBC to be just as likeable as QQ, whereas English users disliked the information density of QQ, suggesting that a site with lower information density is favorable. Accordingly, it appears that web designers can focus on creating one global interface to maximize efficiency.

References

1. Nisbett, R.E., Miyamoto, Y.: The influence of culture: holistic versus analytic perception. Trends Cogn. Sci. **9**(10), 467–473 (2005). https://doi.org/10.1016/j.tics.2005.08.004. http://www.sciencedirect.com/science/article/pii/S1364661305002305. ISSN 1364-6613
2. Ji, L.-J., Peng, K., Nisbett, R.E.: Culture, control, and perception of relationships in the environment. J. Pers. Soc. Psychol. **78**(5), 943 (2000)
3. Miyamoto, Y., Nisbett, R.E., Masuda, T.: Culture and the physical environment: holistic versus analytic perceptual affordances. Psychol. Sci. **17**(2), 113–119 (2006)
4. Monga, A.B., John, D.R.: Cultural differences in brand extension evaluation: the influence of analytic versus holistic thinking. J. Consum. Res. **33**(4), 529–536 (2006)
5. Norman, D.A.: The Design of Everyday Things. Basic Books Inc., New York (2002). ISBN 9780465067107
6. Nielsen, J., Norman, D.: The Definition of User Experience UX. https://www.nngroup.com/articles/definition-user-experience/
7. Pernice, K., Whitenton, K., Nielsen, J.: How People Read on the Web: The Eyetracking Evidence. Nielsen Norman Group (2014)
8. Pernice, K.: F-Shaped Pattern of Reading on the Web: Misunderstood, But Still Relevant. Nielsen Norman Group (2017)
9. Brooke, J., et al.: SUS-A quick and dirty usability scale. Usability Eval. Ind. **189**(194), 4–7 (1996)
10. BBC. http://www.bbc.com/news
11. Top sites ranking for all categories in China. https://www.similarweb.com/top-websites/china

12. Top Sites in China the sites in the top sites lists are ordered by their 1 month Alexa traffic rank. https://www.alexa.com/topsites/countries/CN
13. Dong, Y., Lee, K.-P.: A cross-cultural comparative study of users' perceptions of a webpage: with a focus on the cognitive styles of Chinese. Koreans and Americans. Int. J. Des. 2(2), 19–30 (2008)

Guidelines for Evaluating the Completeness of the Portfolio

Ji Min Ryu[1] and Keeheon Lee[2,3(✉)]

[1] Graduate School of Communication, Yonsei University,
Seoul, Republic of Korea
[2] Underwood International College, Yonsei University,
Seoul, Republic of Korea
keeheon@yonsei.ac.kr
[3] Graduate School of Information, Yonsei University, Seoul, Republic of Korea

Abstract. Design has been expanding its position. The design has been expanding its position. because, the development of technology, to grow demand that solving problems using design methodologies [9, 13]. As a result, the capacity of individual designers is becoming more important, and the importance of 'portfolios' expressing and evaluating their capabilities is increasing. In the industrial society, the portfolio is used as an indicator of competence of designers, but the evaluation method and criteria depend on the subjective view of the evaluator so that the competence of the designer is not objective. Although both designers and evaluators agree on this problem, research on the portfolio itself, as well as the portfolio evaluation area, is very limited [3]. Therefore, this study is based on the priority of the components that should be considered in the evaluation of the completeness of the portfolio by analyzing the components of the portfolio so that the portfolio can be evaluated as an index for evaluating the individual competence of the designer Evaluation guidelines were presented. In order to do this, we conduct surveys and in-depth interviews with designers engaged in the business to understand the needs of the portfolio, and analyze the component data of the portfolio extracted based on the analysis, and prioritize the portfolio components that should be considered for completeness determination This study has significance in that it is presented through data analysis.

Keywords: Design · Portfolio · Artificial intelligence · Data science

1 Introduction

With the recent developments of AI (Artificial Intelligence) technology have caused various changes in various industrial fields [13, 17]. Also, the design industry is also being developed and expanded through various changes [10], and the role of design in the industrial society is increasingly recognized as an important means. Since the design industry is an industry on which human resources are based, one's personal competence is more important than other industries, and the need for competent designers is increasing. Therefore, the completeness of the portfolio, which serves as an indicator for evaluating the personal competence of the designer and as an individual

© Springer Nature Switzerland AG 2019
C. Stephanidis and M. Antona (Eds.): HCII 2019, CCIS 1088, pp. 46–56, 2019.
https://doi.org/10.1007/978-3-030-30712-7_7

career certificate, is becoming more important. As such, we are aware of the importance of the portfolio, but the evaluation criteria depend on the subjective opinion of the evaluator. Therefore, not only the designer but also the evaluator is confused about producing and evaluating the portfolio.

The purpose of this study is to find out the objective index for evaluating the personal competence of the designer as a preliminary study for the AI - based service development that objectively and quantitatively evaluates the portfolio, identifies priorities of components that affect portfolio completeness assessment and provide evaluation guidelines. In order to accomplish the purpose of this study, we have identified the needs of designers and portfolio evaluators who produce portfolios through in-depth interviews and in-depth interviews. Based on this, Python was used to extract and analyze the 820 component data of the portfolio, and the priorities of components to be considered in the portfolio identification were derived. This study is meaningful in that a new direction using data was devised and presented for objectification and quantification of the portfolio evaluation method. As a result of this study, it is expected that designers will provide a guideline to express their competence more effectively in the portfolio and more objective and standardized evaluation criteria to the evaluator. In addition, if subsequent research based on this research is continued, it is expected that AI services for objective evaluation can be constructed in the evaluation of the completeness of the portfolio.

2 Literature Review

2.1 Portfolio and Evaluation Methods

Design is a specialized area for presenting solutions to problems and acting on those tasks. Therefore, compared to other direct groups, designers are each valued for their individual competencies. because the portfolio is the most important material for assessing the competency of individual designers [6]. A portfolio is a communication tool that shows the designer's personal competence and communicates with others as a mirror showing the designer's thoughts and problem-solving methods, rather than simply a completed collection of works. (Kim 2008) was carefully analyzed according to the characteristics of the structural elements of the interior design portfolio and arranged the elements of the portfolio to focus on the way the presentation of the portfolio. (Han [6]) was presented in six categories of guidelines for the objective competency evaluation of designers through portfolios through expert in-depth interviews, looking at portfolios from the perspective of designer recruiters. This study is significant that this is a study that objectively presents the evaluation criteria of the designer through the portfolio. However, the limitations of the study mentioned by the authors of this paper are as follows. 1. Participants in the in-depth interview for the elicitation of needs were limited. All the interviewee were evaluators. 2. Since the evaluation method of the portfolio has already been evaluated as subjective and abstract language, it is difficult to objectify the evaluation method. The guidelines are shown in Table 1.

Table 1. Basic elements of portfolio evaluation guidelines (Han [6])

Designers competency	Elements
Planning power	Portfolio configuration power
Observant	Designed by things, on the phenomenon for observe found
Comprehension	Whether or not you understand and implement the given proposition
Analytical	Optimal design solution implementation for issues analysis
Creativity	Designer your own creativity
Expressiveness	Graphics, communication way

2.2 Changes in the Industrial Sector Due to the Emergence of AI

In addition to recent advances in AI technology, many changes have been taking place throughout the industrial society of Automobiles, robotics, education, etc. In the design area, you can find many examples of using AI. Companies such as Adobe, Microsoft, and Autodesk that produce 3D Tools and 2D Tools that are used primarily by designers provide artificial intelligence-based 'intelligent services' to provide designers with the convenience of using tools. Services such as Google's Quick Draw is to convert complete rough sketches to detailed graphics [12]. And such as 'tailorbrands', 'hatchful' and 'Logoshi' are automatically to create logos. The application of artificial intelligence in the design area has been applied to a variety of areas, from design tools utilized by professional designers to services that make it easier for non-professionals to access the design.

3 Preliminary Survey

A questionnaire survey was conducted on 117 designers. The purpose of this questionnaire is as follow. (1) to understand how designers perceive portfolios. (2) To find out the needs for an objective portfolio evaluation method (Table 2).

Table 2. Items in questionnaire

Items	Investigation contents
General characteristics	Company size, experience, design field
Essentials of designer competency development	Key elements to the designer's required competency and competency representation
Evaluating of portfolio	Recognition and requirements for existing portfolio assessment methods

A total of 117 people participated in the survey, and 2018.09.26–2019.09.30. It took 5 days in total. Data collected from questionnaires were analyzed using the SPSS program, and frequency analysis was conducted. The general characteristics of the questionnaire are shown in Table 3.

Table 3. General characteristics of questionnaire

Contents		Frequency	%
Company size	Major company in-house	14	12.0
	Start-up or small business	66	56.4
	Design agency	29	24.8
	Others	9	6.8
	Total	**117**	**100.0**
Experience	Less than 1 year of experience	66	56.4
	2 years of experience	17	14.5
	3 years of experience	16	13.7
	More than 4 years of experience	18	15.4
	Total	**117**	**100.0**
Design field	UX, UI, GUI	57	48.7
	Industrial design	42	35.9
	Visual design	12	10.3
	Branding	4	0.3
	Others	2	0.2
	Total	**117**	**100.0**

Design skills and design expression (65.8%), design thinking (60.7%), and planning ability (57.3%) were the most frequent factors in the frequency analysis. Design Tool skill & design expression was remarkably high. The creativity of designers was ranked 5th with 31.6% (Table 4).

Table 4. Designer's essential competency (including duplicate votes)

Contents	Frequency	%
Design tool skill & design expression	77	65.8
Design thinking	71	60.7
Creativity	37	31.6
Planning ability	67	57.3
Language skill	10	8.5
Communication skill	61	52.1
Ability to converge in another field	34	29.1

Portfolios, academic backgrounds, and self-introduction were the first, second, and third most important factors in evaluating designer competencies. Among the factors that assess the competence of designers, the portfolio was significantly higher at 98.3%. As a result, it can be seen that designers are aware of 'portfolio' as a tool for expressing their competence. Table 4 also shows that the 'portfolio' is effective in evaluating 'Design Tool & Design Expression', which is an essential capability for designers.

Table 5. Important factors in evaluating a designer's competency (including duplicate votes)

Contents	Frequency	%
Academic level	32	27.4
Language level	15	12.8
Portfolio	115	98.3
Self-introduction letter	27	23.1
Resume	13	11.1
Others	14	12.6

In order to achieve the purpose of this first study, we conducted post interviews on the services needed to develop the competency of the designer. This is because interviewing methods are more effective in identifying the needs of designers. The interview results were coded and the needs were typed as shown in Table 6. The frequency analysis showed that 'Education service (40%)', 'Portfolio service (24%)' and 'Community service (20%)' were ranked first, second and third respectively. Designers want to grow. Thus the need for education services so high. The need for portfolio services was also high. Portfolio service needs were detailed in the order of 'Production Guide', 'Attachment', and 'Objective Evaluation'.

Table 6. Services needed to develop a designer competency

Contents	Service	Frequency	%
Portfolio	Portfolio creation guide service	13	11.1
	Portfolio correction service	8	0.7
	Objective evaluation service	3	0.3
	Total	**24**	**20.5**
Education	Design tool	11	11.1
	Language	3	2.6
	Composition	1	0.9
	Design process	20	17.1
	others	5	4.3
	Total	**40**	**34.2**
Design thinking	Design thinking service	13	11.1
	Total	**13**	**11.1**
Community	Designer community service	20	17.1
	Total	**20**	**17.1**
Q&A	Business Q&A service	9	7.7
	Total	**9**	**7.7**
No answer	-	10	8.5
	Total	**10**	**8.5**
Total		**117**	**100**

This study confirms that the importance of portfolio and objectification of the evaluation method are needed in the industrial structure where a designer's personal competence becomes increasingly important through previous research and pilot questionnaire. Confirms the priority of components affecting the evaluation of portfolio completeness, suggest evaluation guidelines.

4 Method

4.1 RandomForest

Random forest used in this study is to generate several decision trees from data and then to predict the most selected class among the predicted values of each individual tree [1, 16]. In other words, it is an ensemble technique that improves learning performance by applying several simultaneously. The ensemble means harmony or unification in French, and it learns several models in machine learning and predicts better values than one model using the predictions of the models. This method is called an ensemble learning or an ensemble method [14, 16]. Random Forest works by constructing more than 30 datasets from the same data, extracting them from the same data, applying decision trees to each, and collecting the learning results [5]. However, each tree only learns a few of the variables, which is an attempt to increase diversity by making the individual trees view the data differently [14]. Random forest is a way to eliminate the overfitting problem of the training data of existing decision trees. To realize this, it is necessary to make many decision trees [15, 16]. Each tree should be well predicted and distinguished from other trees [14, 16]. Random forests are generated randomly when a tree is created so that the trees are different from each other. There are two ways of randomly choosing the data to be used when creating the tree, and randomly selecting the characteristics in the partitioning test [14, 16].

4.2 Research Procedure

Design portfolio is a critical factor in evaluating the capability of a designer. However, there is no standard way to evaluate a design portfolio. Additionally, there has been no academic study to give a guideline for evaluating a design portfolio. We had an in-depth interview with designers in the field to collect possible criteria for design portfolio evaluation. According to the criteria, we organized the elements that good design portfolios have and made a data-driven classifier for identifying good design portfolios. Eventually, we came up with a guideline for evaluating a design portfolio based on our study. This guideline suggests the priority of the elements that organize good design portfolios.

Step1

Aleading study of portfolio components for portfolio improvement and for the development of business designers' needs (Kim 2008) and the prior art of the evaluation of the Portfolio Assessment guidelines (Han 2011) was, based on this, the required capabilities of the designer were typed into five. Based on the structure of the Korean Design Industry (Korea Industrial Design Statistics Report, Kidp 2017), Survey and In-depth interviews have conducted with 15 designers who were in the office of start-up, Design Agency, and in-house. As a result, it was confirmed that the main evaluation criteria for evaluating the portfolio are different for each group (Table 7). In this study, tried to show between the Designers competency defined by 'basic skills' and portfolio elements are related. Table 8 shows the types of designer competencies evaluated through the portfolio through the interview coding process (Table 8).

Table 7. Evaluation criteria of a portfolio by design industry group

Industry	Designers competencies	Evaluation standard
Start-Up	Creativity	Variety of portfolio Layout
	Originality	How to use the color and text
	Design skills	
Design agency	Understanding	Tracking, leading
	Adaptability	How to use the grid
	Design skills	Main page composition
In-house	Planning ability	Contents of text
	Understanding	Whether to use terminology
	Analytical skills	The Idea of product

Step2. Portfolio Gathering

Behance (behance.net) is an online website that can display and search works created by designers from around the world with Adobe Creative Cloud [2]. Pinterest (pinterest.com) is a social network service that users post and share images with other users. In this study, Using Python, the 900 Portfolios, which is open online, such as 'Behance' (behance.net) and ' Pinterest' (pinterest.com), has been Crawled [2, 11]. Among them, the 820 Portfolios were used in the analysis for convenience in the analysis, the 80 Portfolios which are non-portfolio images and dynamic images (such as a GIF) were excepted. The components of the portfolio are largely divided into images and texts, and each itemized component of the data extracted from the 820 portfolios is shown in Table 9.

Step3. Data Preprocessing

The 820 portfolios are to be used for analysis, 40 were divided as Good and 780 were divided as Normal. Standard of between good and normal has been divided as of whether or not having a 'Behance recommendation label' for the convenience of analysis, the extracted data is encoded with matched with numbers and then, the learning model could process them. The N-gif and N-tool were not encoded because their values are already represented by integers and the values range from 0 to 5. On the other hand, main-color and key-color are encoded the extracted RGB values based on the color tone. A total of five color tones were used as the standard, monotone as 1, pastel tone as 2, vivid tone as 3, deep tone as 4, and natural tone as 5. The value of N-Text is encoded by 200 units, with 0–199 as 1, 200–399 as 2, 400–599 as 3, 600–799 as 4, and 800 or more as 5 (Table 11). We select the portfolio completeness evaluation as the 'target variable' and the six attributes selected in Step 3 as the 'predictor variables'. The variables used for the prediction of the portfolio completeness among

Table 8. Basic elements of portfolio

Characteristics classification	Interview contents
Design skill	Layout, color, typography and other design skills
Typography	Selection of the importance of the text, Basic elements of typography, tracking, leading, etc.
Storytelling	The structure of the design process
Project order	Position and organize the order of importance of content
Identity	Personality and story of a designer individual

Table 9. The data element of portfolio

	Element	Contents
Image	Main-color	The main color used in portfolio making
	Key-color	Point color used in portfolio making
	N-gif	Number of gif images in the portfolio
Text	N-Text	Number of Text in the portfolio
Tool	N-Tool	Number of Design tools used to make the portfolio

the total variables were selected through the preliminary study and the in-depth interview. A total of six variables were selected, one for design skill, one for comprehension and analysis, and one for originality. Selected variables were extracted from 820 portfolios and created a dataset (Table 10).

Table 10. Dataset

	Class	N-gif	Key-color	Main-color	N-Text	N-Tool
1	Good	0	3	1	2	3
2	Good	2	1	1	2	3
3	Good	1	3	1	2	2
4	Good	1	3	3	2	3
5	Good	2	1	1	2	3

Step4. Data Partition

In order to make an ideal model using data mining, it is desirable to create multiple prediction models from one data set and compare and analyze them [7]. Therefore, we divide the whole data into analytical data and verification data, create a model with analytical data, and apply the verification data to the model to compare the performance of the model. In this study, was divided by 7:3. Since random forests arbitrarily select variables to construct a tree, the ratio of analysis data to verification data does not affect the analysis [16].

Step5. Data Training and Evaluation
Random forests can be used to rank the importance of each variable in a classification or regression problem [1, 16]. Feature_importances_ was used to calculate the importance value of predictive variables. The data used in the analysis are unbalanced in the target variable. In the case of unbalanced data in RandomForest, there is a way to compensate overfitting by assigning a weight to a small number of variables [4]. However, in this case, there is a drawback that it is more susceptible to noise, and analysis by a weighted method does not affect the performance of the prediction model [4]. To build a RandomForest model, you must define the number of trees to be created. You can set the number of trees by the n_estimator value of RandomForestClassifier. In this analysis, n_estimator = 500, random_state = 42 was set, and a training model was created using scikit-learn. In order to reduce data noise and reduce the probability of overfitting, we normalized the normalized score to 0 with a mean and a standard deviation of 1. Principal Component Analysis (PCA) was used to build the model.

5   Result

5.1   Feature Importance

RandomForest was used to derive important feature importance for class discrimination and feature priority. As a result, N-Tool, N-gif, and N-Text were ranked first, second and third. This is a significant result because it reflects the latest trend in which the portfolio using dynamic images such as gif and video has appeared. Also, according to a result of in interviews has conducted with 15 designers, there were many opinions that text is important in portfolio evaluation. In other words, the portfolio is recognized as a means of communicating between the designer and the evaluator. so Text is considered more important than Image in the portfolio because the text implies that the value of the designer and the process of solving the idea. Although this study identifies only the number of simple texts, there are limitations, but it is meaningful in that it is in line with the main elements derived through in-depth interviews. The feature priorities for class discrimination are summarized in Table 11 below.

Table 11. Importance of features.

Rank	Features	Contents	Importance (%)
1	N-Tool	The main color used in portfolio making	34.76%
2	N-gif	Point color used in portfolio making	33.16%
3	N-Text	Number of gif images in the portfolio	16.64%
4	Main-color	Number of text in the portfolio	9.32%
5	Key-color	Number of design tools used to make the portfolio	6.12%

5.2   Accuracy Score

Accuracy Score to create an ideal model, data is divided the data set into two parts: 'training data' and 'test data' at a ratio of 3:7 and analysis using RandomForest. As a result, as shown in Tables 12 and 13, the training score is 0.9913 and the test score is 0.959933 (Tables 12 and 13).

Table 12. Training score

Accuracy score: 0.9913 | Average accuracy: 0.9635 | Standard deviation: 0.0194

Classification report

	Precision	Recall	Fl-score	Support
0	0.93	0.95	0.94	41
1	1.00	0.99	1.00	533
Avg/total	0.99	0.99	0.99	574

Table 13. Test score

Accuracy score: 0.9593

Classification report

	Precision	Recall	Fl-score	Support
0	0.62	0.94	0.75	16
1	1.00	0.96	0.98	230
Avg/total	0.97	0.96	0.96	246

6   Conclusion and Suggestion

Portfolios are a fundamental document for assessing the competence of designers, and the importance of the portfolio is rapidly increasing. However, related research is insufficient. In addition, existing research is only a conceptual guideline based on the opinion of the evaluator. Therefore, this study analyzed the literature related to the portfolio evaluation, analyzed and typified the portfolio components through in-depth interview with the working designer, and presented a comprehensive direction considering the specificity of the Korean design industry structure. Based on the results of this study, it is expected that designers will use the dynamic image to create a portfolio that reflects the latest trends in the portfolio and will help improve the expression and evaluation of individuals when considering the weighting of the text in portfolio formulas.

However, this study has the following limitations. the number of portfolio samples used in this study is 820, which is not enough. In the process of creating a dataset as a property of the portfolio, class classification criterion is ambiguous, it is classified as Good & Normal. When evaluated the portfolio through in-depth interviews, confirmed that the main competence such as designer 's understanding and analytical ability was evaluated through the context of the text. but, in this study, attribute describing the text context in the portfolio could not be found.

Acknowledgment. This work has been conducted with the support of the "Design Engineering Postgraduate Schools (N0001436)" program, an R&D project initiated by the Ministry of Trade, Industry and Energy of the Republic of Korea.

References

1. Amit, Y., Geman, D.: Shape quantization and recognition with randomized trees. Neural Comput. **9**(7), 1545–1588 (1997)
2. Behance. https://www.behance.net/. Accessed 15 Dec 2018
3. Blackburn, T.: Korea Design Statistical DATA, pp. 48–58, 223–242. Korea, Seoul (2017)
4. Chen, C., Liaw., Breiman, L.: Using random forest to learn imbalanced data. Technical report, University of California, Berkeley, US (2014)
5. Guido, S., Mueller, A.C.: Introduction to Machine Learning with Python. O'Reilly Media, Sebastopol (2016)
6. Han, S.M.: A study on the objective capability evaluation method through a designer's portfolio -focusing on visual designer-, Sungkyunkwan University, Korea (2011)
7. Jeong, H.K.: Development of a model for preventing informally discharged cancer patients using medical records in a university hospital. Unpublished master's thesis, Chungnam National University, Daejeon (2004)
8. Kim, H. J.: A study on the characteristic contents structure in the interior design portfolio, Sookmyung Women's University, Korea (2008)
9. Kim, J.K., Kim, H.H.: It's Design, Communication books, Korea (2011)
10. Kim, D.Y.: The changes in design area over time: focusing on the changes in the design department name and design profession field, Hong Ik University, Korea (2017)
11. Pinterest. https://www.pinterest.co.kr/. Accessed 28 Dec 2018
12. Quick Draw. https://quickdraw.withgoogle.com/, Accessed 20 Feb 2019
13. Shin, D.J., Kim, H.H.: Some thoughts about expansion of the design area according to change of the times – focused on invisible area. J. Digit. Des. **13**(3), 321–329 (2013)
14. Vanderplas, J.: Python Data Science Handbook : Essential Tools for Working with Data. O'Reilly Media, Sebastopol (2016)
15. Wikipedia. https://en.wikipedia.org/wiki/Decision_tree. Accessed 20 Feb 2019
16. Wikipedia. https://en.wikipedia.org/wiki/Random_forest. Accessed 20 Feb 2019
17. World Economic Forum: The Future of Jobs: Employment, Skills and Workforce Strategy for the Fourth Industrial Revolution. World Economic Forum, US (2016)

CasandRA: A Screenplay Approach to Dictate the Behavior of Virtual Humans in AmI Environments

Evropi Stefanidi, Asterios Leonidis[✉], Nikolaos Partarakis,
and Margherita Antona

Institute of Computer Science (ICS), Foundation for Research and
Technology – Hellas (FORTH), Heraklion, Cretet, Greece
{evropi,leonidis,partarak,antona}@ics.forth.gr

Abstract. Intelligent Conversational Agents are already employed in different scenarios, both in commerce and in research. In particular, they can play an important role in defining a new natural interaction paradigm between them and humans. When these Intelligent Agents take a human-like form (embodied Virtual Agents) in the virtual world, we refer to them as Virtual Humans. In this context, they can communicate with humans through storytelling, where the Virtual Human plays the role of a narrator and/or demonstrator, and the user can listen, as well as interact with the story. We propose that the behavior and actions of multiple, concurrently active Virtual Humans, can be the result of communication between them, based on a dynamic script, which resembles in structure a screenplay. This paper presents CasandRA, a framework enabling real-time user interaction with Virtual Humans, whose actions are based on this kind of scripts. CasandRA can be integrated in any Ambient Intelligence setting, and the Virtual Humans provide contextual information, assistance, and narration, accessible through various mobile devices, in Augmented Reality. Finally, they allow users to manipulate smart objects in AmI Environments.

Keywords: Intelligent conversational agent · Virtual humans · Storytelling · Augmented reality · Ambient intelligent environment

1 Introduction

Virtual Humans are embodied agents, existing in virtual environments, that look, act and interact with humans in a natural way. The incorporation of Virtual Humans (VHs) in Ambient Intelligence (AmI) environments can enhance the social aspects of interaction, offering natural anthropocentric communication [1]. In this context, Intelligent Conversational Agents (ICAs) enable the interaction of the VHs with humans, and can be combined with end-user development (EUD), to author and define the behavior of the agents, as well as the AmI environments [2]. In the context of EUD, providing users with intelligent tools that support authoring and creative processes is important [3], as user-generated content sharing has become a cultural phenomenon and interactive storytelling crafts are the focus of increasing interest [4].

© Springer Nature Switzerland AG 2019
C. Stephanidis and M. Antona (Eds.): HCII 2019, CCIS 1088, pp. 57–66, 2019.
https://doi.org/10.1007/978-3-030-30712-7_8

Storytelling and VHs, as well as game-like interfaces, have been introduced to replace or supplement GUIs [4]. Our focus, however, does not lie on how these stories are created, but on how to enact them, through the VHs; that is, on story telling rather than story creation. Storytelling traditionally relies on a predefined plot, concerning facts and occurrences, and involves presentation means such as speech, poses, and gestures of the narrator, in our case the VH, as well as representations of narration; that means textual as well as visual aids (e.g. pictures, videos, presentations, etc.) [4].

Storytelling is usually based on a script, the "screenplay", a term also used in filmmaking. In "The Screenwriter's Workbook" [5], screenwriter Syd Field defines a screenplay as a story told in words and pictures, so that in addition to reading the dialogue, the reader of a screenplay can read what the camera sees [6]. In our case, the readers are the VHs, who "read" the script, and act appropriately. We thus adapt the concept of screenplay to a conversation between VHs, who coordinate in order to enact a story. According to [7], a conversation is an interactive dialogue between two agents, which in our case are the VHs. In CasandRA, the conversation flow between the VHs is encoded in scripts, dictating their behavior (i.e. actions, movements, etc.).

In this paper we present CasandRA, a framework that enables real-time user interaction with ICAs, in the form of VHs, in Augmented Reality (AR), within AmI environments. These VHs can provide help and information, as well as act as story-tellers. Moreover, they allow users to use natural voice-based interaction to get information, as well as configure and manipulate various smart artifacts of the AmI environment. Our novelty lies in the communication protocol between the VHs, which dictates their behavior and intelligence. This protocol does not limit itself to speech, but also posture, movement, facial animation, etc., as well as the sharing of content with the users (images, video, presentation etc.). One VH (the narrator) is responsible for coordinating both itself and all the other VHs (demonstrators), who may be acting in the same or different devices. This protocol allows real-time interaction and is based on a dynamic script, which resembles a screenplay. The usage of this scripting technique facilitates the scalability and reusability of the script. Each script consists of sections which get selected for execution dynamically during run-time, depending on the interaction with the user.

2   Related Work

Several studies highlight the advantages of VHs, as they can elicit better results with regard to social presence, engagement and performance. In [8, 9] users favored interacting with an agent capable of natural conversational behaviors (e.g., gesture, gaze, turn-taking) rather than an interaction without these features. Moreover, research in [10] demonstrated that an embodied agent with locomotion and gestures can positively affect users' sense of engagement, social richness, and social presence. Finally, with respect to engagement, participants in [11] could better recall stories of robotic agents when the agent looked at them more during a storytelling scenario.

Regarding contextual awareness, and the capability of VHs to interact with their surroundings, [12] discusses the perception of changes to the environment as well as the ability to influence it with a VH, and concludes that this approach can increase social presence and lead to realistic behavior. With respect to environmental awareness, the research in [13–15] indicated that a VH in AR exhibiting awareness of objects in a physical room elicited higher social presence ratings.

VHs are investigated in various research projects, with different systems offering conversational abilities, user training, adaptive behavior and VH creation. For example, the ICT Virtual Human Toolkit [16, 17] offers a flexible framework for generating high fidelity embodied agents and integrating them in virtual environments. Embodied Conversational Agents as an alternative form of intelligent user interface are discussed in depth in [18]. Finally, in [19] Maxine is described, an animation engine that permits its users to author scenes and VHs, focusing on multimodal and emotional interaction.

In the same context, VHs have been proven effective as museum storytellers, due to their inherent ability to simulate verbal as well as nonverbal communicative behavior. This type of interface is made possible with the help of multimodal dialogue systems, which extend common speech dialogue systems with additional modalities just like in human-human interaction [20]. However, employing VHs as personal and believable dialogue partners in multimodal dialogs entails several challenges, because this requires not only a reliable and consistent motion and dialogue behavior, but also appropriate nonverbal communication and affective behavior. Over the last decade, there has been a considerable amount of success in creating interactive, conversational, virtual agents, including Ada and Grace, a pair of virtual Museum guides at the Boston Museum of Science [20], the INOTS and ELITE training systems at the Naval Station in Newport and Fort Benning [21], and the SimSensei system designed for healthcare support [22]. In the FearNot! application VHs have also been applied to facilitating bullying prevention education [23].

Existing approaches have been proven successful but target specific application, communication and information provision contexts. However, in order to unleash the power of Virtual Humans as conversational agents in smart environments, there are still several open challenges imposed by the radically changing ICT domain. Such challenges are mainly stemming from the need to address AmI ecosystems that have dynamic behavior and may offer unstructured and even chaotic interactions with unpredicted user groups in fluid contexts, changing through the dynamic addition and modification of smart devices and services. Current approaches do not provide a holistic method suitable for the broad needs imposed by AmI environments. A step towards this direction is the work in [1], where Bryan is presented, a virtual character for information provision who supports alternative roles and can be integrated in AmI environments.

Regarding the conversation between VHs, [7] presents a system for automatically animating conversations between multiple human-like agents. They focus on how to synchronize speech, facial expression, and gesture, so as to create an interactive animation dialogue. In [24] a new language and protocol for agent communication is described, called Knowledge Query and Manipulation Language, focusing on the dialogue between the agents.

Our approach goes a step further, by delivering CasandRA, a platform that allows multiple VHs to interact with humans in AR, in an AmI environment, by following a straightforward, screenplay-like dynamic script. The behavior of the VHs is dictated by these scripts, allowing them to appear across different mobile devices as well.

Furthermore, our approach enhances the storytelling aspect, as it is performed by multiple VHs collaborating within the AmI environment, to offer a richer and more natural storytelling experience, inspired by the structure of screenwriting scripts in the film and theater industries. CasandRA's infrastructure is implemented in a way that allows scalability, reusability and easy integration of new scripts defining the VHs' behavior and storytelling. Finally, CasandRA allows users to get information about their surroundings in real-time and manipulate smart objects both in the virtual and real world.

3 Requirements

The high-level requirements that CasandRA satisfies have been solidified through an extensive literature review and an iterative requirements elicitation process, based on multiple collection methods, as outlined below:

1. Brainstorming, where mixed groups of developers were involved (AmI usability experts and end users)
2. Focus groups with end users
3. End-users who were requested to perform typical everyday activities, in the context of the "Intelligent Home" simulation space located at the AmI Facility (http://ami. ics.forth.gr/) of FORTH-ICS, in order to evaluate how VHs could be of assistance
4. Scenario building during co-design processes, where experts and end-users were formulating scenarios of use together

The following requirements were derived for CasandRA:

R1. **Human-likeness of the Virtual Humans**: The system should allow for natural, human-like interaction between the VHs and people. This means the VHs should be as realistic as possible, as well as user-friendly.

R2. **Context-awareness**: The VHs should be aware of the context, meaning they should have behaviors corresponding to their context of use; for example, when they are deployed in a smart museum exhibition, they should be aware of the existing artifacts and any relevant stories about them.

R3. **Smart object discovery and manipulation**: The VHs should be able to discover the smart objects in an AmI environment, what can be done with them, and be able to manipulate and configure them.

R4a. **Dynamic dialogue between the VHs**: The conversation between the VHs should be provided through a dynamic script which will dictate their behavior. Dynamic means that different sections of the script are selected to be executed at runtime, depending on the interaction with the user and the dialogue flow that occurs.

R4b. **Hierarchy in the Conversation between the VHs**: The conversation between the VHs should be structured, i.e. follow a hierarchy. There should be:

- One master, the moderator of the conversation (or narrator), who gives "commands" through the dialogue.
- One or more slaves (or demonstrators). They are the ones receiving the commands from the narrator.

R5. **Scalability, reusability, extensibility**: The system's architecture should support: (a) scalability for addition of more complex interaction scenarios, (b) reusability in different applications and AmI contexts, (c) extensibility to support future addition of other AmI services and functions.

4   System Description

CasandRA is a framework enabling VHs to interact with users in AmI environments of various contexts (e.g. Intelligent Homes, Museums), and provide information, smart object manipulation, and storytelling services. This interaction takes place in AR, i.e. users can utilize their mobile devices (smart phones, tablets), to view their surroundings in AR, enhanced with the VHs and the functionalities they provide.

CasandRA is currently deployed in the "Intelligent Home" simulation space located at the AmI Facility (http://ami.ics.forth.gr/) of FORTH-ICS. Inside this environment, everyday user activities are enhanced with the use of innovative interaction techniques, artificial intelligence, ambient applications, sophisticated middleware, monitoring and decision-making mechanisms, and distributed micro-services. A complete list of the programmable hardware facilities of the "Intelligent Home", that currently include both commercial equipment and technologically augmented custom-made artifacts, can be found in [2].

4.1   Architecture

CasandRA's architecture, depicted in Fig. 1, consists of different components, coordinated by the *Agent Behavior Script Manager* (ABSM). The *Scripts* component refers to the dynamic scripts driving the behavior of the VHs and their interactions, which are structured as screenplays, i.e. a dialogue between them. Each Script is comprised of different "sections", which correspond to different interaction scenarios. The Scripts are dynamic, meaning that, depending on the context and the user input, which is processed through the ParlAmI framework [25], different sections of them are executed. ParlAmI namely receives and modifies the raw user input, using Chatscript[1], and is targeted to facilitating the definition of behaviors in AmI spaces.

The ABSM combines ParlAmI input with information from the AmI-Solertis [26] platform, which is used for service and object discovery. With the data that these two frameworks stream to the ABSM, it then instructs the Narrator Script regarding which sections of the Script should be executed at a given moment. The Narrator Script is responsible for communicating with the available Demonstrator(s), and instruct them which section of their Script they should execute; in more detail, each section of the Demonstrator Script corresponds to a specific "line" in a section for the Narrator Script. This means that the Narrator script includes a command (e.g. *Demonstrate Looming technique*), that constitutes a section for the Demonstrator, i.e. it is interpreted to one or more commands for him. This can be better understood by viewing the sample script

---

[1] Wilcox, B.: Chatscript. (2011) http://chatscript.sourceforge.net/.

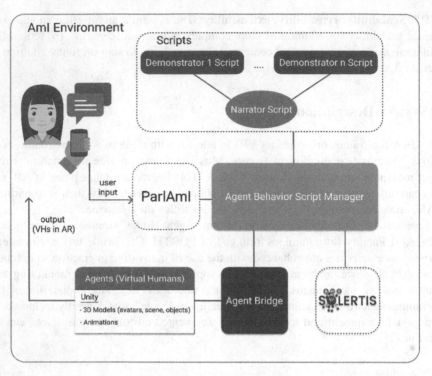

Fig. 1. CasandRA's architecture.

for the Narrator and Demonstrator Scripts in Fig. 2(a) and (b) respectively. We assume the context of an "Arts and Crafts" museum, where storytelling regarding the art of weaving with a loom is taking place. In this example, *Loom Storytelling* and *Behavior Definition* constitute different sections of the Narrator Script, while in the Demonstrator Script, *Demonstrate Looming Technique* and *Demonstrate Used Objects* are also different sections. For instance, when the *Demonstrate Looming Technique* section of the Demonstrator script gets executed, the Demonstrator should walk towards the Loom, sit in front of it, and begin to show how weaving with the Loom is conducted. After that, the Demonstrator should stand up. This is described by the commands visible in the Demonstrator Script below.

The ABSM allows a constant flow of information between all its components; thus, when the Narrator Script dictates that a VH should perform an action (e.g. say something, perform a certain physical movement), this information is passed on to the *Agent Bridge*. While the Narrator and Demonstrator Scripts constitute "high level" abstractions of the behavior of the VHs in natural language, the Agent Bridge (Fig. 2 (c)) converts them into separate "low-level" commands. These commands are then propagated to the Unity engine so as to execute the designated animations of the VHs in the virtual space. In reality, these functions constitute a remote API to an internal Unity module that implements them; for example, *PlayAnimation("StandUp")* is translated through that API to the corresponding Unity code, as depicted in Fig. 3.

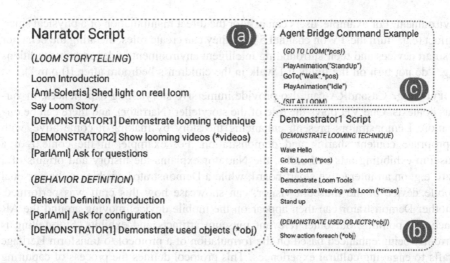

Fig. 2. (a) Example of narrator script. (b) Example of demonstrator script. (c) Example of agent bridge command

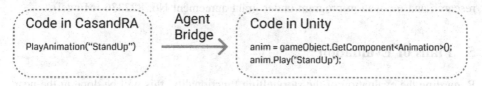

Fig. 3. The agent bridge translates CasandRA commands into Unity commands.

4.2 Use Cases of VHs in AmI Environments

The CasandRA framework can be integrated and used in any AmI environment consisting of smart devices and can provide Virtual Humans who can assist in various context scenarios. This section presents three such examples of VHs powered by CasandRA.

Assistance. The VHs can provide information and assistance to users, or even demonstrate how something works (e.g. tutorial of an Intelligent space or artifact). This kind of interaction is either explicitly initiated, after a user's request (e.g. "how can I use this switch", "what will the weather be like tomorrow", "is John home"), or implicitly, when the agent relies on contextual monitoring to detect when the user needs assistance. In the latter case, users can freely dismiss the agent if they do not want help. As an example of this type of interaction, when the user goes to bed, the agent can suggest turning off the heating or inform the user about any lights that remain switched on. Depending on the user's response, the agent learns to either turn them off automatically, or not bother the user in the future regarding this matter.

Behavior Definition. Besides providing information, the VHs can also be used as "virtual butlers", as a means of defining behavior scenarios in the context of the AmI environment. For example, users can ask for the direct manipulation of a physical smart artifact (e.g. "turn the TV on channel 5"), or they can create rules, dictating the behavior of smart devices and their surrounding intelligent environment under certain conditions (e.g. "do not turn on the lights if I walk in the children's bedroom after 10 p.m.").

Storytelling. CasandRA can also provide immersive storytelling experiences, in various contexts. One VH plays the role of the storyteller (Narrator), and there can be one or more Demonstrators present, enhancing the story by making it come alive, with appropriate content sharing and demonstration. For example, in the context of a museum exhibiting arts and crafts, the Narrator explains the history and origins of a craft, e.g. on an interactive smart board, while a Demonstrator, visible on the personal mobile device of the museum visitor, can showcase how this craft was performed. Another Demonstrator can then appear on the mobile device, moving around the AR space and pointing out other relevant museum artifacts and exhibits. Storytelling is currently being enhanced based on the formulation of a protocol to transform Heritage Crafts to engaging cultural experiences. This protocol defines the process of capturing information from multiple sources including motion capturing, and representing such information appropriately, so as to generate narratives that can be then transformed to CasandRA scripts. This work is conducted under the European Union's Horizon 2020 research and innovation program under grant agreement No. 822336 (Mingei).

5 Plans of Evaluation

Regarding the evaluation of the storytelling functionality, this will be done in the near future in the context of the European Union's Horizon 2020 research and innovation program under grant agreement No. 822336 (Mingei). The main goals will be to validate: (a) the protocol that is used to generate narratives, (b) the ability of CasandRA to transform narratives to engaging stories in intelligent environments, and (c) the exploitation of CasandRA in the context of Heritage Crafts training, where the VH acts as a tutor for craftsmanship education, based on the computer-aided authoring of interactive experiences that involve manual procedures, use of simple machines, and tools in Augmented Reality.

6 Discussion

This paper has presented CasandRA, a framework enabling the interaction between humans and VHs in AmI environments in AR, for information and assistance provision, smart object manipulation, as well as storytelling. It utilizes a novel technique for the definition of the behavior of the VHs, by employing screenplay-like dynamic scripts for the definition of the behavior of the VHs, whose execution can be modified in real-time, according to the interaction with the user. In particular, there are two different types of scripts: (i) the Narrator's script, responsible for orchestrating the behavior of that VH (i.e. directly instructs him what to say and how to act), and dictating the behavior of any Demonstrators; and (ii) the Demonstrators' script, which internally defines their behavior, and is externally exposed to the Narrator, so as to accommodate the overall scenario.

Our immediate plans include a user-based, full-scale evaluation of CasandRA's interface and functionalities, in order to assess its usability. Future improvements involve: (a) the ability to transform the narratives that will be provided by the Mingei project to CasandRA's scripts, for enriching the storytelling aspect of the system; (b) the deployment of the CasandRA framework on actual heritage sites; and (c) the introduction of an Avatar editing module, to enable users to select among available avatars for the VHs (Narrator/Demonstrators), allowing for further customization.

Acknowledgments. Part of the work reported in this paper is being conducted in the context of the European Union's Horizon 2020 research and innovation program under grant agreement No. 822336 (Mingei).

References

1. Birliraki, C., Grammenos, D., Stephanidis, C.: Employing virtual humans for interaction, assistance and information provision in ambient intelligence environments. In: Streitz, N., Markopoulos, P. (eds.) DAPI 2015. LNCS, vol. 9189, pp. 249–261. Springer, Cham (2015). https://doi.org/10.1007/978-3-319-20804-6_23

2. Stefanidi, E., Foukarakis, M., Arampatzis, D., Korozi, M., Leonidis, A., Antona, M.: ParlAmI: a multimodal approach for programming intelligent environments. Technologies **7**, 11 (2019)

3. Riedl, M.O., Rowe, J.P., Elson, D.K.: Toward intelligent support of authoring machinima media content: story and visualization. In: Proceedings of the 2nd International Conference on INtelligent TEchnologies for Interactive enterTAINment, p. 4. ICST (Institute for Computer Sciences, Social-Informatics and … (2008)

4. Spierling, U., Grasbon, D., Braun, N., Iurgel, I.: Setting the scene: playing digital director in interactive storytelling and creation. Comput. Graph. **26**, 31–44 (2002)

5. Field, S., Field, S.: The Screenwriter's Workbook. Dell, New York (1984)

6. Honkanen, S.: Stepping Inside the Story: Writing Interactive Narratives for Virtual Reality (2018)

7. Cassell, J., et al.: Animated conversation: rule-based generation of facial expression, gesture & spoken intonation for multiple conversational agents. In: Proceedings of the 21st Annual Conference on Computer Graphics and Interactive Techniques, pp. 413–420. ACM (1994)

8. Cassell, J., Thorisson, K.R.: The power of a nod and a glance: envelope vs. emotional feedback in animated conversational agents. Appl. Artif. Intell. **13**, 519–538 (1999)

9. Cassell, J., Bickmore, T., Vilhjálmsson, H., Yan, H.: More than just a pretty face: affordances of embodiment. In: Proceedings of the 5th International Conference on Intelligent User Interfaces, pp. 52–59. ACM (2000)

10. Kim, K., Boelling, L., Haesler, S., Bailenson, J.N., Bruder, G., Welch, G.: Does a digital assistant need a body? The influence of visual embodiment and social behavior on the perception of intelligent virtual agents in AR. In: IEEE International Symposium on Mixed and Augmented Reality (2018)

11. Mutlu, B., Forlizzi, J., Hodgins, J.: A storytelling robot: modeling and evaluation of human-like gaze behavior. In: 2006 6th IEEE-RAS International Conference on Humanoid Robots, pp. 518–523. Citeseer (2006)

12. Chuah, J.H., et al.: Exploring agent physicality and social presence for medical team training. Presence Teleoperators Virtual Environ. **22**, 141–170 (2013)
13. Kim, K., Bruder, G., Welch, G.: Exploring the effects of observed physicality conflicts on real-virtual human interaction in augmented reality. In: Proceedings of the 23rd ACM Symposium on Virtual Reality Software and Technology, p. 31. ACM (2017)
14. Kim, K., Maloney, D., Bruder, G., Bailenson, J.N., Welch, G.F.: The effects of virtual human's spatial and behavioral coherence with physical objects on social presence in AR. Comput. Animation Virtual Worlds **28**, e1771 (2017)
15. Kim, K., Schubert, R., Welch, G.: Exploring the impact of environmental effects on social presence with a virtual human. In: Traum, D., Swartout, W., Khooshabeh, P., Kopp, S., Scherer, S., Leuski, A. (eds.) IVA 2016. LNCS (LNAI), vol. 10011, pp. 470–474. Springer, Cham (2016). https://doi.org/10.1007/978-3-319-47665-0_57
16. Hartholt, A., et al.: All together now. In: Aylett, R., Krenn, B., Pelachaud, C., Shimodaira, H. (eds.) IVA 2013. LNCS (LNAI), vol. 8108, pp. 368–381. Springer, Heidelberg (2013). https://doi.org/10.1007/978-3-642-40415-3_33
17. Virtual Human Toolkit. https://vhtoolkit.ict.usc.edu/
18. Cassell, J., Sullivan, J., Churchill, E., Prevost, S.: Embodied Conversational Agents. MIT Press, Cambridge (2000)
19. Baldassarri, S., Cerezo, E., Seron, F.J.: Maxine: a platform for embodied animated agents. Comput. Graph. **32**, 430–437 (2008). https://doi.org/10.1016/j.cag.2008.04.006
20. Swartout, W., et al.: Virtual museum guides demonstration. In: 2010 IEEE Spoken Language Technology Workshop, pp. 163–164. IEEE (2010)
21. Campbell, J.C., Hays, M.J., Core, M., Birch, M., Bosack, M., Clark, R.E.: Interpersonal and leadership skills: using virtual humans to teach new officers. In: Proceedings of Interservice/Industry Training, Simulation, and Education Conference, Paper (2011)
22. DeVault, D., et al.: SimSensei kiosk: a virtual human interviewer for healthcare decision support. In: Proceedings of the 2014 International Conference on Autonomous Agents and Multi-Agent Systems, pp. 1061–1068. International Foundation for Autonomous Agents and Multiagent Systems (2014)
23. Aylett, R., Vala, M., Sequeira, P., Paiva, A.: FearNot! – an emergent narrative approach to virtual dramas for anti-bullying education. In: Cavazza, M., Donikian, S. (eds.) ICVS 2007. LNCS, vol. 4871, pp. 202–205. Springer, Heidelberg (2007). https://doi.org/10.1007/978-3-540-77039-8_19
24. Finin, T., Fritzson, R., McKay, D., McEntire, R.: KQML as an agent communication language. In: Proceedings of the Third International Conference on Information and Knowledge Management, Gaithersburg, Maryland, USA, pp. 456–463. ACM (1994)
25. Stefanidi, E., Korozi, M., Leonidis, A., Antona, M.: Programming intelligent environments in natural language: an extensible interactive approach. In: Proceedings of the 11th PErvasive Technologies Related to Assistive Environments Conference, pp. 50–57. ACM (2018)
26. Leonidis, A., Arampatzis, D., Louloudakis, N., Stephanidis, C.: The AmI-Solertis system: creating user experiences in smart environments. In: Proceedings of the 13th IEEE International Conference on Wireless and Mobile Computing, Networking and Communications (2017)

A Multi-stage Approach to Facilitate Interaction with Intelligent Environments via Natural Language

Zinovia Stefanidi, Asterios Leonidis^(⊠), and Margherita Antona

Institute of Computer Science (ICS), Foundation for Research
and Technology – Hellas (FORTH), Heraklion, Crete, Greece
{zinastef,leonidis,antona}@ics.forth.gr

Abstract. Due to the proliferation of Internet of Things (IoT) devices and the emergence of the Ambient Intelligence (AmI) paradigm, the need to facilitate the interaction between the user and the services that are integrated in Intelligent Environments has surfaced. As a result, Conversational Agents are increasingly used in this context, in order to achieve a natural, intuitive and seamless interaction between the user and the system. However, in spite of the continuous progress and advancements in the area of Conversational Agents, there are still some considerable limitations in current approaches. The system proposed in this paper addresses some of the main drawbacks by: (a) automatically integrating new services based on their formal specification, (b) incorporating error handling via follow-up questions, and (c) processing multiple user intents through the segmentation of the input. The paper describes the main components of the system, as well as the technologies that they utilize. Additionally, it analyses the pipeline process of the user input, which results in the generation of a response and the invocation of the appropriate intelligent services.

Keywords: Conversational agent · Chatbot · Intelligent environment · Intelligent home · Natural language processing · Home automation

1 Introduction

Research in the area of Intelligent Environments is booming over the last several years. The evolution of Internet of Things (IoT) along with the emergence of Ambient Intelligence (AmI) technologies have led to a plethora of web-based services and devices, with which the user interacts on an everyday basis, especially in the context of the Intelligent Home.

In order to achieve a natural and intuitive interaction with the intelligent environment, conversational agents (i.e. "chatbots") can be employed that utilize natural language - in the form of speech or text - to interact with the user. Over the last couple of years, due to advancements in Machine Learning (ML) and Speech Recognition and Understanding (SRU), their capabilities have expanded and their usage has spread, becoming a part of millions of households (118.5 Million Smart Speakers in the US

© Springer Nature Switzerland AG 2019
C. Stephanidis and M. Antona (Eds.): HCII 2019, CCIS 1088, pp. 67–77, 2019.
https://doi.org/10.1007/978-3-030-30712-7_9

alone since December 2018[1]). Popular examples of conversational agents in the form of virtual assistants are Amazon's Alexa[2], Microsoft's Cortana[3], Apple's Siri[4] and Google Assistant[5].

Using a conversational agent to communicate with a smart environment is not a new concept. There are a number of systems that use chatbots for home automation and control, even as kitchen assistants. However, in spite of the continuous progress and advancements in this area, there are still some considerable limitations in existing approaches. In particular, such systems require either user configuration before use, or reprogramming when adding a new service. This is inefficient, time-consuming, prone to errors, and most notably not user-friendly. Furthermore, errors in case of wrong or missing information when communicating with the Chatbot are not optimally handled from a user-centered perspective, thus resulting into a lack of understanding of the user's intent. This can prove to be particularly problematic, considering that errors during a conversation are commonplace. Especially, when speech recognition is involved, noise can easily alter the users input. Additionally, when the user's request is complex (e.g. *"Turn on the oven for 45 min at 180 °C and turn on the air-conditioning for 30 min at 22 °C"*), the necessary information is easily omitted or wrongly provided. Moreover, previous approaches are unable to handle input containing more than one user intents. For instance, the message *"turn off the water heater and play relaxing music in the bathroom"*, should be split into two separate commands, namely *"turn off the water heater"* and *"play relaxing music in the bathroom"* that should be handled consecutively.

The proposed system aims to provide a scalable software framework that can be used by conversational agents in order to facilitate user interaction with any of the available services of the intelligent space (e.g. home, classroom, greenhouse) in a natural manner. To that end, the framework:

- **automatically integrates new services** based on their formal API specification without the need for reconfiguration or user action
- **incorporates fundamental error handling**, by posing a series of follow up questions to the user, in order to acquire the necessary missing information and
- **handles user input containing multiple intents** by splitting it into separate sentences, which are then processed sequentially.

2   Related Work

Nowadays, Conversational Agents are becoming an integral part of our daily lives. A steadily increasing number of applications utilize them to achieve a more natural and seamless interaction between the user and the system. Notable applications that

---

[1] https://www.nationalpublicmedia.com/wp-content/uploads/2019/01/Smart-Audio-Report-Winter-2018.pdf.

[2] https://developer.amazon.com/alexa-voice-service/sdk.

[3] https://developer.microsoft.com/en-us/cortana.

[4] https://developer.apple.com/siri/.

[5] https://developers.google.com/assistant/sdk/.

incorporate Chatbots can be found in numerous fields, such as medicine [1, 2] and education [3–6]. Particularly in Intelligent Environments, populated by multiple heterogeneous devices and different IoT ecosystems, a single chatbot can serve as a common interface [7]. According to [7], this approach can address technological as well as human-centric challenges of IoT systems.

In the context of the Intelligent Home, there have been a number of applications that employ a chatbot or voice commands for the automation and control of the house [8–12]. Some of them accept as input simple commands such as "Turn on" and "Home" [8], while others understand natural language and engage in a conversation with the user [9, 10]. Some systems particularly focus on the Smart Kitchen, developing a conversational kitchen assistant that provides cooking recipes and nutrition information [13, 14]. In [13], the conversational agent can also reason about dietary needs, constraints and cultural preferences of the users, whereas in [14], it can guide the user throughout the cooking process.

For the development of conversational agents, different technologies and frameworks are employed, such as IBM's Watson[6], Google's DialogFlow[7] and Facebook's Messenger Platform[8]. The majority of those technologies rely on intent classification and intent extraction of the user input, using Natural Language Processing (NLP) methods. This entails training a Machine Learning model with multiple examples for each user intent. Another technique used to process user input utilizes keyword and action lists, where the former contains all the possible keywords relevant to the system (e.g. light, TV, temperature) and the latter contains all possible actions (e.g. open, close, increase).

3   System Objectives

The proposed system aims to facilitate Human - Computer Interaction (HCI), in the context of an AmI environment, by utilizing the Natural Language Interaction paradigm. It incorporates a Conversational Agent in the form of a Virtual Assistant with whom the user can interact, not only through text messages, but also through speech. The components of an AmI environment are exposed as services to the system, enabling the user to communicate with the environment through the Conversational Agent in a natural and intuitive manner. In particular, the system's objectives are threefold: (a) provision of information regarding the intelligent environment, (b) execution of commands that affect the intelligent environment, and (c) programming the behavior of the surrounding intelligent environment.

Provision of Information. An integral part of the system is the provision of information about the environment using natural language. For instance, in the context of the Smart Greenhouse, the user can inquiry about the condition of the crops or the environmental conditions inside the greenhouse. The system provides timely

---

[6] https://www.ibm.com/watson.

[7] https://dialogflow.com/.

[8] https://developers.facebook.com/docs/messenger-platform/.

information by communicating with the appropriate service. Consequently, the user can be kept informed and up-to-date about the environment, even remotely.

Execution of Commands. Another essential part of the system is to execute commands issued in natural language. For example, in the context of the Smart Kitchen, the user can turn on the coffee machine, or turn off the oven by expressing that intent. The system understands the task the user wants to perform and calls the appropriate function of the corresponding service. Therefore, the user can perform even complex actions instantly and intuitively.

Programming of the Surrounding Environment. Apart from acquiring information and executing actions, the user can program the environment by defining automations in the form of if-then statements. Through the trigger-action paradigm, users can define triggers that initiate specific actions when their conditions are met. For instance, in the context of the Smart Greenhouse, a trigger could be "*if humidity falls below 50%*", with the resulting action being "*turn on the sprinklers*". Thus, common operations in the user's environment are automated using natural language.

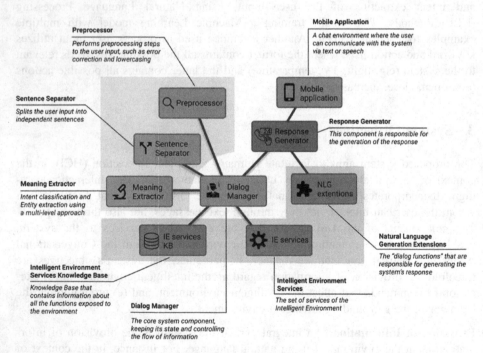

Fig. 1. The overall architecture of the proposed system.

4   System Architecture

As Fig. 1 illustrates, the system comprises of three main categories of components namely: (a) components that process user input aiming to extract its meaning, (b) components that interact with the services of the intelligent environment, and (c) components that manage the conversation flow and communicate with the user.

Preprocessor. It processes the user input before sending it to the Sentence Separator and performs various actions (e.g. lowercasing, lemmatization and error correction) to streamline the subsequent steps of the analysis pipeline.

Sentence Separator. Splits the user input into independent sentences. For example, the input *"turn on the light and the TV"* is split into the sentences *"turn on the light"* and *"turn on the TV"*. This is achieved through a heuristic approach, which incorporates the Dependency Parsing and Part-of-speech (POS) Tagging facilities of the SpaCy[9] framework, along with custom algorithms that aim to generate complete sentences by filling-in any implicitly defined data.

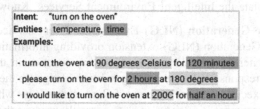

Fig. 2. Part of the definition of the "turn on the oven" intent. Rasa NLU relies on such detailed definitions to understand user input.

Meaning Extractor. This component uses Rasa NLU[10], an open source Python library for intent classification and entity extraction. In particular, three machine learning models are used, which are trained using the training examples that every intelligent service has registered in the IE Service Knowledge Base, as seen in Fig. 2.

- *Level-1* model: a general model that aggregates indicative examples from all the connected services
- *Level-2* service-specific models: they describe which intents a service can accommodate (i.e. the functions that if offers)
- *Level-3* function-specific models: they define in detail the arguments that a specific function of a certain service can have.

In more detail, the Level-1 model is mainly used for deciding the service with which the user wants to communicate, whereas the Level-2 model is primarily used for

---

[9] https://spacy.io: A library for advanced natural language processing in Python.
[10] https://rasa.com.

firstly deciding the function of the service that needs to be called and then extracting its arguments. Finally, Level-3 models are used for extracting the missing or wrong arguments of the initial user input, in a follow-up clarification dialog, when needed. This hierarchical approach is used to improve the accuracy of intent classification as already confirmed in [15]. Moreover, common user intentions such as "greet" and "help" are also incorporated and recognized from these models, with their semantics being model-dependent. For instance, the treatment of the "help" intent differs between the generic Level-0 model and a specific Level-1 model; in the former case the system should provide a general help message to the user, whereas in the latter case, the system should deliver context-sensitive instructions with respect to the given service.

Intelligent Environment Services and Knowledge Base. Each AmI service should provide an API that contains information about all the functions it exposes to the environment (Fig. 3). Concretely, for each function, its definition should contain the function arguments, their type, and their range or accepted values. In addition, it should include training examples of user input that correspond to the specific function being called. These examples are used to train the model that determines which service function needs to be called for a given user input. The set of all the services' formal specifications populate the Intelligent Environment Services' Knowledge Base.

Natural Language Generation (NLG) Extensions. Every service should provide a Natural Language Generation (NLG) extension providing information or the dialogue. Specifically, this extension should supply, for every function in the service, "dialog functions" that are responsible for generating in natural language the system's response upon successful execution or in different failure cases (e.g. when arguments are missing, when an argument is wrong), so as to correctly produce the response that will communicate the outcome to the user (e.g. provide a summary to the user with respect to the lock state of the home's doors, windows and shutters).

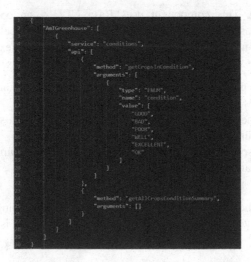

Fig. 3. Part of the formal API specification of an AmI Greenhouse's service.

Response Generator. This component uses ChatScript[11], which is a "next Generation" Chatbot engine with various advanced features and capabilities, in order to generate the responses to be communicated to the user. It invokes the appropriate dialog function from the service's NLG extension, depending on the state of the conversation, to produce the response. For instance, when an argument of a function is missing, it calls the corresponding dialog function which asks the user for that missing argument (e.g. *"Which window do you want to open?"*). The Response Generator also produces the responses to user intents that are not directed to a specific service, but refer to a more general context (e.g. when a user says "thank you" or "hello").

Dialog Manager. It is the core component of the system, keeping the system's state and controlling the flow of information. It communicates with the Meaning Extractor to discover the appropriate service and function and extract any provided arguments. Comparing the currently extracted data with the data that the discovered service requires, it deduces the system's state (e.g. wrong or missing arguments, successful extraction of all required arguments) and delegates control to the Response Generator for the generation of the appropriate response. In addition, provided that the state indicates that an intelligent service has to be invoked and all the required data are in place, the Dialog Manager is responsible of executing the call and forwarding the result to the Response Generator for further processing.

Mobile Application. This component is a chat environment where the user can communicate with the Conversational Agent via text messages or speech through a smartphone, as depicted in Fig. 4.

Fig. 4. Sample conversations between the Chatbot and the user in the context of a Smart Greenhouse.

---

[11] http://chatscript.sourceforge.net.

5   The Analysis Pipeline

The input is processed in consecutive steps in order to understand the user's intentions, invoke the appropriate intelligent service, and generate the response (Fig. 5). The analysis pipeline is used for all three types of user intentions in the context of the intelligent environment, namely the acquisition of information, the execution of commands and the programming of the environment's behavior.

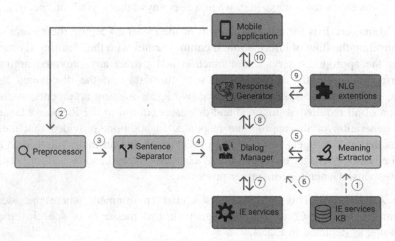

Fig. 5. A high-level view of the analysis pipeline.

Step 1: Initially, the Entity Extractor dynamically trains at run-time its internal recognition mechanisms with the appropriate model(s), based on the current dialog state; the training models are retrieved from the IE Services' KB. In particular, at the beginning the Entity Extractor loads the general Level-1 model that collects indicative examples from all the available Level-2 models (i.e. available Intelligent Environment Services), so as to be able to determine the service that the user most likely refers to. As soon as the desired service is detected (see Step 5), then the service-specific Level-2 model is used for training to facilitate the recognition of the desired function. Finally, if the conversation's state indicates that a number of arguments are missing or are incorrect, then a Level-3 model that corresponds only to the selected function is automatically generated and loaded to aid the extraction of the missing/incorrect data in a follow-up dialog.

Step 2: The user input is forwarded from the UI to the Preprocessor, where it is adapted appropriately.

Step 3: The adapted input is propagated from the Preprocessor to the Sentence Separator, which will split it into sentences if needed.

Step 4: Each distinct sentence is dispatched to the Dialog Manager, where further processing begins to understand the user's intentions and act accordingly.

Step 5: The input is forwarded to the Meaning Extractor component (whose internal recognition mechanisms have been prepared during step 1) to firstly discover which IE service the user wants to use (e.g. Light Service, HVAC Service, Cooking Assistance Service), and subsequently decide to which function of that service the user refers to (i.e. extract the user's intent which uniquely identifies a specific function). During this step, possible entities that correspond to the arguments of the desired function are also extracted. This information is sent back to the Dialog Manager for further processing.

Step 6: Since the desired function is detected, the system knows the exact number of arguments and types that it should anticipate. Subsequently, if any arguments have been extracted during the previous step (i.e. step 5), their types and values are compared with the expected ones; if any mismatches are found (e.g. missing arguments, incorrect types, values outside of the permitted bounds), the dialog's state changes accordingly and the Dialog Manager is notified to act accordingly (i.e. start a follow-up dialog to address these issues).

Step 7: If the system has all the necessary information to execute the function (i.e. no missing or wrong arguments exist), then the actual call to the IE service is carried out. As soon as the remote call returns, the Dialog Manager incorporates any results into the state and forwards control to the Response Generator.

Step 8: The Response Generator examines the dialog's state and schedules the generation of the appropriate response (see Step 9).

Step 9: If the user refers to a specific service, the Response Generator, depending on the state of the conversation, calls the appropriate dialog function from the service's NLG extension in order to produce the response to be sent to the user, namely: (a) ask for a missing argument, (b) notify that a value of an argument is out of range, (c) report the success of a function call along with any returning messages, or (d) report the failure of a function call and any possible error messages; for the two latter cases, the Response Generator retrieves any data posted by the Dialog Manager at step 7 that correspond to the value(s) that the function returned when invoked. For instance, if an argument of a function is wrong, it calls the dialog function that informs the user about the mistake, and asks for the missing argument (e.g. *"The zone number should be between 1 and 7 but you gave 9. So, in which zone do you want to turn on the water pump?"*); on the contrary, if a function call executed correctly, it uses the dialog function that reports the success message to the user (e.g. *"The alarm is set for tomorrow morning at 6:45 AM"*). If on the other hand the user's intent is not directed to a specific service, but belongs to a conversation topic of general interest, then an internal built-in model is used to generate the answer without having to consult any NLG extension.

Step 10: Finally, the response is communicated back to the user via the UI.

6 Future Work

A significant future advancement of the system will be the integration of context awareness. Contextual information, such as the location of the user, his profile, his current activity, as well as the time the conversation is taking place, will further enhance the system's user-friendliness and efficiency. Additionally, the syntactic structure and lexical analysis of the user input is going to be utilized for the improvement of service disambiguation and intent classification. Another future improvement could be the semi-autonomous generation of training examples for the NLU JSON APIs of the services. This will increase the number of the training examples and reduce human effort, while also potentially improving the accuracy of intent classification. Furthermore, the system's sentence separation will be enhanced, in order to deal with more complex cases, where attributes are involved. For example, the input *"turn on the bedroom's lights and TV"* should be split into *"turn on the bedroom's lights"* and *"turn on the bedroom's TV"*, with the attribute *"bedroom's"* being included in both sentences. The system will also undergo user-based evaluation in the setting of simulated intelligent environments.

Acknowledgements. This work is supported by the FORTH-ICS internal RTD Program "Ambient Intelligence and Smart Environments".

References

1. Comendador, B.E.V., Francisco, B.M.B., Medenilla, J.S., Mae, S.: Pharmabot: a pediatric generic medicine consultant chatbot. J. Autom. Control Eng. **3** (2015)
2. Madhu, D., Jain, C.J.N., Sebastain, E., Shaji, S., Ajayakumar, A.: A novel approach for medical assistance using trained chatbot. In: 2017 International Conference on Inventive Communication and Computational Technologies (ICICCT), Coimbatore, India, pp. 243–246. IEEE (2017)
3. Song, D., Oh, E.Y., Rice, M.: Interacting with a conversational agent system for educational purposes in online courses. In: 2017 10th International Conference on Human System Interactions (HSI), Ulsan, South Korea, pp. 78–82. IEEE (2017)
4. Heller, B., Proctor, M., Mah, D., Jewell, L., Cheung, B.: Freudbot: an investigation of chatbot technology in distance education. In: EdMedia + Innovate Learning, pp. 3913–3918. Association for the Advancement of Computing in Education (AACE) (2005)
5. Kerlyl, A., Hall, P., Bull, S.: Bringing chatbots into education: towards natural language negotiation of open learner models. In: Ellis, R., Allen, T., Tuson, A. (eds.) International Conference on Innovative Techniques and Applications of Artificial Intelligence, pp. 179–192. Springer, London (2006). https://doi.org/10.1007/978-1-84628-666-7_14
6. Ranoliya, B.R., Raghuwanshi, N., Singh, S.: Chatbot for university related FAQs. In: 2017 International Conference on Advances in Computing, Communications and Informatics (ICACCI), Udupi, pp. 1525–1530. IEEE (2017)
7. Kar, R., Haldar, R.: Applying chatbots to the internet of things: opportunities and architectural elements. Int. J. Adv. Comput. Sci. Appl. **7** (2016). https://doi.org/10.14569/ijacsa.2016.071119

8. Parthornratt, T., Kitsawat, D., Putthapipat, P., Koronjaruwat, P.: A smart home automation via Facebook chatbot and raspberry Pi. In: 2018 2nd International Conference on Engineering Innovation (ICEI), Bangkok, pp. 52–56. IEEE (2018)

9. Baby, C.J., Khan, F.A., Swathi, J.N.: Home automation using IoT and a chatbot using natural language processing. In: 2017 Innovations in Power and Advanced Computing Technologies (i-PACT), Vellore, pp. 1–6. IEEE (2017)

10. Baby, C.J., Munshi, N., Malik, A., Dogra, K., Rajesh, R.: Home automation using web application and speech recognition. In: 2017 International Conference on Microelectronic Devices, Circuits and Systems (ICMDCS), Vellore, pp. 1–6. IEEE (2017)

11. Zhu, J., Gao, X., Yang, Y., Li, H., Ai, Z., Cui, X.: Developing a voice control system for zigbee-based home automation networks. In: 2010 2nd IEEE International Conference on Network Infrastructure and Digital Content, pp. 737–741. IEEE (2010)

12. Baig, F., Beg, S., Khan, M.F.: Controlling home appliances remotely through voice command. arXiv Prepr. arXiv12121790. (2012)

13. Angara, P., et al.: Foodie fooderson a conversational agent for the smart kitchen. In: Proceedings of the 27th Annual International Conference on Computer Science and Software Engineering, Riverton, NJ, USA, pp. 247–253. IBM Corporation (2017)

14. Rystedt, B., Zdybek, M.: Conversational agent as kitchen assistant (2018)

15. Jenset, G.B., McGillivray, B.: Enhancing domain-specific supervised natural language intent classification with a top-down selective ensemble model. Mach. Learn. Knowl. Extr. **1**, 630–640 (2019). https://doi.org/10.3390/make1020037

Steering Wheel Interaction Design Based on Level 3 Autonomous Driving Scenario

Xiyao Wang[✉] and Jiong Fu

Shanghai Jiao Tong University, Shanghai, China
Essence@sjtu.edu.cn

Abstract. With application and development of advanced technology such as Internet, big data and artificial intelligence in the field of transport vehicles, autonomous driving technology and human-machine interaction (HMI) design for smart vehicles has become the focus of major car companies and technology companies at home and abroad. Before maturation and popularization of autonomous driving technology, the traditional driving devices can be retained to a large extent. Thus, the entity equipment inside a car has great potential of becoming efficient interactive medium. After relevant research and analysis, this paper sorted out the structure of mainstream users' demand for steering wheel interaction of the smart vehicle, and proposed a set of conceptual design to optimize user experience based on the Level 3 autonomous driving scenario, which is likely to be universal in next five years.

Keywords: Steering wheel interaction · Level 3 autonomous driving · HMI

1 Introduction

1.1 Background of HMI

In this era, with the rapid development of Internet and mobile terminal technology, intelligent mobile equipment such as laptops and cell phones has become an indispensable part of people's life. In such an environment, the development of the car, which is one of the most important vehicles, is slowly changing its trajectory.

On the one hand, people hope that cars containing more intelligent devices can provide more convenient and humanized driving experience. On the other hand, emerging Internet car enterprises have opened a new idea of making car with artificial intelligence and network. They cater to demands of the new generation of consumers with more fashionable thinking. The traditional car enterprises need to adjust the inherent mode of research and development (R&D) in the new era to achieve rapid transformation.

HMI is the interaction between people and cars in the scene of driving [1]. Inside of one car is a typical interactive space, where a large amount of equipment needs continuous operation and adjustment. It's vital to HMI research how users control the car, interact with all sorts of equipment and acquire information [2].

© Springer Nature Switzerland AG 2019
C. Stephanidis and M. Antona (Eds.): HCII 2019, CCIS 1088, pp. 78–84, 2019.
https://doi.org/10.1007/978-3-030-30712-7_10

1.2 Development Status of Autonomous Driving

According to the Society of Automobile Engineers International (SAE), autonomous driving cars belong to intelligent vehicles, whose level is from Level 3 (L3) to Level 5 (L5). These cars should be able to perform a complete dynamic driving task (DDT) with automatic driving system (ADS).

L3 is the level of conditional autonomous driving, which means the vehicle can do all the driving actions in situations where conditions permit, and remind the driver to take back the wheel when it's necessary. The most typical L3 driving scenario is where the driver can conduct no operation on the road which is determined by the system to be suitable for autonomous driving, and the vehicle will drive safely toward the destination. When current road conditions are not suitable for autonomous driving, the vehicle will alert the driver and must be taken over. This research is based on this scenario.

1.3 Background of Steering Wheel Interaction

Under the premise that the autonomous driving technology of L3 and above has a long way to be popularized, the steering wheel is still one of the devices that drivers interact most closely and frequently with the vehicle. That means steering wheel interaction design still has great potential for development. In recent years, there has been a lot of academic research, such as a multi-touch steering wheel [3] and Interaction techniques for Input based on thumb operation [4].

2 Research Content and Method

The basic process of this study is to establish research topics, conduct literature research, determine research directions, set up observation and interview outlines, find observed users, conduct observation through interviews, create user journey maps, conduct user grouping, summarize users' needs, conduct questionnaire verification, and propose conceptual design in sequence.

3 Qualitative Research

3.1 User Research Method and Sample Selection

Observation and in-depth interviews are used in this survey. In view of the fact that L3 autonomous driving technology has not been put into practical use, this study selected Shanghai and Shenzhen, two first-tier cities in China, as typical areas. A total of 16 typical car owners were selected for information collection. All of their cars have L2 autonomous driving technology and mature steering wheel interaction system. The whole process is recorded by recording, video and photo taking, and is sorted and analyzed in the follow-up. Each in-depth interview is about 45 min long. After selection, samples are divided into three levels according to the user's proficiency of the steering wheel interaction. Each level recruits five to six users.

3.2   Survey Outline

This survey produced an investigation outline based on users' process of using the steering wheel interaction while driving, which has been revised several rounds based on the results of the trial interview. In the observations and interviews, this study mainly used the POEMS framework (P-people, O-objects, E-Environments, M-Messages) to carry out the key Information extraction and recording.

4   User Research and Requirements Analysis

4.1   Requirements Analysis

Through observation and interviews, this study refers to the division method of KANO model [5], dividing the purpose of steering wheel interaction into two levels: basic quality and performance quality (see Fig. 1).

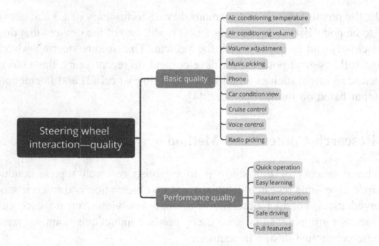

Fig. 1. Basic quality and performance quality

In order to dig deeper into user needs, this study has carried out a more detailed combing according to different driving mode (manual driving or autonomous driving).

What Is worthy of attention in the process of autonomous driving is that, due to more freedom of choice, users have more requirement than in manual driving. Personalized interaction is apparently one of the performance quality. According to interviews, there is a variety of solutions, such as entertainment interaction. Some users take a certain way to satisfy themselves, such as adjusting music by voice, setting commonly used hot spots, and so on. The study found that users' requirement of individualization and concise specification is concentrated and intense. If satisfied, user experience can be significantly improved.

4.2   User Group and Portrait

Based on assessment of 16 samples, this study divided the sample users into groups. In the object coordinate system, the horizontal axis and vertical axis respectively measures users' preference to the functional richness and the flexibility level for the steering wheel interaction. This study got four types of users (see Fig. 2).

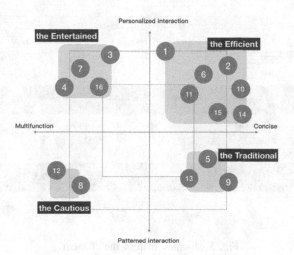

Fig. 2. Four types of users

The Efficient. The Efficient especially attaches great importance to the efficiency in interaction. They hope that operation in inside the car can keep up with the pace of life. They have confidence in the development of the steering wheel interaction, and don't think the basic operation needs to let them removed his hand from the steering wheel. They hope to custom their own efficient interaction system.

The Entertained. The Entertained like interesting interaction system which can be customized according to their preference. They think of their car as a mobile terminal, similar to the mobile phone. Because their require for efficiency of function control is not high, they mainly enjoy the in-car entertainment interaction.

The Cautious. The Cautious have strong learning ability and are good at quickly adapting to the interactive system modeled in the car. They attach more importance to safety than anything else, so they are not willing to customize the interaction in the car. They recognize the rich functions in the interactive system and feel more secure in driving because of them.

The Traditional. The Traditional regard the car as a means of transportation and are less likely to accept operation medium other than physical buttons. They do not have high requirements for in-car interaction and rarely use it. They are more willing to focus on driving itself rather than other things that may affect driving safety.

4.3   Journey Map

This study further researched the journey map of users and summarizes the pain points and chances (see Fig. 3).

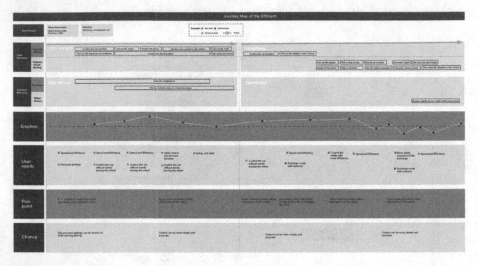

Fig. 3. Journey map of the efficient

5   Concept Design

5.1   Core Requirements and Functions

According to the results of requirement insight, this study determines the scene based on L3 automatic driving, and creates an efficient and personalized steering wheel interactive system, which not only improves the efficiency, but also brings entertainment experience to users by completing interactive function setting with concise and accurate operation.

5.2   Design Prototype

Through two pieces of screen with tactile feedback added to the wheel (see Fig. 4), users can intuitively customize functions in the process of autonomous driving or parking. Users choose the specific function by sliding thumb on the right screen, and by sliding on the left to adjust the specific function. By both the operation of the two dimensions, personalized settings and high efficiency can be realized at the same time. Because of the HUD (Head Up Display), users can efficiently obtain information without looking away from the road ahead, with the functions and information displayed on the front windshield during the driving process (see Fig. 5), so as to ensure that users can keep the mental concentration on driving at any time (see Fig. 6).

Fig. 4. Concept design

When the car is in static state, the system turns on the screen on the steering wheel to display. At this time, the user can freely set the functions and order of operation on the steering wheel to realize personalized adjustment.

When the car is in the state of manual driving, the display of the steering wheel screen is turned off to avoid distracting the driver. At this time, the two screens are equivalent to the touch pad, and the user can still operate, but the interface will be displayed through HUD to ensure driving safety.

Fig. 5. HUD display

When the car is in a state of autonomous driving, the vehicle will only in the necessary time turn driving power to users. The steering wheel screen is on, but this can only operate the car function, not to personalize the function. User interface can be observed through the steering wheel or HUD. When an emergency occurs, the steering wheel and HUD will flash a warning at the same time, with the sound and vibration hint. This design encourages users to remain highly focused on the steering wheel in the process of autonomous driving, without being busy for artificial transition. In order to allow users to operate safely through the steering wheel in the autonomous driving stage, the handover of driving rights can only be determined by the system. The autonomous driving status will not be affected when the user is holding the steering wheel.

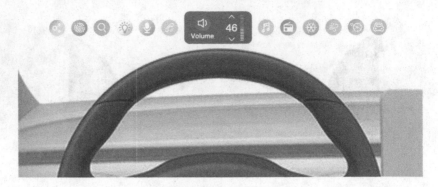

Fig. 6. Using scenario

6   Conclusion

This paper has designed a system of steering wheel interaction based on level 3 Autonomous Driving Scenario and takes into account the driving process and requirement of the target user.

The preliminary experimental results show that steering wheel interaction is surely useful for realizing high efficiency. However, far more usability tests need to be done with more sort of users and scenarios.

References

1. Zhang, P.: Advanced Industrial Control Technology. Elsevier Inc., Oxford (2010)
2. Schmidt, A., Dey, A.K., Kun, A.L., et al.: Automotive User Interfaces: Human Computer Interaction in the Car. ACM, USA (2010)
3. Pfeiffer, M., et al.: A multi-touch enabled steering wheel: exploring the design space. In: Chi 10 Extended Abstracts on Human Factors in Computing Systems, pp. 3355–3360. ACM, USA (2010)
4. Gonzalez, I.E.: Eyes on the road, hands on the wheel: thumb-based interaction techniques for input on steering wheels. In: Proceedings - Graphics Interface, pp. 95–102. DBLP, Canada (2007)
5. Kano Model. https://www.kanomodel.com. Accessed 17 June 2019

How to Optimize the Input Efficiency of Keyboard Buttons in Large Smartphone? A Comparison of Curved Keyboard and Keyboard Area Size

Yincheng Wang[1], Hailin Ai[1], Qiongdan Liang[1], Wenjie Chang[2], and Jibo He[1(✉)]

[1] Tsinghua University, Beijing, People's Republic of China
{wang-yc18, ahl16, lqdl8}@mails.tsinghua.edu.cn,
hejibo666@mail.tsinghua.edu.cn
[2] Wuhan University of Technology, Wuhan, People's Republic of China
narcissusc@live.com

Abstract. Smartphone has been constantly optimizing the user experience of viewing content by increasing screen size. However, larger screen brings about unsatisfactory input issue, especially for one-handed users. Curved QWERTY keyboard and reduced soft keyboard area are proposed to solve the input inefficiency issue of application design in the large smartphones. Following the design of existing curved keyboards, we designed a keyboard application, which could collect all the usage data, to test whether the curved keyboard or reduced-area keyboard could indeed solve the input inefficiency issue. By using within-subject design. we compared 2 screen sizes (5.0 in. vs. 6.5 in.), 2 area sizes (small-area: letter key area is 4.9 mm × 7 mm vs. large-area: letter key area is 6.3 mm × 9 mm), and 2 keyboard layouts (curved QWERTY vs. traditional QWERTY). The results show that the large-area keyboard is significantly better in terms of pairs per minute and reaction time between two keys, at the same time, the curved keyboard performs worse than the traditional keyboard. It indicates that the two design elements are not a common practice.

Keywords: Curved QWERTY keyboard · Reduced input area · Input efficiency · Reachability

1 Introduction

1.1 Input Efficiency Issue

The large screen smartphone is everywhere. Although Steve Jobs insisted that 3.5 in. is the perfect mobile phone size, smartphone designers have been increasing the phone screen sizes to optimize the user experience. From 2007 to 2019, the size of the Apple mobile phone increased from 3.5 in. (iPhone 4) to 6.5 in. (iPhone XS Max), and the similar increases in sizes for the Android smartphone. Among 3774 different kinds of smartphones, 6.5-in. smartphone (e.g., Honor 8X, iPhone XS Max) is larger than

C. Stephanidis and M. Antona (Eds.): HCII 2019, CCIS 1088, pp. 85–92, 2019.
https://doi.org/10.1007/978-3-030-30712-7_11

95.62% smartphones [1], while 5-in. smartphone (e.g., Huawei Changxiang 6S, nova 2) is larger than 13.46% smartphones [2].

Reachability refers to the difficulty and efficiency of touching with a finger for a point on the screen. The increase in the screen of the mobile phone has changed the center of gravity of the smartphone. In order to accomplish the input task, users have to continuously change their hand-grip posture and rapidly flex their fingers to reach the buttons which include some hard-to-reach keys. These hand-grip and reachability issues bring about finger fatigue and joint pain which leads to unsatisfactory input efficiency and experience. People sometimes have to use a phone with one hand (some people are originally one-handed users), such as in a meeting, or being busy with a variety of things, etc., and one-handed operation can improve the convenience of using the mobile phone to a certain extent. In the large smartphone, the above issues exist in different operation styles, however, they are more prominent in one-handed operation posture [3–6].

1.2   Curved Keyboard and Reduced Input Area

Three kinds of approaches were used to optimize the keyboard layout to improve input efficiency, including adaptive keyboards [7, 8], dynamic and static key resizing [9–11], and keyboard optimization [12–16], e.g., IJQWERTY, Quasi-QWERTY, etc. Although several of these approaches have shown some benefits, they all have failed to be widely accepted and have not proven to well solve input inefficiency issue in large smartphones [17, 18].

Researchers found that curved QWERTYand reduced-area keyboards may be useful and helpful. Trudeau, Sunderland, Jindrich, and Dennerlein found that the user performance with soft QWERTY keyboard could be improved by changing its radius of curvature, orientation, and vertical location on the screen [19]. Also, Fitts' Law shows that distance, area, and space are important factors for efficiency [20, 21]. Users have to frequently change their hand posture and move their fingers to reach all necessary regions of the phone screen relevant to their tasks, and the regions were defined as the "functional area" [22]. It indicated increasing the number of buttons in the functional area of the user's thumb could improve the one-handed input efficiency. Based on the above, curved QWERTY keyboard and reduced-area (small-area) keyboard are designed to solve the input inefficiency issue, e.g., Sogou Keyboard, ThumbFan, and WordFlow, etc. (Fig. 1).

Therefore, following the design of existing curved keyboards, we designed a one-handed keyboard application to test whether the curved keyboard or reduced input area could indeed solve the input inefficiency issue on different screen sizes.

2   Method

By using within-subject design, we compared 2 screen sizes (5.0 in. vs. 6.5 in.), 2 area sizes (small-area: letter key area is 4.9 mm × 7 mm vs. large-area: letter key area is 6.3 mm × 9 mm), and 2 keyboard layouts (curved QWERTY vs. traditional

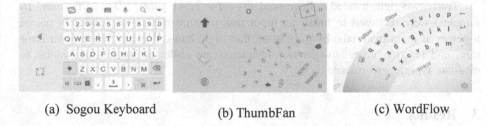

(a) Sogou Keyboard (b) ThumbFan (c) WordFlow

Fig. 1. Existing reduced-area keyboard: (a) Sogou Keyboard. Existing curved QWERTY keyboards: (b) ThumbFan, and (c) WordFlow.

QWERTY), and the apparatus are Honor 8X (6.5-in. screen) and Huawei Changxiang 6S (5.0-in. screen) (Fig. 2).

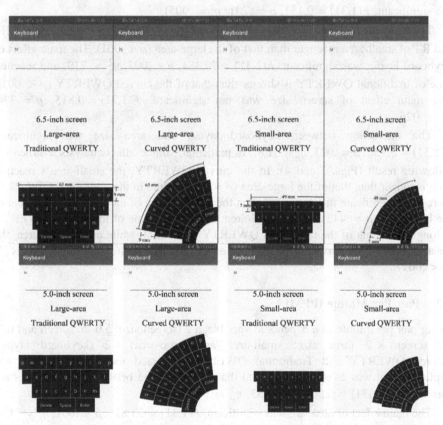

Fig. 2. All the conditions and application interfaces. In each keyboard, the length and width of each letter key are the same, while the functional keys (Space, Delete, and Enter) are twice as wide as the letter key. The parameters of the small-area keyboard depend on iPhone 4 s screen size (3.5 in.). Large-area keyboard, which is 1.3 times of small-area (reduced-area) keyboard, is covered with the width of the screen of the 5-in. smartphone.

Thirty-two right-handed college students (M = 22.41 years, SD = 2.70 years, 16 females) were recruited to finish an input task (two characters are randomly paired together as input materials) by only using their right hand. Pair per minute, pair error rate, and reaction time between two characters are collected by the application to evaluate typing performance.

3 Results

3.1 Reaction Time (RT)

Using reaction time between two characters as a dependent variable, a 2 (screen size: 5.0-in. screen and 6.5-in. screen) × 2 (area size: small-area and large-area) × 2 (keyboard layout: Curved QWERTY and Traditional QWERTY) repeated measures ANOVA was applied, and it was consequently found that the three-way interaction was not significant, $F(1,31) = 0.151$, $p = .701$, $\eta_p^2 = .005$).

The main effect of area size was significant, $F(1,31) = 15.362, p < .001, \eta_p^2 = .331$, and RT of small-area is longer than that of the large-area ($p < .001$). The main effect of keyboard layout was significant, $F(1,31) = 79.384$, $p < .001$, $\eta_p^2 = .719$, and reaction time of traditional QWERTY is shorter than that of the curved QWERTY ($p < .001$). The main effect of screen size was not significant, $F(1,31) = 0.815$, $p = .374$, $\eta_p^2 = .026$.

The interaction between keyboard layout and area size was significant, $F(1,31) = 5.733, p = .023, \eta_p^2 = .156$. In particular, simple-effect analysis returned the following result (Figs. 3 and 4): In the curved QWERTY, the small-area's reaction time is longer than that of the large-area ($p = .001$), while in the traditional QWERTY, there is no significant difference between the reaction time of the small-area and that of the large-area ($p = .442$). In the small-area, the reaction time of the curved QWERTY is longer than that of the traditional QWERTY ($p < .001$), while in the large-area, the reaction time of the curved QWERTY is longer than that of the traditional QWERTY ($p < .001$).

3.2 Pair Per Minute (PPM)

Using pair per minute as a dependent variable, a 2 (screen size: 5.0-in. screen and 6.5-in. screen) × 2 (area size: small-area and large-area) × 2 (keyboard layout: Curved QWERTY and Traditional QWERTY) repeated measures ANOVA was applied, and it was consequently found that the interaction between the three was not significant, $F(1,31) = 0.206$, $p = .653$, $\eta_p^2 = .007$.

The main effect of area size was significant, $F(1,31) = 23.816, p < .001, \eta_p^2 = .434$, and the pair per minute of small-area is shorter than that of the large-area ($p < .001$). The main effect of screen size was significant, $F(1,31) = 7.402$, $p = .011$, $\eta_p^2 = .193$, and the pair per minute of 5.0-in. screen is longer than that of the 6.5-in. screen ($p = .011$). The main effect of keyboard layout was significant, $F(1,31) = 117.422$,

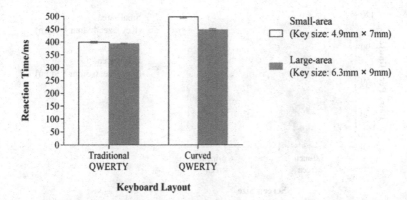

Fig. 3. Difference of reaction time between keyboard layout and keyboard area size. Error bar represents Standard Error of Mean. (Keyboard layout)

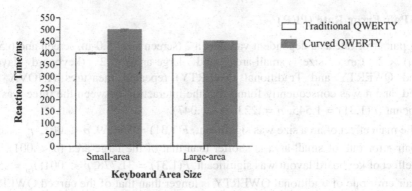

Fig. 4. Difference of reaction time between keyboard layout and keyboard area size. Error bar represents Standard Error of Mean. (Keyboard area size)

$p < .001$, $\eta_p^2 = .791$, and the pair per minute of traditional QWERTY is longer than that of the curved QWERTY ($p < .001$).

There was a significant interaction between screen size and area size, $F(1,31) = 5.704$, $p = .023$, $\eta_p^2 = .155$. In particular, simple-effect analysis returned the following result (Fig. 5): In the 5.0-in. screen smartphone, the small-area's pair per minute is shorter than that of the large-area ($p = .026$), while in the 6.5-in. screen smartphone, the difference between the small-area and the large-area was not significant in terms of pair per minute ($p = .197$). In the small-area, there is no significant difference between the 5.0-in. screen and the 6.5-in. screen smartphone in terms of pair per minute ($p = .991$), while in the large-area, there is no significant difference between the 5.0-in. screen and the 6.5-in. screen smartphone in terms of the pair per minute ($p = .561$).

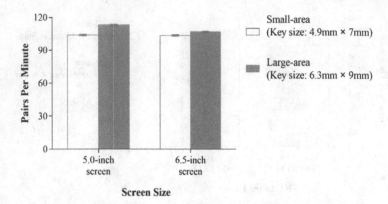

Fig. 5. Difference of pair per minute between screen size and keyboard area size. Error bar represents Standard Error of Mean.

3.3   Pair Error Rate (PER)

Using pair error rate as a dependent variable, a 2 (screen size: 5.0-in. screen and 6.5-in. screen) × 2 (area size: small-area and large-area) × 2 (keyboard layout: Curved QWERTY and Traditional QWERTY) repeated measures ANOVA was applied, and it was consequently found that the interaction between the three was not significant ($F(1,31) = 1.545$, $p = .223$, $\eta_p^2 = .047$).

The main effect of area size was significant, $F(1,31) = 55.269$, $p < .001$, $\eta_p^2 = .641$, and pair error rate of small-area is shorter than that of the large-area ($p < .001$). The main effect of keyboard layout was significant, $F(1,31) = 31.778$, $p < .001$, $\eta_p^2 = .506$, and pair error rate of traditional QWERTY is longer than that of the curved QWERTY ($p < .001$). The main effect of screen size was not significant, $F(1,31) = 0.017$, $p = .896$, $\eta_p^2 = .001$. At the same time, we didn't find other significant two-way interaction.

4   Discussion and Application

Based on the results, we found that the large-area keyboard is significantly better in terms of pair per minute and reaction time. The curved keyboard performs worse than the traditional keyboard in terms of longer reaction time.

In this study, we designed a keyboard application to test whether curved QWERTY keyboard and reduced-area keyboard could optimize input efficiency in large smartphones. The results showed that in the aspect of reaction time between two characters, the traditional QWERTY keyboard is significantly better than the curved QWERTY keyboard, and the large-area keyboard is significantly better in the aspect of pair per minute and reaction time. It means that curved QWERTY keyboard and reduced-area keyboard both perform worse than traditional QWERTY keyboard and large-area keyboard in terms of reachability and input efficiency issue. The reasons might be unfamiliarity with the keyboard, rotation of keyboard letters, and that large area was not covered with the width of the screen of 6.5-in. smartphone, etc. Besides, it indicated that 3.5-in. keyboard is not perfect in the large smartphone, and functional area could be more precisely redefined to enlighten keyboard designers.

In conclusion, although many designers intuitively believed that small-area (reduced-area) keyboard and curved keyboard can solve the reachability and input inefficiency issues of the large smartphone, our data showed no benefits of both small-area keyboard and curved QWERTY keyboard. Perhaps that is why the two design elements are not a common practice.

References

1. ZOL mobile Honor 8X. http://detail.zol.com.cn/1210/1209676/param.shtml. Accessed 13 June 2019
2. ZOL mobile Huawei Changxiang 6S. http://detail.zol.com.cn/1158/1157596/param.shtml. Accessed 13 June 2019
3. Boring, S., Ledo, D., Chen, X., Marquardt, N., Tang, A., Greenberg, S.: The fat thumb: using the thumb's contact size for single-handed mobile interaction. In: Proceedings of the 14th International Conference on Human-Computer Interaction with Mobile Devices and Services, San Francisco, USA, pp. 39–48. ACM (2012)
4. Kim, S., Yu, J., Lee, G.: Interaction techniques for unreachable objects on the touchscreen. In: Proceedings of the 24th Australian Computer-Human Interaction Conference, Melbourne, Australia, pp. 295–298. ACM (2012)
5. Yu, N.H., Huang, D.Y., Hsu, J.J., Hung, Y.P.: Rapid selection of hard-to-access targets by thumb on mobile touch-screens. In: Proceedings of the 15th International Conference on Human-Computer Interaction with Mobile Devices and Services, Munich, Germany, pp. 400–403. ACM (2013)
6. Girouard, A., Lo, J., Riyadh, M., Daliri, F., Eady, A.K., Pasquero, J.: One-handed bend interactions with deformable smartphones. In: Proceedings of the 33rd Annual ACM Conference on Human Factors in Computing Systems, Seoul, Republic of Korea, pp. 1509–1518. ACM (2015)
7. Gkoumas, A., Komninos, A., Garofalakis, J.: Usability of visibly adaptive smartphone keyboard layouts. In: Proceedings of the 20th Pan-Hellenic Conference on Informatics, Patras, Greece, p. 40. ACM (2016)
8. Goel, M., Jansen, A., Mandel, T., Patel, S.N., Wobbrock, J.O.: Context-type: using hand posture information to improve mobile touch screen text entry. In: Proceedings of the SIGCHI Conference on Human Factors in Computing Systems, Paris, France, pp. 2795–2798. ACM (2013)
9. Gelormini, D., Bishop, B.: Optimizing the android virtual keyboard: a study of user experience. In: 2013 IEEE International Conference on Multimedia and Expo Workshops (ICMEW), San Jose, USA, pp. 1–4. IEEE (2013)
10. Nicolau, H., Guerreiro, T., Lucas, D., Jorge, J.: Mobile text-entry and visual demands: reusing and optimizing current solutions. Univ. Access Inf. Soc. 13(3), 291–301 (2014)
11. Rudchenko, D., Paek, T., Badger, E.: Text text revolution: a game that improves text entry on mobile touchscreen keyboards. In: Lyons, K., Hightower, J., Huang, Elaine M. (eds.) Pervasive 2011. LNCS, vol. 6696, pp. 206–213. Springer, Heidelberg (2011). https://doi.org/10.1007/978-3-642-21726-5_13

12. Bi, X., Smith, B.A., Zhai, S.: Quasi-qwerty soft keyboard optimization. In: Proceedings of the SIGCHI Conference on Human Factors in Computing Systems, Atlanta, USA, pp. 283–286. ACM (2010)

13. Bi, X., Zhai, S.: Ijqwerty: what difference does one key change make? Gesture typing keyboard optimization bounded by one key position change from qwerty. In: Proceedings of the 2016 CHI Conference on Human Factors in Computing Systems, San Jose, USA, pp. 49–58. ACM (2016)

14. Dunlop, M., Levine, J.: Multidimensional pareto optimization of touch-screen keyboards for speed, familiarity and improved spell checking. In: Proceedings of the SIGCHI Conference on Human Factors in Computing Systems, Austin, USA, pp. 2669–2678. ACM (2012)

15. MacKenzie, I.S., Zhang, S.X.: The design and evaluation of a high-performance soft keyboard. In: Proceedings of the SIGCHI conference on Human Factors in Computing Systems, Pittsburgh, USA, pp. 25–31. ACM (1999)

16. Smith, B.A., Bi, X., Zhai, S.: Optimizing touchscreen keyboards for gesture typing. In: Proceedings of the 33rd Annual ACM Conference on Human Factors in Computing Systems, Seoul, Republic of Korea, pp. 3365–3374. ACM (2015)

17. Ljubic, S., Glavinic, V., Kukec, M.: Effects of interaction style and screen size on touchscreen text entry performance: an empirical research. In: Stephanidis, C., Antona, M. (eds.) UAHCI 2014. LNCS, vol. 8514, pp. 68–79. Springer, Cham (2014). https://doi.org/10.1007/978-3-319-07440-5_7

18. Zhai, S., Kristensson, P.O.: The word-gesture keyboard: reimagining keyboard interaction. Commun. ACM **55**(9), 91–101 (2012)

19. Trudeau, M.B., Sunderland, E.M., Jindrich, D.L., Dennerlein, J.T.: A data-driven design evaluation tool for handheld device soft keyboards. PLoS ONE **9**(9), e107070 (2014)

20. Fitts, P.M.: The information capacity of the human motor system in controlling the amplitude of movement. J. Exp. Psychol. **47**(6), 381 (1954)

21. Guiard, Y., Beaudouin-Lafon, M.: Fitts' law 50 years later: applications and contributions from human-computer interaction. Int. J. Hum.-Comput. Stud. **61**(6), 747–750 (2004)

22. Bergstrom-Lehtovirta, J., Oulasvirta, A.: Modeling the functional area of the thumb on mobile touchscreen surfaces. In: Proceedings of the SIGCHI Conference on Human Factors in Computing Systems, Toronto, Canada, pp. 1991–2000. ACM (2014)

Cognitive Issues in HCI

Attitude-Behavior Inconsistency Management Strategies in MTurk Workers: Cognitive Dissonance in Crowdsourcing Participants?

Katherine Fritzlen[✉], Dania Bilal, and Michael Olson

University of Tennessee, Knoxville, TN, USA
kfritzle@vols.utk.edu, {dania,molson2}@utk.edu

Abstract. Crowdsourcing refers to an online micro-task market to access and recruit large groups of participants. One of the most popular crowdsourcing platforms is Amazon's Mechanical Turk (MTurk). MTurkers are as reliable as traditional workers yet they receive much less monetary compensation (Pittman and Sheehan 2016). Many MTurk workers consider themselves exploited (Busarovs 2013), yet, despite this, many continue to complete tasks on MTurk. The purpose of this study is to investigate how MTurk workers dealing with inequities in effort and compensation. We experimentally manipulate expected effort and worker payment in order to compare how effort verses wage inequity affects workers' attitudes towards a series of tasks. We found that those paid more rated the task as more enjoyable and important than those paid less. Implications of this study are discussed.

Keywords: Crowdsourcing · Mechanical Turk · Cognitive dissonance · Wage inequity · Social computing

1 Introduction

The Internet has changed the possibilities for social science research. One of the changes is through the rise of crowdsourcing. Crowdsourcing refers to using an online micro-task market to access and recruit large groups of participants. One of the most popular crowdsourcing sites is Amazon's Mechanical Turk (MTurk). Studies have found that MTurkers are as reliable as participants from more traditional sources (Buhrmester et al. 2011), yet they receive much less compensation for their participation than other participants (Pittman and Sheehan 2016).

It is reasonable to believe that MTurk workers experience dissatisfaction over being underpaid for their work. In fact, many MTurk workers consider themselves exploited (Busarovs 2013), yet, despite this, many continue to complete tasks (called "HITs") on MTurk. How then are MTurkers managing this inconsistency between the effort they put into tasks and the payment they receive? We believe that this inconsistency is causing MTurk workers to experience cognitive dissonance (i.e. psychological discomfort) and they are motivated to reduce this discomfort through rationalizations about the importance and enjoyment of their work. We examine this in the current investigation.

© Springer Nature Switzerland AG 2019
C. Stephanidis and M. Antona (Eds.): HCII 2019, CCIS 1088, pp. 95–102, 2019.
https://doi.org/10.1007/978-3-030-30712-7_12

1.1 Cognitive Dissonance Theory

The theory of cognitive dissonance states that when a person holds two relevant cognitions that are in opposition to each other, this causes dissonance (i.e. psychological discomfort) to occur (Festinger 1959). For dissonance to be reduced, without changing the behavior or attitude entirely, one must either: remove or reduce the importance of dissonant cognitions or add or increase the importance of consonant cognitions (Harmon-Jones and Mills 1999). Of the several paradigms used to investigate this theory, the paradigms most relevant to the current investigation are the induced compliance and effort justification paradigm.

Induced Compliance Paradigm. The induced compliance paradigm states that dissonance is aroused when a person does or says something that is contrary with a prior belief or attitude. Based on the prior belief or attitude, it would follow that the individual would not engage in that behavior (Harmon-Jones and Mills 1999). Festinger and Carlsmith (1959) investigated this by testing the hypothesis that the smaller the reward for saying something that one does not believe, the greater the attitudinal change in order to maintain consistency with the behavior (i.e. the lie). In their study, they had participants complete a dull, tedious task. Afterwards, researchers told participants that the confederate for the next session was running late and asked if they would fill in. Specifically they were asked if they would tell the next participant how much they enjoyed the task for either $1 or $20 in compensation. Then, participants were asked to rate their actual enjoyment of the task. Those who were given $1 rated their enjoyment of the tasks as greater than those who were given $20. Participants who received the $1 for lying to the next participant had to justify why they had knowingly told the other person a lie (i.e. that the task was enjoyable) for so little compensation. They justified their lie through changing their cognitions about the task, that is, by increasing their actual enjoyment of the task so their attitudes would be in line with their behaviors.

Applied to the current investigation, dissonance may be aroused in situations when MTurk workers believe they are not being fairly compensated for the work they are asked to perform. In this case, the dissonant cognitions are workers belief that they should be paid fairly for their work and the reality that they are being compensated much less than traditional workers for the same amount of time and effort expended. This may motivate individuals to reduce dissonance by justifying their behavior (i.e. continuing to complete tasks), such as through increased enjoyment and perceived importance of the task.

Effort Justification Paradigm. The effort justification paradigm states that the more effort that individuals exert to achieve an outcome, they will be motivated to justify their effort exertion, and this will result increased liking for the outcome. Aronson and Mills (1959) tested this by having women undergo a severe and mild initiation to gain membership into a group. In the "severe" initiation group, women engaged in an embarrassing activity to join the group while, in the "mild" initiation group, the activity to join the group was not very embarrassing. They found that those in the severe initiation group rated the group as more favorable than those in the mild initiation group. Those in the severe initiation justified the effort they underwent to join the group by increasing their overall liking of the group.

Applying these findings to MTurk, dissonance may be aroused in situations when MTurk workers experience above-average effort exertion on tasks, such that they have to justify their continued participation. Previous research has found that one of the most reported complaints by MTurk workers about requesters was inaccurate task descriptions, specifically, advertising tasks as requiring less time to complete than in actuality (Brawley and Pury 2016). These inaccurate descriptions may cause MTurk workers to perceive such tasks as more time and effort consuming compared to tasks in which descriptions are accurate. If individuals find tasks more effort consuming than anticipated, due to inaccurate task descriptions, they may become frustrated and this frustration may motivate them to justify their effort exertion and continued participation.

1.2 Cognitive Dissonance and MTurk Workers

To our knowledge, only one study has investigated cognitive dissonance in MTurk workers. Lui and Sundar (2018) manipulated participants' perceptions of underpayment for completing a 20-minute study by either telling participants that the researchers had received additional funding and would be able to pay each worker more than the advertised compensation amount (i.e. $1.50 compared to $.50 in Study 1 and $3.00 compared to $.25 in Study 2). They found no differences between conditions in Study 1. In Study 2, found that those offered more than advertised rated task as less important then those who were not offered any more than the advertised amount. They found that increased perceived importance of the task was, in turn, associated with more enjoyment of the task, perceived choice, and less tension.

According to the theory of cognitive dissonance, dissonance is only aroused when a person does something that is contrary with a prior attitude such that, based that attitude, it would follow that the individual would not engage in that behavior. Therefore, dissonance-arousal occurs when individuals are invested enough in an activity to need to justify their continued participation. While Lui and Sundar found group differences in Study 2, they did not get participants invested in the task before manipulating monetary compensation, unlike previous research. Therefore, although they found that differences in monetary compensation were affecting workers task attitudes, we are hesitant to interpret these findings as evidence of cognitive dissonance-motivated attitude change.

1.3 Current Investigation

In the current investigation, we seek to replicate and extend the study by Lui and Sundar by investigating the compound effects of dissonance using both an induced compliance and effort justification framework. Although dissonance occurs in both of these situations, it remains to be tested whether the outcomes of dissonance are the same or perhaps compounded when the dissonance is aroused from two different inequalities (i.e. effort compared to payment) within the same context. In the current investigation we manipulate both perceived task effort and monetary compensation and look at how it affected workers subjective experiences of the task.

2 Methods

2.1 Participants and Setting

This study employed a 2 (Effort: Anticipated vs. Unanticipated effort) x 2 (Payment: High or Low) between groups experimental design and used both quantitative and qualitative measures to gather data about the experiences of workers. The survey was distributed using Amazon's Mechanical Turk in micro-batches over the course of six days. Participants (N = 334) were Mechanical Turk Workers from the United States. Data collection took place online, in a remote location, on an internet-accessing device (phone, desktop, or laptop, etc.).

2.2 Procedure

The study description stated that researchers were using machine learning to digitally transcribe thousands of old and damaged texts, and while the algorithms were adaptive, humans were still needed to inspect the algorithm's accuracy. Participants were informed the purpose of this study was to use human subjects to check the algorithm's text detection and transcription accuracy. Specifically, participants' job was to check that the algorithms were detecting all of the letters and numbers within the texts. Participants were offered $.30 to complete the task.

During the task, participants were shown several pictures of texts and were instructed to count and record how many letters and numbers they contained. This task was purposefully very tedious to make it more effort inducing to participants. The average amount of time in the description was manipulated between participants, which served as our manipulation of perceived effort. Those in the unanticipated effort condition were told the study would only take about 5 min to complete while those in the anticipated effort condition were told the study would take about 15 min to complete. In actuality both groups completed the same study, which took about 15 min to complete.

At the end of this task, participants were told that the study was over but were given the option to complete another, ostensibly unrelated task for additional compensation. Specifically, each participant was given the following information: "Thank you for completing our study. This is a pilot study for a larger experiment we will be conducting. We would like to draw a diverse number of quality participants and we think the best way to attract quality MTurk workers is by using positive evaluations of the task provided by past participants. Therefore we are interested in getting your positive reactions to the letter counting task. You are under no obligation to complete this task, but if you do, you will be additionally compensated $.02 ($.40)." The amount of additional compensation was manipulated between participants. Those in the low payment condition will be offered $.02. Those in the high payment condition will be offered $0.40 to complete this task. Those who opted to complete the task were instructed to write a positive endorsement of the task. Those who opted to not complete the additional task were immediately directed to the final subjective experience questions that participants completed before being debriefed. Participants who completed the additional were paid $.70 for their participation, regardless of what they were offered in the description. Those who opted not to complete the additional task were paid $.30, the amount offered in the initial task description.

2.3 Dependent Measures

The Intrinsic Motivation Inventory scale (IMI; McAuley et al. 1989) was used to assess participant's subjective experiences of the letter counting task across four different factors: importance ("I believe participating in this study could be of value to me"), enjoyment ("This study was fun to do"), perceived choice ("I believe I had some choice in participating in this study"), and effort ("I tried very hard on this activity."). Participants rated their agreement or disagreement of statements on a 7-point Likert Scale ranging from −3 (Strongly Disagree) to +3 (Strongly Agree). The order of items was counterbalanced between participants. Embedded within these items were three attention-check questions that had clear, obvious answers and were used to assess participants' level of engagement and thoughtfulness. Example items include "Please select 'Not at all Descriptive (1)' to answer this item". Attention was assessed based on the inverse of the error rate. Only participants with no errors were included in the final sample.

3 Results

3.1 Exclusionary Criteria

We excluded participants based on two criteria: their accuracy on the counting task and attention check questions. We excluded participants who did not complete the letter counting task as instructed, as evinced by their accuracy. We assessed accuracy by summing each participant's total letter and number counts and then divided their total count with the correct count total to create an accuracy ratio score for each participant. We excluded those whose count ratio was more than 10% off the correct total; less stringent exclusion criteria (e.g., 20%) led to similar patterns of results. A total of 124 participants fell outside this range, leaving a total of 210 participants included in our final sample. The frequency of exclusion did not significantly differ between conditions, $F(3,330) = .370, p = .774$.

To assess how carefully participants were answering questions, we embedded three attention-check questions within the subjective experience items. Only participants who answered all three questions correctly were included in our sample. A total of 27 participants failed at least one of the attention check questions and thus were excluded from analyses. Exclusion did not significantly differ based on condition, $F(3,331) = 1.294, p = .274$.

3.2 Subjective Experience

To assess participants' subjective experiences we created aggregate scores for each participant for each of the four subjective experience subscales. Results from a one-way ANOVA revealed a significant effect of wage condition on participants' enjoyment,

$F(1,166) = 4.135$, $p = .044$, and importance of the task, $F(1,166) = 4.320$, $p = .039$. Specifically, those in the high payment condition showed significantly more enjoyment ($M = 4.45$, $SD = 1.47$) and perceived the task as more important ($M = 4.78$, $SD = 1.48$) than those in the low payment condition ($M = 3.96$, $SD = 1.67$, and $M = 4.27$, $SD = 1.66$, for enjoyment and importance, respectively). Similarly, a marginally significant effect of effort condition on enjoyment emerged $F(1,166) = 3.430$, $p = .066$, with those in the unanticipated effort condition showing less enjoyment ($M = 4.04$, $SD = 1.51$) than those in the anticipated effort condition ($M = 4.49$, $SD = 1.61$). We did not find a significant Wage x Effort interaction on any of the subjective experience measures, all F's < 1.9, all p's $> .17$.

3.3   Positive Endorsement Task

A total of 67 participants (20% of our sample) opted to not complete the additional task. We investigated whether this significantly differed by condition. We found significant differences in those who opted to or not to complete the additional task between conditions, $F(3,331) = 8.856$, $p < .001$, with significantly fewer participants opting to complete additional task when offered \$.02 ($N = 51$) compared to when offered \$.40 ($N = 16$). We counted the number of words in each endorsement to examine whether length of endorsement differed based on condition as a proxy measure of participants' thoughtfulness and effort on the task. The results of a one-way ANOVA showed a significant effect of payment condition on endorsement length $F(1,166) = 10.76$, $p = .001$, with those in the high payment condition ($M = 17.18$, $SD = 13.97$) writing significantly longer endorsements than those in the low payment condition ($M = 12.19$, $SD = 9.64$).

4   Discussion

In the current investigation we manipulated perceptions of effort and monetary compensation and found that, opposite our initial predictions, those offered more monetary compensation rated task as more enjoyable, important, were more likely to write a positive endorsement of the task and wrote longer endorsements compared to those who were offered less money. Similarly, those given accurate descriptions of task length showed marginally more enjoyment of the task. We take these results to mean that, unlike previous research, it appears that fair monetary compensation and accurate study descriptions make individuals enjoy and tasks more, not less. Thus, it appears that MTurk workers are not changing their attitudes to justify inequity but rather are adjusting their attitudes to be consistent with equitable conditions. In other words, when workers feel they are being equitably compensated for their work and provided accurate study descriptions, they show more enjoyment of and perceive the task as more important than when they are not.

   While we did not find evidence that MTurk workers were experiencing dissonance, this may be due, in part, to a manipulation failure rather than a lack of dissonance. While our effort manipulation was supposed to induce differing perceptions of effort in our participants, we did not find any differences on the IMI effort subscale between the anticipated and unanticipated effort conditions (a mean of 6.08 compared to 6.01, respectively). Therefore, it may be that our manipulation was not strong enough to induce differing effort perceptions in participants.

4.1 Online: A Special Context?

Our findings do not suggest that individuals are using similar psychological and cognitive processes to buffer their perception of inequity and create consistency between their behavior and attitudes online as they have demonstrated in the real world. It may be that the online context affected how participants dealt with their dissonance. In Festinger and Carlsmith's (1959) study, none of the participants refused to help out researchers and lie to the next participant compared to the 20% of our participants opted not to complete the additional task. Declining to participate in the additional task may have served as a way for participants to reduce their dissonance (i.e. by changing their behavior). Compared to face-to-face interaction, there are less normative and descriptive pressures online to influence participants' decisions. Thus, the anonymity afforded to individuals in the online context may buffers individuals from social norms and conformity pressures present in face-to-face interactions, and with these reduced pressures, may have allowed them to address dissonance through a change in their behavior (i.e. stopping their participation by saying no the additional task).

It is likely that these participants, if forced to complete the additional task, would show subjective experience scores much lower than those who opted to complete the additional task. This prediction is corroborated by preliminary evidence coming from the differences between those who did and did not opt to complete the additional task. Those who opted to do the additional task did show higher importance and enjoyment scores than those who did not. Specifically, those who opted to complete the additional task rated their enjoyment as 4.26 compared to 2.47 for those who did not complete the additional task, and rated importance as 4.57 compared to 3.18. Therefore, it may be that those who experienced the most dissonance were also those that ended their participation early and opted not to complete the additional task, skewing our results.

4.2 Implications and Conclusions

In the current investigation we did not find evidence that crowdsourcing workers are experiencing cognitive dissonance. We found that paying participants more and providing them with accurate time descriptions of the tasks resulted in greater enjoyment and increased importance of the task. This, in turn, was associated with doing *more* work on tasks. It appears that MTurk workers are adjusting their attitudes to be consistent with equitable work conditions not to justify inequitable conditions. These results suggest that dissonance is less of a problem with MTurk workers than previous research would imply.

The results of our investigation have implications for the future of crowdsourcing platforms as a reliable way to gather data. Our findings suggest that participants' subjective experiences are more positive when they feel they are being compensated equitably, implying that crowdsourcing in its current form is sustainable given that equitable conditions are provided for workers. This sustainability is contingent on researchers' willingness to create such equitable conditions by providing workers with fair compensation for their participation. Research investigating worker experiences is imperative if crowdsourcing is to remain a valid option for researchers to recruit participants.

References

Aronson, E., Mills, J.: The effect of severity of initiation on liking for a group. J. Abnormal Soc. Psychol. **59**, 177–181 (1959)

Brawley, A.M., Pury, C.L.S.: Work experiences on MTurk: job satisfaction, turnover, and information sharing. Comput. Hum. Behav. **54**, 531–546 (2016)

Busarovs, A.: Ethical aspects of crowdsourcing, or is it a modern form of exploitation. Int. J. Econ. Bus. Adm. **1**, 3–14 (2013)

Buhrmester, M., Kwang, T., Gosling, S.D.: Amazon's mechanical turk: a new source of inexpensive, yet high-quality data? Perspect. Psychol. Sci. **6**, 3–5 (2011)

Festinger, L., Carlsmith, J.M.: Cognitive consequences of forced compliance. J. Abnormal Soc. Psychol. **58**, 203–210 (1959)

Harmon-Jones, E., Mills, J.: An introduction to cognitive dissonance theory and an overview of current perspectives on the theory. In: Harmon-Jones, E., Mills, J. (eds.) Science Conference Series. Cognitive Dissonance: Progress on a Pivotal Theory in Social Psychology, pp. 3–21. American Psychological Association, Washington D.C. (1999)

Lui, B., Sundar, S.S.: Microworkers as research participants: does underpaying Turkers lead to cognitive dissonance? Comput. Hum. Behav. **88**, 61–69 (2018)

McAuley, E., Duncan, T., Tammen, V.V.: Psychometric properties of the Intrinsic Motivation Inventory in a competitive sport setting: a confirmatory factor analysis. Res. Q. Exerc. Sport **60**, 48–58 (1989)

Pittman, M., Sheehan, K.: Amazon's Mechanical Turk a digital sweatshop? Transparency and accountability in crowdsourced online research. J. Media Ethics **31**, 260–262 (2016)

On Two Types of Thinking Patterns
in Aviation Safety

Hung-Sying Jing[(⊠)]

Institute of Aeronautics and Astronautics, National Cheng Kung University,
Tainan, Taiwan, Republic of China
hsjing@mail.ncku.edu.tw

Abstract. The theories of flight safety are examined from the thinking pattern point of view. Due to the different evolving environments of western and Chinese cultures, the basic thinking patterns are fundamentally different. The western linear thinking, based on the "event" of flight operation, results in the causal sequential type of flight safety theories such as the domino, accident chain, cheese theories. The Chinese pictographic thinking forms the different theory like the Flight Safety Margin based on the "feature" of flight situation, although which can only represent a very preliminary trial. The flight situation composed of features with many interacting factors included is used to comprehend the accident by the Chinese. How the features are extracted from flight operation still needs to be studied scientifically. How the features are correlated to form the significance of safety is another difficult problem. To clarify the Chinese thinking patterns in aviation safety will be a valuable research field especially after the Chinese C-919.

Keywords: Thinking pattern · Flight safety margin theory

1 Introduction

There is no doubt that aviation technology is totally Western. From the invention of airplane, to the manufacturing, and the standard operation procedures are all Western creations. It will be very reasonable to say that aviation bears almost one hundred percent Western characteristics. Hence, globalization for sure will create serious culture conflict including aviation safety. Although cultural ergonomics has been a discipline in the corresponding fields for many years (Kaplan 2004), serious problem is still there, like B-737 Max. It does represent deeper consideration about culture is needed.

In Western culture, the understanding about aviation safety usually involves sequence. Accident models and explanations contain simple chains of failure events. However, these event-based models developed to explain physical phenomena are inadequate to explain accidents involving organization, social factors, human decisions, and software design errors in highly adaptive, tightly-coupled, interactive complex sociotechnical systems. In addition, the influence from deep level of culture could even never be seen.

Even talking about the so-called system approach, it is still constructed using individual components together with discrete connections representing causal sequence

C. Stephanidis and M. Antona (Eds.): HCII 2019, CCIS 1088, pp. 103–107, 2019.
https://doi.org/10.1007/978-3-030-30712-7_13

between them. In a typical diagram for a complex system (Leveson 2011), there are only two kinds of elements, one is block while the other is arrow. Blocks represent individual components with the arrows discrete connections. For the connection, it can be understood as causal sequence appeared in theories as domino, accident chain, and cheese. In the West, the paradigm shift apparently observed in safety, as understood from event-based model to system model (Leveson 2011), represents only a shift about view point instead of the system itself. For the event-based model, the concentration is placed on the individual block, while the system model places concentration on the arrows, i.e., interactions between components. Obviously, it presents a progress although may not be enough.

In this research, a theory about the thinking pattern is considered. It is believed that the thinking pattern is the most important aspect in cultural study. The reason for the thinking pattern to be so fundamental is that it is the operating system of culture. A simple theory called the thinking pattern theory of culture is proposed from the knowledge of computer science. It is a three layer theory, environment-value-artifact, connected interactively with thinking pattern. The analogy between operating system in computer science and thinking pattern in culture will be provided. Therefore, all the application software in culture, like knowledge, science, music, painting, crafts, medicine, institution, social value, etc., have to be designed based on the thinking pattern, even including aviation safety.

There are two basic types of thinking patterns underlying all human civilizations. They are the one dimensional linear pattern created in ancient Greece, and the two dimensional pictographic pattern used by the Chinese. Both have cyclic form coming from the basic understanding process of human brain. All the human understanding about everything has to be a thinking cycle. Starting from the object to be understood, the process must go through a step of separation of information, followed by the essential "understanding", and through another step of assemblage, then back to the original object. Thus, the complete thinking cycle is then object → separation → understanding → assemblage → object. Although the basic cycles are the same for both the Western and Chinese thinking, because of the written scripts used, the contents are different. For the Western linear thinking, because of the alphabets, to understand means to find the essence of the object. The separation is the induction and the assemblage is the deduction. Therefore, the Western thinking cycle is then phenomenon → induction → essence → deduction → phenomenon. On the other hand, due to the Chinese pictographic written characters, the Chinese thinking is formed as phenomenon → analogy → feature → correlation → phenomenon. It is obvious that the understanding about everything of the Western culture is always through the essence of the object, while the Chinese through the feature. Countless examples can be found to reveal this fundamental difference in almost every aspect in both cultures.

2   Western Linear Thinking and Aviation Safety

In the Western minds, physical aspects of systems are thought to be decomposed into separate physical components whose behavior can be delineated as discrete events over time. And, the traditional scientific methods break the system into distinct parts so that the parts can be examined separately. The decomposition assumes that the separation is feasible, that is, each component or subsystem operates independently, and analysis results are not distorted when these components work altogether as a whole. This assumption implies that the components or events are not subjected to feedback and other nonlinear interactions and that the behavior of the components is the same when examined singly as when they are playing their part in the whole. In this case, the principles governing the assembling of the components into the whole are straight forward, i.e., the interactions among the subsystems are simple enough so that they have no any influence on the subsystems and these subsystems work separately the same as they work in the systems.

Living in the cradle of the ancient civilization, a place full of clay soil and reed, people from Mesopotamia created the most influential written script: cuneiform. All the alphabetical writing systems used today are derived from it. When compared with Chinese characters, there is an obviously striking difference. In cuneiform, there exists basic constructing units! Of course, it is because of the reed pen used. With only a few units, through different combinations, so many different languages can be spelled. Inspired by the concept of basic constructing units for several thousand years, western people instinctively believe that the understanding about everything can be established through the "essence", the basic constructing unit of thought.

With basic constructing units in mind, the domino, link, cheese, also the event can thus be created to construct the understanding model about flight safety. Those models explain accidents in terms of multiple events sequenced as a chain over time, just like languages being different combinations in sequence of alphabets. The events considered almost always involve some type of component failure, human error, or energy-related event. The chains may be branching or there may be multiple chains synchronized using time or common event. Other relationship may be represented by the chain in addition to a chronological one, but any such relationship is almost always a direct, linear one. As such, event-based models encourage limited notions of causality, usually linear causality relationships are emphasized.

The above mentioned methodology about system approach of safety (Leveson 2011) still represents a typical western conception about making sense of reality. Shaped by the alphabetical writing system, western thinking is always automatically looking for something like arche or essence for everything to understand, even when the object is called "system". This is the reason why western philosophy concentrates on metaphysics and ontology before any theory can be established (Jing 2012).

3   Chinese Pictographic Thinking and Aviation Safety

In China, on the contrary, with totally different landscape, the ancient Chinese created the famous oracle bone scripts, the direct ancestor of Chinese characters used today. When compared to cuneiform with obvious basic constructing units, Chinese characters has simply no basic unit! This is exactly the right reason why the Chinese characters do not have alphabets. For several thousand years, in Chinese minds, there is never anything like basic constructing units. Therefore, the Chinese always understand everything as itself, or as a whole, which is called holistic view. However, human brain cannot process all the information entering into the brain, the Chinese thus understand everything by extracting the "feature" of the object, the most representative portion of information.

Opposite to the Western thinking, Chinese thinking is always automatically looking for holistic characteristics for everything to comprehend (Jing 2016). The ideographic thinking is of networking type instead of sequential, with emphasis placed on the connections. This is the most fundamental difference between linear and pictographic thinking, since that linear thinking focus on the substance or entity, as described by Aristotle, while pictographic thinking focus on the correlation among entities. In the Chinese thinking, there is no such thing as individual component and discrete connection. Hence, to have a real Chinese theory for flight safety, the concept of individual component and discrete connection have to be abandoned, at least modified. Otherwise, we will be still discussing event-based model with more complex structure at most.

Operationally, originating from an alphabetical system, the linear mode of thinking of Westerners stresses sequence composed of elements, and values logic, with analytical capability as its specialty. On the other hand, the Chinese pictographic mode of thinking, is holistic with stressing equilibrium between features. The special capability as different from the western counterpart is called insight, finding system features with given only very little information. Moreover, this fundamental difference has already existed for at least two thousand years due to the fostering geographical environments. As long as the Chinese people still use their writing characters, and Western cultures also keep on using alphabets, the difference will definitely persist in the foreseeable future. Consequently, it would be quite helpful to have alternatively a theory derived from the Chinese mode of thinking and create a Chinese theory for flight safety as the insufficiency of the Western linear thinking has already been exposed.

There is still no any rigorous flight safety theory based on the Chinese pictographic thinking even today, although the very crude Flight Safety Margin theory can be recognized as the very first one (Jing and Batteau 2015). The most fundamental reason for this peculiar situation is from the development of philosophy. Basically, philosophy is a kind of knowledge about thinking itself. Ancient Greeks had already spent huge amount of time to clarify the linear thinking pattern, and the result is quite spectacular. However, it never happened in Chinese history because of the separation of the language and the written scripts, and the pictographic nature of Chinese characters. Thereafter, the ancient Chinese intellects had almost never discussed the Chinese thinking itself. This is also the basic reason for the existence of the argument about whether China has philosophy (Jing 2016).

However, after thousands of years of development, it is still very hard to say that the Chinese holistic thinking has being clarified. It is still in the deep midst although it has being used successfully in different fields in the long history of China. This is the reason why some western scholars argued, and agreed by certain amount of Chinese scholars, that there is no philosophy in China. The main reason for this peculiar phenomenon is that the Chinese thinking pattern had being discussed seriously only in a very short period of time two thousand years ago. After that, the discussion ended almost forever. The group of scholars seriously discussed how the Chinese think is called the School of Names. Although the Chinese system thinking is still not clear, the key feature has been already revealed to some extent.

The Flight Safety Margin theory represents the first step to use Chinese thinking in flight safety. To proceed, more typical features of Chinese thinking have to be incorporated. The next step will be to use holistic characteristics to replace individual parameters. Everything must be understood interactively as a whole. Consequently, every flight parameter must be understood as a group of parameters. The term "event" can also be modified to incorporate the Chinese thinking. "Event" means there are certain components going wrong so that something bad happens. In Chinese system thinking, the appropriate term is symptom. Symptom means situation deviating away from normal and being understood from the characteristics point of view, or deviation of a group of parameters with certain characteristics representation. Of course, this step will be very difficult. The reason is that the analogy, similar to the induction in Western thinking, has to be done first for any meaningful step can proceed. Analogy here means we have to identify features, group of interrelated parameters, related to flight safety through comparison with lots of data from accidents and events. Just like the Chinese five operations, wood, fire, earth, metal, water, flight safety symptoms can be defined as well. If that can be done, a real Chinese pictographic theory without individual components and discrete connections, and different from the simple multilinear aggregation of discrete elements, can then be discussed seriously.

4 Future Development

A scientific theory about flight safety based of the Chinese pictographic thinking is surely possible, although it is extremely difficult. Up until now, the process about how the object is decomposed into features through analogy, and how the features are correlated into the understanding of the corresponding phenomena is still in the deep midst. As for flight safety, the flight situation composed of features with many interacting factors included should be used to comprehend the accident. How the features are extracted from flight operation also needs to be studied scientifically. How the features are correlated to form the significance of safety is another difficult problem. To clarify the Chinese thinking patterns in aviation safety will be a valuable research field to be explored along with the increasing influence of China in aviation, e.g., C919. It is expected that it will be a special topic in aviation psychology.

References

Jing, H.-S.: The Critique of Western Philosophy (in Chinese). The Science Monthly Publishing Co., Taipei (2012)

Jing, H.-S., Batteau, A.: The Dragon in the Cockpit – How Western Aviation Concepts Conflict with Chinese Value Systems. Ashgate Publishing Limited, Farnham (2015)

Jing, H.-S.: The Gon Sun Lon and the School of Names – New Interpretation with Pictorial Thinking (in Chinese). The National Cheng Kung University Press, Tainan (2016)

Kaplan, M.: Cultural Ergonomics. Elsevier Ltd., Amsterdam (2004)

Leveson, N.G.: Engineering a Safer World: System Thinking Applied to Safety. The MIT Press, Massachusetts (2011)

Detecting and Identifying Real and Decoy Tanks in a Computer Screen: Evidence from Stimuli Sensitivity and Eye-Tracking

Kari Kallinen[(⊠)]

Finnish Defense Research Agency, Riihimäki, Finland
kari.kallinen@mil.fi

Abstract. In a modern warfare as well as in reconnaissance operations it is on one hand highly important to hide and protect own troops but on the other hand find and target the enemy. Target identification is often based on visual examination of video or still images produced by for example by Unmanned Aerial Vehicles (UAVs) or other means of Intelligence, Surveillance, and Reconnaissance (ISR). In the present study we examined the perception, detection and identification of real and decoy tanks among a total of 28 participants using reaction time tests and eye-tracking recordings during categorizing tasks of images of tanks (real vs. fake; without vs. with camouflage). We found, among other things, that fake and camouflage images of tanks as compared to real and non-camouflage images decreased identification speed. We also found that camouflage images elicited more attention shifting between image and background as compared to non-camouflage images. We argued that this is probable due the fact that as camouflage blurs the image contour and sharpness people seek cues for categorization by switching between image and background. The results are important in understanding the perception and identification of military visual objects in displays and can be used for example in optimization of decoys as well as, in connection with detection, configuring display settings.

Keywords: Target identification · Decoy · Camouflage · Tank · Eye-tracking · Screen

1 Introduction

In a modern warfare as well as in reconnaissance operations it is on one hand highly important to hide and protect own troops but on the other hand find and target the enemy. The protection of armament can be achieved for example by using camouflage and/or decoys. Most visual intelligence information gathered today comes from aerial photographs taken by various means of ISR (e.g., spy satellites, reconnaissance aircraft, UAVs) and presented in different displays. However, photos of dummy and/or camouflage tanks, planes and guns can deceive even trained analysts. In order to be able to hide and seek as well as build good decoys it is important to study the processes behind observing, detecting and identifying military objects. However, even though there is some previous research on camouflage (see for example King et al. 1984), there

© Springer Nature Switzerland AG 2019
C. Stephanidis and M. Antona (Eds.): HCII 2019, CCIS 1088, pp. 108–112, 2019.
https://doi.org/10.1007/978-3-030-30712-7_14

is scarcity of publically available studies especially on camouflage and decoys in military settings.

A military decoy is a low-cost fake military equipment device intended to represent a real item of military equipment to fool enemy forces into attacking them and so protect the real items of equipment by diverting fire away from them. A fake item is usually intended to be visible to enemy. In contrast, military camouflage is the use of camouflage to protect personnel and equipment from observation by enemy forces. In connection with tanks, camouflage differs from personal camouflage in that as the primary threat is aerial reconnaissance the goal is to disrupt the characteristic shape of the vehicle, to reduce shine, and to make the vehicle difficult to identify even if it is spotted. In practice, the main difference between real and fake and without and with camouflage objects is the lack in the details and roughness of shapes and contours visually available for the observer. Therefore, in general we expected that fake and camouflage images of tanks should be harder to detect than images of real and no-camouflage tanks.

On the basis of aforementioned arguments we expected that the sensitivity (i.e., signal-noise ratio) would be better in connection with real and non-camouflage images as compared to fake and camouflage images (Hypothesis 1A). We also expected that the identification speed would be lower and error rate higher for the fake and camouflage as compared to real and non-camouflage images (Hypothesis 1B). In connection with decoys, we expected that because decoys lack the visual details as compared to real objects, fake tanks would involve more attention to the image area and less attention switching between image and background than real tanks (Hypothesis 2A). We also expected that because camouflage disrupts the characteristic shape and contour of the vehicle as compared to the background, camouflage tanks would involve more attention to the outside image area and attention switching between image and background as compared to non-camouflage tanks (Hypothesis 2B).

We investigated the abovementioned hypothesis in two experiments: in the first experiment we examined the categorizations speed and accuracy of real and fake tanks with and without camouflage; in the second experiments we examined the eye-tracking activity associated to the evaluation of the images.

2 Methods

2.1 Participants and Materials

A total of 28 subjects participated to the study. They were 15 men and 13 women aged from 18 to 56 ($M = 38$). Most of them were associated with Finnish Defense Forces (as officers, civilian staff or conscripts). Eight people took part to experiment 1 (categorization speed) and 20 people (divided in two groups of 10 people) in experiment 2 (group 1 for images of real and fake tanks without camouflage and group 2 for images of real and fake tanks with camouflage).

On the basis of expert evaluations, we chose 9 pictures of real tanks and 9 pictures of fake tanks publically available in internet and standardized them to about a size of 600×400 pixels. The camouflage versions of the tanks were produced by 40%

blending by a camouflage image with the tank images using Photoshop image processing software. The real (top-left) and fake (top-right) and their camouflage versions
(bottom left and right) are illustrated in the Fig. 1.

Fig. 1. Images of the real and fake tanks without (top) and with (bottom) camouflage.

2.2 Measures

Demographics (age, gender, etc.) and was assessed with a self-report questionnaire.

Go/No-go test (see e.g., Fillmore et al. 2006) in the Inquisit stimuli presentation
software (millisecond.com) was used to assess the identification speed and accuracy of
images of tanks in experiment 1. A sensitivity index (d prime), identification speed and
error rates were calculated. The d prime sensitivity index was calculated as z-score of
the overall successful hit rate minus z-score of the overall false alarm rate in the
GO/NO test.

In the experiment 2, eye movements were tracked using a head-mounted eye-
tracker "Dikablis" (Ergoneers GmbH, Manching, Germany) with a sampling rate of
60 Hz, scene camera field of view of 120°, using four point calibration, contrast pupil
detection and D-Lab 3.5 recording software. Areas of interests (AOIs) were drawn with
D-lab AOI tool for tank image and background areas and used to examine the visual
activity with-in and between image and background by calculating the attention ratio
and transition times between image area and background.

2.3 Procedure

Before experiment, the participants were properly informed and instructed in the course
of experiment.

In experiment 1 (detection speed), the participant was told to respond as fast as possible to the target type of stimuli by pressing a space button in computer. Stimuli consisted of four blocks of trials. In first block the task was to response as fast as possible for the real tanks (but not for fake tanks); In the second block the task was to response as fast as possible for the fake tanks (but not for real tanks); Block 3 was same as block 1 and block 4 the same as block 2 but with camouflaged images. The order of the blocks was balanced using Lating Square. Each block consisted of a practice session followed by a trial with 50 stimuli (40 go stimuli and 10 no-go stimuli). The stimuli were randomly selected from the set of 18 images without and 18 images with camouflage.

In the experiment 2 (eye-tracking), participants were told to look at the images for six seconds as they were presented the center of the computer screen and then choose a between two radio buttons (real, fake) whether the image that was presented was a fake or a real tank.

After experiment the participants were debriefed and thanked. The experiments took place in a quiet office room and took from 10 min (experiment 1) to 20 min (experiment 2).

2.4   Data Processing and Analysis

Data for the first experiment (identification speed) was analyzed by the Linear Mixed Model in SPSS, with tank type (real, fake) and camouflage (without, with) as fixed factors and sensitivity index, identification speed and error rate, each in turn, as a dependent variable.

The eye-tracking data was analyzed by the General Linear Model (GLM) Repeated Measures procedure in SPSS, with image type (real, fake) and camouflage (without, with) as with-in subjects factors and continuous independent variables (i.e., AOI attention ratio and percentage of transition times), each in turn, as a covariate.

3   Results

As expected and illustrated in summary Table 1 below, the results showed that (1) the sensitivity was higher for real than fake tanks (for camouflage there was no difference), (2) the identification speed was lower for fake and camouflage images as compared to real and non-camouflage images, and (3) the error rate for fake images was higher than for real images (for camouflage vs. non-camouflage there was no difference). Therefore the results supported our Hypothesis 1A (partly) and 1B.

As also expected and illustrated in the Table 1, awe found that fake tanks involved more attention to the image area and less attention switching between image and background than real tanks and that camouflage tanks involved more attention to the outside image area and attention switching between image and background as compared to non-camouflage tanks. Therefore our Hypothesis 2A and 2B were supported.

Table 1. Summary of the results

Variable source	Stimuli type		
Experiment 1	*Real*	*Fake*	
Sensitivity (d prime)	3,55	3,55	N.S
Error rate	0,12	0,13	p = .013
Average identification speed	573,29 ms	599,92 ms	p < .001
Experiment 2 Group 1	*Real*	*Fake*	
Attention ratio (image area/out of image)	84,76%	87,88%	p < .01
Percentage transition time (image/out of image)	26,48%	15,87%	p < .01
Experiment 1	*Non-camouflage*	*Camouflage*	
Sensitivity (d prime)	3,86	3,23	p = .023
Error rate	0,13	0,13	N.S
Average identification speed	557,13 ms	616,07 ms	p < .001
Experiment 2 Group 2	*No camouflage*	*Camouflage*	
Attention ratio (image area/out of image)	88,13%	84,45%	p = .020
Percentage transition time (image/out of image)	19,27%	23,08%	p < .01

4 Discussion and Conclusions

In the present study we examined the perception, detection and identification of real and decoy tanks without and with camouflage. We found, among other things, that fake and camouflage images of tanks as compared to real and non-camouflage images decreased identification speed and that camouflage images elicited more attention shifting between image and background as compared to non-camouflage images. We argue that the results support that in general fake and camouflage images of tanks are harder to detect than images of real and no-camouflage tanks because they lack in the details and roughness of shapes and contours visually available for the observer. A follow-up study is now being conducted to look more thoroughly to which parts of the images people looks and base their evaluation.

The results are important in understanding the perception and identification of military visual objects in displays and can be used for example in optimization of decoys as well as, in connection with detection, display settings.

References

Fillmore, M.T., Rush, C.R., Hays, L.: Acute effects of cocaine in two models of inhibitory control: implications of non-linear dose effects. Addiction **101**, 1323–1332 (2006)

King, M.G., Stanley, G.D., Burrows, G.D.: Visual search processes in camouflage detection. Hum. Factors **26**(2), 223–234 (1984). https://doi.org/10.1177/001872088402600209

How Important Alarm Types for Situation Awareness at the Smart Factory?

Heesung Park[✉], Daehee Park[✉], and Jeongpyo Lee[✉]

Samsung Electronics, Seoul, Republic of Korea
{hux.park, daehee0.park, jp0212.lee}@samsung.com

Abstract. In recent years, manufacturing engineering has been changed rapidly through different parallel running developments. According to the needs of customers have become vary and the market has become being expanded through e-commerce development, manufacturers are willing to produce customized products globally, it induces a higher proliferation of variants, and shorter product life cycles. Endsley (2016) suggested that many systems involve various types of alarms or alerts function in order to call operators' attention to important information. In order to increase the operator's situation awareness, gathering and integrating all kinds of data from the machine are not sufficient. The system applied in the smart factory should involve the specific alarm system which analyses the cognitive processing of the operators, thus it should inform contexts of problems to operators effectively. In this paper, we more focus on designing and evaluating the alarm system, thus, how the system might have an effect on operators' situation awareness that researched in detail level.

Keywords: Smart factory · Alarm system · Situation awareness

1 Introduction

In recent years, manufacturing engineering has been changed rapidly through different parallel running developments. According to the needs of customers have become vary and the market has become being expanded through e-commerce development, manufacturers are willing to produce customized products globally, it induces a higher proliferation of variants, and shorter product life cycles. How fast adapt the new technology leads to the success of manufacturing [1]. Thus, it is one of an important point to adopt new innovative technology to expand variant of products and reduce any errors occurring in the manufacturing process, in order to finally satisfy the customers' needs [2].

2 Smart Factory: Definition, and Intelligent System

According to Weiser (1991), the smart environment consists of various kinds of sensor, actuators, displays and computer elements, which are seamlessly embedded and connected each other [3]. Lucke and Westkamper (2008) insisted that the view of Weiser (1991) can be applied in manufacturing environment [4]. Lucke and West-kamper

(2008) suggested that smart factory is defined as a factory that recognizes and understand the contexts of workers and machines, so that it is able to assist them in the execution of their tasks [4]. Some government of developed countries such as Germany, USA, and the Republic of Korea described that the basic functions of the smart factory system are the Internet of Things (IoT), Big data and data analytics, and system integration [2]. It indicated that manufacturing machine and lines equip sensors and connected each other to collect various kinds of data from the machine and lines. In addition, there is the main control system which integrates all kinds of data from machine, analyses insight and it informs the intuitive alarm system to confront critical problems and avoid manufacturing issues in advance.

3   Smart Factory with Situation Awareness

Endsley [5] suggested that many systems involve various types of alarms or alerts function in order to call operators' attention to important information. As mentioned above, recognizing and understanding the situations occurring around the machine and operators that are regarded as important factors to build a system of the smart factory. In order to increase the operator's situation awareness, gathering and integrating all kinds of data from the machine are not sufficient. The system applied in the smart factory should involve the specific alarm system which analyses the cognitive processing of the operators, thus it should inform contexts of problems to operators effectively. In the factory, the alarm system should consist of a complex set of mental processes. Because there are many types of operators in the factory and their role divided according to the work process. When an event related to work process occurs, the alarm signal should include essential and sufficient information in the environment in order to account for the situation. Endsley suggested that the meaning and significance of the alarm can be comprehended with various factors involving the operator's experience, their mental model and their expectancies [5]. The operators could decide their actions to the event based on their interpretation of the alarm. Designing the alarm system with various big data gathered that regarded as a critical issue in the smart factory since it influences on situation awareness of the operators. In this paper, we more focus on designing and evaluating the alarm system, thus, how the system might have an effect on operators' situation awareness that researched in detail level.

4   Methods

4.1   System Design

We developed a new system which can be applied in the factory. Unfortunately, we cannot reveal the original system screens due to the security issue. However, only some limited functions used to research about how operators being aware of the situation through the system (see Figs. 1 and 2). As suggestion of Blanchet et al. (2018), the smart factory system should consist of four stages; perception (collection of data from sensors → data loading into the system → operators being aware of the events), comprehension (operators understand about the events), projection (operators expect the results of events) and decision (operators decide which solution should be applied to fix it) [6]. There is a research gap between smart factory system and situation awareness. Alarm systems can be assumed as an essential part to research in the smart factory in order to increase situation awareness. In order to augment situation awareness level of operators at the smart factory, effectiveness of each alarm type; no alarm, alarm on the PC system, and alarm on mobile messenger have researched.

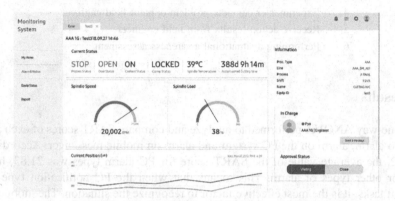

Fig. 1. Example of Monitoring system screen to PC

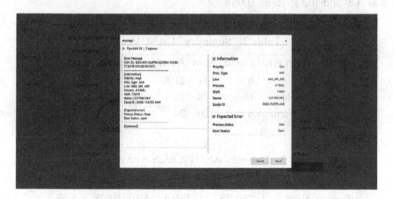

Fig. 2. Example of Alarm contents to PC

4.2 Experimental Design

Six participants who work as an operator at the factory recruited to investigate the effectiveness of alarm types. They have used the new smart factory system for two weeks. The participants were assigned and executed as shown in Table 1.

Table 1. List of tasks given to the experimenter

Step	Task
1	Experimenter to perform other tasks
2	Facilitator notifies experimenter of problem situation task (1) PC: Sound and toast popup based on Web task (2) Mobile: Using Notification Center task (3) No Alarm
3	Experimenter checks the alarm sent by the Facilitator
4	Experimenter contacts problem content field engineer
5	Receive action results from field engineer
6	Performing a situational awareness assessment

5 Results

Then one-way ANOVA performed to analyze and compare SART scores of each alarm type; no alarm, alarm on the PC system and alarm on mobile messenger. According to Table 2, the average value of the SART score for PC alarm types was 21.83, higher than for other types of alarm. This means that when the PC notification type is in different tasks, it is the most effective factor to recognize the situation. The mobile alert type had a lower average score of SART than when it was not notified. It was also indicated that there was a significant difference between alarm types (see Table 3). The F-value was 4.1 and the P-value 0.038.

Table 2. Summary of ANOVA

Alarm type	Count	Sum	Average	Variance
PC	6	131	21.83	27.8
Mobile	6	78	13	58.8
No alarm	6	120	20	8.8

Table 3. One-way ANOVA each type of alarm

Source of variation	SS	df	MS	F	P-value	F crit
Type of alarm	260.78	2	130.4	4.10	0.038	3.68
Error	476.83	15	31.79			
Total	737.61	17				

6 Discussion

The result of the evaluation has shown that the type of PC notification is the most powerful type of alarm to situation awareness. It describes that operators normally work at the desk with PC, thus, alarm on PC leads to increase situation awareness of operators even though they work other duties. According to the understanding score in

Fig. 3, PC alarm was rated as the most understandable element than other types of alarm. In the post-interview, the factory worker commented on the advantages of being an alarm in a PC environment as follows: "We receive a lot of information from the PC, but we check it as soon as the alarm comes in. And details about alarm can also be found right away, which is best for situational awareness."

In the case of mobile alarm, situation awareness is lower than when there is no alarm. This is because in factories, operators in factory work as the main device rather than using multiple devices. In addition, one of the subjects' post-op interviews said: "Because the mobile device is used as a personal communication rather than as a job notification, it is not easy to see during work." As such, the mobile alarm is generally easily ignored or forgotten. Also, the screen size of the mobile phone is not sufficient for operators to be aware of the situation easily (5.7-inch).

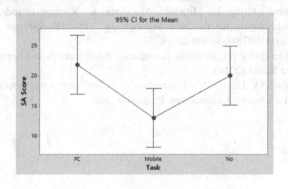

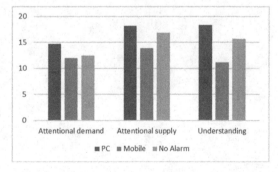

Fig. 3. Situation Awareness Score each type of alarm

7 Conclusion

The purpose of this project is to find out the most effective types of alarm to provide general guidance regarding how to increase situation awareness of operators at the smart factory. We have developed an alarm system when a problem occurs in the factory. And then the situational awareness scores were compared for the three types of alarm. This is because operators normally work at the desk with PC, thus, alarm on PC leads to increase situation awareness of operators even though they work other duties Further research should be discussed on the factors and design forms of effective alerts in the PC environment.

References

1. Gorecky, D., Khamis, M., Mura, K.: Introduction and establishment of virtual training in the factory of the future. Int. J. Comput. Integr. Manuf. **30**(1), 182–190 (2017)
2. Kang, H.S., et al.: Smart manufacturing: past research, present findings, and future directions. Int. J. Precis. Eng. Manuf.-Green Technol. **3**(1), 111–128 (2016)
3. Weiser, M.: The computer for the twenty-first century. In: Scientific American, 09/91, pp. 94–110 (1991)
4. Lucke, D., Constantinescu, C., Westkämper, E.: Smart factory-a step towards the next generation of manufacturing. In: Mitsuishi, M., Ueda, K., Kimura, F. (eds.) Manufacturing Systems and Technologies for the New Frontier, pp. 115–118. Springer, London (2008). https://doi.org/10.1007/978-1-84800-267-8_23
5. Endsley, M.R.: Designing for Situation Awareness: An Approach to User-Centered Design. CRC Press, Boca Raton (2016)
6. Blanchet, K., Lebec, O., Leroux, C., Bouzeghoub, A.: Situation Awareness for Collaborative Robotics in Manufacturing Applications, Feasibility Study

The Impact of Self-efficacy and Gender on Computer Performance

An Eye Tracking Study

Jenny Stein[✉] and Lilia Lajmi[✉]

Ostfalia University of Applied Sciences, 38302 Wolfenbüttel, Germany
jenny.v.stein@gmail.com

Abstract. This paper addresses the role of self-efficacy in human-computer-interaction (HCI) and examines whether there are gender differences in computer performance. This research study is part of the interdisciplinary doctoral program "Gendered Configurations of Humans and Machines. Interdisciplinary Analyses of Technology," funded by the federal state of Lower Saxony, Germany and conducted by the Braunschweig University of Technology, Ostfalia University of Applied Sciences and Braunschweig University of Art. This research project aims to analyze usage contexts, expectations, and behavior in the field of information technology with regard to gender aspects. In order to investigate and identify the key gender variables affecting performance and subjective perception during interaction with a human-computer interface, an empirical study with 30 participants was designed and carried out at the Ostfalia University of Applied Sciences, Faculty of Electrical Engineering. Fifteen female and 15 male participants, aged 21–63, with different educational, social, migration, and cultural backgrounds were asked to perform three different tasks with an unfamiliar software. The participants wore an eye tracker during task processing. Our extended qualitative and quantitative research aggregated a series of potential gender differences. The results showed that there are gender differences in computer performance. Female users aged 35–64 had lower self-efficacy than male users. They were less persistent when a task became challenging and showed a tendency to attribute failure at a task to their own lack of capability, whereas male users attributed this to the difficulty of the task.

Keywords: HCI · Gender · Self-efficacy · Experimental study

1 Introduction

Complex information systems are becoming increasingly important and having significant impact on many areas of life. User-centered system development and usability should therefore play an important role in development of intuitive system use. It is particularly important to understand users in order to evaluate existing systems or develop new concepts. In the research on relevant perception and decision-making processes, therefore, the diverse life experiences and the wide range of life situations of user groups should also be considered. However, in the course of a generalized perception of users and user groups in the software development process, important gender

© Springer Nature Switzerland AG 2019
C. Stephanidis and M. Antona (Eds.): HCII 2019, CCIS 1088, pp. 119–125, 2019.
https://doi.org/10.1007/978-3-030-30712-7_16

aspects are often not taken into account. It can be assumed that through a gender-appropriate design process, target group-oriented and needs-based user interfaces can be developed.

Studies show that female users tend to process information in a comprehensive way and to examine all available indications and information to make a decision, whether the problem is simple or complex. Male users on the other hand, avoid comprehensive information processing on lighter tasks and access heuristics more quickly. Comprehensive information processing is more likely to be carried out by male users on complex tasks [1].

Bandura's self-efficacy construct from the field of psychology describes the personal assessment of one's own competencies in coping with difficulties and barriers. People with low self-efficacy tend to place less effort in challenging situations and show less persistence when encountering difficulties. Self-efficacy plays an important role in the context of the operation of a graphical user interface. Self-efficacy influences many aspects of human activity, such as endurance, use of strategy and even dealing with failure [2]. People who have low self-efficacy tend to use cognitive strategies less and to spend less effort, for example, on a difficult task than people who have high self-efficacy. Some studies show that females have lower self-efficacy than males [3]. There is also a significant correlation between self-efficacy and computer performance for females. This is not the case for males [4].

Furthermore, the process of developing user interfaces is also a very important factor. Without taking gender into account, gender-related problems can occur. An example of this is "I-Methodology," where software developers unreflectively assume their own characteristics, preferences and competencies are representational of many user groups, or they make stereotypes about users without performing an actual requirements analysis with actual users [5].

2 Empirical Methodology

To investigate whether there are gender differences in computer performance, self-efficacy, decision-making, or processing information while using software, an empirical study has been carried out at the Ostfalia University of Applied Sciences in Germany.

Thirty participants took part in the study: 15 females and 15 males between the ages of 21 and 63 (M = 36 years; SD = 14.19 years). The study was conducted on the participants' use of image-editing software. This software was previously unknown to the participants.

First, the participants had 5 min for free exploration of the software. After that, three tasks had to be performed. The tasks differed according to degree of difficulty. Task 3 also aimed to address the major usability problems in the software.

An eye tracker was used to investigate perception and decision-making processes. In addition, the method of "Thinking Aloud" was applied [6].

Here, the participants verbalize all thoughts and impressions regarding the use of the software, while using the software. This enabled conclusions to be made about the cognitive processes during the processing of tasks.

Self-efficacy was measured with the Allgemeine Selbstwirksamkeit Kurzskala (ASKU) questionnaire [7]. The format for the answers of the three items on the ASKU questionnaire was a five-point scale from *does not apply at all* (1) *to applies completely* (5). This questionnaire was given at the beginning of the empirical study.

After completing all three tasks, participants filled out the System Usability Scale (SUS) questionnaire, for measuring the usability of the software [8] and the NASA-Task Load Index (NASA-TLX) that rates perceived workload [9]. A semi-structured final interview was conducted at the end of the study. The interview consisted of a list of questions with the possibility to discuss individual topics and collect in-depth information from direct conversations with the participants.

3   Results

The results of the empirical study presented in this paper focus on the evaluation of objective data (task performance) and the ASKU questionnaire in order to establish a correlation between subjective assessment of self-efficacy and the actual performance of the subjects. Performance was objectively measured with appropriate performance variables. The most important aspects of human performance are the accuracy and speed of the execution of tasks [10]. An important measure of accuracy is the correct handling of tasks. The speed performance parameter could be evaluated from the processing times of task execution.

The data show that female participants had a slightly lower self-efficacy than male participants. In the user group aged 35–64, the differences in self-efficacy are more evident. Here it is also interesting to observe the individual items on the ASKU scale. The item titled *"I am able to solve most problems on my own"* shows little difference in the responses of male and female participants. On the other hand, the difference in self-evaluation of male and female participants is greater for two other items: *"I can rely on my own abilities in difficult situations"* and *"I can usually solve even challenging and complex tasks well"* (Table 1).

Analyzing objective data also shows a difference between both gender groups. In the user group, aged 18–34, female participants were faster at completing two of three tasks (Fig. 1). In the user group aged 35–64 female participants took longer to complete all three tasks than male participants (Fig. 2).

The differences in the third task were clear. A significant correlation was found between the gender of the users and the performance of the third task (r (30) = −0.391, p = 0.05). It is likely that the association with self-efficacy could play a role here.

The results of the NASA TLX questionnaires' shows that on the dimensions of *effort* and *frustration*, female participants reported higher values than male participants (*effort*: male age 35–64 (M = 9.8, SD = 4,02), female age 35–64 (M = 12.28, SD = 6.52), *frustration*: male age 35–64 (M = 7.8, SD = 5.4), female age 35–64 (M = 12.57, SD = 6.6), whereas males aged 35–64 have higher scores in the subjective assessment of task accomplishment *performance* (M = 9, 6, SD = 6.84), female age 35–64 (M = 6.85, SD = 4.29) (Fig. 4). Female participants age 18–34 also rated their performance lower (M = 6,63, SD = 4,24) that male participants age 18–34 (M = 9,1, SD = 5,1) although they actually achieved better results (Fig. 3).

Table 1. Descriptive evaluation ASKU questionnaire. Participants aged 35–64 (Mean and standard deviation)

	Mean	SD
ASKU_I_can_rely_on_my_own_abilities_in_difficult _situations _Male_age_35-64	4.63	.544
ASKU_I_can_rely_on_my_own_abilities_in_difficult _situations _Female_35-64	4.14	.694
ASKU_I_am_able_to_solve_most_problems_on_my_ own _Male_age_35-64	4.22	.452
ASKU_I_am_able_to_solve_most_problems_on_my_ own _Female_age_35-64	4.14	.690
ASKU_I_can_usually_solve_even_challenging_and_ complex tasks_well _Male_age_35-64	4.21	.842
ASKU_I_can_usually_solve_even_challenging_and_ complex_tasks_well _Female_age_35-64	3.85	.643

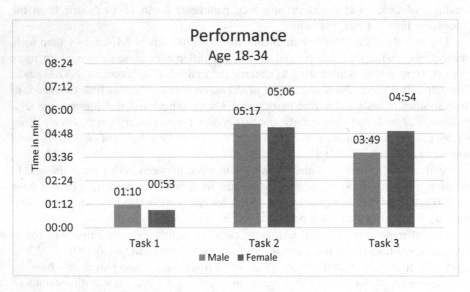

Fig. 1. Mean of task completion time for user group aged 18–34

The results of the SUS questionnaire for the entire software are M = 39.83, SD = 18.14 for male participants and M = 35.83, SD = 19.33 for female, which is a poor result. Values below 60 indicate significant usability issues [8]. The assessments of male and female is very similar.

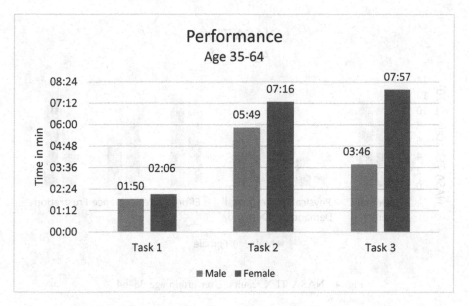

Fig. 2. Mean of task completion time for user group aged 35–64

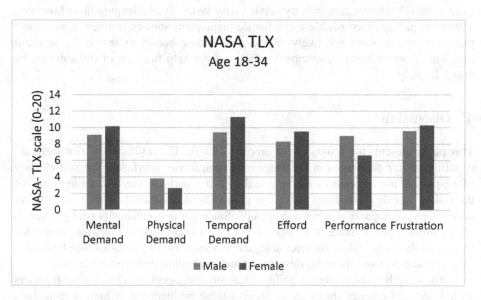

Fig. 3. NASA TLX results. User group aged 18–34

Evaluating the qualitative data from "Thinking Aloud" method it becomes clear that female participant were less persistent when a task became challenging and showed a tendency to attribute failure at a task to their own lack of capability, whereas male participants attributed this to the difficulty of the task.

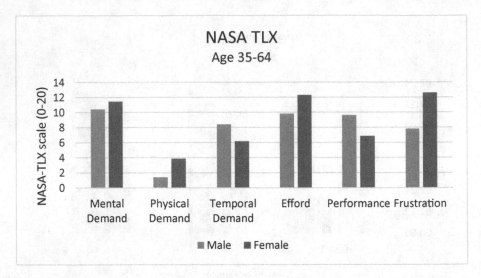

Fig. 4. NASA TLX results. User group age 35–64

Analyzing of the participants' eye movement patterns with eye tracking system show relatively similar approach by solving easy tasks. By challenging tasks however, a different picture emerged. Male and female participants showed different approaches: male participants are more likely to use right mouse button to search for required function, however female participants often use the help function of the software or asked for help.

4 Discussion

This paper presents the results of the empirical study. The results show that there are certainly gender differences in the usage of graphical user interfaces. The self-efficacy of the participants correlates with the actual objective performance (processing times of the tasks). Female participants in the age group 35–64 assessed their skills with lower scores than participants in other user groups. Since low self-efficacy is strongly tied to poor computer performance, it is important to find ways to support this user group. One way to do this is providing software-integrated video tutorials and assistance functions. Future research could focus on developing and evaluating this type of support.

This study has shown that usability problems are especially challenging for users with lower self-efficacy. In order to prevent these problems, it is logical to include gender and diversity research in the development process of information-technical systems in order to ensure user-centered design.

These research results from Germany correspond with the research results from other studies (mostly from the United States). However, it may be important to conduct more research or a replication of the study in different countries with different cultures. There is the possibility of finding different results.

References

1. Beckwith, L., et al.: Effectiveness of end-user debugging features: are there gender issues? In: Proceedings of ACM Conference Human Factors in Computing Systems, pp. 869–878. ACM Press, April 2005
2. Bandura, A.: Self-efficacy: toward a unifying theory of behavioral change. Psychol. Rev. **8** (2), 191–215 (1977)
3. Busch, T.: Gender differences in self-efficacy and attitudes toward computers. J. Educ. Comput. Res. **12**, 147–158 (1995)
4. Beckwith, L., Grigoreanu, V., Burnett, M.M., Wiedenbeck, S.: HCI: what about the software? Computer (2006). https://doi.org/10.1109/mc.2006.382.source. IEEE Xplore
5. Bath, C.: De-Gendering informatischer Artefakte. Grundlagen einer kritisch-feministischen Technikgestaltung. Dissertation. Staats- und Universitätsbibliothek Bremen (2009). http://elib.suub.uni-bremen.de/edocs/00102741-1.pdf
6. Nielsen, J.: Evaluating the thinking aloud technique for use by computer scientists. In: Hartson, H.R., Hix, D. (eds.) Advances in Human-Computer Interaction, vol. 3, pp. 69–82. Ablex (1992)
7. Beierlein, C., Kovaleva, A., Kemper, C.J., Rammstedt, B.: ASKU - Allgemeine Selbstwirksamkeit Kurzskala [Fragebogen]. In: Leibniz-Zentrum für Psychologische Information und Dokumentation (ZPID) (Hrsg.), Elektronisches Testarchiv. Online im Internet (2012). https://www.zpid.de/Testarchiv
8. Brooke, J.: SUS: a "quick and dirty" usability scale. In: Jordan, P.W., Thomas, B., Weerdmeester, B.A., McClelland (eds.) Usability Evaluation in Industry, pp. 189–194. Taylor & Francis, London (1996)
9. Hart, S.: Nasa-task load index (Nasa-TLX); 20 years later. In: Human Factors and Ergonomics Society Annual Meeting Proceedings, vol. 50, pp. 904–908 (2006)
10. Johannsen, G.: Mensch-Maschine-System. Springer, Berlin (1993). https://doi.org/10.1007/978-3-642-46785-1

Research on Competency Model of Flight Operations Quality Assurance Personnel

Xin Wang[✉] and Bin Li

Aviation Safety Research Division, China Academy of Civil Aviation Science
and Technology, Engineering and Technical Research Center of Civil Aviation
Safety Analysis and Prevention of Beijing, Beijing, China
wangxin@mail.castc.org.cn

Abstract. In order to ensure the full matching of flight operations quality assurance personnel and positions, and to meet the post requirements, the job analysis method is used to study, and the competency model of flight operations quality assurance personnel is established in this paper. At the same time, the final competency model of airline flight operations quality assurance personnel is determined by questionnaire method and SPSS statistical tools analysis. The competency model includes 6 dimensions such as education level and work experience, basic competencies, attitudes, flight operations quality assurance specialty knowledge and skills, specialty knowledge, basic skills, which include 36 competency factors. These competency factors are arranged in order of importance. The competency model not only helps airlines to recruit, train, and motivate flight operations quality assurance personnel, but also provides a basis for employees' occupation development. What's more important is that personnel with these competency factors are more able to give full play to their professional expertise, analyze flight quality monitoring data, find safety risks, and provide a guarantee for the safety of civil aviation.

Keywords: Safety management · Human resource management ·
Flight operations quality assurance · Competency · Competency model

1 Introduction

Flight operations quality assurance is one of the internationally recognized important means of ensuring flight safety. It has been widely recognized by the world civil aviation industry, and its important role is self-evident. The level of flight operations quality assurance depends not only on the technical equipment used, but also on the technical capability level of the flight operations quality assurance personnel.

According to the scope and nature of flight operations quality assurance, it mainly includes decoding system management and maintenance, flight procedure development, flight data processing and analysis, flight quality analysis, flight data application, etc. These characteristics of work require that flight operations quality assurance personnel should have the appropriate professional knowledge and skills. However, the current professional background of flight operations quality assurance personnel has a wide variety of backgrounds, and rarely receives systematic flight operations quality

© Springer Nature Switzerland AG 2019
C. Stephanidis and M. Antona (Eds.): HCII 2019, CCIS 1088, pp. 126–134, 2019.
https://doi.org/10.1007/978-3-030-30712-7_17

assurance training. The level of professional skill is limited. Their application analysis of flight quality monitoring data is not deep enough, and flight operations quality assurance cannot be applied with high quality to improve the safety level of airlines and reduce operational risks [1].

At present, some scholars have carried out certain research on the competency model. The research objects are mainly concentrated on management staff [2–4], technical research and development personnel [5, 6], university teachers [7], Certified public accountant [8], Chinese entrepreneurs [9], civil servants [10] and so on. It can be said that all kinds of industry are studying the competency model of enterprise employees, indicating that it is very important to study the competency model of enterprise employees to better play their personal value to meet the needs of the post and contribute to the enterprise. However, at present, there is no research on the competency model of airline flight operations quality assurance personnel at home and abroad. This paper uses the job analysis method to construct the competency model of flight operations quality assurance personnel.

2   The Competency Model

The competency model is a collection of competency items that are required to perform a task well.

$$CM = \{Ci, |i = 1, 2, \ldots, n\}; \tag{1}$$

Among them, CM represents the competency model, Ci is the i-th competency item, and n represents the number of competency items.

Spencer et al. proposed the Iceberg Model after nearly two decades of research and application of competency [11].

As the part under the water surface of the iceberg, we usually refer to the "potential" of human beings. The depth from top to bottom is different, indicating that the degree of difficulty of being excavated and perceived is different. The deeper the water, the less likely it is to be excavated and perceived. The surface part, the knowledge, skills, and behavior of the human being, is easily perceived. The content of competency includes not only the potential part below the surface of the iceberg, but also the knowledge and skills part above the surface.

Based on the understanding of the competency concept [12], the author believes that although there are many competencies of individual employees, what the enterprise needs is not necessarily all the competencies of the employees. Therefore, the employee competency model is not defined or graded for all the competencies. However, according to the requirements of the position and the organization's environment, it is necessary to clarify the competency characteristics that can ensure the employees are qualified for the job and ensure their full potential, that is, the competency that employees should have in the job, which is commonly referred to as qualifications. They include academic qualifications, experience, knowledge, skills, basic abilities and attitudes.

3   The Research Methods

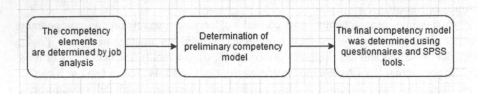

Fig. 1.   Research flow chart

The job analysis method in the human resource management method is used to determine the competency model of airline flight operations quality assurance personnel. The job analysis method is mainly based on the analysis of the duties and job requirements of the airline flight operations quality assurance personnel, and then determines the competency requirements. The questionnaire is mainly for the preliminary competency model determined by the job analysis method, and the importance of each item in the competency model can be obtained, and then the competency item is selected, and the competency model of the flight operations quality assurance personnel is finally determined. The research process is shown in Fig. 1.

4   Determination of the Competency Model

4.1   Using the Job Analysis Method to Study Competency Requirements

Job analysis is the systematic process of determining the job nature, responsibility, authority, cooperation, working environment and qualification conditions of the required staff by conducting thorough investigation, collecting data, analyzing and sorting out the work positions in the organization, and formulating job description [13].

The research objective of this paper is to determine the competency model of flight operations quality assurance personnel, which can be applied to the research method of job analysis that focuses on the post capacity and competency.

Responsibilities of Flight Operations Quality Assurance Personnel. By investigating the duties of each airline's flight operations quality assurance, it is found that some companies will further subdivide the flight operations quality assurance work according to the different focuses of work, including flight quality monitoring, flight data processing, and flight quality analysis. Some companies have not subdivided. After investigation, it is concluded that the main job responsibilities of flight operations quality assurance personnel include the following.

(1) Develop various flight quality related regulations and procedures, such as the development and revision of monitoring items and standards;
(2) Flight data management, such as the implementation of flight data transmission, playback and backup, monitoring flight data collection and transmission, statistics

of each fleet monitoring rate, timely detection of data quality issues; management and maintenance related basic information.

(3) Development and maintenance of flight quality monitoring procedure.
(4) Flight data decoding processing and analysis.
(5) Interpretation and analysis of flight exceedance events.
(6) Write event statistics and trend analysis report, including daily, monthly, annual reports, etc., and unsafe events analysis report.
(7) Maintenance of flight quality monitoring decoding system.
(8) Data application and research, including the development and maintenance of various data application systems; responsible for the data extension and application work such as 3D animation production; participated in the research work of flight big data; mined the safety risk of flight manipulation and summarized the safety risk trend information.
(9) Organize flight quality monitoring meeting, QAR training, etc.

Determine the competency requirements according to the post duty. This paper analyzes the relevant job responsibilities of flight operations quality assurance personnel to determine the competency requirements. Table 1 is an example of flight data analysis to illustrate how to determine competency requirements based on job responsibilities.

Table 1. Example analysis

Classification of duties	Specific responsibilities	Competency requirements
Flight data analysis	1. Develop various flight quality related regulations and procedures a. Develop and revise monitoring items and standards b. Develop flight quality regulations and procedures c. Develop flight data analysis work procedures and exceedance event investigation procedures, etc.	1. Understand the relevant regulations of the Bureau's flight operations quality assurance; 2. Understand each aircraft type monitoring items and standards; 3. Understand the investigation procedures of the bureau's unsafe events; 4. Understand flight operations quality assurance workflow;
	2. Flight data management a. The implementation of flight data transmission, playback and backup work b. Monitor the flight data collection and transmission, collect the monitoring rate of each fleet, discover data quality problems in a timely manner, issue rectification requirements and track improvement	5. Understand the principles of flight data collection and transmission; 6. Understand flight operations knowledge; 7. Understand the principle of event triggering; 8. Ability to write a variety of analysis reports; 9. Ability to make 3D simulations;

(continued)

Table 1. (*continued*)

Classification of duties	Specific responsibilities	Competency requirements
	3. Event analysis and preparation of reports, including daily, monthly, annual reports, and unsafe event analysis report; Carry out exceedance event investigation to ensure efficient flight data management and accurate event analysis	10. Ability to mine data applications; 11. Be able to identify safety risk points; 12. Impartiality; 13. Leadership skills; 14. Learning ability; 15. Have communication and collaboration skills; 16. Ability of statistical analysis; 17. Organizational ability; 18. Have the ability to train and guide; 19. Have writing ability;
	4. Data application and research, including participating in the development and maintenance of various data application systems, taking charge of data extension and application work such as 3D animation production, participating in the research work of flight big data, mining flight manipulation safety risk and summarizing safety risk trend information	
	5. To supervise and inspect the flight data analysis work of all departments of the company, to ensure that the company's flight data analysis work standards are unified and procedures are standardized, and to ensure that the flight data are timely and fully applied	
	6. Participate in relevant training at home and abroad, assist in organizing internal training of the company, coach the flight data analysis business of various departments of the company, and ensure the continuous improvement of the flight data analysis level of the company	

Preliminary Competency Requirements. The above is an example analysis of the relevant job responsibilities of flight operations quality assurance personnel. The author also analyzed other working elements of flight operations quality assurance. Due to space limitations, they are not listed here. Competency requirements are determined based on the job analysis of the flight operations quality assurance, the equipment and tools used, and their work environment. Combined with the results of the above analysis, the competency factors are divided into six categories, including basic competency, attitude, flight operations quality assurance expertise and skills, business knowledge and basic skills. The specific contents are shown in Table 2. Table 2 shows the final competency model. The relevant content analyzed by the job analysis method is similar to the content in Table 2. Due to the limitation of space, the preliminary competency model analyzed here is not described in detail.

4.2 Determination of Competency Model

The Questionnaire Survey. The above competency model is compiled into a questionnaire, which contains 36 competency elements in total, and includes the definition and behavioral performance of these competency elements at the end of the questionnaire. The five-point scale is adopted to assign values to these competency elements from "very important" to "not important" from 5 to 1. The questionnaire also included the education and work experience that flight operations quality assurance personnel should have to be qualified for their positions.

The subjects are the flight operations quality assurance personnel of the airline company and the personnel who are familiar with the flight operations quality assurance work (including superior leaders and subordinate employees). A total of 30 personnel. A total of 30 questionnaires were issued, 28 of which were valid, with an effective rate of 93.3%.

The Data Analysis. This article uses SPSS statistical software for data analysis.

Reliability Test of Questionnaire. The questionnaire reliability was measured by the alpha reliability coefficient. The Scale in SPSS was used to calculate the alpha reliability coefficient. The results showed that the Alpha coefficient of this questionnaire reached 0.8976 and the standard coefficient was 0.8913. ($0.7 \leqq$ Cronbach alpha coefficient < 0.9, very reliable) this indicates that the consistency of this questionnaire is very high, and the measurement results are reliable, which can be used to continue the following statistical analysis.

Descriptive Statistical Analysis. Descriptive statistical analysis is mainly an average analysis of the importance of competency factors. According to the average analysis of all competency factors' importance to work in the total sample, the average score of 36 competency factors is between 3.04 and 4.96. This indicates that the contribution of these competency factors to work performance is above the medium level. Therefore, these competency factors are retained.

The importance score (average score) of competency elements in each dimension was added, and then the average value was calculated, that is, the importance degree of each dimension, and then the value was normalized, that is, the weight of each dimension. The specific results are shown in Table 2. Similarly, the specific competency factors are normalized to obtain the corresponding weight, and the results are shown in Table 2.

According to the result of questionnaire, the expert group and the airlines flight operations quality assurance personnel of superior leadership to discuss, finalized, qualified for flight operations quality assurance position requirements: (1) for system management and data processing personnel, need a bachelor's degree or above, major in civil aviation related business and above 1 years work experience; (2) for data analysts, a bachelor's degree or above is required, with at least 3 years of experience as a captain.

Determination of Competency Model. Based on the above analysis results, the competency model of the airline flight operations quality assurance personnel is finally determined. See Table 2. The serial number in the competency factor is the order of importance of each sub-dimension.

Table 2. The competency model of the airline flight operations quality assurance personnel

Competency category (Weight)	Competency factor (Weight)
Education and work experience	1 Bachelor degree or above, working experience in civil aviation related business for 1 year or more; (system management and data processing personnel) 2 Bachelor degree or above, 3 years or above experience as captain. (data analysts)
Basic Competency (0.198)	1 Language communication ability (0.107); 2 Statistical analysis ability (0.107); 3 Team awareness (0.098); 4 Coordination ability (0.098); 5 Collaboration ability (0.098); 6 Organizational ability (0.089); 7 Good physical quality (0.089); 8 Learning ability (0.084); 9 Logical analysis ability (0.084); 10 Leadership ability (0.071); 11 Training and guiding ability (0.071);
Attitude (0.216)	1 Conscientiousness (0.188); 2 Confidentiality (0.188); 3 Responsibility (0.180); 4 Impartiality (0.158); 5 Carefulness (0.158); 6 Initiative (0.128);
Professional knowledge and skills of flight operations quality assurance (0.205)	1 Monitoring items and standards (0.118); 2 Write various analysis reports (0.118); 3 Proficient in flight data decoding software (0.114) 4 Flight data acquisition and transmission principle (0.109); 5 Principle of event detection (0.100); 6 Civil Aviation Administration and the company's flight operations quality assurance regulations (0.090); 7 Write a monitoring procedure (0.090); 8 Application of flight operations quality assurance in safety management systems(0.090); 9 Making 3D simulations(0.090); 10 Understand risk management knowledge (0.081)
Business knowledge (0.193)	1 Flight operations knowledge (0.193); 2 Flight procedures (0.193); 3 Meteorological knowledge (0.168); 4 Airspace(0.151); 5 Navigation (0.151); 6 Airport operational knowledge (0.143)
Basic skills (0.188)	1 Proficiency in computer operation and computer related knowledge (0.379); 2 Have writing skills (0.328); 3 Have a certain level of English listening, speaking, reading and writing (0.293)

5 Conclusion

Through the job analysis method to study the competency model of flight operations quality assurance personnel, and using the questionnaire method, using SPSS statistical tools to analyze and determine the competency model of airline flight operations quality assurance personnel. The model includes six dimensions of academic qualifications and work experience, basic competency, attitude, professional knowledge and skills of flight operations quality assurance, business knowledge, basic skills, and a total of 36 competency factors. In addition to academic qualifications and work experience, these five dimensions are ranked as attitude, professional knowledge and skills of flight operations quality assurance, basic competency, business knowledge and basic skills.

Each airline can refer to the competency model of flight operations quality assurance personnel established in this paper to build the competency model of the company. The model is conducive to airlines to carry out human resource inventory, clarify the gap between current capacity reserve and future requirements. A benchmarking system has been established to help airlines better select, train and motivate employees who can contribute to the building of their core competitive advantages [14].

References

1. Wang, X., Yu, L.: The status of flight operational quality assurance in airlines and the proposals. China Civil Aviation **211**, 111–112 (2015)
2. Wang, C., Chen, M.: Managerial competency modeling: a structural equation testing. Psychol. Sci. **25**(5), 513–516 (2002)
3. Wang, X.: Study on competency model of safety managers in airlines. J. Nanjing Univ. Aeronaut. Astronautics (Soc. Sci.) **16**(3), 63–68 (2014)
4. Yu, L.: Job analysis of management staff based on competency model. Enterprise Reform Manag. 56 (2016)
5. Cao, M., Wang, R.: Research on competency of enterprise R&D staff. Technoecon. Manag. Res. **2**, 38–40 (2006)
6. Zhang, S.: Job Analysis of Developers' Position Based on Competency Model. Hunan University of Technology (2015)
7. Li, Z., Liu, Z., Zhou, Y.: The contemporary value and Chinese strategies: teacher job analysis in the top American universities. J. Natl. Acad. Educ. Adm. **7**, 88–94 (2018)
8. Wang, J.: Research on the Construction of Chinese CPA Competency Model. Chinese Academy of Fiscal Sciences (2012)
9. Xiong, A.: The construction of quality model for Chinese entrepreneurs. Manag. Technol. SME **14**, 67–70 (2017)
10. Fang, Z., Tang, J.: Senior civil servant competency model-international experience and reference. Adm. Reform **12**, 78–83 (2018)
11. Spencer, L.M., Spencer, S.M.: Competence at Work: Models for Superior Performance. Wiley, New York (1993)

12. Liu, L.: Research on the Construction and Application of Employee competency Model under the Condition of Knowledge Economy, pp. 10–14. North China Electric Power University (2004)
13. Zhao, Y., Zhu, Y., Deng, D.: Job Analysis and Design. Shanghai Jiaotong University Press, Shang Hai (2006)
14. Li, R.: Research on the Construction Theory and Application of competency Model, pp. 21–27. Xi'an University of Architecture and Technology (2005)

Accessibility and Universal Access

A Haptic Virtual Kitchen for the Cognitive Empowerment of Children with Autism Spectrum Disorder

Erik Almaguer[(✉)] and Shamima Yasmin[(✉)]

Eastern Washington University, Cheney, WA 99004, USA
ealmaguer@eagles.ewu.edu, syasmin@ewu.edu

Abstract. Research works have been carried out on how children with autism spectrum disorder (ASD) react to different virtual environment (VE) stimuli. It is hypothesized by psychologists that children with ASD will be cognitively empowered while interacting in a VE, as it can offer positive reinforcement and a better sense of engagement to keep the child's interests awake. This research will explore the development and refinement of virtual kitchen applications in an immersive environment by incorporating the sense of touch. A tangible VE lets users touch, grasp, and manipulate virtual objects with the help of a haptic force feedback device. The Unity game engine will be integrated with the existing haptic pipeline to build a full-fledged haptic virtual kitchen. Once developed, the software will be tested by children with and without ASD under a psychologist's observation. Monitoring will be done by tracking users' progress while learning different steps of cooking in a haptic VE; transfer of knowledge from a VE to the real world will be closely observed.

Keywords: Haptic feedback · Virtual environment · Autism spectrum disorder

1 Introduction

Virtual reality (VR) is currently being used to address physical and mental disabilities [1]. The use of VEs has become a popular solution for patients who have lost motor ability of limbs and require proper rehabilitation to regain a better control of them [2]. Psychologists are currently exploring the immersive effects of VR for cognitive behavioral therapy [3]. VEs are being used for immersion therapy to combat phobias and social behavioral simulation applications to train children with social disorders to cope with anxiety and regulate emotions [4].

This paper mainly addresses cognitive rehabilitation in a haptic VE. Several rehabilitation applications have been developed using haptic VEs but few address cognitive impairments. This paper aims to enrich the abilities, lives, and self sufficiency of children with ASD by providing an immersive haptic space to experiment, learn, and explore their abilities in a sandbox-like kitchen setting. A child with ASD can freely interact within a VE since there are minimal consequences to their actions. VEs allow someone with ASD to practice social skills an unlimited number of times without anxiety and discomfort. In combination with cognitive behavioral therapy, VEs can

© Springer Nature Switzerland AG 2019
C. Stephanidis and M. Antona (Eds.): HCII 2019, CCIS 1088, pp. 137–142, 2019.
https://doi.org/10.1007/978-3-030-30712-7_18

offer children with ASD a safe immersive space where they are allowed to make social mistakes without fear of rejection [4, 5]. This sparks development of applications that simulate social settings where a child can practice social skills [4]. This paper mainly addresses one such application.

2 Background

A number of research works have been carried out to address cognitive ability of autistic children. Some online VR platforms are already available that can be catered to the need of children with autism [6].

Mace et al. emphasized collaborative VE for physical training where a team was composed of healthy and impaired subjects so that a healthy participant can assist the impaired one. The game consisted of a ball on a beam with players on both ends trying to balance the beam by varying their power-grip force. Players received credits counted by the number of stars collected that worked as an incentive to make further progress in the game [2].

Christiansen et al. designed a virtual kitchen where patients were required to follow a number of steps in order to prepare a can of soup [3]. The VR system was comprised of a PC platform and a head mounted display (HMD); the user interacted with the environment using either a mouse or joystick.

Goršič et al. developed a cooperative cooking application for upper limb rehabilitation [7]. In this application, multiple tasks were performed by multiple participants to prepare one dish, but each task was performed by a single participant. The Bimeo arm rehabilitation system was used to track movements of arm, forearm, and wrist with embedded sensors [8]. The application requires the user to drag ingredients specific to a dish to a bowl/pan. Some challenges such as swatting away flies was also introduced into the cooking environment. This application mainly focused on mobility impairment and movements of the limbs as well as teamwork. This application was not evaluated by the target group.

Didehbani et al. created a VR application to help children with high functioning autism (HFA) to practice socializing using a keyboard and mouse [4]. This application focuses on putting the user into specific social situations such as consoling friends, participating in a classroom, and more. Participants were represented as self-avatars who were able to run, jump, and use a variety of arm and body gestures. Along with the self-avatars, other avatars were included and controlled by participants or trained clinicians to provide immediate feedback to the user.

Cheng et al. exposed ASD subjects to social scenarios such as a restaurant, let them explore empathy by understanding social contexts and respond accordingly. The application used an interactive collaborative VE where users could select a 3D avatar for their representation. The empathy scenario included various 3D animated social events to elicit empathy in different situations, such as waiting in line to order food while observing slips and falls of a passer-by. Participants' responses to different events were observed and later, measured from a baseline to gauge the effectiveness of the system [5].

Mesa-Gresa and her research group conducted an extensive survey on the effectiveness of virtual reality for children and adolescents with ASD and provided moderate evidence about the effectiveness of VR, but encouraged VR to be utilized to develop new VR-based treatments for children with ASD [9].

In this paper we mainly focus on cognitive rehabilitation of children with ASD who need to practice social skills or daily chores in a relaxed and stress-free environment. A virtual kitchen was chosen to address the issues of autism in a non-competitive environment. In order to make the VE more immersive, haptic force feedback was used along with the scope of multiplayer cooperative interactions. For further immersion and engagement, a head mounted display (HMD) was also introduced into the system.

3 Proposed Approach

The proposed approach focuses on the following issues:

- A cooperative VE that involves multiple participants.
- A non-competitive sandbox-like VE to minimize stress and anxiety.
- An immersive VE which allows users to be fully engaged inside the virtual world.

Figure 1 demonstrates different components of the proposed approach. A common kitchen setting from daily life has been selected to practice cooking in a stress-free environment. Two participants can be involved in cooking in the virtual kitchen in a cooperative manner. For example, one user can chop vegetables, while another can cook ingredients on a stove. The use of an HMD will offer users an immersive experience while interacting in the virtual kitchen. Haptic devices will add depth to their experience by allowing them to touch and grab virtual objects.

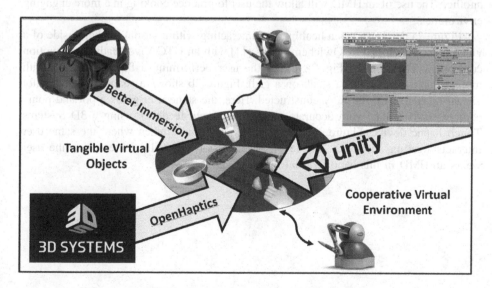

Fig. 1. Proposed approach at a glance.

4 Implementation and Results

This project uses the Unity game engine for fast and easy high-level VR development. 3D Systems [10], has already developed a plugin for Unity to interface with haptic devices. With this plugin, an HMD can be easily combined with haptic virtual reality for a more immersive experience. The proposed virtual kitchen will be equipped with all modern kitchen appliances, and an assortment of dishes and utensils. In the virtual kitchen, participants will be required to follow a number of steps to prepare a particular dish. This involves grabbing vegetables from a refrigerator, taking a knife and cutting board from a drawer, slicing vegetables, turning on a stove, placing a pan on the top of it, pouring cooking oil, spices, and vegetables into the cooking pan, and so on. With a haptic force feedback device, precise movements can be made while grabbing or touching virtual objects, which is an advantage over motion controllers, joysticks, or mouse-based interaction. The haptic VE will simulate the feeling of a kitchen and objects inside it while handles of haptic devices will represent different cooking items such as knives, spatulas, tongs, and more.

Objects can be assigned physical properties such as solid/hard or soft/elastic feeling. Objects will have accurate depictions of friction, viscosity, and weight. For example, during the process of mixing cake batter with other ingredients, the batter alters from a thin and runny state to a thick viscous substance. The user will be able to navigate the entirety of the virtual kitchen and interact with objects using the haptic device.

With two haptic devices, this virtual kitchen allows for a single player to interact with multiple objects simultaneously with both hands. The cooking team can also be composed of healthy-impaired participants or impaired-impaired participants depending on the severity of a patient's disorder. This will allow one participant to mentor another. The use of an HMD will allow the user to practice cooking in a more engaging environment.

Figure 2a demonstrates a healthy user interacting with a virtual kitchen inside of a video game developed by Owlchemy Labs [11] with an HTC Vive headset and motion controllers. The inset of Fig. 2a shows the user performing a flipping motion with motion controllers to flip a steak on a grill. Figure 2b shows a snapshot of our pilot virtual kitchen yet to be fully constructed. Here, the same user grabs a pot and pours contents onto a plate with accurate motion and force feedback using a 3D Systems Touch haptic device. Figure 2c shows the same virtual kitchen where the same user interacts wearing an HMD. The level of immersion gradually increases as the user wears an HMD in this haptic virtual kitchen.

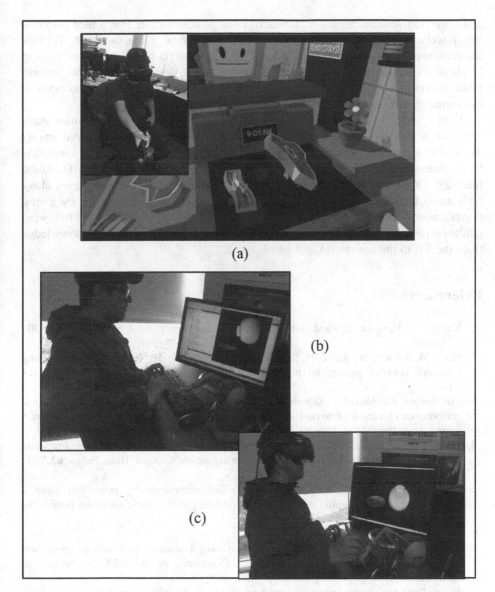

Fig. 2. (a) A virtual kitchen in a video game developed by Owlchemy Labs, (inset) a healthy user preparing a steak and performing flipping motion to cook both sides of the steak. A healthy user is interacting with the proposed pilot haptic virtual kitchen (b) without HMD and (c) with HMD.

5   Conclusion and Future Works

For addressing cognitive impairments such as ASD, a stress-free VE is preferable over a competitive VE. A virtual kitchen is an ideal environment to address ASD among children. A cooperative virtual kitchen may help ASD children practice daily chores and socialization simultaneously. Research findings demonstrate that a user performs better while playing a therapeutic game in a cooperative game mode [2, 7]. This incomplete pilot virtual kitchen has already been tested by a healthy user and varying levels of immersion have been observed. With a haptic device, the user can perform more accurate motions while receiving haptic force feedback. For a cooperative environment, this application will support multiple haptic devices.

Future works will involve building a full-fledged virtual kitchen, and user study will include the target group. Different levels of immersion will be observed among users while interacting with different VEs i.e., a non-haptic VE with motion controller-based interaction, a haptic VE without HMD, and a haptic VE with HMD. Audio feedback will be integrated for better guidance. Different steps will be displayed along with audio feedback. Level of performance and effort can be measured by giving players points and rating their accuracy. Accuracy will be measured for following guidance properly and completing steps successfully. Lastly, transfer of knowledge from the VE to the real world will be observed.

References

1. Yasmin, S.: Virtual reality and assistive technologies: a survey. Int. J. Vir. Real. **18**(2), 30–57 (2018)
2. Mace, M., Kinany, N., Rinne, P., Rayner, A., Bentley, P., Burdet, E.: Balancing the playing field: collaborative gaming for physical training. J. NeuroEng. Rehabil. **14**(116), 1–18 (2017)
3. Christiansen, C., Abreu, B., Ottenbacher, K., Huffman, K., Masel, B., Culpepper, R.: Task performance in virtual environments used for cognitive rehabilitation after traumatic brain injury. Arch. Phys. Med. Rehabil. **79**(8), 888–892 (1998)
4. Didehbani, N., Allen, T., Kandalaft, M., Krawczyk, D., Chapman, S.: Virtual reality social cognition training for children with high functioning autism. Comput. Hum. Behav. **62**, 703–711 (2016)
5. Cheng, Y., Chiang, H., Ye, J., Cheng, L.: Enhancing empathy instruction using a collaborative virtual learning environment for children with autistic spectrum conditions. Comput. Educ. **55**(4), 1449–1458 (2010)
6. VRChat Homepage. https://www.vrchat.net/
7. Goršič, M., Tran, M., Novak, D.: Cooperative cooking: a virtual environment for upper limb rehabilitation. In: 40th Annual International Conference of the IEEE Engineering in Medicine and Biology Society 2018, pp. 3602–3605 (2018)
8. Bimeo PRO neurological rehabilitation. https://sstrehab.club/bimeo-pro-en/
9. Mesa-Gresa, P., Gil-Gómez, H., Lozano-Quilis, J-A., Gil-Gómez, J-A.: Effectiveness of virtual reality for children and adolescents with autism spectrum disorder: an evidence-based systematic review. Sensors **8**(18), 2486 (2018)
10. 3D Systems Homepage. https://www.3dsystems.com/
11. Owlchemy Labs. https://owlchemylabs.com/

LipSpeaker: Helping Acquired Voice Disorders People Speak Again

Yaohao Chen[1]([⊠]), Junjian Zhang[1]([⊠]), Yizhi Zhang[2]([⊠]), and Yoichi Ochiai[1]([⊠])

[1] Digital Nature Group, University of Tsukuba, Tsukuba, Ibaraki, Japan
{yaohao.chen,tyookk,wizard}@digitalnature.slis.tsukuba.ac.jp
[2] Applied Analytics, Columbia University, New York, USA

Abstract. In this paper, we designed a system called LipSpeaker to help acquired voice disorder people to communicate in daily life. Acquired voice disorder users only need to face the camera on their smartphones, and then use their lips to imitate the pronunciation of the words. LipSpeaker can recognize the movements of the lips and convert them to texts, and then it generates audio to play.

Compared to texts, mel-spectrogram is more emotionally informative. In order to generate smoother and more emotional audio, we also use the method of predicting mel-spectrogram instead of texts through recognizing users' lip movements and expression together.

Keywords: Accessibility · Disabled people · Lipreading

1 Introduction

Currently acquired voice disorder people communicate with others mainly in three methods. The first is through sign language. The second is communicate through paper and pen. The last method is to use smartphones or computers as medium.

However, all three methods have their own flaws. The first method requires others to be proficient in sign language but few people know sign language. The second method requires literate people but not all the people are literate. Furthermore, it is inconvenient to create writing environment on the road. The third method requires the users to master the basic keyboard input which is not applicable to all the people.

In order to solve the above problems, we have designed a new interactive solution- LipSpeaker: a system that uses the movements of the user's lips to generate speech. What the user need to do is simply face the camera on his smartphone. LipSpeaker uses the facial landmark detector to capture images of the user's lips. With the time sequence frame of the lips captured as input, the deep neural network can generate the text of the user's speech. With LipSpeaker, acquired voice disorder users can communicate with other people without the need for sign language, literacy or any keyboard input.

C. Stephanidis and M. Antona (Eds.): HCII 2019, CCIS 1088, pp. 143–148, 2019.
https://doi.org/10.1007/978-3-030-30712-7_19

2 Related Work

Benefited from the development of deep neural networks in recent years, the field of lipreading has also been greatly developed. Among the well-known contributions are LipNet [1] of Assae et al. and Lip Reading in the Wild [2] by Chung et al.

Word Error Rate (WER) is an important indicator in training and evaluating the accuracy of lipreading using GRID corpus [3] dataset. Compared to Wand's WER in Lipreading with long short term memory [4] in 2016 is only 20.4%, the WER in LipNet is 4.8%. In Lip Reading in the Wild, the WER even reached 3.0%. At the same time, Assae et al. indicated that the accuracy of lipreading using deep neural network is 4.1 times higher than that of artificial lipreading. Proving that using deep neural networks to predict text through the movement of the lips is feasible.

At this stage, we also use the GRID corpus dataset to train deep neural networks. The text results are predicted by inputting the motion sequence frame of the user's lips into the lipreading deep neural network model, and the audio playback is synthesized through Text-To-Speech (TTS) system. However, there is a disadvantage in generating audio in this way: the tone of the user's speech will be filtered directly into a text while our ultimate goal is to generate emotional audio based on the user's lip movements.

Inspired by Tacotron2 [5] by Jonathan Shen et al., we are trying to predict mel-spectrogram using the lipreading deep neural network model instead of predicting texts. Together with mel-spectrogram, we can generate emotional audio with WaveNet [6].

3 Implementation

The implementation of LipSpeaker is divided into two major steps: training phase and evaluation phase. Training phase runs on Ubuntu. We use tensorflow as a framework for deep learning, training the lipreading deep neural network with the GRID corpus dataset, and obtaining a well-trained model after training. In the evaluation phase, we convert the well-trained model into the model of Apple's deep learning framework Core ML, and then run the model onto the phone.

Since loading and running a well-trained model on the smartphone produces a relatively large amount of computation, it will result in high performance requirements for the smartphone. In order to alleviate the burden of computation on Text-To-Speech (TTS), we use Apple's AVSpeechSynthsizer provided by AVFoundation to generate audio. Compared to the TTS system such as Tacotron2, AVSpeechSynthsizer improves the generation speed and reduces the amount of computation at the expense of audio fluency and naturalness. AVSpeechSynthsizer is sufficient at this stage to verify the validity of the system.

In order to improve the accuracy of lipreading. In the pre-processing, we did mouth detection on the input image and cropped the user's mouth area as input.

Since the training device is PC and the actual running device is smartphone. In order to ensure the consistency of mouth detection results between training and running, we use dlib [7] to crop the position of the lips.

In terms of deep neural network models, we have adopted a network structure similar to LipNet since it has three advantages over the network structure of Lip Reading in the wild. First, the overall result it gets is better. Second, its network structure is simpler and the amount of computation is much less, and third, the network structure is End-To-End, which is more suitable for running on smartphones.

See the Fig. 1 for the specific Network Architecture. We adopt Connectionist Temporal Classification [8] (CTC) loss as our loss function. For optimizer we use AdamOpimizer.

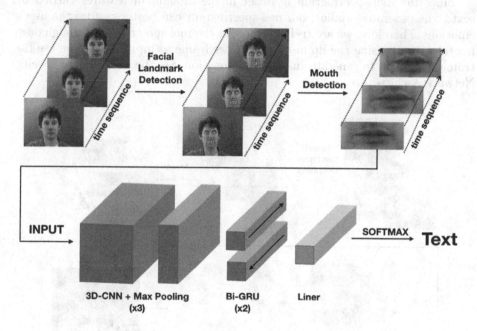

Fig. 1. Lip reading deep neural network architecture.

The accuracy of the model after training is similar to that in the LipNet. The WER of the prediction results for the overlapped speaker is about 7%, and the number for the Unseen Speaker is about 14%.

4 Future Works

We will use the same evaluation method as TTS to verify the validation of Lip-Speaker using the Mean Opinion Score (MOS). In this experiment, each group will consist of an acquired voice disorder participant and a non-disabled participant. The two users will communicate in three ways: pen and paper, keyboard input and LipSpeaker. Both users in each group score the three methods respectively with the score ranges from 1 to 5, and each group generating six numbers. Through multiple sets of experiments, the MOS of each communication method is calculated and compared to verify the effect of LipSpeaker on the acquired voice disorder participants and non-disabled participants.

As mentioned in Sect. 2: predicting text with lip motion sequence frames can result in loss of features of the user's emotions. Therefore, we have improved the network structure inspired by Tacotron2. Tacotron2 is a system for TTS that consists of two major parts. The first part uses deep neural network to predict mel-spectrograms through text sequences. The second part uses the obtained mel-spectrogram to generate audio through another deep neural network WaveNet.

Since the mel-spectrogram is richer in the amount of features carried by texts, the generated audio from mel-spectrogram can better restore the user's emotions. Therefore, we are trying to predict the mel-spectrogram through deep neural network using the lip motion sequence frame as input. Lastly we use the trained WaveNet to generate audio with intonation. See the Fig. 2 for the specific Network Architecture.

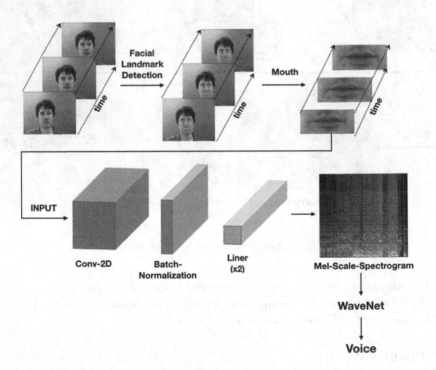

Fig. 2. The approach of predict mel-spectrogram by deep learning network architecture.

Natoki Kimura et al.'s SottoVoce [9] successfully predicted the Mel-scale spectrum using the ultrasound picture sequence frames of the tongue. Since the lip motion sequence frame has more features than ultrasound picture sequence frames of the tongue, we highly believe it is feasible for lip motion sequence frame. Up until now, we have tried to generate mel-spectrogram using 3D Convolutional Neural Networks [10] (3D-CNN). In order to achieve the expected accuracy, further experiments are still needed.

5 Conclusion

The system LipSpeaker we designed shows a new way of human-computer interaction. LipSpeaker can use the deep neural network to predict text by identifying the lip motions of the acquired voice disorder people and use it to generate speech in conjunction with TTS. LipSpeaker can help acquired voice disorders people to communicate more easily with others in their daily life. The WER of the model reached 7% in the laboratory environment, demonstrating the effectiveness of the method.

However, at the same time, the model is greatly affected by the environment. In the case of poor lighting conditions or the user's lip pictures are not clear, the accuracy will drop dramatically. The reason may be that the trained GRID corpus datasets data is obtained in an environment where the light is always sufficient and the participant is always facing the camera at the front face. In future work, we will try to add more training data to improve this situation.

Since the mel-spectrogram is richer in the amount of features carried by the text, the generated audio by mel-spectrogram can better restore the user's feelings. Inspired by the network structure of Tacotron2, we proposed to predict the mel-spectrogram through the lip motion sequence frame and use WaveNet to generate smoother audio with more intonation. In order to achieve the expected accuracy, we will conduct further experiments based on 3D-CNN.

References

1. Assael, Y.M., Shillingford, B., Whiteson, S., de Freitas, N.: LipNet: End-to-End Sentence-level Lipreading. arXiv e-prints, page arXiv:1611.01599, November 2016
2. Chung, J.S., Senior, A., Vinyals, O., Zisserman, A.: Lip Reading Sentences in the Wild. arXiv e-prints, page arXiv:1611.05358, November 2016
3. Cooke, M., Barker, J., Cunningham, S., Shao, X.: An audio-visual corpus for speech perception and automatic speech recognition. Acoust. Soc. Am. J. **120**, 2421 (2006)
4. Wand, M., Koutník, J., Schmidhuber, J.: Lipreading with Long Short-Term Memory. arXiv e-prints, page arXiv:1601.08188, January 2016
5. Shen, J., et al.: Natural TTS Synthesis by Conditioning WaveNet on Mel Spectrogram Predictions. arXiv e-prints, page arXiv:1712.05884, December 2017
6. van den Oord, A., et al.: WaveNet: A Generative Model for Raw Audio. arXiv e-prints, page arXiv:1609.03499, September 2016
7. King, D.E.: Dlib-ml: a machine learning toolkit. J. Mach. Learn. Res. **10**, 1755–1758 (2009)

8. Graves, A., Fernández, S., Gomez, F., Schmidhuber, J.: Connectionist temporal classification: labelling unsegmented sequence data with recurrent neural networks. In: Proceedings of the 23rd International Conference on Machine Learning, ICML 2006, pp. 369–376. ACM, New York (2006)
9. Rekimoto, J., Kimura, N., Kono, M.: SottoVoce: an ultrasound imaging-based silent speech interaction using deep neural networks. In: ACM CHI (2019)
10. Ji, S., Xu, W., Yang, M., Yu, K.: 3D convolutional neural networks for human action recognition. IEEE Trans. Pattern Anal. Mach. Intell. $35(1)$, 221–231 (2013)

A Study on the Use of Motion Graphics and Kinect in LMA (Laban Movement Analysis) Expression Activities for Children with Intellectual Disabilities

Sung Hee Hong[✉] and Tae Woon Kim

DongYang University, Youngju, Gyeongbuk, South Korea
hongsungh22@hanmail.net

Abstract. The purpose of this study is to the motion expression activities of children with intellectual disabilities using motion graphics and Kinect. In the process of recognizing movement expression activity using motion graphics and Kinect, the effect of performance was shown when the movement expression activity through the body was properly performed. The subjects were 8 children with intellectual disabilities, and conducted the program twice a week for 10 weeks. The research design utilized video screen and theme music as contents of musical works. 42 actions were performed randomly. When the movement is perfectly represented, the score is displayed along with the sound. As a research method, Laban Movement analysis was used as a motion expression activity program. It is analyzed by four elements of LMA: Body, Effort, Shape, and Space. We observed the connectivity, body structure, body movements, progress, gestures and postures of each part of the body measured by LMA and figured out what the content of movement was. When the anatomical position of the body is divided into upper/lower (vertical) (average: 34/42: total score), left/right (horizontal) (average: 23/42: total score), and front/back (sagittal) (average: 13/42: total score). Through this study, it is shown that the movement of the children with intellectual disabilities can be induced by using the motion graphics and the functional game using Kinect to train the body structure and movement direction in daily life and to induce the change of the internal attitude.

Keywords: Motion graphics · Kinect · Laban Movement Analysis · Intellectual

1 Introduction

1.1 LMA (Laban Movement Analysis)

One of the practical methods of representing motion research is the motion analysis proposed by Rudolph Laban, which is already being used by infants and children with disabilities. Motion analysis education can present creative programs and it can be done as a treatment program for children with disabilities through movement. However, the development of movement has not been proven in children with disabilities. In this study, it is meaningful that the analysis of Laban movement using ICT is verified in

© Springer Nature Switzerland AG 2019
C. Stephanidis and M. Antona (Eds.): HCII 2019, CCIS 1088, pp. 149–154, 2019.
https://doi.org/10.1007/978-3-030-30712-7_20

actual field for children with disabilities. It is a motion analysis system based on LMA (Laban Movement Analysis) [1] theory. It is a key element of all natural and artificial movements in the world, from various movements expressed in virtual space, the presentation in Table 1 is mainly addressed in Laban's motion analysis. Linder [2] based on the discovery that there are common elements in all movements of Laban's approach to motion. The analysis and records used in the study of movement were to be found in previous unrelated movements this suggests that movement is not simply a physical activity, which means that human activity has always been viewed as a means of conveying internal attitudes or internal responses of the mind [3]. Tables 1 and 2 depicts emotions and thoughts in human movements, and refers to internal motivation, which is expressed by external expressive movements. The movement of the body is to convey various information to the mind and to interact and express it outwardly. In addition to the structure of movement such as movement direction, speed, distance, weight, etc., the port analyzes and records the characteristics of how the effort reflecting the inner psychological state is utilized. The concept of the will is expressed as a core concept [4]. Laban can be classified as 'natural behavior and unnatural act' when he or she approached 'disorder' by movement. By studying human movements, we have argued that we can understand human internal conflicts, in the method of expression and communication that expresses by movement, human beings move to satisfy desire. The basic physical experience emerges from the function of simple transmission to the expression of emotional experience as well as the movement of human life from confirming the existence of life. This is consistent with Hong [5] study. Study on the educational effect analysis of motion expression in motion graphics of Kim [6]: Laban's Movement Analysis as in the centered study, Laban's movement theory was tried in motion graphics, but the limit in motion graphics is dance. The dancer's intentional intentions and motivational movements, expressed directly through the body, are presented through ICT only in a way that expresses emotional and psychological aspects differently from the intention of expressing it directly. The purpose of this study is to present the movement of Laban's movement in the movement of physical activity of children with intellectual disabilities using Kinect and motion graphics.

Table 1. Key elements of Laban Movement Analysis

Configuration	Contents	
Body	Body part	External parts: head, shoulders, arms, legs, etc.
		Internal parts: heart, muscle, bones, joints, etc.
	Body motion	Movement vs non-movement
		Lifting vs lower
		Push vs band

Figure 1 shows the effects of the movement activities on the emotional and psychological aspects of the movement of the children with mental retardation. It is possible to present a study of the program of movement expression activities by

Table 2. Effort element that reconstructs time, space, flow on three steps

Movement element	Effort element		
Time	Speed	Normal speed	Slow
Space	Straight	Little flexible	Flexible
Flow	Stop	Flowing	Growing

interacting with ICT through learning through experiencing confident and movement expressive activities to children with disabilities.

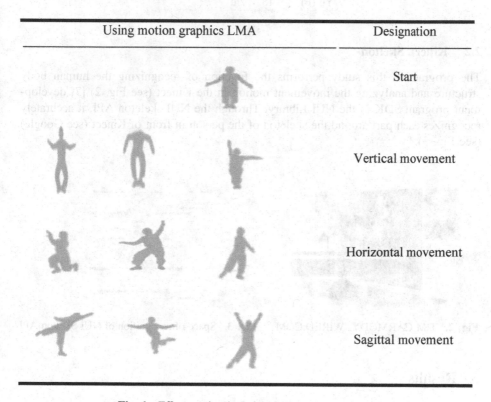

Using motion graphics LMA	Designation
	Start
	Vertical movement
	Horizontal movement
	Sagittal movement

Fig. 1. Effort motion in Laban Movement Analysis

2 Research Design

2.1 Subject

Students with intellectual disabilities were children with disability grade 2 and 3, ages 10 to 18, and 8 children (3 males and 5 females). We participated in the game 20 times (twice a week) in 10 weeks (January ~ March 2018). Table 3 shows the rating characteristics of each participant in the game.

Table 3. Characteristics of participants in the game

Name(sex)	Age	Disability grade
Ko (F)	18	3rd
Ko (M)	16	2rd
Bang (F)	18	3rd
Jeon (F)	16	2rd
Jang (M)	10	3rd
Kim (M)	18	2rd
Park (F)	14	3rd
Yu (F)	18	2rd

2.2 Kinect, Skelton

The program in this study performs the function of recognizing the human body structure and analyzing the movement motion in the Kinect (see Fig. 2) [7] development program SDK in the NUI Library. Through the NUI skeleton API, it accurately recognizes each part around the skeleton of the person in front of Kinect (see Google) (see Fig. 3).

 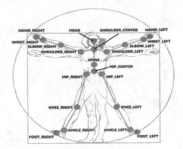

Fig. 2. TIM CARMODY, WIRED.COM   **Fig. 3.** Space of recognition of NUI Skelton API

3 Results

The purpose of this study is to investigate the motion graphics of kinematics of children with intellectual disabilities and the kinesthetic activities of Kinect. The participating children did not have experience of games at all, and the space where the physical activity was encountered was mainly indoor activities rather than outdoor activities, educational movements programs participating in physical activity are children who have difficulty in experiencing environmental factors. Movement activities were based on the anatomical postures of the body as a result of physical activity of vertical, horizontal, and sagittal (center shift). Vertical movement showed the highest score in children with intellectual disability when divided into vertical movement, horizontal movement, and sagittal movement (average score)/Total score: 8.2 points/10 points), followed by a horizontal movement score (average score/total score: 6.1 points/10 points). The lowest score was the sagittal movement (average score/total score: 4 points/10 points). In Table 4, the evaluation criteria for the 10-point scale were set by 10 selected motions with 1 preparation, 3 vertical motions, 3 horizontal motions, 3 front and back motions, And the average of the score values of each performed action.

Table 4. Motion representation activity vertical, horizontal, sagittal (movement)

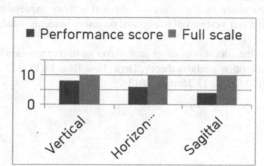

In the movement analysis, the children with disabilities preferred the private space rather than the general space. Vertical movement and horizontal movement. These results show that the movement activities of the children with disabilities are also the most preferred and confidently represented by the non-movement movement.

Also, in the body movement center movement activity, it showed higher score in non - movement than center movement. It is suggested that the activities of expressing the preference of the children with disabilities are represented by the vertical activities indicated by the high scores, and when they are expressed with the vertical direction of the body structure in daily life, And the horizontal direction, that is, the direction that moves left and right, shows the internal attitude of 'communication' as a posture requiring a stability of the body. Finally, the sagittal movement that moves forward and backward, which is the movement of the center movement, is somewhat difficult to express to children with disabilities due to the characteristic of movement that has the lowest attitude of inner will or approach when performing the concentration and operation of a certain work, And the internal attitude of the activity. This study suggests that the presentation of the program that can induce the internal attitude change of the body movements can be used for the education of the movement of the body expressing activity as the educational function of the psychological element to the children with the disability. In particular, it can be used variously in education games for the disabled and the disabled, and for the elderly people in the movement learning and dementia prevention education. By presenting the study of practical educational game programs, it is expected that continuous research should be linked.

Acknowledgements. This work was supported by the Ministry of Education of the Republic of Korea and the National Research Foundation of Korea (NRF-2017S1A5B5A07063616).

References

1. Laban, R.V.: The Mastery of Movement. Plays Inc., Boston (1971)
2. Linder, T.W.: Transdisciplinary Play-based Assessment: A Functional Approach to Working with Young Children (Rev. edn). Brunner-Routledge, New York (1993)
3. Lee, K.: The meaning of motion evaluation in dance motion therapy (centered on Laban motion analysis). Korean Dance Res. Assoc. **60**(3), 123–138 (2016)
4. Shin, S., Kim, J.: Reading body and movement. Ewha Women's University (2010)
5. Hong, S.-H.: A case study on the effects of physical activity expression activity on self - expression ability and self - esteem of intellectual disability students. Stud. Korean Arts Educ. **15**(1), 127–140 (2017)
6. Kim, H.: A study on the educational effect analysis on motion expression in motion graphics - focused on Laban's motion analysis theory. Digit. Des. Res. **14**(1), 427–436 (2014)
7. Carmody, T.: WIRED.COM, 12 January 2012

Tingling Cast: Broadcasting Platform Service for Stuttering Children

HyunJin Jo(✉) ⓘ, YeonJi Kim, and JaeYoung Yun(✉)

Hongik University, Seoul 04066, South Korea
guswls1994@gmail.com, yjikim117@gmail.com,
ryun@hongik.ac.kr

Abstract. HIRA (Health Insurance Review & Assessment Service) in South Korea showed that 70% of patients treated for stuttering were children last year. In general, stuttering treatment is more effective the earlier post-onset it is provided to the child. However, several obstacles have found in standard stuttering treatment related to visual recording also limitations have found in existing digital treatment services for stuttering children. In this paper, the case study introduced "Tingling Cast" application to confirm stuttering symptoms and to help promote and maintain speech fluency in children. Based on the case study with a stuttering child and interviews with speech therapists, the case study showed that the "Tingling Cast" service had a positive impact on children's stuttering treatment motivation and in promoting speech fluency. In light of these positive results from qualitative data, the case study proposes this service to confirm stuttering symptoms and to help promote and maintain speech fluency in children.

Keywords: Service design · Interaction · Stuttering · Symptom identification · Behavior change · Children

1 Introduction

In recent years, HCI researchers have shown potentials of using interactive technologies to support people with disorders. However, we have found that there has been a severe lack of study in digital tools that involves people who stutter [2]. According to the Health Insurance Review & Assessment (HIRA) Service in South Korea, a total of 423 individuals sought medical treatment for stuttering in 2017, and 291 (68.7%) of them were children. The younger the children experiencing speech difficulties are, the more favorable the prognosis for stuttering. However, treatment services for speech fluency impediments (e.g. stuttering, cluttering, etc.) are mainly confined to adults. With this in mind, this case study set out to propose treatment services to promote practical fluency improvement for stuttering children.

2 Background

2.1 Definition and Causes of Stuttering

Stuttering is a condition marked by the repetition of sounds that impede one's speech. The causes of this impediment are usually complex and are often due to environmental

© Springer Nature Switzerland AG 2019
C. Stephanidis and M. Antona (Eds.): HCII 2019, CCIS 1088, pp. 155–161, 2019.
https://doi.org/10.1007/978-3-030-30712-7_21

and psychological factors. Stuttering usually appears in children from 1.6 years to 12 years old and occurs most frequently in children aged between 2 and 5. In 80% of all cases of stuttering appearing during a child's language development, symptoms subside naturally after 3 years or more, with symptoms persisting throughout the elementary school in the remaining 20% of cases [4]. In most cases in which stuttering persist throughout a child's elementary school years, there is a risk of evolution into a chronic speech impediment. Therefore, it is critical to have a speech therapist monitor and diagnose whether a child's stuttering will subside on its own or if active speech therapy is required [1].

2.2   Treatment for Stuttering

There are three main approaches to stuttering treatment: 'stuttering modification', 'fluency shaping', and 'integrated or hybrid intervention'. 'Stuttering modification' teaches children to "stutter with fluency"—i.e., to recognize instances of stuttering and to reduce any associated fears of speaking by building the confidence to self-correct when necessary. 'Fluency shaping' is a multi-step approach that reduces unnecessary stuttering-related behaviors in order to improve fluency. Finally, the 'integrated or hybrid intervention' combines these two forms of intervention. The 'stabilization' stage included in the integrated therapy is characterized by a crucial step that focuses on reducing the rate of relapse during and after treatment [3].

2.3   Limitations of Existing Treatment Services for Stuttering

Applications and services for children were significantly less than for adults. There were only a few services shared with the therapist for continuous care. Furthermore, most of these services involved voice recordings and DAF (Delayed Auditory Feedback) functions, rather than objective feedback from speech therapists. Some applications provided word lists for pronunciation practice. However, it is hard to practice speaking in real life by training pronunciation based on word or sentence. Among the types of apps used for language therapy, a simulation that implements everyday communication situations and problem-solving apps that apply acquired speech and language learning should make more efforts since it is only at 0% of the total [2].

3   Tingling Cast

3.1   Service Background

Through the interview process involving experts with speech disorder consisting of four speech therapists, the head of speech-language therapy and aural rehabilitation department at WooSong University in South Korea, and a director of Shin's Speech-Language Clinic in South Korea, we have found several problems with existing treatment for stuttering. During the 'symptom identification' stage, the first stage of 'stuttering modification' treatment, the therapist uses video taking to help children to identify their symptom. However, children are uncomfortable to see themselves and even deny their stuttering. Speech therapists face a heavy emotional burden as they try to assess the speech conditions of children while also being considerate of children's emotions. The final stage of treatment, 'stabilization', requires prolonged and continuous monitoring of children to maintain treatment results and to avoid the high risk of relapse. The therapist often takes a video to observe the patient during the stage and expects the patient to be aware of it. However, children show a lack of focus on treatment activities due to a long journey of treatment. Moreover, there are limitations when therapists treat the patient one-on-one. The longer the treatment, the more challenging to come up with different treatment activities. These problems cause difficulty to produce the results of fluency practices.

To overcome obstacles, we have considered two methods. First, we implemented the content creation experience to the service. Recently, much attention has been paid to reports of elementary students indicating "media creator" as their dream job. This is because teenagers use video media significantly. Data shows that teenagers spend three times longer on YouTube than on KakaoTalk (the most commonly used free mobile instant messaging application in South Korea) [5]. Demonstrating that video is the most common medium of content they access and the most popular medium of content creation. The children from the Shin's Speech-Language Clinic who encouraged this case study were familiar with YouTube and even expressed a desire to create YouTube content in the future. Taking these factors into consideration content creation was selected as an effective means to create to capture children's interest. Second, we applied the everyday problem-solving practice to the service. When using the "Tingling Cast" application, speech therapists can select either symptom identification or fluency examination as a customized objective for each child. Moreover, these objectives can meet the specific practice of each child by considering everyday situations, questions, and conversations. This allows speech therapists to decide on an appropriate course of therapy adapted to each individual. It also gives the children an opportunity to become aware of their own speech patterns and engages them to participate in everyday conversations and scenarios to further promote fluency development and preservation.

3.2   Service Content and Operation

We propose a service that helps maintain fluency in the stage of "identification" and "stabilization" using Van Riper's therapy [3]. The "Tingling Cast" operates as follows. First, children who experience stuttering become media content creators and record their own content on the application. They select one of several objectives set by a speech therapist before they begin recording (Fig. 1) and can even purchase special effects (Fig. 2) from the game store to make their content more unique. After completing their recording, the children can click on their recorded videos to start the process of symptom identification. When they find their stuttering or secondary behavior (e.g., eye blinks, looking away from the listener, etc.), they click the button. The button used a comma icon to express a metaphorical sense of 'taking a moment to pause when speaking.' When children click the button, an icon is displayed in the video progress bar (Fig. 2). After completing the symptom identification, the subscribers increase as basic compensation. It rises each time when they finish video taking regardless of their stuttering. However, stuttering subtracts subscribers from the total number of subscribers (Fig. 3). Children who earn a certain number of subscribers will unlock new special effects that they can use in their content creation. Speech therapists can keep track of their patients through the "Tingling Cast" and can add age-appropriate treatment objectives for each child. These objectives are then saved on the server, and they can be shared with other speech therapists. Shared data would be useful for other speech therapists when they confront a hard time creating new contents for children's objectives. Therapists can view the video content created by their patients and leave comments on each child's progress (Fig. 4).

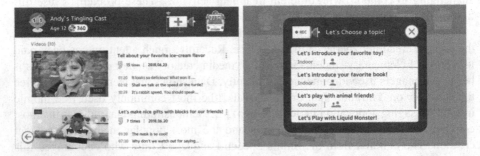

Fig. 1. Main and topic selection page

Fig. 2. An effect shop and symptom identification page

Fig. 3. Reward pages

Fig. 4. Therapist's pages: main and children's comments page

4 The Case Study

The subject of this case study was a 12-year old boy who is a 6th-grade elementary student and has been getting treatment at Shin's Speech-Language Clinic for more than a year. He met with a speech therapist at the clinic twice a week to record practice videos and to observe his own speech fluency preservation. Also, the child received homework to practice at home and recorded his speaking to get feedback from the therapist. The results of the observation showed that even though conducting this treatment for approximately one year evidenced promising results within a structured setting, it was difficult to determine the impact of the treatment on the child's everyday life. The child and his parent visited the clinic to engage in the case study. Also, we and the therapist participant were present during the service observation. We are researchers conducting the case study, and the therapist participant was a speech therapist with a master's degree in speech pathology who had experience in assessing speech fluency disorders in children.

"Tingling Cast" is a mobile app developed using Unity and installed in Samsung tablet to take a case study. To assess the interactions using "Tingling Cast", the tablet was arranged in the separated room at Shin's Speech-Language Clinic with additional props related to objectives that the research subject has to perform (see Fig. 5). First, we explained the intent and purpose of the study to the child and his parent. Next, the child entered the room and was asked to select one of the objectives presented by the speech therapist to take a video by using the app for more than 15 min. The child selected one of the objectives (e.g., "Tell us about your favorite movie character") and recorded himself with a prepared prop (e.g., "Marvel Avengers guide book") within the guidance of us. The child introduced his favorite movie and explained about movie characters using "Tingling Cast" following the process explained above (3.2. Service Operation and Content). He completed his video taking within 1 h including 'symptom identification' process. Then, the therapist participant took the video recorded by the child and reviewed it. After examining the video, the therapist participant assessed the child's performance and gave specific feedback during the next treatment.

Fig. 5. User test setting at Shin's Speech-Language Clinic

During the case study, we observed the interaction between the child and "Tingling Cast" and analyzed the accessibility of the service. After the case study, we interviewed the child about the usability and attractiveness of "Tingling Cast" service. Also, we showed the result of the child's video to the parent and interviewed for the value of the app. Lastly, the therapist participant reviewed the child's video and checked whether he performed his treatment activity considering his treatment goals. Then, the therapist participant answered the questionnaire asking about the effectiveness of treatment through the app.

5   Results

5.1   The Therapeutic Value

Qualitative data from the case study with the therapist participant, the child, and the parent support our findings. The therapeutic value of "Tingling Cast" was evaluated by the therapist participant through reviewing video taken from the child. The therapist participant fulfilled the questionnaire assessing therapeutic value and gave detailed feedbacks to us. Results regarding the confirmation of the identification of stuttering showed that the child was already aware of his speech patterns, but that he came to recognize accompanying behaviors upon reviewing his recordings. The speech therapist rated the effectiveness of the service highly in helping the child quickly acknowledge his own speech patterns and their accompanying behaviors without burden. The speech therapist also observed that the child applied the lessons he had learned to preserve speech fluency when proceeding video taking. Furthermore, he was able to practice and engage in more various and enjoyable activities than those offered by existing treatment methods.

5.2   The Ease of Functions

The accessibility of "Tingling Cast" was assessed by us observing the child in the case study. And the attractiveness of "Tingling Cast" was evaluated by the interview between us and the child. Results regarding the functionality and effectiveness of the service showed that "Tingling Cast" possess the functions within the reach of the child. "Tingling Cast" interaction design induces the child to control the app and the app responded to the child's manipulation accurately. Also, through the observation, it was confirmed that the relevant menus and icons are appealing to and simple enough for the child. The child expressed interest in and enjoyed the feature of adding special effects to his content, stating that he wanted to "increase [his] number of subscribers so that [he] could try out other stickers." Since the child's records have been accumulated and kept, it was possible for the parent to check the child's treatment progress. Positive feedback had received from parents who want to continue to receive treatment progress while outside of the center. The parent showed delight since her child could continue practicing at home.

6 Conclusion

This case study aimed to provide a service to effectively identify symptoms and maintain fluency in stuttering children. The results of the case study showed that the "Tingling Cast" service motivated the child to participate in treatment and promoted greater awareness of their stuttering, while also teaching the child skills needed to actively learn to maintain their own speech fluency. The parent commended the service for enabling them to keep track of the child's progress throughout the treatment course and to receive feedback from speech therapists. Furthermore, speech therapists highlighted the fact that children showed an observably greater interest in participating actively in their therapy sessions. Based on these findings, the use of "Tingling Cast" can be beneficial in the treatment of speech fluency for, and the language development of, stuttering children. Subsequent studies will be conducted to offer more advanced services for stuttering children to enjoy their treatment and also to reduce the inconvenience of speech therapists assessing the stuttering.

Acknowledgments. This study was conducted in collaboration with Shin's Speech-Language Clinic in South Korea 2018-19.

References

1. Lee, S.-B.: The longitudinal study of treatment effect predictors in early childhood stuttering. Ph.D. Ewha Woman's University, Seoul, Korea (2014)
2. Lee, Y.: Analysis of mobile application trends for speech and language therapy of children with disabilities in Korea. Phonetics Speech Sci. **7**(3), 153–163 (2015)
3. Lee, S.: Fluency Disorder. Sigma Press, Seoul, Korea (2005)
4. Amborse, N., Yairi, E., Cox, N.: Genetic aspects of early childhood stuttering. J. Speech Hear. Res. **36**, 701–706 (1993). https://doi.org/10.1044/jshr.3604.701
5. The Kyunghyang Shinmun, The golden age of 1 media creators. http://news.khan.co.kr/kh_news/khan_art_view.html?art_id=201803040944031. Accessed 04 Mar 2018

A Software Tool for the Deaf and Hard-of-Hearing to Learn How to Speak

Robert Moreno(✉) and Shamima Yasmin

Eastern Washington University, Cheney, WA 99004, USA
rmorenonv@gmail.com

Abstract. This project aims towards the empowerment of the deaf and hard-of-hearing (DHH) in social communication by providing them a software tool to learn how to speak. As the DHH will closely monitor and mimic other's facial expressions on the software, they will also explore how tongue placement is used to create the correct sounding words. The software application uses simple technologies and can be used in computers or mobile phones with the help of embedded cameras and microphones. Hence it is portable and easily deployable with everyday gadgets, i.e., laptops, mobile phones, and so on. The application also comes in handy for the DHH to develop better communication skills by providing a flexible learning environment.

Keywords: Deaf · Hard-of-hearing · Assistive technologies

1 Introduction

Existing research on the accessibility to language learning software mainly focuses on sign language. On the other hand, learning how to speak could be beneficial to the DHH because they would have another way of communicating their needs to others who may not know sign language. A secondary benefit to this would be that as they learn how to speak, they also become more proficient in lipreading which could eventually expand their communication skills. With reduced communication barriers, more opportunities arise. A software tool as proposed could help the DHH to practice communication skills to enhance social interaction capabilities, and integrate into mainstream society through improved understanding and evaluation of the surroundings [1].

2 Background

More than 85% of the DHH go to regular schools; about 95% of DHH children have speaking and hearing parents but have a limited access to practice speaking [2]. When these children start school, they have significant delay in language development in comparison with their peers that do not have hearing loss. After reaching middle school. They learn as much from text as they do from sign language or spoken language in school. Current research works in this field are limited as user studies were carried out on a small sample population.

C. Stephanidis and M. Antona (Eds.): HCII 2019, CCIS 1088, pp. 162–167, 2019.
https://doi.org/10.1007/978-3-030-30712-7_22

In the recent past, a user study was conducted with 500 DHH students who were not identified with any other disability other than hearing impairment [2]. This study aimed to isolate variables specifically tied with hearing impairment and academic achievement. Participants were tested on comprehension, math, social studies, and science skills. Better speaking ability was found to be positively related to achievement scores across all the tests. DHH students who attended only regular schools, even those who were in self-contained classrooms, performed better across all achievement measures than those who attended either special schools or a mix of regular and special schools.

Another study was conducted with 101 5-year-old DHH children who are accustomed to hearing aid devices and use speaking as their main form of communication [3]. These children were found to have greater phonological awareness on average which has been associated with increased reading ability when compared to other DHH children. However this study removed some variables (i.e., socio-economic background, age group, developmental disorders, and more) that could have been associated with variances in data for a better conclusion.

Another study performed at a school for DHH children analyzed the predictors of reading achievement as the receptive and expressive components and considered 78% of the variance in reading achievement scores [4]. The findings did not correlate speech scores to reading scores significantly; it only correlated the proficiency in English language to their reading achievement.

Research findings clearly indicate that DHHs need to have more opportunities to be exposed to the social environment; social avoidance and isolation can affect them in a negative way. This paper aims to enrich the abilities, lives, and self-sufficiency of the DHH.

3 Proposed Approach

The proposed approach consists of the following steps:

1. Live or pre-recorded video data of news anchors or interaction partners to be captured by a camera.
2. Convert audio feedback to video captions in real time with the existing speech recognition libraries (Fig. 1).
3. Extract, demarcate, and enhance facial features (e.g. lips) with existing graphics and images processing libraries such as OpenGL and OpenCV (Fig. 2).

It is hypothesized that the DHH will closely monitor and mimic other's facial expressions and explore how tongue placement is used to create the correct sounding words. Simultaneous video captions or subtitles will help them better enunciate the words. Hence the proposed approach mainly consists of close monitoring of the visemes and pronounce the captions accordingly to be able to speak properly as demonstrated in Figs. 1 and 2. This software should be portable and could be used on computers, tablets, and mobile phones which allows the user to use it whenever and wherever is convenient and comfortable for them.

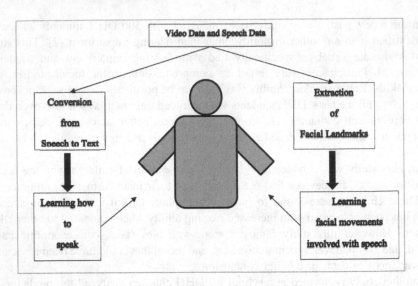

Fig. 1. The proposed approach at a glance

Fig. 2. Visemes to be considered for correct pronunciation of words [5].

4   Implementation and Results

Python 3.7 was used in conjunction with a speech recognition library. The speech recognition library (SpeechRecognition 3.8.1) uses Google Speech to Text API. This software uses OpenCV to either show a prerecorded video feed or a live feed of the user. The software at its current stage can extract audio and video data properly. Audio feedback is displayed onto the screen as subtitles along with the video of the user. Below are some results from this work-in-progress.

The user in Fig. 3 is an international student with severe hearing impairment who learned how to speak at a very young age. His speaking ability developed during his time at a deaf school and he continued to practice even after attending regular schools. Now he is a junior in a computer science program at Eastern Washington University. He leads a very social life with very little assistance from any devices, i.e., cell phones, computers, hearing aids, writing, and others.

Figure 4 demonstrates the use of the software by a normal user. Though some words were mispronounced intentionally, the speech recognition library could handle it

Fig. 3. The software in use by a user who has severe hearing impairment, but he can speak, and the software is able to translate what he has said correctly.

properly. For example, the user pronounced "wittle wady went to the mawket" and it was translated correctly with this software to "little lady went to the market".

Fig. 4. This caption "little lady went to the market" was pronounced "wittle wady went to the mawket" and it was translated correctly by this software.

This tool does make mistakes depending on the quality of microphone available and pronunciations. Mistakes happen most often because of mispronunciations, for example if you say "yellow stone" too quickly it might translate to "Yellowstone" which have two different meanings. This would be important if the user is trying to convey a location or an object that contain the same words but are pronounced differently.

As part of the future works of this project, facial features for different facial movements (i.e., lips) will be checked against ideal facial movements. Ideal facial movements will be demonstrated on one side of the screen. Next, the software will take in sound from either the microphone or a prerecorded audio file and translate it into text where it can be checked against the expected word or phrase to give appropriate feedback. Finally, with the combined feedback as provided by the software, users will be able to practice as much as they would like to improve speaking and lip reading skills.

5   Conclusion

It is obvious as more tools are available for the DHH, their avenues of communication can be broadened accordingly. This will assist them academically and in their careers. This will allow them to seek healthcare options that are not readily available for them in areas that lack proper resources to provide quality services for the DHH community [6].

The proposed approach can be used primarily to gather data about speech patterns specific to the DHH. A speech recognition software could become easier to implement with a large data set. Datasets could be specific to age group, severity of hearing loss, time when hearing loss acquired, or the information provided by the users. This could give more insight into how to provide more options to the DHH based on their specific needs.

This program could help bridge the communication gap by providing a tool to the DHH to practice speaking and lip reading with a smartphone, tablet, or computer that has a microphone and a camera. Additionally, it could provide an alternative way of expanding their means of communication. With more means of communication opportunity, the DHH would have increased accessibility to needed services. This is especially relevant to people in rural areas who do not have reasonable access to services specific to their needs [6].

References

1. Kafle, S., Huenerfauth, M.: Evaluating the usability of automatically generated captions for people who are deaf or hard of hearing. In: Proceedings of the 19th International ACM SIGACCESS Conference on Computers and Accessibility, ASSETS 2017, New York, NY, USA, pp. 165–174. ACM (2017)
2. Marschark, M., Shaver, D.M., Nagle, K.M., Newman, L.: Predicting the academic achievement of deaf and hard-of-hearing students from individual, household, communication, and educational factors. Except. Child. **81**(3), 350–369 (2015)
3. Cupples, L., et al.: Predictors of early reading skill in 5-year-old children with hearing loss who use spoken language. Read. Res. Q. **49**(1), 85–104 (2014). https://www.jstor.org/stable/43497638
4. Nielsen, D.C., Luetke, B., McLean, M.: The English-language and reading achievement of a cohort of deaf students speaking and signing standard English: a preliminary study. Am. Ann. Deaf **161**(3), 342–368 (2016)

5. https://www.web3.lu/phonemes-phones-graphemes-visemes/
6. Tate, C., Adams, S.: Information gaps on the deaf and hard of hearing population: a background paper. [ebook] Western Interstate Commission for Higher Education (2019). https://www.wiche.edu/pub/12452. Accessed 13 June 2019

A Systematic Literature Review on User-Centered Design (UCD) Interface of Mobile Application for Visually Impaired People

Hammad Hassan Qureshi and Doris Hooi-Ten Wong[✉]

Razak Faculty of Technology and Informatics, Universiti Teknologi Malaysia,
54100 Kuala Lumpur, Malaysia
h.qureshi-1979@graduate.utm.my, doriswong@utm.my

Abstract. In modern mobile application development, User-Centered Design (UCD) is a key success. Mobile devices are becoming an integral part of daily life. Nowadays it is very much difficult and tricky to use the mobile application. A task like sending data from one application to another application is too much difficult. Normal people who use these mobile applications, sometimes they feel difficult to use them. Hence, there is a clear point that visually impaired people need much more efforts to use these applications. In the past years, there are many types of research try to improve the mobile application for visually impaired people. All the mobile applications produced from these researches are focusing in technocentric approach, in which they ignore the analysis of actual needs from visually impaired people. In order to improve the quality of mobile application for visually impaired people, the UCD interfaces are more valuable. It can provide more freedom for visually impaired people to perform their daily tasks. It is really helpful for visually impaired people who access their needs with minimum physical and mental effort, and least effect on their natural activity. This paper provides a Systematic Literature Review (SLR) of the present studies on UCD interface of mobile application for visually impaired people. The first aim is to identify current problems facing by visually impaired people when using the mobile applications. The second aim is to summarize the possible solutions to resolve the problems facing by visually impaired people when using the mobile applications. The third aim is to find the problem in UCD interface of mobile application manufacturing. This research will also beneficial for future research in UCD interface of a mobile application for visually impaired people. UCD of a mobile application can bring marvelous changes in the life of visually impaired people. These interfaces and new strategies expected to improve the quality of life for visually impaired people.

Keywords: Visually impair · Mobile application ·
Visual impairment · Systematic Literature Review ·
Human-computer interaction · User interface

© Springer Nature Switzerland AG 2019
C. Stephanidis and M. Antona (Eds.): HCII 2019, CCIS 1088, pp. 168–175, 2019.
https://doi.org/10.1007/978-3-030-30712-7_23

1   Introduction

In the year 2018, World Health Organization (WHO) measured that there are approximately 285 million visually impaired people worldwide. From which 39 million people are blind and 246 million have low vision called visually impaired. In developing countries, there are about 65% of people have suffered from visual impairment over the age of 50 years. The main reason for visual imparity is refractive errors, cataracts, and glaucoma [1]. A research shows that the prevalence of nearsightedness will increase to around half the population of the world in 2050 [2]. Visual impairment has a great impact on the quality of life, including to develop a personal relationship and their ability to work. There are almost 48% of people cut off moderately or completely from the things and people around them due to visual impairment. The UCD of mobile application helps the visually impaired people to reduce those problems, that they faced in their daily life.

1.1   User-Centered Design (UCD)

It is a very complex task that selecting the user requirements, in which a huge number of errors are disposed of. In Information System (IS) literature it has been documented widely [3,4]. UCD is a policy that highlights the role of user requirements and analysis and their exact gathering. In the year 2004, a methodology for designing a product in which the final outlook of that product is according to the end-user is described [5]. According to the researcher, this methodology is called UCD, which is one of the main perceptions that appeared from the early researches of HCI. In the last era of the 1980s after the introduction of UCD, a vast number of researchers have to take part in the construction of this preliminary theory idea and accept that UCD is one of guiding ideologies [3,6]. In the year 2011, UCD is one of guiding ideologies that described in this era for designing the useable technologies [7]. The iterative stages of UCD are (1) theoretical, (2) requirements analysis, (3) consolidation, design and validation, and (4) evaluation.

1.2   Mobile Device

Mobile phones are the devices that used as a part of daily life, but sometimes the usage is so much tricky. If take a simple view of the previous era, featured mobile phone was introduced at the end of the 90s. They had many new features like mobile games, wallpaper, ringtones that are the customizable and mobile camera. In the year 2002, the era of smartphones started. They included all the previous era phones features. The only changes was having a bigger screen size. In the year 2007, the most recent era starts when the iPhone launched by Apple [8,9]. The multitouch simple display was introduced with mobile interaction. The Android operating system was introduced as a competitor to iPhone a couple of years later. These mobile phones have many cost-effective technologies for visually impaired people. These mobile phones were used frequently for visually impaired people and suitable software is needed for them.

1.3   Categories of Visual Impairment

There are many types of visual imparities, such as diabetic retinopathy, Age-related Muscular Degeneration (AMD), cataract and glaucoma [1]. It is very difficult to describe their vision for the people having a visual impairment. It is also difficult for someone to describe their vision spot. There is a tool called mock-optics that can be used to some understanding of how visual impairments can be felt. The tool mock-optics describes five different types of visual impairments that are shown in Fig. 1. The first picture mark with 0 is the original picture. The second picture mark with 1 demonstrates the diabetic retinopathy visual imparities which can be described with as blurry vision. The third picture mark with 2 demonstrates cataract, which involves the lens became cloudy. It is quite similar to the diabetic retinopathy but these are two different diseases. The fourth picture mark with 3 demonstrates age-related macular degeneration (AMD), which causes central vision loss. This is the common type in old age and it is identifying that 25% of all people over age 75 [1]. The fifth picture mark with 4 demonstrates a narrow vision filed which can be the result of many different diseases, but glaucoma is most common. An occurrence of this disease is 4% at the age of 75 years. The last picture mark with 5 demonstrates vision impairments result in light only, this type of visual imparities is called blindness.

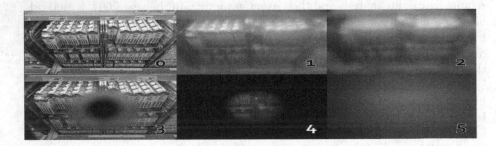

Fig. 1. Vision impairments simulated with mock optics. 0 - Full vision. 1 - Diabetic retinopathy. 2 - Cataract. 3 - Age-related macular degeneration (AMD). 4 - Narrow field of view i.e. retinitis pigmentosa (RP). 5 - Only light vision

The remaining part of this paper is organized as follows: Sect. 2 explains the SLR research method. Section 3 discusses the results of the research questions, regarding the problem facing by visually impaired people when using the mobile applications, possible solution to resolve their problems and problem in UCD interface of mobile application manufacturing. Section 4 concludes this work with the remarks on the research direction.

2   Systematic Literature Review

A SLR conducted using detailed search approaches, in order to overcome such problems during combination and classification phase in our study. In this study, the focus is to identify current problems facing by visually impaired people, summarize the possible solutions to resolve the problems facing by visually impaired people when using the mobile applications and find the problem in UCD interface of mobile application manufacturing. The evaluating and understanding all available research relevant to spectacle of interest, topic, to a particular research question is called SLR [10]. SLR has been conducted to follow the different guidelines. These guidelines are mainly from Charters and Kitchenham in 2007. The three main points included in the SLR are (i) an initial list of studies (ii) judgment relevance and (iii) data exploring. In the account of data resource and search approaches only English written and online available paper are searched. In the policy of search, there is the inclusion of different surveys, electronic databases, and conference proceedings. Following are the electronic databases that have been used.

1. Google Scholar (http://scholar.google.com.pk/)
2. IEEE Xplore (www.ieeexplore.ieee.org/Xplore/)
3. Springer Link (www.springerlink.com/)
4. ACM Digital library (www.portal.acm.org/dl.cfm)
5. Wiley InterScience (www.interscience.wiley.com/)
6. Elsevier Science Direct (www.sceincedirect.com/)

According to research title 'user-centered design of a mobile application for visually impaired people,' the papers searched in different conference proceedings, editorials, features, and seminars. At each database searched out the following keywords, from that search the result will get the article that contains the words 'mobile application' and 'disabilities'. In order to find the complete text of conference proceedings and journal articles, these logical queries were used. There are many queries intelligence that was able to manage the distinction of many words such as 'disability' and 'disabilities', 'impaired' and 'impairment' (like, 'disability' or 'visual impair', and 'User-Centered Densing of Mobile application' or 'Mobile applications', or 'UCD application design' or 'Mobile application for Visually Impaired people'). After that, wisely separated the title, keywords, full text, and abstract. Around 505073 papers were found on disabilities from these search queries but there were only 4906 papers found on UCD mobile application, visually impaired, mobile application interface on visually impaired. Total 1331 paper were found on the impact of the UCD interface of a mobile application for visually impaired people. Then from the primary list, relevant papers were selected manually, irrelevant papers are removed after reading the titles, keywords, abstract and full text. The following are the elimination standards used to remove the papers from the primary list.

1. UCD did not focus on these articles.
2. The papers were not related to the visually impaired community.
3. Duplication was found in some papers.
4. Insertion conditions were not fulfilled by papers.
5. Experimental evidence did not prove by the papers.
6. Insertion of Non-English papers was not approved.

7. Consequences of papers were not according to mobile applications for visually impaired people.
8. Paper published before 2010.
9. Paper's full text was not available.
10. The objective of our criteria did not complete by the papers.

3   Result

Dyba and Dingsoyr's citation management procedure is followed in this study [11]. Firstly, q refer to total number of paper, (q = 1331) are stored using end-notes. A spreadsheet was used to import all these citations. In this spreadsheet recorded all the sources of each citation and decision of consequent insertion or extraction. In order to determine the relevance of studies with SLR, the title of all 1331 papers has been analyzed in the second step. Secondly, 500 relevant papers were identified and all nonrelevant or out of scope papers were discarded. Nevertheless, the title of a paper can not always represent paper content. Thirdly, the 179 paper's abstract was included and promising in the visually impaired people's domain. These papers were extracted from reviewing the 500 papers. At the end of third step, only 50 papers remained for the selection process in the final step. In data removal and combination only 27 papers were selected shown in Fig. 2. For more identification and analysis 27 papers were selected.

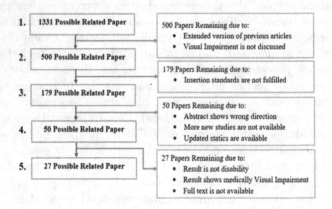

Fig. 2. The steps in the screening criteria of papers.

The research topic is addressed by using the following standards after the screening criteria.

1. What are the current problems facing by visually impaired people when using the mobile applications?
2. What are the possible solutions to resolve the problems facing by visually impaired people when using the mobile applications?
3. Does a paper describe any challenges handled by this user center mobile interface of the mobile application?

3.1 What Are the Current Problems Facing by Visually Impaired People During Using the Mobile Applications?

Visually impaired people are facing the problems in using the mobile application. Different mobile applications are focused according to the new era. These mobile applications are Globonews, WhatsApp, Facebook and mobile phone embedded application. In Globonews application, visually impaired people had some difficulties in identifying the item, due to unclearly show the labels of descriptions. Components were not identified properly, some of them are 'Button A' and 'Button B' [16]. The screen orientation changes and numbering order of saved playlist did not warn by the application. Hence, the idea of the interface to their users was not provided by the application. Visually impaired users required to count the screens to accessing their required tasks. Another problem faced by the user in this application was the HOME button or link is not provided by the application. In order to perform this step, firstly close all the applications then reached home [16]. The second application that was discussed here is WhatsApp. The first problem in this application is to find out a new contact. Due to the delay in updating the new contact and this delay does not warn the user. Picture sending in this application was another problem, the picture's sending label on button did not present. The confirmation of image capture is also affected due to the lack of sound and tactile [17]. Facebook application, there was one problem that the characters were not entered in the text field and the application did not warn about this problem [18].

3.2 What Are the Possible Solutions of Problems Facing by Visually Impaired People During Using the Mobile Applications?

When a character is entered by the user then it must be heard to the user. The chosen item and images names must be heard to the user, because of they are touched. It is necessary that in the response of all interactions a clear voice or event sound must be provided and screen reader must be a presence. A home button must be provided by a system. On the control pad, the identification of this button can be very quickly and easily. That's why the user itself able to work in the interface. In order to start the mobile operations that home key could be used as an initial command. A specific position of this key is represented on the touch screen mobile devices and it is used some kind of actions in the mobile interface [12]. In order to reduce the mistakes, the mobile screen must offer the documented equivalence when text is read from the mobile. The media must be translated into a text form that produces a similar idea if other media like photo, buttons, movie, maps, and sounds are being used. The information alerts should be provided by the system, that is used from other communication channels instead of visual.

3.3 Why UCD Interface Is Necessary for Manufacturing the Mobile Application for Visually-Impaired People?

Visually impaired people have unique interactive experiences while using smartphones. This uniqueness consequently causes a gap between the ideas of designers of mobile application technology and the needs of visually impaired people [13]. During the design process, there is a 'lack of thoughts' about user needs, it becomes a cause of the gap between ideas of mobile application and requirements of visually impaired people. In the development of new mobile applications, this gap is a challenge. In developing the mobile phone applications for visually impaired people, there is a need to evaluate the application according to UCD requirements [14]. The enhancement in the needs of visually impaired people's in the area of mobile application development is truly required. The position of UCD is supported by visually impaired people saying that 'I know what is better for me' [15]. The true potential of a mobile application for visually impaired people can be used more effectively with the help of UCD methods.

4   Conclusion and Future Work

This SLR directed to recognize and categorize different demanding components that describe the problems of visually impaired people when using mobile applications, the proposed solution of problems and the problems in UCD interface of mobile application manufacturing. Finding are described in two stages: in the preliminary stage, quantitative classification about the number of publication published in every year from 2010 till 2019. In the secondary stage, explore the answer to research topics that were addressed by using the screening criteria.

An empirical study will be needed to strengthen the findings of SLR, that explore the current implementation of UCD model of a mobile application for visually impaired people in order to verify the findings of the SLR. This empirical study aims to describe, explore, and evaluate the difficulties of visually impaired people in using mobile applications.

References

1. Whoint (2018). https://www.who.int/news-room/fact-sheets/detail/blindness-and-visual-impairment. Accessed 18 Oct 2018
2. Holden, B.A., et al.: Global prevalence of myopia and high myopia and temporal trends from 2000 through 2050. Ophthalmology **123**(5), 1036–1042 (2016)
3. Nielsen, J.: Usability Engineering. Morgan Kaufmann, San Francisco (1993)
4. Hackos, J., Redish, J.: User and Task Analysis for Interface Design. Wiley, New York (1998)
5. Abras, C., Maloney-Krichmar, D., Preece, J.: User-centered design. In: Bainbridge, W. (ed.) Encyclopedia of Human-Computer Interaction. Sage Publications, London (2004)
6. Mayhew, D.: The Usability Engineering Lifecycle. Morgan Kaufmann Publishers, San Francisco (1999)

7. Haklay, M., Nivala, A.-M.: User-centred design. In: Haklay, M. (ed.) Interacting with Geospatial Technologies, pp. 91–106. Wiley, Chichester (2011)
8. Kjeldskov, J.: Mobile computing. In: The Encyclopedia of Human-Computer Interaction, 2nd edn. Interaction Design Foundation (2014). https://www.interaction-design.org/literature/book/the-encyclopedia-of-human-computer-interaction-2nded/mobile-computing
9. Fling, B.: Mobile Design and Development. O'Reilly Media, Sebastopol (2009)
10. Brereton, P., Kitchenham, B.A., Budgen, D., Turner, M., Khalil, M.: Lessons from applying the systematic literature review process within the software engineering domain. J. Syst. Softw. **80**(4), 571–583 (2007)
11. Dyba, T., Dingsoyr, T.: Empirical studies of agile software development: a systematic review. Inf. Softw. Technol. **50**(9–10), 833–859 (2008)
12. McGookin, D., Brewster, S., Jiang, W.: Investigating touchscreen accessibility for people with visual impairments. In: Proceedings of the 5th Nordic Conference on Human-Computer Interaction, pp. 298–307 (2008)
13. Baptista, A., Martins, J., Goncalves, R., Branco, F., Rocha, T.: Web accessibility challenges and perspectives: a systematic literature review. In: 2016 11th Iberian Conference on Information Systems and Technologies (CISTI), pp. 1–6. IEEE (2016)
14. Coelho, T., Barbosa, G.A.R., Silva, I.S., dos S. Coutinho, F.R., da Silva, F.R.: An overview of researches on digital accessibility before and after the great challenges of SBC 2006–2016. In: Proceedings of the 16th Brazilian Symposium on Human Factors in Computing Systems, IHC 2017, pp. 1–10. ACM Press (2017)
15. Kim, W.J., Kim, I.K., Jeon, M.K., Kim, J.: UX design guideline for health mobile application to improve accessibility for the visually impaired. In: 2016 International Conference on Platform Technology and Service, PlatCon 2016, pp. 2–6 (2016)
16. Korbel, P., Skulimowski, P., Wasilewski, P., Wawrzyniak, P.: Mobile applications aiding the visually impaired in travelling with public transport. In: Proceedings of Federated Conference on Computer Science and Information Systems, pp. 825–828 (2013)
17. Siebra, C., Gouveia, T.B., Macedo, J., et al.: Toward accessibility with usability. In: Proceedings of the 11th International Conference on Ubiquitous Information Management and Communication - IMCOM 2017, pp. 1–8. ACM Press (2017)
18. Siebra, C., et al.: Usability requirements for mobile accessibility: a study on the vision impairment. In: Proceedings of the 14th ACM International Conference on Mobile and Ubiquitous Multimedia, pp. 384–389 (2015)

Learning and Games

Focus on the Human Dimension: Constructing Sustainable Experiential Learning Solutions for Small Unit Leaders

Lauren Hallal-Kirk(⊠), William A. Ross(⊠), and Roger N. Daigle(⊠)

Cognitive Performance Group, Orlando, FL 32828, USA
{Lauren, Bill, Roger}@cognitiveperformancegroup.com

Abstract. The US military is committed to an Information Age strategy that focuses on how to advance the state-of-the-art in training by leveraging adult learning theories, instructional technologies and talented trainers. Adult learning solutions and advanced instructional technologies are an investment that prepares Service members for the challenges of the Future Operating Environment (FOE) more effectively and more efficiently. Because the FOE is dynamically complex, simply training or preparing small unit leaders using an Industrial Age, crawl-walk-run approach to training just doesn't result in necessary critical thinking or more adaptive leaders. This pivot from knowledge and skill acquisition to the development of cognitive performance is critical for overmatching the near-peer threats and takes off the gloves when sparring with a thinking Opposing Force (OPFOR) at the live training sites and the virtual training battle space. This paper describes methods and processes for creating experiential learning cases, which result in more adaptive behaviors, more effective performance and more sustainable results among small unit leaders. Effective experiential learning means more than using a virtual simulation or conducting a live training simulation. To improve human performance, training solutions must incorporate rich content, create relevant contexts, and implement meaningful measures.

Keywords: Military · Training · Scenario development · Adult learning

1 Introduction

The United States military is committed to an Information Age strategy that focuses on how to advance the state-of-the-art in training by leveraging adult learning theories, instructional technologies and talented trainers. Adult learning solutions and advanced instructional technologies are an investment that prepares Service members for the challenges of the Future Operating Environment (FOE) more effectively and more efficiently. Because the FOE is dynamically complex, simply training or preparing small unit leaders using an Industrial Age, crawl-walk-run approach to training just doesn't result in necessary critical thinking or more adaptive leaders. This pivot from knowledge and skill acquisition to the development of cognitive performance is critical

© Springer Nature Switzerland AG 2019
C. Stephanidis and M. Antona (Eds.): HCII 2019, CCIS 1088, pp. 179–183, 2019.
https://doi.org/10.1007/978-3-030-30712-7_24

for overmatching the near-peer threats and takes off the gloves when sparring with a thinking OPFOR at the live environment training events and simulated battle space.

This paper describes methods and processes for creating experiential learning cases, which have been shown to result in more adaptive behaviors, more effective performance and more sustainable results among small unit leaders. Effective experiential learning requires more than a virtual simulation or a live environment training scenario. To improve human performance, training solutions should incorporate rich content, relevant contexts, and meaningful measures. The challenge of immersing learners in situations that prepare them to perform successfully across the range of military operations has been addressed in a several ways.

1.1 Squad OverMatch (SoVM)

The purpose of Squad Overmatch, 2013 to 2017, was to design, develop and assess a training curriculum that focused on accelerated learning of tactical skills by small unit leaders and their squads. The demonstrations and experiments were conducted over a 5-year period and involved by US Army and USMC training audiences. During that time, the nature of the research shifted from early assessments of training technologies, to pilot testing of training strategies, and to the incorporation of an integrated training architecture. Tactical scenarios were developed and validated, so that the research team could assess individual changes in four competencies: (1) Team Development (TD): the development of high performing teams; Advanced Situation Awareness (ASA): the development of analysis and pattern recognition skills; Resilience/Performance Enhancement (RPE): the development of individual self-regulating skills; and Tactical Combat Casualty Care (TC3): the development of skills to reduce the died of wounds rate on the battlefield. This research was conducted at Ft. Benning, using classroom instruction; coaching and skill development in the simulation laboratory; and practice and experiential learning at the McKenna MOUT site.

2 Experimental Learning Approach

Beyond the traditional crawl- walk- run- model of adult learning model, [1] we capitalized on the dynamic context of naturalistic training in military domains to accelerate learning Thus, our method for creating live environment and computer simulated scenarios serves the performance of immersing squads and squad leaders in cognitively authentic situations. The goal is to present each learner with problems and provide them time to interact with their environment, solve the problem, react to stimuli, reflect on their performance, and incorporate these learning experiences into their mental models.

Instead of publishing a series of events which generates a recognizable pattern, our model for scenario development creates conditions where participants engage in critical thinking and adaptive cognitive behaviors. The focus of our scenarios on cognitive performance promotes the development of qualities such as resourcefulness and resilience which feed into higher order cognitive responses. Instead of training a set of skills which may or may not be relevant during a combat situation, we create a training solution that promotes problem solving.

A key ingredient of the scenario is the operational stressor. These were derived from the Walter Reed Army Institute for Research (WRAIR, which compiled and catalogued those events that increased battlefield stress. Participants are exposed to the operational stressors in a variety of ways [2, 3] so that they are prepared to adapt tactically or manage the psychological effects associated with the event. In this manner, scenario events created the conditions and allowed the research to focus on the fundamental aspects of resilience and decision-making. Central to the training solution was a set of interrelated tactical stories, which were supported by tactical artifacts e.g., fragmentary orders, intelligence summaries, maps and overlays, and a Road to War.

3 Scenario Creation

Focusing on developing computer simulated and live environment training scenarios was deeply rooted in using the United States Army Training and Doctrine Command's (TRADOC), Future Operating Environment – Winning in a Complex World, TRADOC's Decisive Action Training Environment (DATE), and United States Army and Marine Corps doctrinal training publications.

Developing the scenarios for Squad Overmatch training in Fiscal Year (FY) 2018 was directed by the United States Army Pacific (USARPAC) Commander. His focus was ensuring forces that operated in the Indo-Pacific Theater were prepared for a near-peer threat operating in subterranean and Chemical, Biological, Radiological, and Nuclear (CBRN) warfare. In some instances, these conditions were combined into a single scenario. CBRN missions focused on recognizing, adapting and responding to threat employment of chemical weapon.

Scenarios were prepared for implementation in computer simulated and live training simulations. For live environment training we prepared nine scenarios, i.e., three Subterranean, three CBRN, and three Subterranean missions that included a CBRN threat and event. In addition, two subterranean and two CBRN scenarios were prepared for implementation in virtual reality simulations, but they were not used.

The process of developing the scenarios was a five-step process of (1) analyze the **tactical tasks** and cognitive skill requirements, (2) generate **mission threads** and conditions that align with the learning requirements, (3) depict the events as multi-dimensional **story arcs**, (4) create a training **use case** for the tactical tasks and objectives, and (5) prepare the **tactical artifacts** needed to define the context for training. Once each scenario has been constructed, transition statements are used to integrate all scenarios into a continuous mission thread. The scenario development process is illustrated below (Fig. 1).

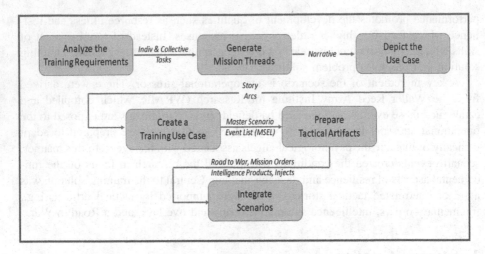

Fig. 1. SOvM scenario development process.

As an initial step, *Analyze the Training Requirement*, we performed a front-end analysis to determine what individual and collective tasks would be trained. This involved working with the leaders and researchers, since the training had to be relevant to the mission essential tasks. And because the training required the development of problem solving and decision-making skills, we also identified specific cognitive skills that were likely to be evident in the training. We linked this performance to the Army's Warrior Leader Tasks or the USMC Training and Readiness (T&R) Manuals. One challenge was determining the learning requirements for CBRN and Subterranean Operations, since the ATP 3-21.51 Subterranean Operations was in draft. In this manner, we determined that the training would be relevant, and we could proceed with the development process.

We proceeded to the second step, **Generate Mission Threads**. Once we had a validated list of individual and collective training requirements, we identified the tactical tasks that would support the training. Our team prepared narratives that described the situation from the perspective of the adversary, the friendly (training) unit, and the civilian population. This allowed us to frame the environment in a way that realistically represented the problem set. It also allowed us to identify how to paint the context in which the tactical tasks would be performed. The product of this step is a 7–8 page narrative.

Our third step, **Depict the Use Case**, was a multi-dimensional illustration of the narrative, which we called a 'story arc'. A use case is a systems engineering technique for describing the actions and interactions that occur to achieve a goal. Our use cases were depicted as story arcs. This steps results in story arcs that support three levels of understanding for the training developer and researcher: (1) the sequence of events from STARTEX to the ENDEX that portrays what will happen; (2) the tactical triggers which will drive the participants to a decision or actions that contributes to performance measurement, and (3) the degree of stress or tension in a situation that builds to a culminating point and requires the use of resilience skills.

The fourth step, **Create a Training Use Case**, transforms the mission threads, narratives and story arcs into a Master Scenario Events List (MSEL). The MSEL is a knowledge product that organizes information about the scenario to support implementation and can be accessed like a database. There are several entry arguments depending on your role in the training.

1. Location: The area in which a tactical task is expected to take place.
2. Tactical Task: The Squad performance under a specific condition.
3. Tactical Trigger: The decision point, where the performance of interest will be demonstrated and observed.
4. Measure of Performance: The desired performance of a tactical task based on a defined standard.

The fifth step, **Prepare Tactical Artifacts**, involves the preparation of a set of materials used to ground the participants in the tactical context. The overarching framework is provided through a detailed Road to War, an Operations Order (OPORD), Intelligence Annex, role player biographies, and mission cards to support the squad. These documents were produced to enable the Squad to plan and execute their mission across all scenarios.

Scenario specific artifacts were prepared and included a Fragmentary Order (FRAGO) and, the Intelligence Summary (INTSUM). The FRAGO was written using the Army five paragraph format, i.e., Situation, Mission, Execution, Sustainment, and Command and Signal. The INTSUM was modified to have five paragraphs of (1) General Enemy Situation, (2) Enemy Activities with sub-paragraphs of Ground, Air, Irregular, and CBRN, (3) Priority Intelligence requirements, (4) Weather and (5) Analysis and Discussion with the sub-paragraphs of Enemy Capabilities and Enemy Vulnerabilities.

4 Conclusion

In settings that require continuity and the capability to demonstrate long term cause and effect relationships, scenarios can be woven together and linked through transition statements. This requires integration of story lines and time jumps that allowed the training audience to remain engaged or immersed in the tactical operation. We employed several vehicles to enable continuity including updated narratives, intelligence summaries and updated graphics.

References

1. Kenner, C., Weinerman, J.: Adult learning theory: applications to non-traditional college students. J. Coll. Read. Learn. **41**(2), 87–96 (2011)
2. Moore, B.A., Mason, S.T., Crow, B.E.: Assessment and management of acute combat stress on the battlefield. In: Military Psychology. Clinical and Operational Applications, pp. 73–92 (2012)
3. Stetz, M.C., et al.: Stress, mental health, and cognition: a brief review of relationships and countermeasures. Aviat. Space Environ. Med. **78**(5), B252–B260 (2007)

Atlanta Code Warriors: A CS Engagement Pilot Initiative

Earl W. Huff Jr.[1], Jaye Nias[2], Robert Cummings[3], Naja A. Mack[4(✉)], and Kinnis Gosha[3]

[1] Clemson University, Clemson, SC 29634, USA
earlh@clemson.edu
[2] Spelman College, Atlanta, GA 30314, USA
jnias@spelman.edu
[3] Morehouse College, Atlanta, GA 30314, USA
{robert.cummings,kinnis.gosha}@morehouse.edu
[4] University of Florida, Gainesville, FL 32611, USA
najamac@ufl.edu

Abstract. The STEM workforce is vastly growing, however, underrepresented groups only account for under 12% of those in science and engineering occupations and for many in these jobs and industries, a 4 year degree is the most reasonable path. It is through this research that we seek to focus and address the challenges that inhibit minority populations in K-12 levels from the motivation and preparation that will align them with future computer science/IT college and career pathway (C-STEM) career fields. Prior research has shown that beliefs around self identity in STEM fields can positively impact behavior and achievement of students in computing disciplines, while increasing African American students belonging can decrease the student achievement gap. The initiatives presented in this paper seek to leverage the inherent value of minority student presence on the campus of a Historically Black institution as a means to normalize student perception of college access and future C-STEM identity.

Keywords: Mentor · Computer science · STEM · IT · Middle school

1 Introduction

According to the 2017 NSF report on women, minorities, and persons with disabilities in Science and Engineering, Asian and Caucasian populations still dominate the share of degrees in those disciplines. While the STEM workforce is growing, under-represented groups account for under 12% of those in science and engineering occupations [1]. Although there is an increase in the numbers of Bachelors and Masters degrees obtained by minority groups in the past four years, there is a need to address the challenges that prohibit students from entering and completing degrees in STEM based disciplines since that is vital in the

C. Stephanidis and M. Antona (Eds.): HCII 2019, CCIS 1088, pp. 184–191, 2019.
https://doi.org/10.1007/978-3-030-30712-7_25

effort to level the professional field. It is through this work that we seek to focus and address the challenges that inhibit minority populations in K-12 levels from experiences that increase motivation and preparation that will lead them toward a future in a C-STEM career field.

Prior research has shown that beliefs centered on self identity in STEM fields can positively impact behavior and achievement of students in computing disciplines [2]. Likewise, the research notes that an increase in African American students' feelings of belonging can decrease the student achievement gap [3]. The following initiatives presented seek to leverage the inherent value of minority student presence on the campus of a Historically Black institution as a means to normalize student perception of college access and future C-STEM identity.

As a subsequent goal, the presence of African-American mentors, both male and female, served to eliminate any social identity threat from the middle school students. For underrepresented minority students in STEM and higher educational programs, near-peer mentor relationships in educational environments have been shown to optimize student academic performance and social engagement [4,5]. Near-peer mentors, which are mentors closer in age and class, are instrumental in establishing trust and positive engagements needed for successful mentoring relationships. Near-peer teachers have a better understanding of the age and stage-appropriate context that enables them to better clarify problems for students [6]. In addition to the curricular support provided by the near-peer mentors, they also presented the middle school students with the opportunity to ask their near-peer, AUC mentors questions about career goals, college life, and why they, the student, should choose computing as their career path.

Similar outreach programs have been implemented to improve computer science identity for underrepresented groups. However, very few programs focus on the development of computer science identities in African American, middle school students through mentor-supplemented, computer programing outreach. Measuring sense-of-belonging, motivation, confidence, and satisfaction, multiple outreach programs have been conducted in computer science using pre-post intervention research methods for female groups [5,7,8]. Garcia has used the programming language Scratch to implement hands-on coding interventions to diverse populations of high school students. Supplemented with discussions and student-led demos, the interventions improve high school students' programming performance and provide knowledge about the social components of computer programming and their application [9,10].

2   Program Design

Although access to STEM-based curriculum channels are increasing for K-12 students, many middle school students, particularly those who come from low socioeconomic (income?) backgrounds, are often isolated from exposure to broader academic and scientific communities. The main benefit of this program is the exposure to academic (Clark Atlanta University), industrial (Google Atlanta Headquarters), and local school communities for programming efforts. For the pilot program, the focus was on two middle schools, Woodland Middle School (3/10 low income rating) [Woodland] and Charles Drew Charter School (7/10 low income rating) [11]. Atlanta Code Warriors (ACW) recruited 25 students in addition to a teacher or staff member from each middle school to serve as representatives and coordinators for their school. Moreover, the program recruited AUC faculty as well. All faculty and staff went through an orientation period to learn Google's Computer Science 1st platform (CS First), which provided the curriculum to teach students computer science. The students' transportation from the schools to the AUC and Google headquarters was provided as well as breakfast and lunch during the program sessions. Snacks were also provided during the school meetings. In order to maintain engagement in activities, raffles, where participants had the chance to win prizes in the form of gift cards. During the program, Coordination and communication among all parties was provided by Advantage Consulting, LLC., who also supplied a collection of student performance and satisfaction data for the program.

The Atlanta Code Warriors program was born out of the 2016 United Negro College Fund (UNCF) Coding Better Futures Initiative. The program was developed to provide systemic interventions and to increase the number of African-American students in the computer science/IT college and career pathways (C-STEM). Another major effort of this initiative is to increase cross-sector collaborations and access to African-American mentors for the students being served. For this pilot initiative, the industry, higher-education, and K-12 collaborators created the ATL-CS Node, which consisted of partnerships between UNCF, Google, Morehouse College, Spelman College, Clark-Atlanta University, Georgia Institute of Technology, Drew Charter School and the Atlanta Public School Systems.

During this 4-week program, students convened every Saturday. The program began with a kickoff event at Google Headquarters, and, in the following weeks, there were two working sessions. During the working sessions, students worked primarily on CS First, Scratch projects, and additional activities. Most of the activities were team-based, which helped students with developing problem solving skills within a group, and encouraged them to design and build complex projects. The Sound & Music theme was chosen from the CS First platform as a means to address the desire to provide C-STEM engagement in a culturally competent context. Within this theme, students were exposed to computational thinking, coding, problem-solving, and design thinking. Students learned concepts like variables, loops, conditionals, and other procedures used to build programs that incorporated musical themed-interactive multimedia projects.

During the weekday, school meetings were held at each middle school by the staff to continue program activities. The last event of the program was a showcase and celebration at Clark Atlanta University, where students demonstrated their projects and were recognized for their work. Concluding the program, there was a post-program evaluation to learn how it affected the middle school participants' views on computer science and their desire to actually pursue a career in computer science or a related field.

Table 1. Pre/post-assessment questions

Questions
(1) I am interested in computer science
(2) I do not feel comfortable using a computer to accomplish tasks
(3) I feel confident in my ability to solve difficult problems
(4) Learning new computer science skills is something I do not feel excited about
(5) Having the skills to do well in computer science classes is important to me
(6) I am likely to seek out new experiences and opportunities that I may not know a lot about
(7) I don't see people who look like me in technology/computer science careers
(8) I can see myself pursuing education and/or career opportunities in STEM/STEAM
(9) I am aware of the requirements and skills necessary to obtain a career in STEM/STEAM
(10) I do not like programming
(11) I am most excited about Google's online games for learning computer science skills
(12) I am most excited about the weekly interactive skill-building sessions and group projects
(13) I am most excited about after-school program sessions with teachers from my school

Note: The table displays the questions on the pre-assessment and post-assessment middle school students completed before and after the Atlanta Code Warriors intervention.

3   Method

Thirty-eight middle school students participated in this research study. The students were provided a pre-assessment to complete, which measured computer science identity in the variables of sense of belonging, computing interest, self-efficacy, and computing knowledge/skill. The pre-assessment also included three questions on the CS1st activities and ACW programming (see Table 1). Each question used a 5-point Likert scale measuring students' agreement. After the pre-assessment, students completed the intervention. At the end of the final day, the participants completed a post-assessment, which was identical to the pre-assessment. The results from the assessments were analyzed through a t-test to determine significant variance in program over time.

Table 2. Mentor student observation & program operations survey

Questions
(1) How effective was the Code Warriors' scheduling of events, food/drinks, and communication from organizers?
(2) How was your experience mentoring your group of MS students?
(3) What was effective in getting the MS students interested in CS education?
(4) What did not work in getting the MS students interested in CS education?
(5) What could the Atlanta Code Warriors do in the future to better engage students in CS education?
(6) Is there anything else you would like to share with us?

Note: The table displays the questions on the post-assessment undergraduate for mentors after the Atlanta Code Warriors intervention.

Sixteen upperclassmen computer science undergraduate mentors completed an open-ended survey during the post-assessment time to record their observations of middle school student behavior and program operations over the course of the program (see Table 2). Three mentors, one from each represented school, were interviewed more in-depth on experiences and rationales for the responses of the mentor survey and their recommendations to improve the program. Results from the open-ended surveys and interviews were analyzed through qualitative content analysis determining codes for student behavior, program operations, and recommendations.

Table 3. Computer science identity and program satisfaction

Assessment					
Variable		Pre (n = 32)	Post (n = 32)	t-value	prob
Computing identity & ACW satisfaction	M	53.25	52.00	2.04	.085
	SD	(7.88)	(10.82)		

Note: The table displays the results of a t-test analyzing any significant variance between the pre-assessment and post-assessment.

4 Results

There was a dropout of six participants (Pre-assessment n = 38, Post-assessment n = 32). Only participants who completed both the pre-assessment and post-assessment scores were used. A one-way repeated measure ANOVA was conducted to compare the effects of the CS1st program on middle school students' computer science satisfaction. The CS1st program did not significantly affect middle school students' satisfaction of computer science at the $p<.05$ level two-tailed from pre-assessment (M = 53.25, SD = 7.88) to post-assessment (M = 52, SD = 10.82) conditions [t(31) = 2.040, p = 0.085] (see Table 3). Holistically, these results suggest that middle school students were not satisfied with the Atlanta Code Warriors program. The students generally were interested in the field of computer science, but not in the practice of programming. The middle school students generally felt a sense of belonging in computer science and STEM, though this did not significantly change due to the program; and had relatively positive informed self-efficacy in career decision making and problem solving abilities. Middle school students were not more excited for Google's programs and sessions.

General observations of middle school student behaviors and program management were conducted from the thirteen mentors, in which student learning and performance was observed. Generally, students completed the motions of the program in its entirety. Some students caught on to concepts faster than others; many students who took a longer time to understand the instruction grew impatient. Students would lose focus and experienced fatigue at various moments during the program. Additionally, students were lethargic and had trouble getting back to work after heavy lunches. Students did not go above and beyond in learning the functionalities of Scratch. Finally, some students were more prepared (both technically and socially) for the main presentation than others.

The interaction between the students and the mentors was observed as well. Students could comprehend when mentors were not excited or not giving off positive attitude. Students became comfortable with mentor, enough to ask questions about the program activities, but not enough for non-technical questions. Students also took time to get comfortable with each other. Other program experiences in which student behavior was observed and recorded include students being most excited during the first day, some students may have been lost, observed through tardiness in attendance, and some students were notably interested in particular segments such as coding or music; a few were not interested in the program at all.

Although the program ran relatively smooth, there were a few challenges. Students were assigned in groups of three to a single computer, and the assigned computer lab did not have Flash to run the CS1st program, which proved to be ineffective. CS1st on Scratch was separated from supplemental videos, which took additional time going back and forth between the two. Many of the mentors were not familiar with App Inventor or CS1st. Food was delivered significantly late on two days of the program.

Mentors recommended changes to improve a future program, and they suggest that all mentors need to maintain authority with students to keep them focused. A one or two students per computer model should be more effective. Students should be provided a "cheat" sheet for the supplemental videos so that they would not have to go back and forth between ideas and Scratch. Mentors also suggested that future mentors be better trained in Scratch, should conduct icebreakers for students to learn and be comfortable with each other, and should always come in with a positive attitude. Other recommendations suggested by mentors include providing students with better maps, signs, and human guides so they can navigate campus better, include more breaks to reduce fatigue, show relevant, impressive Scratch demos to motivate students to figure out more functionalities of Scratch, rotate students through activities, and host practice presentations before the final presentation.

5   Discussion

The Atlanta Code Warriors program was not statistically effective in improving computer science identity and computing tool user experience for African-American middle school students. Student learning and performance observations inform computing outreach coordinators that fatigue, focus, and impatience are challenges and variables associated with disinterest and result-focus rather than process-focus [12–14]. Student exposure to Scratch and similar programs was not assessed, however it can be assumed that students lack of or limited exposure to Scratch made it so students were not aware of what they didn't know, thus there was very little, if any effort associated with trying to create works outside of the box. Additionally, students' comfort with the mentors was at the level of a participant and a facilitator, and not of a mentee and a mentor. More energy needs to be exerted from mentors, students, and program design to develop the role of the team facilitator to that of a mentor [4,5]. Students exhibited varying interest and affinity towards areas of the program such as music, however nothing in the program was designed to allow students to flourish in particular areas.

Overall, middle school students should be informed at orientation of program participation, to try and stay on track, to communicate with mentors and explain why and where they are losing interest, and what they think could make the program more interesting. Students should also be open to interact with one another and their mentors on both program activities and personal affairs. Undergraduate student mentors should ask about and respond to middle school students' questions about their personal interests, as well as introduce themselves incorporating their own personal interests. Mentors need also be knowledgeable about CS1st and all program segments, or one segment each and allow mentors to manage that station as students rotate. Additionally, mentors need to incorporate high energy to support students' diminishing excitement for the program. Program organizers should expose students to all elements, but also allow students to thrive in the elements in which they are interested. Logistically, having smaller lunches, more rest periods, or a two-snack period structure may improve the productivity of students. It is also always essential to check the technical requirements for any activity and outreach program's plan to execute prior to booking a space, to ensure organizers have capability to run the program.

There were few research limitations in this study. The scale adopted from Google's CS1st program by the Advantage Consulting, LLC. was used to measure computer science identity variables rather than using other established validated scales. Furthermore, though thirteen of the sixteen undergraduate mentors completed the open-ended questionnaire, only three mentors were interviewed to provide more extensive observations. Finally, the small sample size for middle school students is convenient, but not very generalizable.

6   Conclusion

Although the Atlanta Code Warriors program was unsuccessful at improving computer science identity in African-American middle school students, findings from the program can be used to improve future studies. Many of the challenges in the program are easily avoidable; concentrating on interest and process-focused learning is recommended and imperative for successfully improving computer science identity. Mentorship needs to be active in order to be effective and is suggested to be implemented within the structure of the program to yield positive results. Academic institutions, particularly historically black colleges and universities (HBCUs) partnering with national organizations such as the United

Negro College Fund are important in mobilizing outreach for underserved and underrepresented minorities, and for building effective research infrastructures at HBCUs and minority serving institutions.

References

1. National Science Foundation, National Center for Science and Engineering Statistics: Women, minorities, and persons with disabilities in science and engineering (2017)
2. Scott, M.J., Ghinea, G.: Measuring enrichment: the assembly and validation of an instrument to assess student self-beliefs in CS1. In: Proceedings of the Tenth Annual Conference on International Computing Education Research, pp. 123–130. ACM (2014)
3. Walton, G.M., Cohen, G.L.: A question of belonging: race, social fit, and achievement. J. Pers. Soc. Psychol. **92**(1), 82 (2007)
4. Zaniewski, A.M., Reinholz, D.: Increasing stem success: a near-peer mentoring program in the physical sciences. Int. J. STEM Educ. **3**(1), 14 (2016)
5. Ericson, B.J., Parker, M.C., Engelman, S.: Sisters rise up 4 CS: helping female students pass the advanced placement computer science a exam. In: Proceedings of the 47th ACM Technical Symposium on Computing Science Education, pp. 309–314. ACM (2016)
6. Bulte, C., Betts, A., Garner, K., Durning, S.: Student teaching: views of student near-peer teachers and learners. Med. Teach. **29**(6), 583–590 (2007)
7. Ericson, B., Engelman, S., McKlin, T., Taylor, J.: Project rise up 4 CS: increasing the number of black students who pass advanced placement CS A. In: Proceedings of the 45th ACM Technical Symposium on Computer Science Education, pp. 439–444. ACM (2014)
8. Ericson, B., McKlin, T.: Effective and sustainable computing summer camps. In: Proceedings of the 43rd ACM Technical Symposium on Computer Science Education, pp. 289–294. ACM (2012)
9. Garcia, D.D., Harvey, B., Segars, L.: CS principles pilot at University of California, Berkeley. ACM Inroads **3**(2), 58–60 (2012)
10. Garcia, D.D., Ding, W., Cohen, J., Ericson, B., Gray, J., Reed, D.: One-day activities for K-12 face-to-face outreach. In: Proceedings of the 46th ACM Technical Symposium on Computer Science Education, pp. 520–521. ACM (2015)
11. Explore Charles Drew Charter School Ja/Sa in Atlanta, GA, October 2018
12. Varma, R.: Making computer science minority-friendly. Commun. ACM **49**(2), 129–134 (2006)
13. Dweck, C.: Carol Dweck revisits the growth mindset. Educ. Week **35**(5), 20–24 (2015)
14. Ibe, N.A., Howsmon, R., Penney, L., Granor, N., DeLyser, L.A., Wang, K.: Reflections of a diversity, equity, and inclusion working group based on data from a national CS education program. In: Proceedings of the 49th ACM Technical Symposium on Computer Science Education, pp. 711–716. ACM (2018)

Using Multi-touch Multi-user Interactive Walls for Collaborative Active Learning

Ghislain Maurice N. Isabwe[1(✉)], Renée Schulz[2], Frank Reichert[1], and Morgan Konnestad[1]

[1] University of Agder, Jon Lilletuns vei 9, 4879 Grimstad, Norway
{maurice.isabwe,frank.reichert,
morgan.konnestad}@uia.no
[2] Osaka University, 1-5 Yamadaoka, Suita, Osaka 565-0871, Japan
renee.schulz@ist.osaka-u.ac.jp

Abstract. Active learning has been advocated for enhancing students' higher order cognition in social constructivist learning settings. However, with the increasing use of student-owned computing devices in face-to-face classrooms, there are risks of limited student-student interactions. Students are likely to be distracted by non-academic activities, hence becoming inactive with regards to the learning tasks. This article presents a technology enhanced learning approach, in which students perform group learning tasks using shared digital workspace while in a physical classroom. The workspace comprises of a 9-m wide screen wall with multi-touch, multi-user interfaces supporting multimodal interactions with and among learners through tactile, visual and auditory perceptions. While using the interactive wall to support group learning activities, the learners also perform various motoric actions, including gestural communications about the learning content as well as full body motion. An investigation into the role of interactive learning surfaces for supporting in-class collaborative learning and the user experience was conducted at University of Agder. The findings indicate that, through the use of the shared workspaces, students were more actively involved in collaborative learning. The practice of using an interactive wall contributed to increased interactions among students, critical thinking abilities and creativity. The study participants expressed satisfaction with regards to the usefulness of the interactive wall as a technology solution. It is suggested that designing relevant learning tasks for optimum technology use could potentially increase student engagement and the quality of user experience in collaborative learning.

Keywords: Interactive wall · Multi-user interaction · Active learning

1 Collaborative Active Learning in a Digital Age

Active learning has been advocated to increase the achievement of intended learning outcomes in general and develop higher order cognitive skills in particular. Christie and de Graaf (2017) argued that, philosophically, active learning would be considered as a tautology given that the learning does not happen unless the learner is actively engaged in meaningful activities. There are several approaches to active learning in higher

C. Stephanidis and M. Antona (Eds.): HCII 2019, CCIS 1088, pp. 192–199, 2019.
https://doi.org/10.1007/978-3-030-30712-7_26

education, whereby learners get engaged in learning activities that require reification of the learning. Some of the popular approaches consist of group learning activities, with clear indications of roles and responsibilities of each individual learner in a learning activity. Group activities can include tasks such as finding relevant learning materials, trying out different techniques and using appropriate tools to solve a real-world problem. Fundamentally, active learning stems from the constructivist learning theory which suggests that learners can make sense of the existing knowledge as well as create new meanings of their own. Learners carry out activities which require them to interact with the learning materials and explore diverse possibilities while devising ways of understanding phenomena or tackling challenging enough yet solvable tasks. Active learning through group works and problem-based learning has been successfully implemented in traditional brick and mortar learning environments, where students had limited or no access to personal, Internet connected devices. However, during the last 10 years, many institutions of higher learning are rapidly adopting the "bring-your-own-device (BYOD)" approach to technology enhanced teaching and learning. Despite the claimed benefits of BYOD (Song and Kong 2017), it can be challenging to keep the attention of all students and get them fully engaged with the learning activities while interacting on individual devices. It is quite common to observe students getting distracted by applications which are not necessarily educational, hence reducing their engagement in learning. On one hand, it can be argued that students may not have sufficient intrinsic motivation to prioritize the learning activities while using their own devices; on the other hand, it is challenging to maintain collaboration within the group without a common, shared user interface.

2 Multitouch Interactive Surfaces in Education

The last two decades have seen an increased use of interactive surfaces, commonly referred to as "Smart whiteboards" or "Interactive whiteboards". The key interest of using such surfaces in education is to increase in-class student collaboration, learner-to-content interaction through direct manipulation of digital learning materials. The interactive surfaces also help teachers to better present the content, with support for multimedia content. However, room size interactive learning surfaces are not yet very common, even though they may present additional learning opportunities and improved in-class learning experience. Stoodley et al. (2017) observed that learners interacting with a large screen were actively engaged as they learned through exploration. Collaborative learning took place as learners directly communicate with each other, engaging in activities to advance the learning. The interactive wall supports active learning through multiple functionalities. Depending on the size of the interactive surface, multiple resources can be shown and interacted with at the same time. Those resources can have different modalities, as well as interaction possibilities. Although large sizes may present educational benefits, it is important to take into consideration certain usability aspects (Nutsi and Koch 2015): keeping different interaction zones in mind, digital workspace and physical personal space, accessibility and readability, audio sources and noise levels. This work attempts to answer the following research questions:

- Which teaching and learning activities can be supported through the use of interactive learning surfaces?
- What are the affordances of large interactive surfaces to mediate learning for both on-site and off-site students?

3 Methodology

3.1 Research Approach

This work is an action research carried out during Autumn semester of 2018. It is based on the "Interaction Design" course for master students in Multimedia and Educational Technology programme at University of Agder. Learning tasks included the design of an interactive system (high fidelity prototype). An online survey instrument was used to collect data from students who used an interactive wall and other interactive boards during the course. The survey comprised of closed-ended questions with net promoter scores (NPS), users' opinions on 6-points Likert scale and open-ended questions. 20 out of 30 students responded to the survey shared through the learning management system (LMS) and student e-mail. Respondents (10 men and 10 women, 18–54 years old) could remain anonymous, but 7 out of 20 respondents did not choose that option. Additionally, classroom observations and interviews were conducted with 3 teachers.

3.2 Study Setup: The Future Classroom

Future Classroom is an integration of physical and virtual learning spaces for enabling high quality learning experiences. This facility at UiA campus Grimstad, supports both on-campus and off-campus learners using a combination of Internet-connected large-sized multi-touch multi-user interactive learning surfaces and personal computing devices. The classroom offers many possibilities to increase meaningful interactions for effective collaborative learning and co-creation of knowledge. It is equipped with multimodal digital collaboration and communication tools as well as movable furniture for flexible classroom arrangements. With a 25 people sitting capacity, the classroom features among other things, a 9-m wide interactive wall, the "Nureva Wall[1]".

Figure 1 shows a teaching scenario where a teacher presents the learning materials using the interactive wall. The wall is equipped with three short-throw

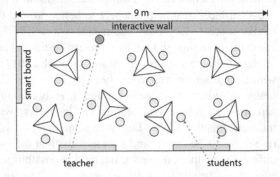

Fig. 1. Teaching/lecture scenario with the teacher as sole user of the interactive wall

---

[1] http://agder-ikt80.uia.no/futureclassroom/nureva/.

projectors connected to two computers supporting multipanel connectivity. This interconnectivity allows presentations from multiple sources of content, for instance slides presentation and web content in multiple browser windows. The supporting software ("Span Workspace"[2]) provides possibilities to move content from one area of the wall to another, as well as direct manipulation of the visual content. This helps to better present and discuss content with leaners.

Applying a social-constructivist approach, student-centred learning effectively achieved, whereby students are invited to learn through group tasks. The technology solution caters for visual collaboration, and given the possibilities to directly manipulate content, student groups use the interactive wall to mediate group discussions for collaborative learning. The interactive wall has 15 touchpoints, which can allow up to 15 people to use it simultaneously, for example writing with their fingers. Figures 2 and 3 illustrate students working with group tasks. Assuming that a group size of 3 would allow effective participation of each student, and the size of the interactive wall, up to 4 groups are working on the wall. The rest of the class use the three smartboards provided in the classroom.

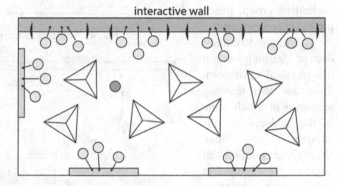

Fig. 2. Small group work: 3 students per group.

Fig. 3. Students visual collaboration.

---

[2] https://www.nureva.com/visual-collaboration/span-workspace.

Once students are done with working in small groups, each group presents their work to the entire classroom as shown in Fig. 4. This increases student-student interactions as the audience asks questions and give feedback to the presenting group, hence increasing engagement.

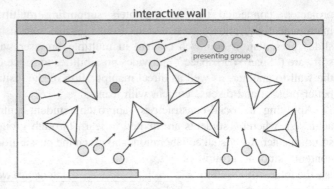

Fig. 4. Students group presentations

In addition to collaborative learning within the physical classroom, there are also learning scenarios in which some of the students are off-campus. Using Span Workspace solution, all students are engaged in collaborative learning as those in the classroom directly interact with the Span wall, whereas those off-campus interact through a web interface and note application as shown in Fig. 5.

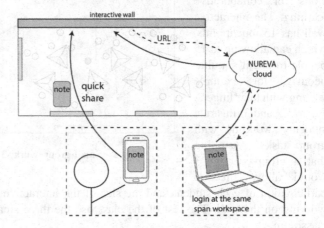

Fig. 5. On-campus and off-campus group collaboration

Further on, using the Span Workspace solution, students using the interactive wall can share their work with students on other interactive boards and vice-versa as indicated in Fig. 6. Furthermore, it is noted that the interactive boards support proprietary solutions to share workspaces for in-class and off-campus (cloud-based) visual collaboration.

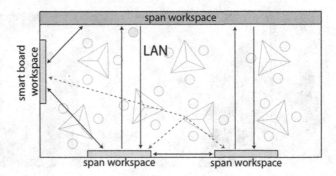

Fig. 6. In-class visual collaboration with multiple interactive surfaces

4 Findings and Discussions

This study explored how large size interactive surfaces could support teaching and learning activities, focusing on the usability of the technical tools and collaboration learning. On the question of familiarity with interactive whiteboards, 16 out of 20 respondents to the survey were detractors whereas 4 were passive (−80 NPS). It is suggested that users may need at least a short training for optimum use of the tools. Common challenges for teachers and students include getting the technology to work properly, finding the right modality and cases of losing work in progress as a result of experimenting new tools/features. Students expressed noticeable level of dissatisfaction with regards to the expected interface designs and system responsiveness.

The survey results suggest that it was challenging for the students to use the interactive wall as shown in Fig. 7.

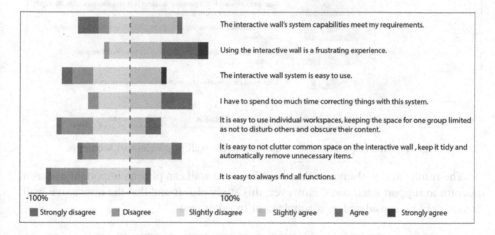

Fig. 7. Students' opinions on the interactive wall usability

Working with the interactive wall has proven to be rewarding yet challenging for teachers. They mostly use it as a standard projection screen. However, it was also said that using the interactive wall, it was possible for the course teacher to see group works of 3–4 groups at the same time. The teacher was able give quick feedback on the learning progress, seeing the performance of each group in relation to the assessment criteria but also in comparison with the achievements of other students' groups. It was also observed that students from different groups had opportunities to discuss about the task and give each other some hints. The interactive wall facilitated increased interactions within and among the student groups. The interactions were enriched by both verbal and written communications. However, in peer review process, students provided direct oral feedback supplemented by written feedback via other communication channels such as Facebook Messenger. Students also used GoogleDocs platform to co-create, and comment on the same document streamed from one of the students' computers to the group interactive surface. Everyone could make a contribution from their computers while the changes were visible to the entire group. This way of working stimulated critical thinking abilities and gave each group member the possibility to contribute. The teacher could keep an eye on the learners, providing guidance and engaging students through socratic questioning (Paul and Elder 2007) and provoking techniques.

While the interactive wall is mostly perceived as useful in educational scenarios as indicated in Fig. 8, the focus should not be on the technology but *"what lectures and assignments actually require such technology, and how it can be most efficiently utilized. In other words, not making a technology room just for the technology, but rather for the tasks it's meant to assist."*

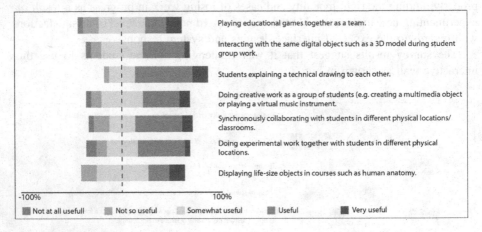

Fig. 8. Perceived usefulness of the interactive wall in educational scenarios

The results in Fig. 9 suggest that the interactive wall can play an important role as a medium to support interaction. However, this study also found that the interactive wall should only be considered as a supplement to other tools.

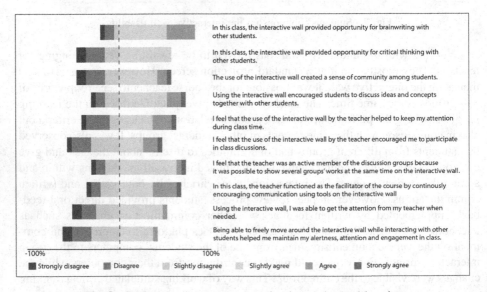

Fig. 9. Students' opinions on supporting interaction and learning

5   Summary and Future Directions

This article discussed an investigation into the use of large-size interactive surfaces for collaborative learning. The presented scenarios of use include the majority of students being in face-to-face teaching and learning on campus, while a few students could be off-campus. A wall-wide multi-touch multi-user interactive screen has been in use over one semester and proved to be useful for group learning. Students' interactions are increased through multimodal communication, with possibilities of direct manipulation of learning content as well as human-human verbal and gestural communication. Three additional multitouch interactive surfaces were also used in the same physical class-room, allowing the sharing of workspaces for multiple student groups and off-campus students through cloud-based solutions. The study suggests that the use of shared workspaces can encourage students to discuss ideas and concepts together with others, while the teacher serves as a course facilitator, hence supporting student-centred learning. The results show a potential to use the interactive wall in collaborative creative work, such as graphics design and user interfaces design. However, the technology solution still presents several usability problems, and more tailored learning tasks are necessary for optimal use.

Future research should focus on group learning tasks design, to use the natural user interfaces and multimodality support for increased interactions. Further on, it would be interesting to study the impact of using such advanced technology tools on the learning performance over more than one semester.

References

Christie, M., De Graaff, E.: The philosophical and pedagogical underpinnings of Active Learning in Engineering Education. Eur. J. Eng. Educ. **42**(1), 5–16 (2017)

Song, Y., Kong, S.C.: Affordances and constraints of BYOD (Bring Your Own Device) for learning in higher education: teachers' perspectives. In: Siu, C.K., Wong, T.L., Yang, M., Chow, C.F., Tse, K.H. (eds.) Emerging Practices in Scholarship of Learning and Teaching in a Digital Era, pp. 105–122. Springer, Singapore (2017). https://doi.org/10.1007/978-981-10-3344-5_23. ISBN 978-981-10-3342-1

Stoodley, I., Abdi, L.S., Bruce, C., Hughes, H.: Learning experiences in a giant interactive environment: insights from The Cube. J. Furth. High. Educ. **42**(3), 402–414 (2017). https://doi.org/10.1080/0309877X.2017.1281888

Nutsi, A., Koch, M.: Multi-user usability guidelines for interactive wall display applications. In: Proceedings of the 4th International Symposium/Pervasive Displays (PerDis 2015), pp. 233–234. ACM, New York (2015)

Paul, R., Elder, L.: Critical thinking: the art of Socratic questioning. J. Dev. Educ. **31**(1), 36 (2007)

Shaping the Intelligent Classroom
of the Future

Maria Korozi, Eleni Stefanidi, Georgia Samaritaki,
Antonis Prinianakis, Antonis Katzourakis, Asterios Leonidis$^{(\boxtimes)}$,
and Margherita Antona

Institute of Computer Science (ICS), Foundation for Research
and Technology – Hellas (FORTH), Heraklion, Crete, Greece
{korozi,leonidis,antona}@ics.forth.gr

Abstract. This paper explores the general concept of the classroom of the future from a technological perspective, and proposes a set of indicative key facilities that such an environment should incorporate. Over the years, there has been an abundance of related research work aiming to build a "smarter" classroom, initially incorporating distance learning, educational games, and intelligent tutoring systems. More recently, many approaches have revolved around the advancements in the domains of Ambient Intelligence and Internet of Things, resulting in the enhancement of the traditional classroom equipment and furniture with processing power and interaction capabilities (e.g. intelligent desk, smart whiteboard) and the integration of emerging solutions in teaching and learning methods (e.g. AR, VR). The proposed intelligent classroom though is a holistic approach towards a student-centric educational ecosystem, which will incorporate state-of-the-art technologies to support (among others) alternative pedagogies, learning through immersive hands-on experiences and collaboration via flexible class layouts. To that end, this paper reports the various ambient facilities of the classroom and the accompanying software, while a prototype of this environment is currently under development in the AmI Facility of FORTH-ICS.

Keywords: Intelligent Classroom · Smart Classroom · Ambient Intelligence

1 Introduction

Over the past few years, many researchers have investigated the effect of information and communication technologies (ICTs) on the domain of education. Indicatively, when used appropriately, different ICTs are claimed to help students engage in the classroom, increase their involvement in learning, enhance their interest and alleviate boredom [1]. Additionally, it is well established that technology encourages communication, interaction and collaboration amongst students [2], while it allows access to unlimited information, enables teachers to offer a wide and flexible curriculum [19], and permits students to easily share resources. These features help to make learning and teaching an engaging, active process connected to real life [3].

© Springer Nature Switzerland AG 2019
C. Stephanidis and M. Antona (Eds.): HCII 2019, CCIS 1088, pp. 200–212, 2019.
https://doi.org/10.1007/978-3-030-30712-7_27

In the past, learning with the use of ICT was strongly related to concepts such as distance learning [4], educational games [5], intelligent tutoring systems and e-learning applications [6]. However, recent advances in the domain of Ambient Intelligence (AmI) and the Internet of Things (IoT) have led to the emergence of the "Smart Classroom" paradigm. Currently, there are several approaches that foster a variety of ambient facilities and utilize state of the art technologies (e.g., virtual reality, augmented reality) aiming to enhance the educational process. In more details, the hardware infrastructure of a "Smart Classroom" may include both commercial (e.g., touch sensitive interactive whiteboard) and custom-made artifacts (e.g., technologically augmented student desks [7]), which - in some cases - are embedded into traditional classroom equipment and furniture. Finally, the underlying software enhances and augments educational activities through the use of pervasive and mobile computing, sensor networks, artificial intelligence, robotics, multimedia computing and appropriate middleware [8].

2 Related Work

2.1 Immersive Educational Experiences

An immersive environment creates new situations that would be impossible to create solely in a traditional or in a digital environment. To this end, creating immersive experiences inside a classroom would be beneficial for its students, since it could enable interaction with the real world in ways that were not possible before.

There are several research efforts as well as commercial products that focus on creating immersive educational experiences. On the one hand, immersion is achieved either by creating CAVE-like stereoscopic projected environments or with the use of interactive wall displays that surround the users. Hence, the walls in the future classroom, will be a mediator of the interaction between students and educational contents and material, rather than having the traditional "separation role" [9]. On the other hand, state of the art technologies, such as Virtual Reality (VR), Augmented Reality (AR) and X Reality (XR) are employed to create highly compelling and memorable experiences.

Indicatively, the work in [10] reports that the simulation of a rainforest - distributed across several large displays - inside a classroom, engaged students and promoted learning. Similarly, AquaCAVE [11] aims to enhance the swimming experience by immersing students into computer generated environments, such as coral reefs, underwater caves, etc. Furthermore, the Advanced Classroom system uses lights, sounds and video to transform any gym into an engaging, immersive video game [12].

A representative example of using AR in the classroom is SESIL [13], that offers unobtrusive, context - aware student assistance by performing recognition of book pages and of specific elements of interest within a page, and by perceiving interaction with actual books and pens/pencils, without requiring any special interaction device. Additionally, the work in [14] tries to overcome barriers in distance learning by proposing a 3D user avatar in an augmented classroom, so that the teacher can interact with the remote students just like interacting with the local students. Finally, in [15] the author suggests that VR can provide unparalleled educative experiences to students e.g. in biology and astronomy. For instance, The Body VR [16] is an educational virtual reality experience that takes the user inside the human body to travel through the bloodstream and discover how blood cells work to spread oxygen throughout the body.

2.2   Technologically-Enhanced Furniture

An agile and highly flexible classroom layout allows its users (i.e. teachers, students) to modify the arrangement according to their needs, so as to form groups, collaborate, share and create new knowledge [17], and can accommodate different learning goals. For that to be achieved, the furniture and any technologically-enhanced artifacts should be able to easily adapt to support learning activities of varying degrees of collaboration (i.e. individual tasks, small-group activities, class-wide activities), while their appearance and affordances should minimize the effort needed by the students to access their enhanced functionality.

A number of research attempts concern intelligent desks that aspire to enhance the learner's experience in the classroom. In particular, in [18] a system is proposed which is embedded in a smart desk and identifies probable connections between learner behavior and task performance, with the aim to improve student performance and aid the learning process by unobtrusively observing and determining specific needs. Similarly, the work in [19] presents an Augmented School Desk that accommodates numerous educational applications in order to support learning activities.

Another topic that has attracted the researchers' attention over the years and has been extensively used in thousands of educational setups is the Interactive Whiteboard. It constitutes a giant sensitive whiteboard that is connected to a computer and a digital projector, which reflects the computer's image onto a big touch-enabled computer screen controlled by an electronic pen, a finger or other kinds of physical objects (e.g. sponge). Research has confirmed that using smart boards increases students' engagement and the interactions among the students, the teacher and the educational content [20], with specific examples showcasing their benefits. In particular, [21] and [22] have demonstrated that the use of an IWB had a positive result on students' motivation, interest, participation and even performance in certain cases.

Finally, with respect to the educator, [23] introduces an advanced teacher's workstation that relies on an intelligent multi-agent infrastructure to unobtrusively monitor the students' activities in order identify potential learning weaknesses and pitfalls that need to be addressed, either at an individual or at a classroom level.

2.3   Robots and Other Technologies

Robots have been actively used as an innovative educational tool or even as teaching assistants. A robot called Elias, which was used for language and math learning provides a typical example. Elias has been programmed to encourage students to dance and sing along with him, based on the fact that having fun is an important element of effective learning. Elias can speak and understand 23 different languages and so far all the experiments showed that students are reacting positively to it [24]. Kindergarten Social Assistive Robotics (KindSAR) robot is another example that illustrates how a novel technological artifact can offer kindergarten staff an innovative tool for achieving their educational aims through social interaction. In a relevant experiment, the robot served as a teaching assistant by telling prerecorded stories to small groups of children, while incorporating songs and motor activities in the process. The experiment's findings showed that children reacted positively to the robot and enjoyed interacting with it [25].

Lego Mindstorms is an easily programmable robot accompanied by a great variety of bricks, motors, sensors and other equipment, which permits students to build small-scale fully functional models of creatures, vehicles, machines and inventions [26]. In an investigation of the effectiveness of Lego Mindstorms as a tool for introducing to students' basic principles of programming through game-play activity, researchers found that the robots had a positive influence on the children's problem-solving skills, creativity, motivation and interest.

Apart from educational robotics, various technological solutions have been deployed in educational environments to enhance students' innovation. Specifically, several publications have shown that the use of 3D printing technology in schools promotes active learning, encourages student's creative and critical thinking and develops problem-solving skills [27–29]. To that end, various general-purpose solutions exist that are also suitable for education, such as Robo C2, Dremel Digilab 3D45 Idea Builder and XYZPrinting da Vinci Jr. Pro 1.0 [30]. These technologies have classroom-friendly features, like enclosed printing area, wide connectivity options and even incorporation of STEAM-based lessons directly from their manufacturers.

Wearables have started to penetrate the classroom as well. In [31], the authors propose the Experience Recorder and an iBand as two ubiquitous devices for an intelligent learning environments. The former is an embedded system that records the paths followed by a student in a classroom and the latter is a wearable device that collects and exchanges information about the students. Finally, given the amount of electronic artifacts in the classroom of the future, a charging solution to successfully power them is needed [32]; to that end, various solutions exist ranging from charging cabinets to charging carts [33, 34].

Fig. 1. Overview of (a) an Intelligent Classroom and (b) a special purpose room featuring interactive walls, ceiling, floor, windows and various X-Reality Gadgets

3   The Classroom of the Future

3.1   Ambient Facilities

Intelligent Walls, Windows, Ceiling and Floor. The classroom of the future will have the ability to create immersive experiences (see Fig. 1). Immersion will be achieved through a collaboration between different "devices", such as projectors (e.g. CAVE-like stereoscopic environments) or using the surrounding interactive displays (e.g. interactive walls and ceiling). Additionally, ambient lighting and projection on the ceiling (e.g. showing the sun's position, the sky or the stars) will further enhance the feeling of immersion; that way the students will be able to interact with the real world in ways that were not possible before. The role of the classroom walls will be dual; on the one hand they will act as interactive smart boards (see Fig. 5), where typical educational content (e.g., multimedia, notes, exercises) can be presented, and on the other hand they will be able to immerse the students into any environment relevant to the course's syllabus (e.g., a cave or a rainforest).

Apart from the walls, enhanced glass technology (see Fig. 2) will allow natural sunlight to be the primary source of light in the classroom - since it reduces headaches and improves learning rates - but will also control the amount of light entering the classroom based on the context of use (e.g. minimize light when watching an educational video). Such technology will be able to transform the windows into secondary displays presenting supplementary content (e.g. classroom's schedule, multimedia, announcements, notes) according to the context of use. Additionally, the windows will also have the ability to be a part of the immersion mechanism by either displaying the same environment as the surrounding wall, or by creating the illusion that the classroom is being transferred to another location.

Fig. 2. View of the classroom's intelligent windows and the intelligent garden

Finally, special purpose rooms (see Fig. 3) with two or three interactive walls, ceilings and floors will be available to the students not only for educational purposes, but also for creating playful, fun and also calming environments (e.g. a student playing frisbee with a dog inside a park). The interactive floor will contribute to the sense of immersion, but it will also offer the opportunity to dynamically create playgrounds anywhere in the room aiming to support collaboration and full-body interaction.

Fig. 3. A special purpose room will dynamically create playgrounds anywhere aiming to support collaboration and full-body interaction, and offer players memorable experiences

Intelligent Desk and Teacher's Workstation. The student desk (see Fig. 4b) will feature a modular design where customizable surfaces can be added or removed on demand in order to support the needs of different courses. Such desks will further enhance students' engagement and motivation, offering hands-on experience and providing personal study spaces with specialized equipment.
Indicative dedicated surfaces are:

- **Geography:** featuring a globe dome, a compass and multiple secondary display
- **Chemistry:** featuring smart flasks, test tubes, scales, a Bunsen burner and basic accessories
- **Physics:** featuring equipment to accommodate experiments and secondary displays
- **Geometry:** featuring a calculator and a set of smart mathematical instruments such as a ruler, protractor etc.

The surfaces will be designed in such a way that the cables, chargers, electronics and microprocessors will be hidden from the students. This will not only make the desks safe for use by young children, but it will also reduce distractions. In order to facilitate rearrangement of classroom desks - addressing the changing demands of different teaching scenarios (e.g. two adjacent desks can be connected to create a larger interactive workspace and promote teamwork) - desks will be designed for single use.

The teacher on the other hand will be able to monitor and manipulate every aspect of the intelligent classroom (e.g. ambient facilities, educational software, intelligent behavior, automations) from a comfortable workstation (see Fig. 4a) (e.g. an armchair with an embedded tablet). Additionally, the future intelligent classroom will be able to interoperate with commercial wearables (e.g. smartwatch) in order inform the teacher regarding important events that occur during a lesson (e.g., a watch vibrates to alert the teacher that the student's do not pay attention).

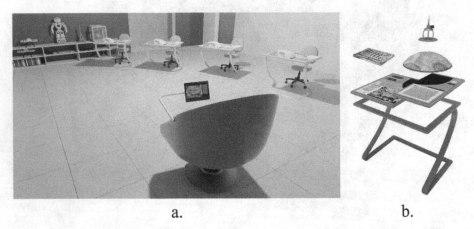

a.   b.

Fig. 4. (a) A comfortable workstation for the teacher with an embedded tablet, and (b) the student desk will feature a modular design with customisable surfaces

Intelligent Garden. Each student will be responsible for a smart pot (see Fig. 2) that will track the plant's progress (measure humidity, soil richness, growth information). Such stem tools aspire to strengthen the student's feeling of responsibility, motivation to learn, teach them action and accountability and other relevant 21st century skills by granting them exclusive rewards when their plants thrive.

Intelligent Bookcase. Physical books will still be present in the classroom of the future due to their indisputable educational value. However, selection and retrieval will become a much more sophisticated and entertaining processes via robotics, AI and AR technologies. Students for example, will be able to search for a specific book or a category via an interactive screen and then moving mechanical parts of the bookcase will fetch the desired books or place them on a designated shelf of the bookcase (see Fig. 5).

Educational Robots. Robots have been used and will continue to be a part of in-class activities (see Fig. 6). Robots can take on the role of the personal assistant for the students, monitoring their actions and supporting them according to their needs and weaknesses. Additionally, they can function as a teaching assistant or be themselves a subject of interest (e.g. robotics class).

Fig. 5. View of the Classroom Board and the Intelligent Bookcase

Prototyping Facilities. Students in the classroom of the future will be able to design and manufacture their own ideas as well as objects and tools needed for the lesson, aided by advanced 3d-printing technologies (see Fig. 6). Those technologies will enable students to give shape to their wildest ideas and direct their own learning, thus contributing to the development of their creativity and sense of accomplishment.

X-Reality Gadgets. Advanced X-Reality technologies (see Fig. 7) will be employed and be available to students in order to change the way students learn. In conjunction with the immersive environment of the classroom, those technologies will be used to create highly compelling experiences, through which students can improve and explore different skills and practices.

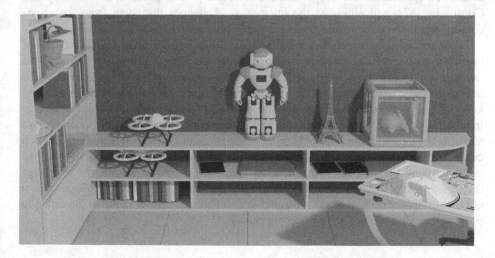

Fig. 6. The corner of Robotics and Prototyping Facilities

Fig. 7. The corner of X-Reality Gadgets

3.2 Intelligent Educational-Oriented Software

The future Intelligent Classroom should heavily depend on contextual information in order to make informed decisions (e.g., course, topic, syllabus). Since a typical classroom consists of different students with varying backgrounds, personalities, behaviors, needs and learning patterns [35], a solid profiling mechanism would be of utmost importance, since it would permit the delivery of personalized material and assistance to each individual.

Since a wide range of technologically augmented artifacts will equip the Intelligent Classroom of the future, a mechanism that transforms the classroom into a unified working environment rather than a group of isolated units is required [36]. In more details, an application host respecting the concepts of Composition, Consistency and Continuity [37], will eliminate the interaction challenges that stem from the cross-device migration of the available educational applications.

As passive listeners, people generally find it difficult to maintain a constant level of attention over extended periods of time, while pedagogical research reveals that attention lapses are inevitable during a lecture; according to [38], student attention will drift during a passive lecture. Ideally, the future Intelligent Classroom should be able to keep students engaged in the educational process. To this end, a mechanism that detects inattentive behaviors and selects appropriate interventions in order to help or support students throughout the educational process seems as an essential feature [39]. In such context, interventions are system-guided actions that subtly interrupt a course's flow so as to (i) draw the educator's attention in problematic situations, and (ii) re-engage distracted, unmotivated or tired students in the educational process (e.g., instantiate a quiz with appropriate content). A suitable mechanism is also required in order to present the selected interventions appropriately.

As far as the end-user applications are concerned, the students should have access to an inventory of educational applications (e.g., calculator, dictionary, multimedia viewer), as well as the digital representations of physical books and exercises. That way, they will be able to (i) get personalized assistance on exercises, (ii) retrieve additional resources about something interesting (e.g., an image displayed on the book), (iii) have access to assistive applications (e.g., calculator, dictionary, etc.), (iv) have access to multimedia, (v) maintain a personal area with access to board's history, homework's history, electronic materials, etc. Additionally, a suite of educational games should not be absent from the classroom of the future; that is because through games students become engaged with the learning process while developing a variety of important skills such as creative thinking, problem-solving and teamwork.

Special software should be available for the teachers so as to support complete classroom overview, automation of trivial tasks and suggestion of engaging activities [23, 40]. Additionally, a sophisticated mechanism that collects learning analytics and statistics of students interacting with the educational applications would enable teachers to easily monitor their performance and detect learning difficulties [41].

Finally, a Classroom Operating System (ClassroomOS) would be invaluable for the Intelligent Classroom of the future. Such a middleware will handle fundamental issues such as heterogeneous interoperability of intelligent artifacts and services, synchronous and asynchronous communication, resilience, security and context aware orchestration [42].

4 Future Work

The above systems are currently under development and deployment in the "Intelligent Classroom" simulation space at the AmI Facility (http://ami.ics.forth.gr/) of FORTH-ICS. The process towards its realization comprises the following steps: requirement analysis to identify state of the art and future trends, design and evaluation of inter-active prototypes, implementation, integration and evaluation with users of the solutions in the educational environment. Such process will be followed iteratively for each individual space, component and service. Specifically, the requirements elicitation will be conducted using multiple methods such as interviews, brainstorming, focus groups, storyboards and journey maps, which will be carried out along with various stake-holders, including industrial designers, engineers, interaction designers, UX experts, educators and students. Afterwards, a feasibility analysis of the identified solutions and prototyping will take place during the design phase. Subsequently, a formative expert-based evaluation of the prototypes will be carried out in context to assess their usability and usefulness. Thereafter, the revised solutions will be implemented and deployed in the classroom simulation space, where finally, a summative, user-based evaluation with educators and students will be conducted in vitro, in order to assess the effectiveness of each system, as well as the classroom environment as a whole.

Currently, prototypes of the smart desk have been developed and the infrastructure of the immersive environment (e.g. interactive wall displays, X-Reality gadgets) is in place, while the first interactive demos have already been deployed. The immediate next steps include the construction a dozen of intelligent desks that will host the table tops accommodating the classes of physics, geometry and robotics, the intelligent board and the prototype design of the teacher's workstation.

Acknowledgements. This work is supported by the FORTH-ICS internal RTD Program "Ambient Intelligence and Smart Environments". Moreover, the authors would like to thank Emmanouil Apostolakis, Antonis Chatziantoniou, Antonis Dimopoulos, Thodoris Evdaimon, Spiros Paparoulis, Nikolaos Stivaktakis, Emmanouil Stamatakis and Emmanouil Zidianakis for their valuable contribution.

References

1. Kurtz, G., Tsimerman, A., Steiner-Lavi, O.: The flipped-classroom approach: the answer to future learning? Eur. J. Open Distance E-Learn. **17**, 172–182 (2014)
2. Business tools: how technology can help with team collaboration. https://www.turbinehq.com/blog/tech-team-collaboration
3. Tinio, V.L.: UNDP Asia-Pacific Development Information Programme, E-ASEAN Task Force: ICT in Education. E-ASEAN Task Force; UNDP-APDIP, Manila; Kuala Lumpur (2003)
4. Bates, A.T.: Technology, E-learning and Distance Education. Routledge, New York (2005)
5. Cross, N., Roy, R.: Engineering Design Methods. Wiley, New York (1989)
6. Brooks, C., Greer, J., Melis, E., Ullrich, C.: Combining ITS and e-learning technologies: opportunities and challenges. In: Ikeda, M., Ashley, K.D., Chan, T.-W. (eds.) ITS 2006. LNCS, vol. 4053, pp. 278–287. Springer, Heidelberg (2006). https://doi.org/10.1007/11774303_28
7. Savvaki, C., Leonidis, A., Paparoulis, G., Antona, M., Stephanidis, C.: Designing a technology-augmented school desk for the future classroom. In: Stephanidis, C. (ed.) HCI 2013. CCIS, vol. 374, pp. 681–685. Springer, Heidelberg (2013). https://doi.org/10.1007/978-3-642-39476-8_137
8. Cook, D.J., Das, S.K.: How smart are our environments? An updated look at the state of the art. Pervasive Mob. Comput. **3**, 53–73 (2007)
9. The Classroom of the Future: A New Phygital Space | Acer for Education. https://eu-acerforeducation.acer.com/innovative-technologies/the-classroom-of-the-future-a-new-phygital-space/
10. Lui, M., Slotta, J.D.: Immersive simulations for smart classrooms: exploring evolutionary concepts in secondary science. Technol. Pedagogy Educ. **23**, 57–80 (2014)
11. Aquacave: Augmented swimming environment with immersive surround-screen virtual reality. In: Proceedings of the 29th Annual Symposium on User Interface Software and Technology, pp. 183–184. ACM (2016)
12. Lü Interactive Playground—Advanced Classroom Technologies. https://advclasstech.com/lu-interactive-playground
13. Margetis, G., Zabulis, X., Koutlemanis, P., Antona, M., Stephanidis, C.: Augmented interaction with physical books in an ambient intelligence learning environment. Multimed. Tools Appl. **67**, 473–495 (2013). https://doi.org/10.1007/s11042-011-0976-x
14. Shi, Y., Qin, W., Suo, Y., Xiao, X.: Smart classroom: bringing pervasive computing into distance learning. In: Nakashima, H., Aghajan, H., Augusto, J.C. (eds.) Handbook of Ambient Intelligence and Smart Environments, pp. 881–910. Springer, Boston (2010)
15. Virtual and Augmented Reality in the Classroom | Saturday Academy. https://www.saturdayacademy.org/about/news/virtual-augmented-reality

16. The Body VR: The Body VR: Journey Inside a Cell - HTC Vive Trailer (2016)
17. Mäkitalo-Siegl, K., Zottmann, J., Kaplan, F., Fischer, F.: Classroom of the Future: Orchestrating Collaborative Spaces. Sense Publishers, Rotterdam (2010)
18. Hernández-Calderón, J.-G., Benítez-Guerrero, E., Rojano, R.: Towards an intelligent desk matching behaviors and performance of learners. In: Proceedings of the XVIII International Conference on Human Computer Interaction, pp. 29:1–29:6. ACM, New York (2017)
19. Antona, M., et al.: Ambient intelligence in the classroom: an augmented school desk. In: Khalid, H., Hedge, A., Ahram, T. (eds.) Advances in Ergonomics Modeling and Usability Evaluation, pp. 609–619. CRC Press, Boca Raton (2010)
20. Al-Sharhan, S.: 14 smart classrooms in the context of technology-enhanced learning (TEL) environments. In: Transforming Education in the Gulf Region: Emerging Learning Technologies and Innovative Pedagogy for the 21st Century, p. 188 (2016)
21. Using an Interactive Whiteboard in Vocabulary Teaching – ScienceDirect. https://www.sciencedirect.com/science/article/pii/S187704281400295X
22. Interactive whiteboard and virtual learning environment combined: effects on mathematics education - Heemskerk - 2014 - Journal of Computer Assisted Learning - Wiley Online Library. https://onlinelibrary.wiley.com/doi/full/10.1111/jcal.12060
23. Mathioudakis, G., et al.: Real-time teacher assistance in technologically-augmented smart classrooms. Int. J. Adv. Life Sci. 6, 62–73 (2014)
24. How to use robots in education. https://www.lasserouhiainen.com/how-to-use-robots-in-education/
25. Fridin, M.: Storytelling by a kindergarten social assistive robot: a tool for constructive learning in preschool education. Comput. Educ. 70, 53–64 (2014). https://doi.org/10.1016/j.compedu.2013.07.043
26. Atmatzidou, S., Markelis, I., Demetriadis, S.: The use of LEGO Mindstorms in elementary and secondary education: game as a way of triggering learning, 9 p. (2008)
27. 4 Benefits of 3D Printing for Schools | The Educator K/12. https://www.theeducatoronline.com/k12/technology/e-learning/4-benefits-of-3d-printing-for-schools/245670
28. 5 Benefits of 3D Printing in Education. https://www.makerbot.com/stories/education/5-benefits-of-3d-printing/
29. Trust, T., Maloy, R.W.: Why 3D print? The 21st-century skills students develop while engaging in 3D printing projects. Comput. Sch. 34, 253–266 (2017). https://doi.org/10.1080/07380569.2017.1384684
30. 12 Best 3D Printers for Schools and Education in 2019. https://all3dp.com/1/best-3d-printer-for-school-education/
31. Winters, N., Walker, K., Roussos, G.: Facilitating learning in an intelligent environment. Presented at the IEE Seminar on Intelligent Building Environments (2005)
32. 7 EdTech Tools Every Smart Classroom Needs. http://www.aver.com/AVerExpert/7-edtech-tools-every-smart-classroom-needs
33. AVer Charging Carts and Sync Carts | AVer Global. http://presentation.aver.com/lines/tablet-storage-and-charging?_ga=2.176573093.1868001760.1562405843-1184187599.1561463407
34. Charging Solutions. http://rise-edu.com/charging-solutions/
35. Felder, R.M., Brent, R.: Understanding student differences. J. Eng. Educ. 94, 57–72 (2005)
36. Ntagianta, A., Korozi, M., Leonidis, A., Stephanidis, C.: A unified working environment for the attention-aware intelligent classroom. In: EDULEARN 2018 Proceedings, pp. 4377–4387 (2018)

37. Wäljas, M., Segerståhl, K., Väänänen-Vainio-Mattila, K., Oinas-Kukkonen, H.: Cross-platform service user experience: a field study and an initial framework. In: Proceedings of the 12th International Conference on Human Computer Interaction with Mobile Devices and Services, pp. 219–228. ACM (2010)

38. McKeachie, W., Svinicki, M.: McKeachie's Teaching Tips. Cengage Learning, Boston (2013)

39. Korozi, M., Leonidis, A., Antona, M., Stephanidis, C.: LECTOR: towards reengaging students in the educational process inside smart classrooms. In: Horain, P., Achard, C., Mallem, M. (eds.) IHCI 2017. LNCS, vol. 10688, pp. 137–149. Springer, Cham (2017). https://doi.org/10.1007/978-3-319-72038-8_11

40. Stefanidi, E., Korozi, M., Leonidis, A., Doulgeraki, M., Antona, M.: Educator-oriented tools for managing the attention-aware intelligent classroom (2018)

41. Rigaki, A., et al.: Learning analytics for AmI educational games targeting children with cognitive disabilities. https://www.researchgate.net/publication/332287424_LEARNING_ANALYTICS_FOR_AMI_EDUCATIONAL_GAMES_TARGETING_CHILDREN_WITH_COGNITIVE_DISABILITIES

42. Leonidis, A., Arampatzis, D., Louloudakis, N., Stephanidis, C.: The AmI-Solertis system: creating user experiences in smart environments. In: 2017 IEEE 13th International Conference on Wireless and Mobile Computing, Networking and Communications (WiMob), pp. 151–158. IEEE (2017)

Exploring the Needs and Preferences of Underrepresented Minority Students for an Intelligent Virtual Mentoring System

Naja A. Mack[1(✉)], Robert Cummings[2], Earl W. Huff Jr.[3], Kinnis Gosha[2], and Juan E. Gilbert[1]

[1] University of Florida, Gainesville, FL 32611, USA
{najamac,juan}@ufl.edu
[2] Morehouse College, Atlanta, GA 30314, USA
{robert.cummings,kinnis.gosha}@morehouse.edu
[3] Clemson University, Clemson, SC 29364, USA
earlh@clemson.edu

Abstract. Many reports highlight a significant lack of minority representation in graduate computing programs. However, effective mentorship has been heavily documented in research as pivotal for students aspiring to persist and excel in computing. Research suggests that virtual mentoring, a form of mentorship between a human user and a computer/software agent, viably supplements existing mentoring practices, which removes the inconveniences of meeting in-person and addresses the lack of willing and suitable mentors. The aim of this research is to develop an intelligent virtual mentoring system (VMS) and to help prepare minority students for matriculation through graduate computing school. In order to design and develop an effective intelligent virtual mentoring system, it is critical to improve the understanding of existing mentoring relationships and user preferences. This paper presents findings from focus groups with minority graduate students and explores their needs and preferences in a mentor.

Keywords: Intelligent virtual mentoring systems · User experience · Underrepresented minorities

1 Background

1.1 Underrepresented Minorities Pursuing Graduate Degrees in Computing

There is a significant lack of minority representation in graduate level computing programs and careers [1,2], and there are many attributing theoretical factors that continue to influence this deficit. The two most substantial factors are: (1) inadequate sense of belonging and (2) insufficient self-efficacy [3,4].

© Springer Nature Switzerland AG 2019
C. Stephanidis and M. Antona (Eds.): HCII 2019, CCIS 1088, pp. 213–221, 2019.
https://doi.org/10.1007/978-3-030-30712-7_28

The lack of minority representation in computing departments and the rarity of minority-focused research contributes to reduced feelings of belonging in the computing arena identified by prospective underrepresented minority computer scientists [5]. Additionally, both ethnic stereotype threats and the lack of effective resources geared toward preparing underrepresented minority students for computing careers and higher education contribute to a fragile state of academic and work performance [6,7].

1.2   Virtual Mentoring

Research suggests that effective mentorship is pivotal for student persistence and achievement, particularly for underrepresented minorities in STEM. Active mentorship helps mitigate the performance deficit of underrepresented minorities in computing by establishing an ongoing support system and guiding direction [8,9]. Mentor relationships are effective when the interaction between mentor and mentee consists of personal connections, matching personalities, and relatability, given the mentor's advisement and expertise is credible [10–12]. However, due to the lack of underrepresented minorities in the field, pairing students with more relatable mentors is challenging [13,14]. Students accessing virtual mentoring systems viably supplements existing mentoring practices [15]. Virtual mentoring is the use of human mentors, distance technology, and computer programming to facilitate a mentoring relationship [15]. Conversational agents (or chatbots), a particular virtual mentor system of interest, are computer programs that use natural language conversations to communicate and advise human users [16]. Due to its accessibility and adaptability, conversational agents as supplemental mentoring are quite useful because they utilize different platforms such as social media and short message service (SMS), which increases accessibility. Content is interchangeable with different subjects, allowing for the advisement of students with varying interests and backgrounds, given a robust expert or intelligent design [17].

There have been very few conversational agents that have been used for advising and teaching Black computing students. Conversational agents on social media, SMS, and web-based programs have been used to discuss race and ethnic differences in health-related topics [18–20] as well as to provide HBCU students with general information on undergraduate prep, completion, and graduate school topics [21–23]. However, there has not been an intelligent system that understands its underrepresented minority users' preferences and their background to mentor users with advisement and resource-sharing, making it to and succeeding in graduate school or a computing career. In order to build such a system, it is critical to improve the understanding of existing mentoring relationships of underrepresented minority computing students and user preferences.

2   Method

2.1   Participants

Twenty volunteers participated in the study during a conference, focusing on black and underrepresented minorities in computing. The focus groups were housed in two rooms, where focus group facilitators recruited conference attendees to volunteer to take part in the study. These volunteers were offered $40 gift cards to participate in the research. All participants were Ph.D. students or Ph.D. candidates in computing and were underrepresented minorities (Black and LatinX). Participant ages ranged from 22–54.

2.2   Procedure

The lead authors facilitated the two focus groups, and a semi-structured model was used for each group. Each focus group lasted one hour to discuss how African-American computing students view mentors and their recommendations for developing an effective virtual mentoring system. The participants were asked to describe their current mentors and how they interact and deliver advisement, as well as how they reacted to being mentored and if they were satisfied with their mentoring relationships. To follow, participants were asked about their previous experiences with virtual mentoring systems and how they would develop an intuitive, useful tool to reflect a supplementary mentor. The focus group was audio recorded and later transcribed for data analysis.

2.3   Analysis

A direct hybrid inductive-deductive thematic analysis was employed to examine the transcriptions from the focus groups [24]. A code manual was developed by synthesizing literature suggestions on significant factors for mentoring underrepresented minority students in computing, and the factors that contribute to developing effective virtual mentoring systems [11]. Transcribed responses were inductively summarized into initial themes prior to being categorized by the codes from the code manual. Common themes were synthesized and theme definitions were revised for further legitimization.

3   Results

3.1   Current Mentor Description

The participants reported that their current mentors were more knowledgeable than them. According to one participant, a mentor is "Someone who's a little bit more senior than you, who's been in the business, who knows how to code in Java or knows the system a little better than you and basically that provides this day-to-day interaction." In many instances, a mentor is assigned to the mentee at work without consideration of their social or personal background, "being a new coder on entry level, they always assign you a mentor." In agreement, all participants expressed how mentors are great for making connections that could advance their professional careers. Participants also described themselves having multiple mentors for different aspects of their lives, "I feel that a lot of times when I'm in different positions, I try to find someone who I can connect with".

3.2   Mentor Communication Delivery

The responses for mentor advice delivery ranged from very positive interactions to very negative interactions. Some participants recommended having more than one mentor so "depend[ing] on how you feel", you can cater the kind of advice you receive. For instance, one participant stated that sometimes they "need to tough love. So [they] go with somebody who can give [them] tough love. Or ... [they] feel ... very down and [they] need someone to encourage [them]." One participant described their experience as a respectful one, "never condescending." However, on the opposite end of the spectrum, another participant described their experience with advice delivery as negative, and stated that the advisor was "... very direct ... it can come across condescending, or it can come across as not necessarily encouraging." In a similar sense, many participants felt their advisors were straightforward when delivering advice.

3.3   Mentee Reaction

Overall, the mentee reaction to human advisement was positive. One mentee highlighted the importance of person-to-person interaction when they exclaimed, "...you are getting the advice, or the response from like a real person." It was reiterated that having multiple mentors is most helpful because "... whenever there's a problem, or situation, or concern, or want feedback on something, [they] get multiple perspectives every time." Claims have also been made that the advisement process has helped some mentees with becoming less sensitive to constructive criticism. One of the participants stated that they "... used to take stuff personal, like, when [they] first started [their] Ph.D. program ... ", which is when they met their mentor.

3.4   Mentee Satisfaction of Advisement

Some participants believed having a mentor that they could identify with is important to forming a strong relationship. One participant attended "an all black, male HBCU", so in his opinion, he was "fortunate enough to have mentors that looked exactly like me, black males"; on the contrary, some participants valued having a mentor that experienced situations similar to theirs, however they found it challenging to make a connection with one. Others felt that it was acceptable to not have a mentor that looked like them. Mentoring relationships stem from a mentor wanting to help guide or advise someone: "Everyone wants a mentor that will pull them up through the ranks, but not every mentor will see something worth cultivating in every individual that approaches them, which makes whomever they choose to enter that relationship unique."

3.5   Experience with Virtual Mentor Systems

The participants expressed little to no experience with using a virtual mentoring system. One of the participants reported: "I have zero experience with it. But one of my Co-PI, he was showing me this site. Basically it's kind of like an outsourcing agent." As a whole, the participants expressed that virtual mentors cannot be used as a blanket for multiple subjects, or for in depth questions: "it's not like a full mentor, but it's just if you need help right now, type in your question or can you give me advice instantly? And it's something automated ...It's a good tool for certain instances. But I don't think it's a coverall."

3.6   Virtual Mentor System Recommendation

We received a large amount of feedback regarding the virtual mentor system. The most prominent recommendation was to develop a more personal relationship. For instance, one participant stated that trust was an important part of mentorship and that the system lacks "rapport" in addition to having those things that you build from, like "interactions." Another noteworthy recommendation was having a larger range of predetermined information. A participant stated that "... it's hard to have a dynamic conversation with a virtual mentor unless it's a real person", so in order for the system to be most efficient and to understand exactly what [users are] looking for, have "... as much predetermined information as possible for any wide range of topics, that may come up."

4   Discussion

Many participants were engaged in ongoing mentoring relationships; mentorships are suggested as beneficial and sometimes necessary for successful pursuit of computing careers [8,9]. Mentors have teachable skill sets and work experience that aided their advice credibility [11]. The mentors' age ranged; a few participants had a near-peer mentor who had recently obtained their Ph.D. Some participants did not have what they considered a mentor, but all agreed that a mentor whom you could connect with was essential for a healthy mentoring relationship [12]; thus the idea of mentors with welcoming and friendly personalities and approaches was highlighted. To accommodate, the mentor system will require a very clear description of its scope and responses with a conversational flow that is highly intuitive. Few participants had assigned mentors from work, research experiences, or academic programs, but all mentoring relationships formed from these experiences. Given this, it will be useful for the intelligent conversational agent to be introduced through a work, research, or academic experience. Advisement was delivered in a considerate, constructive, relatable, and straight-forward approach [12,14,15]. As a relatable system, serious planning needs to occur to ensure users feel the system is speaking to them as a human on an individual personality level, as well as with a sociocultural lens. In addition, further research must be done to understand what considerations are necessary to fine-tune the information needed to be obtained from users. One participant described how their mentor used humor: "being able to share a joke with them afterwards. Or during. Because that's how I receive information. I receive information, that's when I feel like we're having a conversation that matters. But it doesn't have to be so constricting that I have to feel like we can't talk like human beings." A humor feature would need to be further researched and developed to determine its benefits, appropriateness, and suggested dosage to make the feature effective.

Participants appreciated their mentors' advice, encouraging them to think critically and were even used to receiving information that they may not have expected, as it motivates and humbles them [10,15]. Mentees also enjoyed feeling their mentor cared and showed humility and honesty [10,15]. An intelligent mentoring system must not only be accurate, but also deliver the message in a way that makes the user feel like the creators want them to succeed and modestly may not always have the best advice for them. Participants discussed how their satisfaction in a mentoring relationship is also influenced on the overall availability of the mentor. As a primary rationale for the system [18], an intelligent virtual agent would need to be accessible on many platforms and devices at as much time and in as many locations as possible. It is expected that the system would be accessible anytime at any position that supports a user's service on the varying platforms and the devices that possess it. One participant discussed how they liked that their mentor visually and socially reflected them [7,9]. Having a system be reflective of the user is very important and can be approached in many different ways, such as using location based subjects, examples, terminology, and allowing users to choose a mentor avatar that they feel most comfortable with. Mentees did not take joy in their mentors having a disdainful tone and being unfair or unreasonable. Being careful in the word choice of responses based on the subject matter, flow, and timing of the conversation is essential to maintaining a supportive user experience.

Quite a few participants never used a virtual mentor, however there are those who have used supplemental video conferencing and screen sharing with a person, personal assistants like Siri, and automated chatbots. Their experiences with them varied. Participants claimed their interactions were a waste of time, describing their system as uncommitted and untrustworthy with its responses and ability to retrieve classified information. Others believed it was interesting and helpful, though not always necessary. Confidentiality must be explicitly stated, describing proof of privacy for some users to trust a developed mentoring system, and there were many recommendations for developing this system. Being highly secure and having individual sign-in access helps to maintain the sense of privacy and confidentiality as well. Having evidence-based responses and direct resources from the internet is essential to resource-sharing capability, and being weary of bias and stereotyping is critical for the relatability and demographic target of the tool. The system intends to be mapped with SMS and social media, which will be automatic, and establishing a website portal is very useful as well. Integrating through social media allows for more user information to be collected to better tailor intelligent responses. Voice activation and functionality helps to expand the reach of the tool as well as the usability. Having an image to accompany voice and messaging is essential to allow users to feel as if they are connected with a person rather than a computer. Other interesting and more reaching suggestions included having the conversational agent have the same personality as the mentee, integrating users' music playlists, and having random social interaction.

There were few limitations in this study, including that the sample only contained Ph.D. students and candidates. This is great for giving recommendations and sustained mentoring experiences with the profession of computing, however this is limited as it does not address undergraduate students, a likely user demographic. It also does not include underrepresented minorities working in industry. Furthermore, the sample was small, consisting of a total of 20 participants amongst the focus groups. Though the codebook was developed through validated literature suggestions, an existing validated codebook was not used.

5   Conclusion

This study explored the mentoring relationship of underrepresented minority computing students to provide a baseline for design considerations for an intelligent conversational agent to mentor those who would like to pursue a career in computing or enter and complete a graduate program. This study also gauged underrepresented minority computing students' experiences and recommendations for virtual mentoring systems. Findings will be used to develop an intelligent mentoring conversational agent for underrepresented minority computing undergraduate and graduate students. Findings are also useful for mentoring and computing outreach professionals interested in supporting underrepresented minority computing students.

References

1. U.S. Census Bureau Quickfacts: United States, July 2018
2. Dillon Jr., E., Gilbert, J., Jackson, F., Charleston, L.: The state of African Americans in computer science - the need to increase representation. Comput. Res. News **21**(8) (2015)
3. Hargrove, D.T.: This is how we did it: a study of black male resilience and attainment at a hispanic serving institution through the lenses of critical race theory (2014)
4. Smith, W.A., Allen, W.R., Danley, L.L.: "Assume the position... you fit the description" psychosocial experiences and racial battle fatigue among African American male college students. Am. Behav. Sci. **51**(4), 551–578 (2007)
5. Harper, S.R., Kuykendall, J.A.: Institutional efforts to improve black male student achievement: a standards-based approach. Change Mag. High. Learn. **44**(2), 23–29 (2012)
6. Bridges, E.: Racial identity development and psychological coping of African American males at a predominantly White University. Ann. Am. Psychother. Assoc. **13**(1), 14–28 (2010)

7. Khalifa, M.A., Gooden, M.A., Davis, J.E.: Culturally responsive school leadership: a synthesis of the literature. Rev. Educ. Res. **86**(4), 1272–1311 (2016)
8. Brown II, M.C., Davis, G.L., McClendon, S.A.: Mentoring graduate students of color: myths, models, and modes. Peabody J. Educ. **74**(2), 105–118 (1999)
9. Main, J.B., Schimpf, C.: The underrepresentation of women in computing fields: a synthesis of literature using a life course perspective. IEEE Trans. Educ. **60**(4), 296–304 (2017)
10. Newman, C.B.: Rethinking race in student-faculty interactions and mentoring relationships with undergraduate African American engineering and computer science majors. J. Women Minor. Sci. Eng. **21**(4), 323–346 (2015)
11. Berk, R.A., Berg, J., Mortimer, R., Walton-Moss, B., Yeo, T.P.: Measuring the effectiveness of faculty mentoring relationships. Acad. Med. **80**(1), 66–71 (2005)
12. Ericson, B.J., Parker, M.C., Engelman, S.: Sisters rise up 4 CS: helping female students pass the advanced placement computer science a exam. In: Proceedings of the 47th ACM Technical Symposium on Computing Science Education, pp. 309–314. ACM (2016)
13. Charleston, L., Gilbert, J., Escobar, B., Jackson, J.: Creating a pipeline for African American computing science faculty: an innovative faculty/research mentoring program model. J. Fac. Dev. **28**(1), 85–92 (2014)
14. Gilbert, J.E., Jackson, J.F., Dillon Jr., E.C., Charleston, L.J.: African Americans in the US computing sciences workforce. Commun. ACM **58**(7), 35–38 (2015)
15. O'Neil, D.K., Gomez, L.M.: Online mentors: experimenting in science class. Educ. Leadersh. **54**(3), 39–42 (1996)
16. Benotti, L., Martínez, M.C., Schapachnik, F.: Engaging high school students using chatbots. In: Proceedings of the 2014 Conference on Innovation and Technology in Computer Science Education, pp. 63–68. ACM (2014)
17. Kenny, P., Parsons, T.D., Gratch, J., Rizzo, A.A.: Evaluation of justina: a virtual patient with PTSD. In: Prendinger, H., Lester, J., Ishizuka, M. (eds.) IVA 2008. LNCS (LNAI), vol. 5208, pp. 394–408. Springer, Heidelberg (2008). https://doi.org/10.1007/978-3-540-85483-8_40
18. Carter, L., Corneille, M., Hall-Byers, N.M., Clark, T., Younge, S.N.: Exploring user acceptance of a text-message base health intervention among young African Americans. AIS Trans. Hum. Comput. Interact. **7**(3), 110–124 (2015)
19. James, D.C., Harville, C., Sears, C., Efunbumi, O., Bondoc, I.: Participation of African Americans in e-health and m-health studies: a systematic review. Telemed. e-Health **23**(5), 351–364 (2017)
20. Sheats, J.L., Petrin, C., Darensbourg, R.M., Wheeler, C.S.: A theoretically-grounded investigation of perceptions about healthy eating and mhealth support among African American men and women in New Orleans, Louisiana. Family Community Health **41**(1), S15–S24 (2018)
21. Hampton, L., Gosha, K.: Development of a twitter graduate school virtual mentor for HBCU computer science students. In: Proceedings of the ACMSE 2018 Conference, p. 42. ACM (2018)
22. Julian, L., Gosha, K., Huff Jr., E.W.: The development of a conversational agent mentor interface using short message service (SMS). In: Proceedings of the 2018 ACM SIGMIS Conference on Computers and People Research, pp. 123–126. ACM (2018)
23. Gosha, K., Gilbert, J.E., Middlebrook, K.: Virtual graduate school mentoring using embodied conversational agents (2015)

24. Fereday, J., Muir-Cochrane, E.: Demonstrating rigor using thematic analysis: a hybrid approach of inductive and deductive coding and theme development. Int. J. Qual. Methods 5(1), 80–92 (2006)

Leaving Hints: Using Player In-Game Hints to Measure and Improve Learning

Elizabeth S. Veinott[1]([⊠]) and Elizabeth Whitaker[2]

[1] Michigan Technological University, Houghton, MI, USA
eveinott@mtu.edu
[2] Georgia Tech Research Institute (GTRI), Atlanta, GA, USA
elizabeth.whitaker@gtri.gatech.edu

Abstract. Student reflection has been shown to be important for learning in educational domains. In this study, we embedded a student reflection task into a video game to diagnose how players were constructing new knowledge. The game took place in a space station in which odd things had been happening. In order to secure a position on the space station, players had to improve their decision making and solve the mystery. As part of the game narrative, players reflected on each learning opportunity or mini-game by providing hints for future players at the end of each round. A corpus of 674 hints from 41 players, playing a 60-min version of the game were coded independently by two coders. Coding covered four levels of understanding in the hints and ranged from a simple restatement of information to a deeper reflection that integrated ideas and created new knowledge. Analyzing hints provided an in-game learning measure that may complement other measures and a way to understand game play experience that did not interrupt game flow. This study provides some recommendations for the design of embedding user hints into video games.

Keywords: Self-explanation · Adaptive learning environment · Video games

1 Introduction

Video games have the potential to improve learning, but the multimedia complexity of games can make it difficult to capture that learning [4, 7, 14, 21]. There is a growing body of research demonstrating that certain game features, introduced into well-designed video games [11, 12, 19, 24] or multi-media simulations [6, 10, 20], improve learning. One method for managing a multi-media learning environment is to couple it with an intelligent tutoring system (ITS) that tailors the student learning experience based on a player's initial knowledge of a phenomenon, and in-task performance [8, 26, 27]. ITSs have been used mainly in math and physics domains, and few have been implemented in a video game [1, 8, 12]. Van Lehn describes a set of alternatives for improving learning that works in human tutoring, but has yet to be fully examined in the ITS literature [23]. One such example is introducing self-reflection or self-explanation into a learning environment.

© Springer Nature Switzerland AG 2019
C. Stephanidis and M. Antona (Eds.): HCII 2019, CCIS 1088, pp. 222–230, 2019.
https://doi.org/10.1007/978-3-030-30712-7_29

In this paper, we analyze a set of open-ended hints left by players for themselves and future players, and make some recommendations for using hints in a serious game. Our analysis contributes to the ITS and self-explanation research in two ways. First, based on our literature review, it is one of the few studies on self-explanation, generated by players, in a serious video game. Given the dynamic nature of games, if this approach is useful it could contribute to playtesting methodology and game design. Second, it examines self-explanation in a new context (i.e., inferential reasoning) [16].

1.1 Self-explanation

Self-explanation is an effective strategy for learning in multimedia environments [2, 5]. Generating one's own explanations of a phenomenon supports metacognitive learning [1, 2, 6, 12, 17, 18, 28]. A recent review showed that self-explanation implementations vary from generative, open-ended self-explanations to explanations that students choose from a menu [28]. In Mayer's review of the effectiveness of game features on learning, he reported that five of six experiments involving self-explanation, found a positive effect for learning (average Cohen's d = .83). For three of those experiments, more structured, menu-based self-explanations were involved. Participants who selected an explanation from a menu for an electric circuit game task outperformed those who did no self-explanation [12]. Leaving hints for future players is common in commercial video game forums and it fits nicely as a way to operationalize self-explanation within a game narrative. Player hints are easy to collect and may provide useful information for evaluating training design.

1.2 Current Research Questions

In our exploratory study, we examined the hints left by players in a game in order to understand the range and function of these self-explanations. The game objective was to improve players' decision making by training them to avoid or mitigate three cognitive biases [15, 22]. What is the nature of the open-ended, self-explanations (i.e., hints and can we use them for evaluating learning potential? For example, if a hint is simply a restatement of information, then we would not expect it to reflect a deeper understanding [17]. By coding and analyzing the hints provided, we explored the following research questions:

R1: Are the hints left for players understandable and useful? This question evaluates the feasibility of collecting hints in a game.
R2: To what extent does self-explanation vary by cognitive biases? To what extent do hints reflect in-game prescriptive mitigation strategies? This question evaluates the impact of the hints for learning.
R3: Does hint quality change over time? This question also addresses the feasibility of using hints in a game in terms of learning and fatigue.

To explore these questions, we analyzed a corpus of 674 hints left by players of a serious game.

2 Methods

Participants. Hints were collected as part of a larger program [25]. For that study, both gamers and non-gamers were recruited and none knew that they would be playing a video game. Forty-one participants (47% male) were randomly assigned to the ITS version of the game that incorporated self-explanation.

Serious Video Game. Players played an early version of the game, *Heuristica: The Return*. It is a 3D, immersive, serious game that uses the Unreal 3 game engine. The game had seven different, re-playable, learning opportunities or mini-games (Fig. 1) that provided about 60 min of game play. The game goal was to improve decision making and critical thinking by training players to avoid or mitigate three cognitive biases [13, 22]. The game narrative had players competing for a position as commander of a space station. Weird things had been happening on the station, and in order to secure the position, players had to improve their decision making and solve the mystery. Players made decisions and assessments of other players, non-player characters, and reports provided as part of the game narrative. In other words, players learned by doing (e.g., making decisions) in the game [1, 3]. In addition to game play feedback (e.g., sounds, scores), this version of the game included self-explanation and an ITS to manage game play by tracking players' mastery of the material and performance in the game. Our game was designed so that players learned by doing, then we introduced self-explanation based on the prior ITS literature [1, 3, 8, 23, 27, 28]. The video game was fully instrumented to provide experimental control [13].

Fig. 1. Screenshot of a game learning opportunity

Cognitive Biases. As mentioned, the objective of the serious video game, *Heuristica: The Return*, was to improve each player's knowledge and ability to avoid or mitigate the effects of the three cognitive biases [22]. These biases were:

- *Anchoring* is a tendency to rely too heavily, or "anchor," on one trait or piece of information when making decisions. The information is often numeric and can be relevant or irrelevant [22].
- *Representativeness* is a tendency to make judgments based on how *similar* an instance is to a class (e.g., a tall person is to a basketball player) [22].

- *Projection* is a tendency to focus on one's own beliefs, when estimating what others will think [9].

These cognitive biases were elicited when players were making estimates, predictions, and solving problems in the game.

Hint Corpus. The corpus of 674 hints left by the 41 players across seven different learning opportunities were analyzed.

Explanation Coding Scheme. Two independent coders, familiar with the game, analyzed each explanation and coded each for informational value. Any coding discrepancies, the coders discussed and resolved. Our coding scheme (Table 1), adapted from [16], captured four levels of explanation relevant for our task.

Table 1. Explanation level coding scheme

Level	Code with definition and examples
Level 0	**No information:** No hint or a hint with limited information
	Examples: "I'm not getting any better at this one." Can't remember, burned out."
Level 1	**Restatement:** Hint restates information, provides no evidence of understanding
	Examples: "Bias is common everywhere." "Objective info vs. guessing." "Projection is easy to do."
Level 2	**Understanding:** Hint demonstrates some understanding of the cognitive bias, but no recommendation for mitigation (e.g., warning without a strategy for improving)
	Examples: Pay attention to actual statistics, not stereotypes. *(Representativeness)*
	"Perspective of others not your [own] is the key." *(Projection)*
	"Don't be distracted by irrelevant numbers in the environment." *(Anchoring)*
Level 3	**Mitigation:** Hints demonstrate a deeper understanding of the cognitive bias and include a mitigation strategy
	Examples: "Avoid thinking that others will think as you do." *(Projection)*
	"Take a large sample before making a judgment." *(Representativeness)*
	"Avoid using numbers that are irrelevant to making a judgment." *(Anchoring)*

Intelligent Tutoring System. An ITS was integrated into the game and managed a Student Model of each learner. See [26, 27] for more details on this aspect of the project. Briefly, content mastery was recorded and dynamically updated for each learner as he or she played the game. The Student Model used scores from the learning opportunities to infer a player's strengths and weaknesses. Through the analysis of the game log and the use of inference techniques, the Student Model was updated after each learning opportunity to represent the current state of a player's ability or mastery of the material. If mastery was low for a concept, a player received additional mini-games. Our ITS included learner explanation by prompting players to leave hints.

Procedure. After each mini-game in *Heuristica: The Return*, players were invited to reflect on their learning in the form of leaving a hint for a future player. To maintain the game narrative, players were instructed to "Leave behind hints or strategies for the next cadet." Each hint was tied to a single cognitive bias, and a round in the game. These hints were coded for the level of detail and mitigation strategy provided.

3 Results

Each player left between 12–27 hints per game session (one per mini-game) across three different biases for a total of 674 hints. There were 229 hints related to anchoring, 298 related to representativeness, and 147 related to projection (Table 2). There were more hints for representativeness because there are more varieties of this cognitive bias than projection bias. Analyzing the time between hints, we determined that hints were recorded, on average, every 3 min (SD = .002).

R1: *Are the hints left for players understandable and actionable? To what extent do hints reflect in-game prescriptive mitigation strategies?*

Hint quality ranged from 0 to 4, with a mean score of 1.88 (*SD* = .64) across players (Fig. 2). This mean indicates that players are generating a range of explanations and that there is room to improve. A level 2 hint is understandable, but may not help a player mitigate a cognitive bias, while most level 3 hints would be understandable and provide guidance to a new player. A one-way ANOVA indicated a main effect of cognitive bias on explanation degree, $F(2,623) = 3.047$, $p = .048$. Further planned comparisons with a Tukey correction revealed the effect was driven by a statistically significant difference between anchoring and representativeness, $t(525) = 3.5$, $p = 0.001$.

Why might players' self-explanations for mitigating representativeness be better than those for anchoring? One possibility is that the anchoring mitigation strategies were less clear in the game. Reviewing and revising these strategies in the game might be a next step. Alternatively, this pattern may reflect something more fundamental about each cognitive bias. For example, anchoring may be a harder concept to master than representativeness. While this study cannot determine which interpretation is

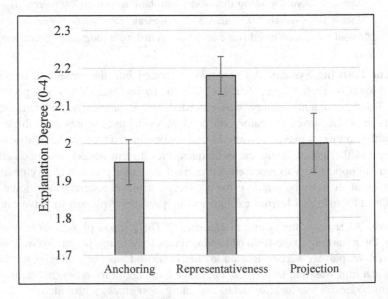

Fig. 2. Mean (SE) explanation scores by three cognitive biases

correct, this analysis provides useful information to support game design and playtesting in either case.

To further measure the quality of the hints, we analyzed the percentage of hints that included our pithy mitigation strategies (e.g., a streak is not a freak). Of the 674 hints, only 28% of the hints included the mitigation sayings we provided.

R2: *To what extent does self-explanation vary by cognitive biases? Or mini-games?*

We compared the distribution of the explanations across the three cognitive biases and found that degree of explanation was associated with the cognitive bias. A statistically significant chi-square indicated that the type of cognitive bias and the degree of explanation were associated, $\chi2(6) = 29.61$, $p = 0.001$. Players provided more mitigation strategies for representativeness than the other two cognitive biases with 49.1%

Table 2. Distribution of explanation level percentages within each cognitive bias

Cognitive bias	Number of hints	Level 0	Level 1	Level 2	Level 3
Anchoring	229	2.4	30.0	38.1	29.5
Representativeness	298	6.5	17.8	26.2	49.1
Projection	147	4.6	26.2	33.8	35.4

being level 3 explanations, compared to 29.5% for anchoring, and 35.4% for projection (Table 2). Because mini-games were different for each cognitive bias, these data also suggest differences across learning opportunities.

There are several things to note regarding the Table 2 distribution of mitigation strategies. First, about a third of the explanations are likely not useful to the player or future players because the hints provide no information. Second, another third of the explanations provide information that may help the player, but cannot be used easily by a future player. Finally, level 3 explanations represented fewer than 50% of the explanations for each cognitive bias. One explanation for this pattern of explanation level is that the type of mitigation strategies provided for representativeness were easier to remember. If the performance outcome data showed a similar pattern, then this conclusion may be appropriate and it did [25]. Not only did the distribution of explanation levels differ across biases, they also differed across learning opportunities. This suggests that some learning opportunities were teaching players to mitigate bias more than others. Regardless of whether one has outcome data, this analysis suggests there is room to improve learning. Recommendations to improve learning in the game would include revising some of the mitigation strategies and learning opportunities.

R3: *Does hint quality change over time?*

It is possible that hint quality could improve over time, suggesting deeper learning. Alternatively, if in-game explanations are too frequent they may decrease the quality of the explanations over time, suggesting that players were getting tired or annoyed. Average explanation quality scores for early, middle and late trials did not statistically differ, $F(2, 674) = 2.25$, $p = 0.11$. Across these groups of trials, explanation quality hovered at a level 2. Similarly, a chi-square of the distribution of explanation levels by trial groups was not statistically significant, $\chi 2(24) = 15.18$, $p = 0.915$, indicating that the two were not associated. Based on these analyses, it seems that asking players to reflect briefly on their learning did not negatively affect the overall explanation quality.

Effect of Hints on In-Game Mastery and Learning. While the learning and mastery analysis were not the focus in this paper, they are briefly reported. Post-game learning was measured using a pre-post questionnaire design that captured players' ability to mitigate the three cognitive biases [see 25 for more details] and compared to two baseline conditions: one where the Student Model was off (SM-OFF) and one with the Student Model was on, but there was no explanation (SM-ON). Mastery scores (ranging from 50–100) represented cumulated in-game performance across concepts and learning opportunities and were used by the Student Model (SM) to monitor in-game learning [26]. Mastery was analyzed using a MANOVA design comparing three conditions (SM OFF, SM-ON, SM-ON PLUS Explanation). Participants in the SM Plus condition, who chose what to learn next and reflected on their learning in the game by leaving hints, achieved statistically higher in-game mastery scores than those in the SM OFF or SM-ON conditions, $F (2, 3365) = 13.2$, $p < .001$. A 1×3 Student Model condition (SM-OFF, SM-ON, SM-ON PLUS Explanation) ANCOVA design, revealed no effect of condition on post-game learning, $F (2, 85) = 0.92$, $p > .05$. Hints improved in-game mastery, but did not achieve far transfer to a questionnaire outside the game.

4   Discussion

In this study, we analyzed in-game, self-explanations or hints and used them to evaluate game experience and learning. This corpus of hints came from an early version of the game, and showed that this method was both feasible and informative. People's hints did not deteriorate over time (due to fatigue), but it also showed there was room for improvement. We showed that people leave different types of hints ranging from no information to useful information that future players could use to improve their game play. Our results indicate that explanation quality differed by cognitive bias and learning opportunities, so could be used to evaluate the quality of a learning opportunity (e.g., are we teaching what we expect to be teaching?). Hints may be one way to manage the distractibility in a video game environment [11, 16]. This work contributes some new evidence to the literature on the feasibility and effectiveness of self-explanation in the context of intelligent tutoring systems [8, 28] and games [23, 27]. While the hints were informational and generating them improved player's in-game mastery, we do not know how it affected players who received those hints. Future research should examine whether hints left behind were remembered by later players and supported learning.

Our recommendations for designing hints into video games are preliminary and more research is needed. Hints need to be part of the game narrative and the instructions need to be simple. Our approach was one way to evaluate hints, but not the only way. This type of evaluation can identify differences in the concepts that were being trained, and identify individual learning opportunities that need work. Hints did not need to be provided in person, so this method could work for on-line playtesting or in-person playtesting. This lightweight approach of analyzing hints provides an in-game learning measure that does not interrupt game flow, helps understand game play experience, and complements other measures. While the focus of this paper was the use of hints in a serious video game, the approach is general and can apply in other training mediums.

Acknowledgement. This work is part of a larger team effort in which the Virtual Heroes Division of ARA developed the serious game, and Georgia Technology Research Institute developed the intelligent tutoring system embedded in the game. We would like to thank our sponsor. This research was supported by Intelligence Advanced Research Projects Activity (IARPA) via Air Force Research Laboratory Contract #FA8650-11-C-7177 to ARA, Inc. The U. S. Government is authorized to reproduce and distribute reprints for Governmental purposes notwithstanding any copyright annotation thereon. Disclaimer: The views and conclusions contained herein are those of the authors and should not be interpreted as necessarily representing the official policies or endorsements, either expressed or implied, of IARPA, AFRL, or the U.S. Government.

References

1. Aleven, V., Koedinger, K.: An effective metacognitive strategy: learning by doing and explaining with a computer-based cognitive tutor. Cogn. Sci. **26**(2), 147–179 (2002)
2. Atkinson, R.K., Renkl, A., Merrill, M.M.: Transitioning from studying examples to solving problems: effects of self-explanation prompts and fading worked-out steps. J. Educ. Psychol. **95**(4), 774 (2003)
3. Anzai, Y., Simon, H.A.: The theory of learning by doing. Psychol. Rev. **86**, 124–140 (1979)
4. Bell, B.S., Kozlowski, S.W.J.: Active learning: effects of core training design elements on self-regulatory processes, learning, and adaptability. J. Appl. Psychol. **93**, 296–316 (2008)
5. Chi, M.: Constructing self-explanations and scaffolded explanations in tutoring. Appl. Cogn. Psychol. **10**, 33–49 (1996)
6. Cooke, N., Shope, S.: Designing a synthetic task environment. In: Schiflett, S.G., Elliott, L. R., Salas, E., Coovert, M.D. (eds.) Scaled Worlds: Development, Validation, and Application, pp. 263–278. Ashgate, Surry (2004)
7. Gee, J.P.: What Video Games Have to Teach Us About Learning and Literacy. Palgrave Macmillan, New York (2003)
8. Graesser, A., Hu, X., Sottilare, R.: Intelligent tutoring systems. In: The International Handbook of the Learning Sciences, pp. 246–255. Routledge, New York (2018)
9. Holmes, D.: Dimensions of projection. Psychol. Bull. **69**, 248–268 (1968)
10. Kozlowski, S.W.J., DeShon, R.P.: A psychological fidelity approach to simulation-based training: theory, research, and principles. In: Schiflett, S.G., Elliott, L.R., Salas, E., Coovert, M.D. (eds.) Scaled Worlds: Development, Validation, and Application, pp. 263–278. Ashgate, Surry (2004)
11. Mayer, R.E., Griffity, E., Naftaly, I., Rothman, D.: Increased interestingness of extraneous details leads to decreased learning. J. Exp. Psychol. Appl. **14**, 329–339 (2008)
12. Mayer, R.E.: Computer Games for Learning: An Evidence-Based Approach. MIT Press, Cambridge (2014)

13. Mullinix, G., et al.: Heuristica: designing a serious game for improving decision making. Paper Presented at the IEEE Games Innovation Conference (IGIC), Vancouver, BC, pp. 250–255 (2013)

14. O'Neil, H.F., Wainess, R., Baker, E.L.: Classification of learning outcomes: evidence from the computer games literature. Curric. J. **16**, 455–474 (2005)

15. Payne, J.W., Bettman, J.R., Johnson, E.J.: Adaptive strategy selection in decision making. J. Exp. Psychol. Learn. Mem. Cogn. **14**(3), 534–545 (1988)

16. Renkl, A.: Learning from worked-out examples: a study on individual differences. Cogn. Sci. **21**, 1–29 (1997)

17. Renkl, A., Stark, R., Gruber, H., Mandl, H.: Learning from worked-out examples: the effects of example variability and elicited self-explanations. Contemp. Educ. Psychol. **23**, 90–108 (1998)

18. Roll, I., Aleven, V., Koedinger, K.R.: The invention lab: using a hybrid of model tracing and constraint-based modeling to offer intelligent support in inquiry environments. In: Aleven, V., Kay, J., Mostow, J. (eds.) ITS 2010. LNCS, vol. 6094, pp. 115–124. Springer, Heidelberg (2010). https://doi.org/10.1007/978-3-642-13388-6_16

19. Roose, K., Veinott, E.: Roller coaster park manager by day problem solver by night: effect of video game play on problem solving. In: Extended Abstracts Publication of the Annual Symposium on Computer-Human Interaction in Play, Amsterdam, Netherlands, pp. 277–282. ACM (2017)

20. Salas, E., Wildman, J.L., Piccolo, R.F.: Using simulation-based training to enhance management education. Acad. Manag. Learn. Educ. **9**, 559–573 (2009)

21. Steinkuelhler, C., Squire, K., Barab, S.: Games, Learning, and Society, pp. 271–442. Cambridge University Press, Cambridge (2012)

22. Tversky, A., Kahneman, D.: Judgment under uncertainty: heuristics and biases. Science **185**, 1124–1131 (1974)

23. VanLehn, K.: The relative effectiveness of human tutoring, intelligent tutoring systems, and other tutoring systems. Educ. Psychol. **46**, 197–221 (2011)

24. Veinott, E., et al.: The effect of camera perspective and session duration on training decision making in a serious video game. In: 2013 IEEE International Games Innovation Conference (IGIC), pp. 256–262. IEEE (2013)

25. Veinott, E, et al.: The effect of cognitive and visual fidelity on decision making: is more information better? In: 2014 IEEE International GEM (Formerly IEEE Games Innovation Conference (IGIC)), Toronto, ON, pp. 1–6 (2014)

26. Whitaker, E., et al.: The effectiveness of intelligent tutoring on training in a video game. In: IEEE International Games Innovation Conference (IGIC), Vancouver, BC, pp. 267–274 (2013)

27. Whitaker, E., Trewhitt, E., Veinott, E.S.: Intelligent tutoring design alternatives in a serious game. In: Sottilare, R., Schwarz, J. (Eds.) First International Conference for Adaptive Instructional Systems as Part of HCII 2019, pp. 151–165. Springer, Cham (2019)

28. Wylie, R., Chi, M.: The self-explanation principle in multimedia learning. In: The Cambridge Handbook of Multimedia Learning, Cambridge, UK, pp. 413–432 (2014)

HCI in Health and Rehabilitation

The Long-Term Effect of Health-Related Online Use on Healthcare Utilization and Expenditures Among Older Adults

Soyeon Guh[✉], Tae Hyon Whang, Betsy Keller, and Phil Fiero

Welltok Inc., Burlington, MA 01803, USA
soyeon.guh@welltok.com

Abstract. The study objective is to assess the long-term effect of registering for an online-based wellness program on healthcare utilization and expenditures among the elderly. The associational relationship was measured using a combined propensity score matching (PSM) and interrupted time series (ITS) method. We utilized expansive data—online activity data of the wellness program, administrative claims data, and consumer data—of 332,911 adults aged 65 and older with Medicare Advantage coverage from a health plan, who had one year of data from the pre-registration period (2016) and two years of data from the post-registration period (2017–2018). After using PSM to control for demographic and health characteristics, and insurance type between registered persons and persons without online access (reference group), we found lower costs of $86 per member per month (PMPM) among registered seniors in the second year of online registration, compared to seniors without online access ($p < 0.001$). We also observed fewer emergency room visits among the registered group ($p < 0.001$), but no significant difference in hospital admission rates.

Keywords: Online wellness program · Elderly · Healthcare utilization · Healthcare expenditure · Propensity score matching · Interrupted time series

1 Introduction

Over the past few decades, the internet has become an indispensable part of daily life. In America, 89% of households owned computers and 82% used internet in 2016. Older adults were not far behind: 75% of elderly households (65 years and older) had desktop, laptop, or smart phone and 68% had an internet subscription [1]. Among internet/online users who are US Medicare beneficiaries aged 65 years and older, 45% conducted health-related tasks: searching information on health conditions, ordering or refilling prescriptions, contacting medical providers, and handling health insurance matters. Also, 51% used internet to manage everyday life such as online bills, online banking, and online shopping; and 86% sent emails or texts in 2011, based on a nationally representative sample from the National Health and Aging Trends Study [2].

The objective of this study is to estimate the long-term effect of health-related internet use among elderly on their healthcare utilization and expenditures, using a rigorous method, a combined PSM and ITS as the strongest, quasi-experimental design to evaluate such effect over time.

© Springer Nature Switzerland AG 2019
C. Stephanidis and M. Antona (Eds.): HCII 2019, CCIS 1088, pp. 233–240, 2019.
https://doi.org/10.1007/978-3-030-30712-7_30

2 Methods

2.1 Program Description

A health plan offered its Medicare Advantage (MA) members access to wellbeing resources through CaféWell, an interactive web and mobile tool developed by Welltok. A centralized, digital platform was launched in 2016 for this study population, providing personalized resources that support physical, emotional, financial, and social health. To receive personalized health and wellbeing services, as well as rewards, eligible MA members were asked to register online.

2.2 Data Sources

Segmented regression analysis requires data to be collected regularly over time and organized at equally spaced intervals. Monthly or annual health care records of utilization and/or expenditures are commonly used sources of time series data. A sufficient number of time points before and after the intervention is needed to conduct ITS analysis. A general recommendation is for 12 data points before and 12 data points after the intervention. A minimum of 100 observations is also desirable at each time point to achieve an acceptable level of variability of the estimate [3].

We linked three different data sets at an individual level: administrative claims data, online registration data from the CaféWell program, and consumer data. We used 4 years of administrative claims and enrollment data of all adults enrolled in an MA plan, covering the period 1/1/2015 to 12/31/2018. One year from January to December 2016 was considered the pre-intervention period and the two years between January 2017 and December 2018 were considered the post-intervention period. We also integrated online registration records for the CaféWell program from January 2017 to December 2018. We determined who had no online access using Welltok's proprietary consumer database.

2.3 Definition of Internet Use

We defined two different measures of internet use: active health-related internet use and non-online access. The intervention group is defined as aged adults who actively use internet for health-related activities, specifically the CaféWell program. The control group is defined as aged adults who did not have online access using the consumer data.

2.4 Healthcare Utilization and Expenditures

To measure the effect of internet use, we used healthcare utilization and expenditures as outcome measures. Monthly emergency department (ED) visit rates and hospitalization rates, and healthcare expenditures, allowed amount, per member per month (PMPM) were calculated on a rolling 12-month basis. For example, PMPM of rolling year at the data point of January 2016 is calculated as the aggregated healthcare expenditures for the period 2/1/2015 to 1/31/2016, divided by 12 months.

2.5 Study Sample

Inclusion criteria for the study sample are listed:

1. Continuous enrollment for 48 months during pre- and post-intervention periods;
2. Age 65 years and older in 2016;
3. Annual healthcare expenditures, allowed amount, less than $56,000 (98 percentile) in 2016, to reduce the influence of outliers.

The intervention group then required continuous registration in the CaféWell program during the post-intervention period for assessment of the program effect, while the control group who met the inclusion criteria but did not have online access, was identified (see Fig. 1).

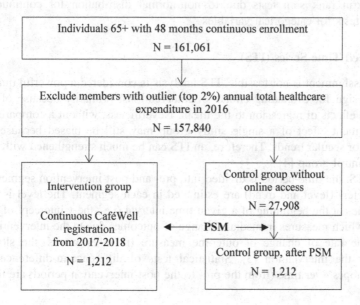

Fig. 1. Sample selection step

2.6 Propensity Score Matching (PSM)

Assessing the effect of health-related internet use on health care utilization and expenditures requires controlling for factors that influence a user's decision to use the internet. Such decision can reflect both observed and unobservable differences in characteristics between online users and non-online users. Studies that examined determinants of internet use found that older adults who were younger, non-Hispanic white, and of higher socioeconomic status were more likely to use the internet [5, 6].

Using a logistic regression model, we estimated the propensity score of registering in the CaféWell program for all individuals based on a set of observed covariates, without interactions or nonlinear terms. On the premise that the expenditures and utilization trends would be similar between the intervention and control group during the pre-intervention period, the control group were then matched to the intervention group. PSM was used to control for cost and utilization during the pre-intervention period; age; gender; number of chronic conditions; co-morbidities including diabetes, hypertension, mental disorder, chronic kidney disease (CKD), and cancer; and insurance type (HMO vs. PPO). Specifically, the Greedy matching algorithm was used.

All persons who registered in the CaféWell program were then matched to persons who did not have internet access, based on their propensity scores, using caliper of 0.2 standard deviations. To examine the quality of the match, we used either the Mann-Whitney-Wilcoxon rank sum tests due to non-normal distribution for continuous variables or $\chi 2$ tests for categorical variables.

2.7 Interrupted Time Series (ITS)

When random assignment is not feasible, ITS analysis is considered a powerful quasi-experimental design for evaluating effects of interventions, primarily because of its control over the effects of regression to the mean. Nevertheless, without a comparison group, the treatment effect of a single study group may still be biased because of selection issues or secular trends. Therefore, an ITS can be much strengthened with the addition of a control group [4].

In a basic ITS, the time-period is divided into pre- and post-intervention segments, and two parameters (level and trend) are estimated in each segment. The level is the value of the series at the beginning of a given time interval (i.e., the y-intercept of the first segment), which measures immediate change of outcomes due to the intervention. The trend is the rate of change of outcome measure (in other words, the slope) over time after the intervention [3]. Statistical tests of difference-in-difference in intercepts and slopes over time (from the pre- to the post-intervention period) are then carried out.

3 Results

Out of 332,911 adults, a total of 29,120 persons met all inclusion criteria. Their characteristics are shown in the first three columns of Table 1 (labeled before matching). On average, aged adults without online access were older and female, compared to health-related online users. Those without online access were more likely to have HMO coverage, more likely to have heart disease and mental disorders. They had higher PMPM ($), as well as higher rates of ED visits and admission.

Table 1. Characteristics of the study sample before & after propensity score matching

N	All	Before matching[a]		After matching[a]	
		Control group	Intervention group	Control group	Intervention group
	29,120	27,908	1,212	1,212	1,212
Demographic characteristics					
Age[b]	80.51	80.69	76.37***	77.07	76.37
Female[c]	62%	62%	53%***	54%	53%
HMO[c]	44%	44%	37%***	37%	37%
Health characteristics					
Diabetes[c]	21%	21%	25%***	24%	25%
Heart disease[c]	22%	23%	18%***	17%	18%
Hypertension[c]	72%	73%	71%	72%	71%
Mental disorder[c]	21%	21%	19%*	19%	19%
Cancer[c]	17%	17%	17%	18%	17%
CKD[c]	8%	8%	7%	7%	7%
Healthcare utilization and expenditures					
PMPM ($)[b]	661.32	662.76	628.29***	628.24	628.29
Having admission[c]	11%	11%	8%***	8%	8%
Having ED visits[c]	21%	22%	15%***	17%	15%

Note: [a]Statistical tests examine the null hypothesis that the intervention group had same characteristics as the control group; [b]Mann-Whitney-Wilcoxon rank sum test due to non-normal distribution; [c]Chi-square test; the symbols ***, **, and * indicate a significance level of 1%, 5%, and 10%, respectively.

The final study sample consisted of 1,212 health-related online users and 1,212 persons without online access who were successfully matched using PSM. Because residual differences in demographics, health characteristics, and healthcare utilization and expenditures between the two groups were not statistically significant, adequate balance was attained (labeled after matching of Table 1).

One of the greatest strengths of interrupted time series studies is the intuitive graphical presentation of results, and a visual inspection of the series over time is the first step when analyzing time series data [3]. Using the matched sample, we conducted two-group interrupted time series analysis (ITSA) for annual ED rates. Looking at the data points during the pre-intervention period in Fig. 2, we found similar ED rates between online users and non-online users, as expected.

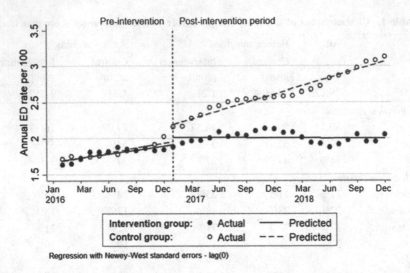

Fig. 2. Two-group ITSA of annual mean ED rates per 100

After the online registration, the average annual ED rates of the intervention group were expected to be changed in its level and/or trend, compared to the control group. Before the intervention, initial ED rates were on average 1.687 per 100 annually and had an increasing trend of 0.023 per year.

Table 2. Parameter estimates, standard errors from the segmented regression models

Parameter	Coef.	S.E.	t-stat	p-value
Annual mean ED rate per 100				
Difference-in-difference of level	−0.135	0.059	−2.31	0.024
Difference-in-difference of trend	−0.034	0.007	−5.18	<0.001
Average PMPM ($)				
Difference-in-difference of level	−65.9	14.87	−4.43	<0.001
Difference-in-difference of trend	−8.7	1.49	−5.83	<0.001
Annual mean admission rate per 100				
Difference-in-difference of level	−0.361	0.06	−6.02	<0.001
Difference-in-difference of trend	−0.001	0.007	−0.22	0.83

The parameter estimates from the linear segmented regression model confirmed that annual ED rates of online-users (intervention group) decreased from the pre- to the post-intervention period, compared to the control group, in level by 0.135 (difference-in-difference of level in Table 2, $p = 0.024$), as well as in trend by 0.034 (difference-in-difference of trend in Table 2, $p < 0.001$).

When expressing the results of segmented regression modelling, we can either report level and trend changes like those in Table 2, or we can express the intervention effect as the absolute difference in values. Using the coefficients of the ITS model [7],

Table 3 shows the estimated effect of health-related online use on ED rates. In December of 2017 and 2018, one year and two years after the intervention, annual ED rates decreased by 0.515 ($p < 0.001$) and 0.977 ($p < 0.001$), respectively.

Table 3. Intervention effects 1 year and 2 years after the intervention.

	Annual ED rate/100	PMPM	Annual admission rate/100
Dec., 2017	−0.515***	−$22.47***	−0.023
Dec., 2018	−0.977***	−$85.91***	−0.043

Note: ***, **, and * indicate a significance level of 1%, 5%, and 10%, respectively.

The second panel of Table 2 shows parameter estimates measuring the effect of health-related online use on annual average PMPM ($). We found a significant decrease in level of $65.90 ($p < 0.001$) and in trend of $8.70 per year ($p < 0.001$) among online users, compared to aged adults without online access. Visual inspection of annual mean PMPM over time clearly suggests lower cost among online users for health-related activities, compared to non-online users (Fig. 3).

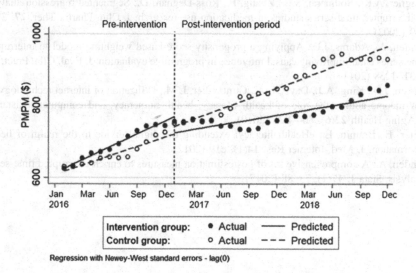

Fig. 3. Two-group ITSA of annual mean PMPM ($)

The estimated intervention effect on PMPM one year and two years after CaféWell registration was a healthcare cost savings of $22.47 and $85.91, respectively (Table 3). Considering the initial mean PMPM of $617.31 before the intervention, healthcare expenditures decreased by 4% and 14%, respectively. However, there was no statistically significant change in annual hospital admission rates (Table 3).

4 Conclusion

We estimated the long-term effect of health-related online use among aged adults on healthcare expenditures and utilization over time, using a rigorous method. To our best knowledge, this is the first published evidence of such effect using this novel study design and time series data. We found reduction in healthcare expenditures one year after the intervention. Cost savings were driven possibly by reductions in ER visits. We have not observed any significant changes in hospital admission rates. In other words, utilization of online health resources among older adults was associated with lower healthcare utilization and expenditures. Our findings also highlight the importance of long-term evaluations to measure such effect, as well as the need for payers to take a long-term investment view when considering an online-based program.

References

1. U.S. Census: Computer and Internet Use in the United States: 2016 (2018)
2. Choi, N.G., DiNitto, D.M.: Internet use among older adults: association with health needs, psychological capital, and social capital. J. Med. Internet Res. 15(5), e97 (2013)
3. Wagner, A.K., Soumerai, S.B., Zhang, F., Ross-Degnan, D.: Segmented regression analysis of interrupted time series studies in medication use research. J. Clin. Pharm. Ther. 27, 299–309 (2002)
4. Linden, A., Adams, J.L.: Applying a propensity score-based weighting model to interrupted time series data: improving causal inference in programme evaluation. J. Eval. Clin. Pract. 17, 1231–1238 (2011)
5. Jensen, J.D., King, A.J., Davis, L.A., Guntzviller, L.M.: Utilization of internet technology by low-income adults: the role of health literacy, health numeracy, and computer assistance. J. Aging Health 22(6), 804–826 (2010)
6. Neter, E., Brainin, E.: eHealth literacy: extending the digital divide to the realm of health information. J. Med. Internet Res. 14(1), e19 (2012)
7. Linden, A.: A comprehensive set of postestimation measures to enrich interrupted time-series analysis. Stata J. 17(1), 73–88 (2017)

Emotion Aware Voice-Casting Robot
for Rehabilitation Evaluated with Bio-signal
Index

Kodai Matsumoto, Reiji Yoshida, Feng Chen, and Midori Sugaya[✉]

Shibaura Institute of Technology, Koto City, Tokyo, Japan
doly@shibaura-it.ac.jp

Abstract. As part of nursing care, there is physiotherapist's physical exercise recovery training (walking training, etc.), which is aimed at restoring athletic ability that is called rehabilitation. In rehabilitation for the practitioners, there is a problem that it is difficult to maintain motivation trough their work. In this paper, we propose "voice-casting robot" that provides support for guide the route of the practitioners and to main their motivation, select the appropriate phrase for voice-casting based on the emotion estimation with pulse sensor's data analysis result of them. The previous voice-casting robot was not considered the arousal revel of arousal, and would not obtain the effectiveness. In this study, we consider the arousal degree of the rehabilitation, and the effect measurement of performing the corresponding vocalization. As a result, it was suggested that it is more effective to consider the degree of arousal and to make a voice-cast than to the case of voice-cast only when negative valence.

Keywords: Emotional communication · Bio-emotion estimate method · Conscious feelings · Unconscious emotion

1 Introduction

The rehabilitation population of the elderly is increasing [1]. Maintaining motivation is essential for effective rehabilitation [2], the practitioners are burdened with pain and mental pain, it is difficult to maintain motivation. In order to maintain motivation at rehabilitation, Itoh et al. proposed a "voice-casting robot" which changes a voice call phrase according to emotion of the practitioner [3]. They designed and implemented a robot that vocalizes different voices according to the state of emotion of the subject, using the value of valence that is calculated on the sensor value of pulse sensor. As a valence evaluation value, they use pNN50 which is an indicator of human autonomic nervousness. The value has been used as to evaluate the emotional state [4], which value is increasing if they feel relax, and decrease if they feel opposite. The experimental results of Ito's work, shows that the most comfortable state was obtained when combining the use of phrases according to emotion of experimental collaborators and supportive behavior [3].

In the research of Ito et al., it is measurement of comfortable discomfort and voice based on it, and they do not consider the arousal state of human. It is reported that anger is high as a state of high arousal degree among discomfort, and it is reported that voice clashing will be the opposite effect in this state [5]. From this, it is possible that the voice call will have the opposite effect. Therefore, in this research, we realize a new voice-over robot adding awareness and verify its effect.

The paper is organized as follows. In Sect. 2, we firstly present related work, then Sect. 3, describe proposal. In the Sect. 4, we showed the experiment using the proposed robot, and results. Finally conclude the paper in Sect. 5.

2   Related Work

Wada et al. proposed "robot therapy" which mental care through touching with an animal-type robot [4]. Robot therapy has an advantage that it can be carried out more easily than animal therapy by using a safety and sanitary animal robot instead of an animal in animal therapy. The seal-like robot Paro [4] realizes tactile, visual, auditory, and balance senses with its internal sensors, and by combining these data, it can learn people's names and actions. With Paro, we can gradually build up the relationships between Paro and its owners through interactions, and the owners are expected to interpret it as if Pharaoh had feelings. It is recognized that animal therapy has mainly (1) psychological effects: an increase in smiles and motivation, mitigation of "depression," etc., (2) physio-logical effects: a decrease in stress, blood pressure, etc., and (3) social effect: an increase in communication, etc. Wada et al. have demonstrated experiments using Paro robots and have shown that they have been effective. However, Paro is mainly healing patients with its singing voice and appearance. It does not, for example, improve specific motivation of patients in rehab by speaking a natural language. On the other hand, one of the factors that enhance the rehab effect is the ambitious effort by the rehab patient himself. Motivation is the driving force of action, and the necessity of activity. Declining motivation, often a problem in everyday life, is an obstacle to implementing rehab. Therefore, Kimishi et al. selected commonly-heard spoken words at a rehab hospital, conducted a questionnaire survey on the staff (physiotherapists, occupational therapists, physicians, etc.) and rehab patients, and investigated the degree of motivation for rehab patients [5].

Using the idea of improve the motivation of rehabilitation, Itoh et al. proposed a "voice-casting robot" which changes a voice call phrase according to emotion of the practitioner [3]. They showed the experimental results, that shows the most comfortable state was obtained when combining the use of phrases according to emotion of experimental collaborators and supportive behavior.

In the research of Ito et al., it is measurement of comfortable discomfort and voice based on it, and they do not consider the arousal state of human. It is reported that anger is high as a state of high arousal degree among discomfort, and it is reported that voice clashing will be the opposite effect in this state. From this, we consider that it is possible that the voice casting would have the decline the motivation of the subject.

3 Proposal

In this study, we consider emotion not only negative/positive from the valence value, but also consider the arousal state of the practitioners. Since as we describe on the previous section, the existent research shows the possibilities of improvement of the motivation of the rehabilitation of the subjects, when the voice-casting robot makes changes the voice over phrase according to the subject's auto nerves state that indicate the positive/negative valence. The result showed that effectiveness of the robot voice-casting with subject's emotion compared to without using the emotion of subjects. However, the effectiveness is limited, since Ito et al. only consider the positive/negative valence state of the subjects, it contains both of the angry and sad emotion without consider the arousal classification in the Russell's model (Fig. 1). The emotions that in the high arousal area in negative valence would evaluated as some frustrated state of patients for rehabilitation. For this case, sometimes encouraging voice-casting would not be effective for them. Even though there are several discussions, there are not sufficiently evaluated to compare the state of the voice casting for the subject's state.

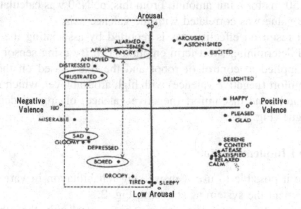

Fig. 1. Russell's model and focused emotion

To solve the problem, we propose a design and implemented a voice-casting robot that cast the appropriate phrase based on the estimation of additional classification by the arousal level.

3.1 Bio-signal Information Analysis

To achieve the purpose, we use the bio-emotion estimation method that has been proposed by Ikeda et al. [8] as a method of estimating emotion according to the status of people. The values obtained from the brain waves and pulses were calculated so as to correspond to the Arousal axis and the Valence axis of Russell's circumplex model [9], and the values of Arousal and Valence were plotted on the two-dimensional coordinate.

The brain wave value associated with the Arousal axis was measured using an electroencephalograph called NeuroSky's MindWave Mobile [10]. We used the value Attention and Meditation calculated by this electroencephalograph. Attention and Meditation are each a value indicating the degree of concentration and the resting degree of the person, and are calculated at the level of 0 to 100. From this, in this study, we assumed that the difference between the value of Attention and Meditation was appropriate to express the degree of arousal of a person and corresponded to the value of arousal axis of Russell's circular model.

The value of the Valence axis was correlated with the pulse rate earned by the Sparkfun's Pulse Sensor. This sensor measures pulse rate by photoelectric volumetric pulse wave recording method, and pNN50 was used as a pulse value corresponding to the Valence axis. The pNN50 shows the rate at which the difference between the 30 adjacent RR intervals exceeds 50 ms. Generally, pNN50 is said to indicate the degree of tension of the nerve, and the smaller the value, the more tense/uncomfortable a person is. Therefore, it can be said that when someone is normal/pleasant, the RR interval exceeds 50 ms for a fair amount. From this, pNN50 was calculated at a rate of 0 to 1.0, and the value was correlated with the valence axis.

An empirical result on effectiveness is reported by associating the state of autonomic nerve and determining short-term emotion [11]. By using sensor values in real time, it can be applied to control of robot and the like. Based on the method, we distinguish discomfort (negative valence) with high arousal level, which is the problem of previous research, and discomfort (negative valence) of arousal degree including sadness and fatigue (Fig. 1).

3.2 Design and Implementation

In order to make it possible to use it in walking rehabilitation in various places, we design and implement the system as shown in Fig. 2.

There are mainly two parts. The one is robot control unit, the other is emotion detected and select phrases unit. (1) The robot control unit first determines the moving direction and sends a serial command from Raspberry Pi to Arduino for motor control, and (2) classify the emotion from the pulse and the brain wave and to determine the phrases to play.

(1) In the determination of the direction of moving, forward and backward switches between walking and feedback/calling, Arduino sends a turn command each time to run. In addition, after the feedback, it was stopped, and it was made the specification to resume moving after calling out. In this experiment, it was assumed that the drive unit mounted this time traveled at 0.5 km/h at the maximum speed at which stable moving can be achieved.

(2) We describe the part that performs voice reproduction from emotion classification. First, the Arousal level and the average value of 10 immediately before Valence (pNN50) are compared. When the comparison value falls below the threshold, the

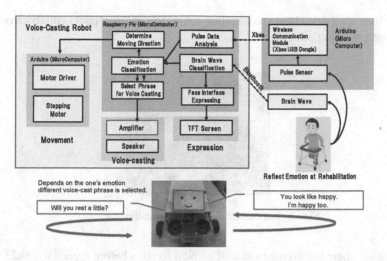

Fig. 2. Voice-casting robots based on the bio-estimated emotion

support operation (moving control) is executed. Then, select and execute the appropriate voice response according to the emotion. The pNN50 was defined as less than 0.23 as the threshold of valence, and the arousal degree was less than 0 was used as the sleepiness dominant.

In addition, the function to write the time when the voice call was made in the data together with the biological information data was also implemented, making it easy to analyze the biological information at the time of voice conversion. In this experiment, the last voice was performed so that 4 to 5 voices were performed within a 10 m walk to prevent the voices being played continuously and the effects of each voice being obscured. In the 20 s from the time of the application, the specification was not used to make calls even if it was below the threshold.

The data of pulse sensor and electroencephalograph were mounted by wireless communication. The communication method uses Bluetooth and Xbee standardly installed in Raspberry Pi 3. The electroencephalograph used Mindwave Mobile of NeuroSky company which can communicate data by Bluetooth. In addition, as a pulse sensor, pulse sensor of Switch Science, Inc., RN4020 of Microchip's Xbee module was used to communicate sensor values with Raspberry Pi.

4   Experiment

4.1   Preliminary Experiment

We firstly execute the preliminary experiments with the aim of investigating the biological reaction by robot's voice call. In a voice call, we conducted a follow-up that showed effectiveness in previous studies. In the evaluation, emotional evaluation was performed using an electroencephalograph and a pulse rate meter. After setting a resting time of 1 min for stabilizing the pulse for experimental collaborators (20 s, 7 people), they are guided by a voice calling robot, and an experiment collaborator walks 6 m using a walking aid (Fig. 3).

Fig. 3. Experimental scene of rehabilitation robot

The case where the average value of pNN50 for 10 s before speech was 0.23 or less was defined as negative valence and used for voice (Table 1). In addition, based on the value acquired by brain waves, the state judgment of a person was classified as negative valence in the case of low arousal degree and negative valence in case of high arousal degree.

Table 1. Appropriate voice based on their emotion status

	In the case of displeasure (pNN50 < 0.23)	In the case of pleasures (pNN50 >= 0.23)
At the start	Thank you in advance.	Let's work hard again today.
During walking	Will you rest a little?	You look like happy. I'm happy too.
	It's okay. Don't be rushed.	Just a bit more.
At the finish	Let's keep up the good work.	See you tomorrow.

4.2   Result

As shown in Fig. 4, in the negative valence (including anger and irritation) with high arousal level on the left, a significant trend was observed in the direction in which the value of pNN50 declined before and after voice calling ($p < 0.10$). On the other hand, in the negative valence (sorrow and fatigue) state with low arousal level in the right figure, there was a significant difference ($p < 0.05$) in the direction in which the value of pNN50 rises before and after voice call. From these facts, although it is effective to voice-casting in previous research on people with negative valence with low arousal level, for people with a high level of arousal, a voice of encouragement in previous research would be considered not to be effective.

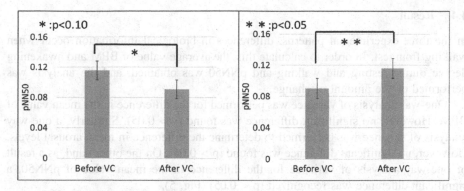

Fig. 4. t-test of before voice-casting and after vice-casting at the time of high arousal level + negative valence (anger/irritation, etc.) condition (left), low arousal level + negative valence (sadness/fatigue etc.)

4.3   Comparison with the Negative Valence and Low Arousal Status

Preliminary experiments have suggested that the voice-casting would not be effective to highly arousal level cooperators. In addition, based on the expert's advice that it is important to keep the state of high arousal at the time of rehabilitation, we evaluate the effectiveness of voice-casting when the degree of arousal decreases (sleepy dominance).

After providing a rest period of 1 min for pulse stability for the experimental collaborators (5 persons in 20's), they receive guidance of a vocalization robot, and the experimental collaborators walk using a walking aid. The walking distance was a 10-m course that was found to be effective in the 6-min walking test [12]. Moreover, in order to add a load to walking, a weight was attached to the ankle of the experiment cooperator. Furthermore, from the expert's advice, in order not to lower the gaze of the gait line too much, the robot and the experiment cooperator were separated by 2 m and walked to maintain the interval.

In this experiment, we set up the three types of conditions: one that does not take account the arousal level and no voice-casting, one that does not take into account the arousal level, but does take into account the negative valence, and the one take into account the arousal level low and voice-casting. We implemented the three patterns. The experimental patterns implemented are summarized below.

I: No voice-casting
II: At negative valence, voice-casting
III: At low arousal, voice-casting

In addition, it is assumed that the follow-up action of the support action is performed before the vocalization.

4.4   Result

In the three experimental patterns, differences in biological information occur when walking from rest. In order to calculate this, the average value of BPM and awakening degree during resting and walking and pNN50 was obtained, and the analysis was performed on the amount of change.

One-way analysis of variance was performed for the difference in the mean value of BPM. However, no significant difference was found ($p > 0.05$). Similarly, a one-way analysis of variance was performed to determine the difference in mean arousal levels. However, no significant difference was found ($p > 0.05$). On the other hand, as a result of one-way analysis of variance for the difference in the mean value of pNN50, a significant difference was recognized ($p < 0.05$) (Fig. 5).

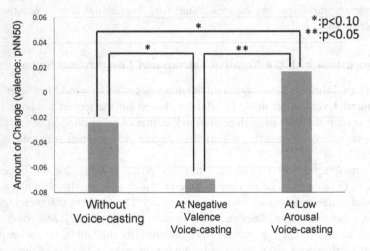

Fig. 5. Comparison with the I No voice casting, II at negative valence voice-casting, III at low arousal voice-casting

Moreover, as a result of performing multiple comparison by Tukey HSD test in order to compare the difference of the mean value of each group, a significant difference is recognized in pattern II and III ($p < 0.05$), pattern I and II and pattern I There was a significant tendency in and III ($p < 0.10$).

4.5   Discussion

There was no significant difference in one-way analysis of variance between the difference in the mean of the BPM and the difference in the mean of the arousal level. This is considered to be because the load does not change just by the presence or absence of a voice, since it is an experiment in which every pattern travels the same distance at the same speed.

In addition, significant differences were found in the one-way analysis of variance for differences in the mean values of pNN50, and significant differences and significant trends were found in multiple comparisons for each combination. From this result, it can be considered that the use of voice-casting only when drowsiness is significant makes the value of pNN50 positive valence.

In addition, it was found that it is more likely to be negative valence when voice-casting only when it is offensive than when no voice-casting. From this, it is more effective to support the rehabilitation executor by giving a voice-casting in consideration of the arousal level, and the action to perform a voice-casting without considering the arousal level is more unsupportive than no voice-casting. This is considered to be unpleasant for the rehabilitation implementer to be voice-casting only when it is offensive.

5   Conclusion

In this study, in addition to the heart rate index pNN50 used in the previous study, we evaluated the robot that by taking into account the degree of the arousal that can be acquired from EEG. As a result, it was found that a voice-casting taking into account the degree of arousal more pleasantly than the action that does not voice-casting or the action voice-casting when disgusting makes people feel better. From the results, it is considered possible to realize a more supportive system and a general-purpose rehabilitation robot by considering the arousal degree and the issues described in the next chapter.

References

1. Cabinet Office: Heisei 20-year Aging White Paper, 26 July 2018
2. Imperial South Rehabilitation Clinic: How do you respond if your motivation declines during rehabilitation? Reference date 26 July 2018
3. Ito, T., Tobe, Y., Sugaya, M.: Supportive voice-casting robots using bio-estimated emotion for rehabilitation. In: The 15th International Conference on Intelligent Environments 2019, Rabat, Morocco, 24–27 June 2019
4. Takunori, S., Wada, K.: Clinical and demonstration experiment of the effect of robot/therapy by seal type robot - Paro. J. Robot. Soc. Jpn. **29**(3), 246–249 (2011)
5. Kibishi, Y., Takahashi, Y., Sasaki, K.: About effective communication to patients in rehabilitation. Professional Rehabilitation Study Group, Professional Rehabilitation No. 3, pp. 25–29 (2004)
6. Shi, H., Yang, L., Zhao, L., Liu, C., et al.: Differences of heart rate variability between happiness and sadness emotion states: a pilot study. J. Med. Biol. Eng. **37**(4), 527–539 (2017)
7. Encouraging words that do not give pressure unsatisfactory is the opposite effect. Reference date 26 July 2018
8. Ikeda, Y., Horie, R., Sugaya, M.: Estimate emotion with biological information for robot interaction. Procedia Comput. Sci. **112**, 1589–1600 (2017)
9. Russell, J.A.: A circumplex model of affect. J. Pers. Soc. Psychol. **39**(6), 1161–1178 (1980)

250   K. Matsumoto et al.

10. NeuroSky Mindwave Mobile. https://store.neurosky.com. Accessed 19 Jan 2019
11. De Carvalho Abreu, E.E.M., De Souza Alves, R., Borges, A.C.L., Lima, F.P.S., De Paula Júnior, A.R., Lima, M.O.: Autonomic cardiovascular control recovery in quadriplegics after handcycle training. J. Phys. Ther. Sci. **28**, 2063–2068 (2016). Method. COMPSAC (2), 601–660 (2018)
12. Kawamoto, R., et al.: Is the 6-minute walk test of the 10 m course useful? In: The 44th Japanese Physical Therapy Congress Abstracts, vol. 36, no. 2, p. 2480

Cities for All Ages: Singapore Use Case

Mounir Mokhtari[1,2(✉)], Antoine de Marassé[1,2], Martin Kodys[3,4],
and Hamdi Aloulou[1,5]

[1] Institut Mines-Telecom (IMT), Paris, France
mounir.mokhtari@imt.fr
[2] National University of Singapore (NUS), Singapore, Singapore
[3] University Grenoble Alpes, Grenoble, France
[4] IPAL, Paris, France
[5] University of Monastir, Monastir, Tunisia

Abstract. *Healthcare & well-being needs a revolution - and it is needed now.*
In the coming years, the relationship between people and digitized systems is
going to change due in large part to the adoption of ambient technologies in
daily life and to the considerable development in AI (Artificial Intelligence).
This includes emerging 5G technologies, small medical devices, non-invasive
new sensing technologies, collaborative robots (e.g. Amazon Echo, Google
home, etc.), Internet-of-Things (IoT) applications, and secured data exchange
mechanisms (e.g. Blockchain). Over the next 20 years there will be demographic shift from predominantly younger populations to older ones. Current
models of care and pathways need to be transformed to become more citizen
focused as well as to support greater community resilience and sustainability.
This will require different approaches to innovation in information technologies
to improve quality of life for people as they age, to reduce onset of frailty as well
as to better support those with long term conditions employing self-management
and prevention strategies. This paper describes on-going project between NUS,
IMT, HDB (Housing Development Board), and AXA Insurance, and aiming at
preserving patient health and avoid deterioration of their quality of life (and also
of their families) by fully utilizing disruptive information & communication
technologies. Additionally, the goal is to help improve the quality of life of
citizens while reducing the health-care expenditure.

Keywords: Smart living · Human-environment interaction · IoT · AI ·
Ageing & wellbeing people

1 Introduction

1.1 Public Health vs. Wellbeing

The WHO Regional Office for Europe now embraces Wellbeing as a vital public health
metric. The 2015 WHO European Health Report stated[1]: "Health 2020 implementation
is gaining momentum, but broader monitoring is needed to capture its true impact,

---

[1] https://www.cdc.gov/hrqol/wellbeing.htm.

© Springer Nature Switzerland AG 2019
C. Stephanidis and M. Antona (Eds.): HCII 2019, CCIS 1088, pp. 251–258, 2019.
https://doi.org/10.1007/978-3-030-30712-7_32

including concepts such as community resilience, empowerment and sense of belonging"

Why is wellbeing useful for public health?

1. Wellbeing integrates mental health (mind) and physical health (body) resulting in more holistic approaches to disease prevention and health promotion.
2. Wellbeing is a valid population outcome measure beyond morbidity, mortality, and economic status that tells us how people perceive their life is going from their own perspective.
3. Wellbeing can provide a common metric that can help policy makers shape and compare the effects of different policies (e.g., loss of green space might impact wellbeing more so than commercial development of an area).
4. Measuring, tracking and promoting wellbeing can be useful for multiple stakeholders involved in disease prevention and health promotion

Cities and governments are increasingly placing emphasis on Wellbeing in public policy and urban planning. This is consistent with the paradigm shift that has taken place in public health – from a focus on morbidity and mortality to a focus on health and wellbeing.

1.2   Behavior Change

Aging natural process is associated with significant behavior change and continuous decline in physical and cognitive abilities. To be more specific, we consider the distinct phases of aging from active aging to dependent aging through frailty targeting three age groups as following (see Fig. 1): **Active ageing**: 55+ considered as future aging. **Pre-frail and frail**: 60+ considered also as active people, but facing chronic diseases (e.g., diabetes type 2, respiratory disease, etc.). **Dependent**: 65+ might face cognitive and physical decline.

Fig. 1. Aging trajectories of health and functions

Detecting behavioral change, and predicting corresponding risk, in early evolution stages is a keystone to better adapt intervention on elderly people and improve their quality of life. Nevertheless, existing psychogeriatric methods diagnose a limited number of possible changes at assessment time and in assessment place [7].

2 Non-invasive Based Technologies

Our ambition is to focus on Non-invasive based technologies to monitor and assess aging people over extended periods in their living environment [1] and detect insights of long-term changes in their behavior based on key geriatric factors [2]. This involves, as illustrated in figure below (see Fig. 2), **Sleep quality monitoring** through bed-based sensors, (for example, micro bend optical fiber sleep mat), and/or wearable devices, such as Fitbit; **Fall detection and prevention** using the inertial measurement unit of a smartphone attached to the subject's body with the signals wirelessly transmitted to a cloud-based server or non-invasive new sensing technologies (ex. using ambient WIFI signals, smart meters); **Mobility monitoring** using wearable activity trackers (smart watches) and urban low energy communication (e.g. Beacons, Sigfox, LORA).

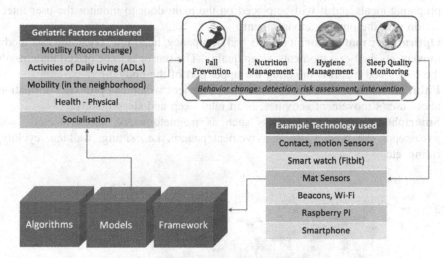

Fig. 2. Use cases for monitoring and assessment of human behavior based on key geriatric factors.

Generic human activity recognition system for smart living - One of the main problems of current activity recognition systems is that the models learned for a given environment and user cannot be used in another context. Given the great heterogeneity of data acquisition systems for smart cities and the number of potential users, that lack of generality can be disastrous. To make activity recognition systems available for smart cities, this project will conduct research on generic recognition systems. Our approach is to capture the inherent semantics of sensor activations. For example, when a binary sensor that monitors the state of a given door gets activated, we will register a "door open" action. Developed framework and associated integrated sensors, where deployed in real life condition in close collaboration with Housing Development Board (HDB) and Senior Activity Centre in the area of Tech Ghee (Ang Mo Kio) in Singapore.

3 Singapore Test Bed and Preliminary Results

3.1 Sensing and Data Collection Indoor

In order to enlarge the audience of the project to the research community and industry players, numerous events and briefing sessions were organized to share about the project at its local scale and internationally. Several types of sensors where deployed in 20 homes of people living in the area of Teck Ghee Neighbourhood with the support of Senior Activity Centre, Town Council and HDB (see Fig. 3):

- **Motion sensor**: it detects indoor movements and it will be in the main room, bedroom, kitchen, and bathroom.
- **Contact sensor**: it will be placed on the fridge to infer kitchen activity such as preparing meals and it will be placed on the main door to monitor the user inter-action with the outdoor environment.
- **Optical fiber mat sensor**: it detects bed occupancy, heart rate, breathing rate, body movements, bed-exit moments, sleep quality. The sensor is to be placed underneath the user's bed mattress targeting the upper part of the body.
- **Fitbit and similar**: it is a wearable type of devices which can provide information about user's movement activities, heart rate, sleep and sleep quality.
- **Smartphone**: embedded sensors such as magnetometers, accelerometers, and gyroscopes can predict user's movement pattern, i.e., sitting, walking, cycling, riding. etc.

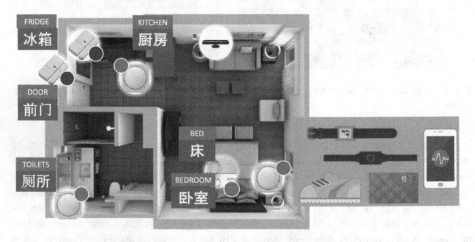

Fig. 3. Distribution of the unobtrusive sensors in a typical user's home

3.2   Sensing and Data Collection Outdoor (Neighborhood)

Beside de deployment indoor in the home of frails people, we managed to deploy about 15 Beacons (Bluetooth Low Energy), in the same area, in several places of interest (Food Court, bus station, physical activities areas, Senior Activity Centre, Town Council premises, etc.) to monitor outdoor location activities (Fig. 4). Additionally some participants where provided with a Fitbit to monitor physical activities.

Fig. 4. Deploying a local neighborhood - community partners

Indoor and outdoor data, including open data (Air Quality, weather conditions) where analyzed and integrated in a dashboard for experts and end-users.

3.3   Dashboard and Mobile App Intervention

Several personalized dashboards, for data analytics and community monitoring, and Apps, for individual data collection and intervention, were designed to target several key players: end-users, family members, formal and informal caregivers, organizers, professionals, technical experts, and so on could monitor, be reminded/notified, to activate corresponding action (Human and/or system intervention). For example, Figs. 5 and 6 gives an example of a user-friendly interface displaying some activities of daily living (sleep time, kitchen activity, and toileting time) and some personalized tips, and urban data (air quality, weather, bikes location etc.).

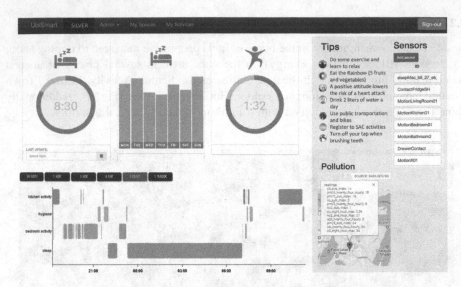

Fig. 5. Distribution end-users and caregivers' dashboard

The dashboard is facilitating the observation of different geriatric factors groups over time. Caregivers can select one category and display more details, for example in term of Instrumental Activities of Daily Living (Cooking, hygiene, …) and Motility (ability to move across rooms, rooms number of visits and time spend…). The different curves bring to sub-sections of the geriatric groups. Data can be seen with the granularity of the low elementary actions and measures (set of sensor events transferred to the data repository and displayed in this dashboard).

3.4   Preliminary Results

More than 70 participants were actively involved: 21 elderly people equipped (sensors deployed in their own homes), 5 caregivers equipped (using the App and Dashboard), 12 experts (involved in the design and in the validation phase), and more than 35 interviewed (understanding the users requirements).

Historical data can be correlated using the Senior Activity Center's presence sheet, activity logs, visit observations and updates about the participants to the caregivers (ex: hospitalization, family visit, holiday trip) (see Fig. 6). This data can be annotated by the local caregivers in order to keep track to the evolution of the monitored factors. When a peak is observed, the data is crossed checked with other sub-category data and external datasets (including third parties' knowledge).

Fig. 6. Data annotation related to change of behavior (for example no activity in July 2017 due to holiday)

4 Related Work

In the medical field, behavior change refers to abandoning health-compromising behaviors (e.g., drink, smoke and over-eat), and maintaining health-improving behaviors (e.g., physical exercise, weight control, preventive nutrition and dental hygiene). Geriatricians use psycho-geriatric scales and questionnaires to analyze elderly people behavior and detect possible health changes. They study question replies and task executions, such as "How many falls did you have in the last 6 months?" [3], "Have you dropped many of your activities and interests?" [4] and "Do you perform your activities of daily living independently (A), not spontaneously or not totally or not correctly or not frequently (B), only with help (C)?" [5]. These scales compute psycho-geriatric scores evaluating physical, emotional, nutritional, social and cognitive abilities. However, Psycho-geriatric scales are insufficient to follow-up health status on a daily basis [6] as subjective information and missing details might influence assessment results [7]. Therefore, Thus, geriatricians need technological services to acquire new objective observations that complete their medical observations [8]. Monitoring technologies can help follow-up elderly people at home and in the city, in order to early detect possible health changes [9].

5 Conclusion

Singapore pilot site team is deploying its technological platform for Ambient Assisted Living. This platform enables to gather the raw signals from deployed sensors and to interpret the data (reasoning engine, rule-based algorithms). This technology infers several measures on Activities of Daily Living and other parameters such as mobility. From this platform, the team co-designed a set of tools to be used by the "caregivers" with the help and guidance of several partners: academic partners working on ageing, community organizations and user caregivers themselves (from partner Senior Activity Centers).

The team have performed interview sessions with elderly participants and with caregivers in order to assess the system overall acceptance and quality of the intervention. Preliminary results are encouraging as most of caregivers saw the impact of such a solution in their daily routine activities. Even if most of the end-users adopted the system, they still didn't perceive an impact on their daily activities. Large scale deployment strategy needs to be performed to provide appropriate impact analysis of people lifestyle.

This project is funded by AXA Research Fund under agreement JRI 2018-EXTENDED (Extending Living Space for Frail and Dependent Ageing People).

References

1. Aloulou, H., et al.: Deployment of assistive living technology in a nursing home environment: methods and lessons learned. BMC Med. Inform. Decis. Mak. **13**(1), 42 (2013)
2. Kaddachi, F., Aloulou, H., Abdulrazak, B., Fraisse, P., Mokhtari, M.: Long-term behavior change detection approach through objective technological observations toward better adaptation of services for elderly people. Health Technol. **8**(5), 329–340 (2018)
3. Tardieu, É., et al.: External validation of the short emergency geriatric assessment (SEGA) instrument on the safes cohort. Geriatrie et psychologie neuropsychiatrie du vieillissement **14** (1), 49–55 (2016)
4. Parmelee, P.A., Katz, I.R.: Geriatric depression scale. J. Am. Geriatr. Soc. (1990)
5. Barberger-Gateau, P., Commenges, D., Gagnon, M., Letenneur, L., Sauvel, C., Dartigues, J.-F.: Instrumental activities of daily living as a screening tool for cognitive impairment and dementia in elderly community dwellers. J. Am. Geriatr. Soc. **40**(11), 1129–1134 (1992)
6. Lökk, J.: Lack of information and access to advanced treatment for Parkinson's disease patients. J. Multidiscip. Healthc. **4**, 433 (2011)
7. Holsinger, T., Deveau, J., Boustani, M., Williams, J.W.: Does this patient have dementia? Jama **297**(21), 2391–2404 (2007)
8. Wilson, D., Consolvo, S., Fishkin, K., Philipose, M.: In-home assessment of the activities of daily living of the elderly. In: Extended Abstracts of CHI 2005: Workshops-HCI Challenges in Health Assessment (2005)
9. Acampora, G., Cook, D.J., Rashidi, P., Vasilakos, A.V.: A survey on ambient intelligence in healthcare. Proc. IEEE **101**(12), 2470–2494 (2013)

The Development and Usability Testing of a Decision Support Mobile App for the Essential Care for Every Baby (ECEB) Program

Siddhartha Nuthakki[1]([✉]), Sherri Bucher[2], and Saptarshi Purkayastha[1]

[1] Indiana University Purdue University Indianapolis, Indianapolis, IN, USA
{snuthakk, saptpurk}@iu.edu
[2] IU School of Medicine, Indianapolis, IN, USA
shbucher@iu.edu

Abstract. mHealth is a pervasive and ubiquitous technology which has revolutionized the healthcare system for both health providers and patients (Wang et al. 2016). Each year, globally, about 15 million babies are born too soon (premature) or too small (low birthweight small for gestational age); among these 2.7 million newborns die every year due to complications from prematurity (Every New Born 2014). Common complications of prematurity like feeding problems, and hypothermia lead to high rates of morbidity and mortality among prematurely born babies each year. Delivery of evidence-based essential newborn care interventions, from birth through the first 24 h of postnatal life, has been shown to improve health and well-being, and reduce mortality, among newborns. However, due to a variety of barriers, bottlenecks, and challenges, many babies born in resource-limited settings do not receive the full complement of these lifesaving interventions. In order to address these challenges, the American Academy of Pediatrics (AAP) has developed an integrated educational and training curriculm for health care providers and family stakeholders in LMICs called Essential Care for Every Baby (ECEB). ECEB has an Action Plan, which serves as a decision support tool and job aid for health care providers. (Figure 1), by synthesizing research over a decade on helping babies survive (Essential Care for Every Baby 2018). This program teaches health care providers essential newborn care practices to keep all babies healthy from the time of birth to discharge from the facility. Yet, the nuances of monitoring, tracking and taking care of multiple babies simultaneously in neonatal wards has a big cognitive load on nurses, who must perform tasks every few minutes on each baby. The care is divided into three phases based on the time after birth: Phase 1 (0–60 min), Phase 2 (60–90 min), Phase 3 (90 min-24 h). We iteratively developed and tested the usability of the ECEB action plan, as part of the mobile Helping Babies Survive (mHBS) suite of apps, and plan to field test the app in the near future.

Keywords: ECEB · mHBS · DHIS2 · Cordova · Framework7

© Springer Nature Switzerland AG 2019
C. Stephanidis and M. Antona (Eds.): HCII 2019, CCIS 1088, pp. 259–263, 2019.
https://doi.org/10.1007/978-3-030-30712-7_33

1   Introduction

According to Central Intelligence Agency (CIA) infant mortality deaths are over 15 per 1,000 live births in more than 100 countries in 2017. United States itself has reported 23,000 infant deaths in 2016 as per Centers for Disease Control and Prevention (CDC) (Infant mortality 2018). One of the leading causes of death is preterm birth.

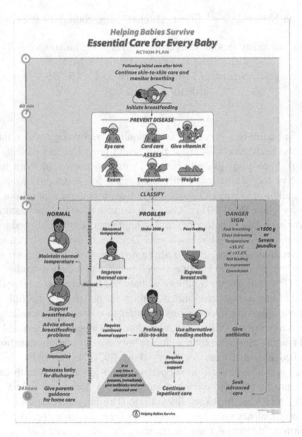

Fig. 1. Essential Care for Every Baby (ECEB) action plan

In recent years, several efforts have taken by both government and private research institutes to improve infant's health after birth often called Essential Newborn Care (ENC). Many infant deaths are reported during first day or week due to lack of this essential care. To overcome this, American Academy of pediatrics (AAP) has come up with a decision chart titled 'Essential Care for Every Baby' as part of Helping Babies Survive (HBS) program. The ECEB aims to educate all health care providers, assist mothers and families by providing knowledge and skill related to most elements of ENC. The ECEB action plan contains care that needs to be given immediately after birth to 24 h post birth based on the different baby conditions. The ECEB action plan covers all the essential new born care like ensuring warmth, skin-to-skin care, breastfeeding, umbilical cord care, immunization, vitamin K administration and eye care. The care plan in ECEB is divided based on specific times like 90 min after birth while others follow observations like body temperature, eye care etc. (Essential Care for Every Baby, Facilitator Flip Chart).

Although the care plan is perfectly designed, the application of care is more strenuous. In environments with limited resources (health care providers), adhering to every step of the care for each baby is arduous. However, mobile health (mHealth) is growing in popularity for its ease of care and benefits which has shown to improve quality of care at a low cost. mHealth has shown to have positive outcomes in Asthma, Cardiac Rehabilitation, Congestive Heart Failure, Chronic Lung disease, Chemotherapy, Hypertension and Diabetes and other common diseases. Along with positive outcomes it has also shown to have increased adherence to treatment for patients with diabetes (Marcolino et al. 2018). Hence the aim of the study is to build a mobile application using ECEB action plan, track the care given to each new born, analyze the care and eventually identify the areas where care should be enhanced.

2 Methods

Data about each newborn is captured using mHBS powered by District Health Information Software 2 (DHIS 2). DHIS 2 is an open-source health management information system, which is used to track health programs in over 60 countries, and by over 100 global NGOs. The ECEB app makes uses of DHIS2's webservice to login health workers and display the resources that are available in their facility. We also provided a facility login, where multiple nurses might be able to share a single tablet or phone device to manage the babies delivered at a neonatology ward. The software development was started by doing a needs analysis that was based on the already developed and successful mHBS app, which is based on other programs of the AAP. A pediatrician and pediatric researcher who was involved in designing the ECEB Action Plan for AAP was interviewed to understand the workflow and the ECEB Action Plan. Based on the content analysis of the interview, we created wireframe mockups of all screens, which further guided the development of the app. We selected Cordova as the framework for app development, as the developer/designer team was comfortable and well-versed with HTML/CSS and JavaScript. In order to document the care given to the baby as per the ECEB action plan, we provide a baby details registration page, which includes baby identifier, bed number, sex, mother's name, and birth time. Once the baby is registered through the app, the healthcare provider is redirected to the different phases of the care, based on time after birth.

Each page in the mobile app consists of title (denoting phase of the baby), mothers name and running timer followed by a list of actions based on the respective phases. Phase 1 consists of checkboxes for each action completed by the nurse (shown in Fig. 2). Phase 2 consists of preventive care given as checkboxes and validated fields (numeric/option etc.) to submit physical assessment of the baby. Based on the data entered in phase 1 and phase 2, a decision support dialog box, which implements the ECEB Action Plan care processing algorithm, is displayed, from which available care options in phase 3 is shown. These include Normal, Problem and Danger Sign care classification of the baby (shown in Fig. 3). Normal stage simply repeats the set of action items that can be completed as a list of checkboxes. Problem stage consists of three sub-phases: Abnormal temperature, under 2000 g and poor feeding. Danger Sign stage includea different reasons for the danger sign, followed by the care to be provided. Based on baby's condition, health care providers are directed to the appropriate stage and care plan.

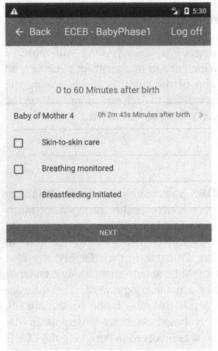

Fig. 2. Check boxes for care provided   **Fig. 3.** Decision support bialog box showing available care options

The data collected through each step of this app is saved to backend database immediately after navigating to the next page. Successful storage of data in the database is confirmed by green color 'tick' mark before the title on each page. Once data is entered in the database, for security and auditing purposes, it cannot be rewritten. All edits are also saved in the database.

Unique features of this mobile application are:

1. Offline Push alerts: These are notifications that are sent using the Android notification system, but still work in offline mode and do not need data services. Clicking on the alert will direct the user to the appropriate phase.
2. ECEB Action Plan Algorithm: These reduce cognitive load on nurses and reminds them when a baby needs to receive specific care intervention.

3. Data Security: Once data is sent to DHIS2, at the end of 24 h or discharge of the baby, all the details of the respective baby are deleted from the mobile application. This prevents ambiguity and makes the application user friendly.

3 Conclusion

The ECEB mobile app was developed through an iterative action-research approach, which enables a simple decision support tool for nurses and clinicians to provide appropriate and essential care for newborns. It helps reduce cognitive load of managing multiple babies and helps identify any gaps in health care professional's performance. This in turn helps to design a better and efficient care plan.

References

Wang, Q., Egelandsdal, B., Amdam, G.V., Almli, V.L., Oostindjer, M.: Diet and physical activity apps: perceived effectiveness by app users. JMIR mHealth uHealth **4**(2), e33 (2016). https://doi.org/10.2196/mhealth.5114

World Health Organization: Every NewBorn – An Action Plan to End Preventable Deaths. WHO Press, Switzerland (2014)

Essential Care for Every Baby. https://www.aap.org/en-us/advocacy-and-policy/aap-health-initiatives/helping-babies-survive/Pages/Essential-Care-Every-Baby.aspx. Accessed 13 Oct 2018

Marcolino, M.S., Oliveira, J., D'Agostino, M., Ribeiro, A.L., Alkmim, M., Novillo-Ortiz, D.: The impact of mHealth interventions: systematic review of systematic reviews. JMIR mHealth uHealth **6**(1), e23 (2018). https://doi.org/10.2196/mhealth.8873

Infant Mortality. Center for Disease Control and Prevention (CDC). https://www.cdc.gov/reproductivehealth/maternalinfanthealth/infantmortality.htm. Accessed 25 Mar 2019

The World FactBook. Central Intelligence Agency (CIA). https://www.cia.gov/library/publications/the-world-factbook/rankorder/2091rank.html. Accessed 25 Mar 2019

The HARP App: Tracking Hypoxia Made Simple

Mitch Tindall[✉], Eric Peterson[✉], and Jacob Entinger[✉]

NAWCTSD, Orlando, USA
{mitchell.tindall, eric.k.peterson,
jacob.entinger}@navy.mil

Abstract. Hypoxia is a dangerous and impaired state [1] that is a highly idiosyncratic experience (i.e., can present differently from person to person or experience to experience), making it especially challenging to study. In an effort to understand the nuanced effects of hypoxia, research was conducted to investigate the relationship between its physiological and subjective indicators. The research design included the tracking and recording of 21 possible symptoms and their associated severity, self-report data, continuous physiological data, and system data. In a quasi-experimental design, observing and recording a large number of variables presented a significant challenge for researchers. To help decrease the load on the researcher, a unique application was created to time stamp, synchronize, streamline, and import/export the numerous variables of the research. The team developed the Hypoxia Assessment and Recording Program (HARP) application to streamline the collection of symptomatic data. An efficient and lightweight scripting engine processed the data gathered from the test subjects. A browser-based interface made the application platform independent and provided native support for the convenient, touch enabled interface. The HARP has practical applications for cross-discipline research beyond this study, especially for researchers interested in collecting subjective and physiological data in applied settings. HARP can be tailored for use in either clinical or applied settings for both experimental and quasi-experimental designs. The technology used in this study enables the user to collect more data reliably while also decreasing the burden on the user. Ultimately, HARP has the potential to increase the efficiency and quality of data gained from observational research.

Keywords: Hypoxia · User-interface · Data synthetization

1 Introduction

Recent events such as the grounding of the Navy's T-45 training squadron [2] have motivated a renewed interest in studying aviation-based physiological events. One of the more commonly reported physiological events is hypoxia [1]. In order to better

The views expressed herein are those of the authors and do not necessarily reflect the official position of the DoD or its components.
NAWCTSD Public Release 19-ORL032—Distribution A: "Approved for public release distribution is unlimited".

understand hypoxia, the researchers investigated the relationship between physiological and subjective indicators of hypoxia. The research design included tracking and recording 21 commonly experienced symptoms of hypoxia, symptom severity, self-report data, continuous physiological data, and various system data (see Table 1 for a detailed list). Data were collected from participants going through hypoxia awareness and mitigation training at various Aviation Survival Training Centers (ASTCs). The researchers observed and recorded symptoms as they occurred during a normal training session. Trainees were also asked to wear physiological data monitors for the duration of the training event.

Table 1. List of variables tracked during research

Variable	Method of collection
Symptoms (observed)	Researcher input on HARP
Severity (observed)	Researcher input on HARP
Event time start	HARP
Event time stop	HARP
Total elapsed time	HARP
Time of symptom occurrence	HARP
Symptoms (self-report)	Participant
Severity (self-report)	Participant
Altitude	HARP
O_2	HARP
Heart rate	Physio data monitor
Breath rate	Physio data monitor

Researching hypoxia symptomology in an applied context such as during aviation survival training presents unique time-related challenges. Traditional data collection methods can be slow and time consuming (e.g., written surveys, video recording, hand written notes). When conducting research in an applied setting where there is less control than in a laboratory setting, these previous approaches to collecting data can be inconvenient and detrimental to the internal validity of the study. To address some of the practical concerns associated with traditional data collection methods, the researcher has the choice to collect fewer variables, run fewer participants at a time, or risk the accuracy and completeness of the data. The training done at the ASTCs is considered critical to the safety of the military's future and current pilots and aircrew. Thus, the impact of our study to the training had to be minimal in that we would have to find a way to collect data without adding or taking away from the training in a significant way.

Environment aside, the challenge of tracking, recording, and synchronizing multiple variables had to be addressed. In the current research, trainees were encouraged to describe symptoms they were experiencing as they became aware of them. Additionally, instructors were asked to probe the trainees for their symptoms to ensure sufficient data collection. Using a traditional method, the researcher would be responsible for recording symptoms as they occur along with the reported severity, time of occurrence, time elapsed, et. In the event that multiple symptoms were being reported or observed the researcher would be hard pressed to capture every data-point. When collecting both subjective data via observation and physiological data via automatic monitors, timing is crucial to ensure the data can be appropriately synchronized after collection. In order to efficiently and accurately collect data in a time sensitive environment where multiple variables are being collected and monitored at the same time, it is essential to have a tool that enables the user to streamline this process. Simply put, traditional paper-based approaches to collecting data are impractical and reduce the amount and accuracy of data collected.

The solution presented by the authors is the creation of the Hypoxia Assessment and Recording Program (HARP) application. The HARP app was developed to enable researchers to track, streamline, and organize data for analysis. The HARP app is a dynamic web-based application designed to help track both subjective and physiological data related to aviation-based physiological events. It is expected that HARP will help facilitate data collection in both applied and laboratory settings while increasing efficiency and accuracy of the data collected. HARP's utility goes beyond this one study. HARP can be used to tackle one of the issues facing cross-disciplinary research, namely threats to internal validity (i.e., instrumentation). HARP provides a way to enable collection of synced-up objective and subjective data while strengthening internal validity of the data.

2   Methods

2.1   Front-End (User) Design

A web-based interface ensured the application's deployability on any platform capable of running a web browser or web view. Hardware required that DoD Windows 10 baseline serve as the host operating system in the current iteration. A single executable program launches a Chrome browser, which connects to a locally hosted Express server. When opened, the initial screen provides two toggle switches to choose from (i.e., slow or dynamic profile). Toggle buttons were chosen for ease of access and to let researchers be sure of which profile was chosen. The initial screen also contains a box to enter the participant identification number and proceed to data collection. After entering the participant data, the user is navigated to the main symptom recording screen. This main data collection screen of the application contains 21 selectable boxes for each symptom of hypoxia (i.e. air hunger, apprehension, belligerence, blurred vision, cold flashes, confusion, cyanosis, difficulty concentrating, difficulty speaking, dizziness, euphoria, fatigue, headache, hot flashes, lack of coordination, nausea, numbness, pressure in face, stress, tingling, twitching) four selectable boxes for each symptom severity levels, cancel, submit, and end boxes, a notes section, and a button to advance to the next stage in the profile. A dialogue box was placed at the bottom of the app that displays the current elapsed time, the last symptom and severity selected, and the time, altitude, and O_2 level when the symptom occurred. The main collection screen is used first by the researcher to collect symptomology data during a training event. At the conclusion of the event, the researcher ends the session and begins the recovery period. During the recovery period the screen opens a dialogue box informing the researcher the recovery period has begun and initiates a stopwatch function that is displayed for the user. Once the participant has recovered, as indicated by two thumbs up to the instructor, the user must click to end the recovery period and HARP will navigate back to the main collection screen where the participant will enter any symptoms they can recall.

2.2 Back-End Design

When running, HARP is capable of logging 21 unique symptoms while simultaneously tracking incoming data from a running profile. Two different profiles were programmed into HARP; slow and dynamic. The profiles come directly from the Reduced Oxygen Breathing Device (ROBD) used in hypoxia training. The slow profile gradually brings trainees up to a simulated altitude of 25k ft. over the course of ten minutes. The dynamic profile is programmed to bring trainees up to a simulated high altitude within two minutes and then hold them at that altitude. Training profile data in the data collection application is time stamped to be synchronous with the ROBD program. Changes in simulated O2 and altitude levels are reflected to the second. When designing how the exported data would appear, it was important to keep in mind the end-user (i.e., the researcher) of the data. All data reports were converted to.csv files to allow use in excel and formatted in two distinct ways. First, the data file was formatted to import in order of recorded symptom, severity of that symptom, simulate O2 level, time (elapsed seconds), and altitude at which the symptom occurred, any notes entered, and the actual time the symptom occurred. The first formatted data file displays as a list type and allows the user to have a broad overview of all symptoms that occurred for the participant. The second data file that is generated is formatted to match the database that was created for the specific statistical analysis software used in the research. By auto populating the data to match the created database, the time required to enter data into the statistics software is drastically reduced. All variables collected using HARP for a given training event are populated in rows versus columns so all the user needs to do is copy and paste the data into the statistical software database.

2.3 Design Methodology

The HARP team applied a top down design. The application needed to capture and export observed symptom data synchronized with the ROBD data in a CSV format. A touch-enabled interface was developed for ease of use and ubiquity of available platforms. Node, with its robust collection of middleware and uncomplicated deployment was a natural choice to handle the back-end web service and data processing. Once these systems were in place, stepwise refinement of each system contributed to the success of HARP.

3 Results

Creating HARP was a process whereby the engineer and end-user worked hand-in-hand during the creation and refinement processes. In lieu of a survey-based usability evaluation of HARP, the design team took an iterative approach to development. End-user feedback was integrated into each phase of development and refinement. The users relied on past literature [3–5] to formulate a heuristic guide for facilitating adequate usability. The heuristics used to guide development include graphic design and aesthetics, effectiveness of developmental characters, user efficiency, and consistency. The principles discussed here were considered in each iteration of HARP to simplify and coordinate the data being collected. The following describes each phase and the changes that were made as a result of user-based evaluations.

3.1 Phase 1

The original requirements for the program were to build a digital survey capable of tracking 21 symptoms of hypoxia (e.g., air hunger, dizziness, nausea, light-headedness) and associated severity of those symptoms on a four-point scale. Output from the survey were designed to be provided on a spreadsheet in tabular form. That is, symptom categories and severity would make up the columns of the spreadsheet making it easier to integrate and analyze later on. A mockup of the initial design of the program (See Fig. 1) was provided to the software engineer in order to start building the basic architecture of the program while the same mockup was also provided to the broader aviation physiological episode research community to attain functional and usability feedback. The community recommended the application also account for training profile (e.g., slow and dynamic), time, altitude and oxygen concentration. These same variables were also added to the spreadsheet.

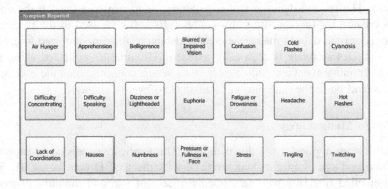

Fig. 1. Initial HARP configuration

3.2 Phase 2

After the completion of the initial application, HARPs functionality and usability were tested during a pilot event. A second mockup (See Fig. 2) was provided to the software engineer based on feedback from the broader research community and information collected during the pilot testing. This second iteration of the software focused mainly on functionality enhancements and less on usability. The aforementioned additional variables (i.e., profile type, time, altitude, oxygen concentration) were requested. These additions would enable the complete and accurate synchronization of variables of interest, which was crucial for guaranteeing the internal validity of the research.

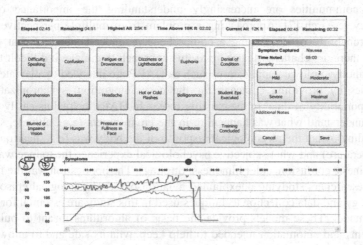

Fig. 2.   Secondary HARP mockup

3.3   Phase 3

The addition of the new variables had very specific implications for data exporting into the tabular spreadsheet. After the phase two iteration of the software the new variables were simply added to the spreadsheet in a specific order. For the purposes of the research it was crucial that symptoms were grouped by profile type, when they occur in the session, what altitude was being simulated, and what O_2 concentration the trainee was breathing. Ordering the data in this manner further improved the ability of the application to ensure the synchronization. In addition to improving synchronization, this feature also streamlined analysis. Organizing data output in such a manner enabled the researchers to match the format of the destination statistical software.

4   Discussion

The iterative process used for the development of HARP increased the likelihood that it would meet the objectives to complete our cross-disciplinary research on hypoxia. The resulting application's architecture could easily be adapted to any context in which there is a need to easily integrate and synchronize data. The outcome of this effort helped inform the design of a graphic-user interface used in a next generation hypoxia trainer. These trainers use many of HARP's design features and capabilities, which result in a richer, more meaningful debrief after training.

Human research is notoriously challenging. This is exacerbated when data are collected in applied settings. While the digitization of subjective survey-based data is not new, the need to collect that data and synchronize it with other variables (e.g., time, altitude, simulated O_2 level, profile) is of interest to researchers studying physiology and psychology simultaneously. The HARP application addresses a unique need. Research communities are increasingly understanding the importance of cross-disciplinary research [7]. Approaching a problem from multiple perspectives increases the probability of developing a comprehensive understanding of that problem. However, there are challenges specific to this approach that make it difficult to ensure internal validity. Software applications such as HARP are intended to alleviate some of these issues by providing a means for the easy integration, synchronization, and import/exportability of data. In the existing research, HARP helped us easily integrate and then understand what was happening in the environment (e.g., altitude, simulated O_2 level, time), what the physiological response of the body was (e.g., heartrate, breath rate, temperature) and what subjective psychological experience the trainee was having (e.g., dizziness, confusion, color blindness, tingling). The application was the first of its kind for researchers studying unexplained aviation-based physiological episodes. The methodology and data collection techniques used in this study are essential for building a causal model. These models provide the basis of algorithms meant to build future alert systems and automation intended to help keep aviators safe and to allow them to focus solely on their mission. Cross-disciplinary research is logistically challenging. Hence, the large-scale execution of this type of research is yet to happen. Capabilities such as HARP can overcome some of the logistical challenges of this research making it more likely to occur in the future.

References

1. Artino Jr., A., Folga, R.V., Swan, B.D.: Mask-on training for tactical jet aviators: evaluation of an alternate instructional paradigm. Aviat. Space Environ. Med. **77**, 857–863 (2006)
2. Seck, H.H.: Navy's T-45 fleet indefinitely grounded after pilot strike. https://www.military.com/daily-news/2017/04/09/navy-t45-fleet-indefinitely-grounded-after-pilot-strike.html. Accessed 19 Mar 2019
3. Nielsen, J.: Heuristic evaluation. In: Nielsen, J., Mack, R.L. (eds.) Usability Inspection Methods, pp. 25–62. Wiley, New York (1994)
4. Nielsen, J.: Enhancing the explanatory power of usability heuristics. In: ACM Computer Human Interaction (CHI) Conference, Boston, MA (1994)
5. Ravden, S.J., Johnson, G.I.: Evaluating Usability of Human-Computer Interfaces: A Practical Method. Halsted Press; Wiley, New York (1989)
6. Shneiderman, B.: Designing the User Interface: Strategies for Effective Human-Computer Interaction. Addison Wesley Longman, Reading (1998)
7. Pennington, D.D.: Cross-disciplinary collaboration and learning. Ecol. Soc. **13**, 8–20 (2008)

The Service Design of Medication Administration System Based on IoT

Xiu Fan Yang, Zhen Yu Gu[(⊠)], Rong Jiang, Dong Wang, and Cheng Hong Yang

Design Department, Shanghai Jiao Tong University, Shanghai, China
875883287@qq.com

Abstract. Medication is the most common way for patients to combat illness, and following the doctor's advice on taking medication has a tremendous impact on a patient's healing speed. But due to a variety of conditions, many patients' medication compliance is less than optimal, which will not only result in less effective treatment but also in a significant waste of medical resources. In addition, the medical system that is closely related to patients gradually exposes some problems in the process of social development. For example, the policy of benefiting nationals and people like medical insurance often gives some criminals opportunities to do something illegal. Han Zheng, party secretary of Shanghai, once said that it is necessary to push forward the reform and development of the city's health care system in a down-to-earth manner. The goal of this project is to design a new medical service system to solve the existing problems. An excellent service design should proceed from the overall situation of the society and emphasize the independence and initiative of design. Furthermore, it should seek for the possibility of building a better society and aim at maximizing the overall social benefits, while reducing total costs and creating new values. This is also the guiding principle of service design for this project. In addition to the design of the service system, the project also studied the design of user terminals, including a service terminal device for reminding users and monitoring user behavior, as well as a mobile App visualizing various information and facilitating user operations.

Keywords: Service design · Medical system · Medication compliance · Maximize social · Benefits

1 Introduction

The aging of population is one of the major problems facing all countries in the world. Middle-aged and elderly patients with chronic diseases have strong dependence on drugs, and their gradually declining memory and action ability makes it particularly difficult to adhere to normal medication [1]. Non-compliance with medication leads to increased incidence of chronic patients, reduced quality of care and unnecessary economic losses, such as excessive hospitalization, or higher drug treatment, etc. [2]. In addition, there are still some loopholes in drug regulation, resulting in a lot of waste and lawlessness. Illegal drug acquisition is absolutely not allowed by law, but the

© Springer Nature Switzerland AG 2019
C. Stephanidis and M. Antona (Eds.): HCII 2019, CCIS 1088, pp. 271–279, 2019.
https://doi.org/10.1007/978-3-030-30712-7_35

circulation of second-hand drugs is often seen in the market, which not only pollutes the environment, but also poses a serious threat to the life and health of patients.

By observing and recording users' behaviors on the spot, this paper finds out the existing problems, comprehensively understands users' life trajectory and is familiar with the operation process of different users in different environments. Due to service design will involve many aspects, so to interview for all aspects of the relevant personnel, understanding their needs, and in the interests of the various aspects situation, under the current system to consider under the new service system, whether the interests of all parties and losses in the acceptable range, for example, patients, hospitals and government aspects and so on. Finally, the service system in this project is summarized by using the service blueprint, and the steps of each user in the operation of the whole service system are analyzed, so as to clearly control the roles of the involved stakeholders in the process and contact points of the service system.

2   Related Work

At present, the health industry is getting more and more attention from the public all over the world, whether it is product and interaction design (such as E-pill and other reminder medicine boxes) or service design (such as Pillpack and other medicine packaging and distribution services). Medical experts have also come to realize that the patient's recovery process is inseparable from the monitoring and intervention of others (especially medical staff), so various institutions have begun to focus on the services and terminal devices for user monitoring. Intel has teamed up with Flex to develop a new Platform called the Health Application Platform for remotely monitoring patient activity. This telemedicine service can help doctors more accurately understand the medical needs of patients, and carry out targeted treatment, which can be more timely and scientific detection of the condition of elderly patients. Current related products and services mostly focus on individual reasons, lack of multi-dimensional system of user guidance and psychological driving mode and the overall macro service design, it is difficult to really effectively improve the user's medication compliance.

There is sufficient evidence to prove that cognitive function is related to adherence to medication. The most common reasons for non-compliance are forgetting, changeable medication schedule and busy life [3]. Many studies have proved that as people grow older, they are more and more prone to chronic diseases. At the same time, cognitive function is slowly experiencing problems (reaction speed, attention, working memory capacity, ability to accept new information and ability to retrieve information, etc.), which will lead to difficulty in taking drugs in full compliance with doctor's orders. [4] In addition, with the continuous increase of the course of the disease and the economic input of the patients, many patients will have negative emotions such as anxiety and depression, coupled with long-term physical discomfort, which will stimulate the patients' disappointment in the treatment process and further lose confidence in the recovery. Therefore, they treat the treatment passively, do not take medicine according to the doctor's advice, and neglect their care, thus forming a vicious circle. At present, most of the applications do not focus on reducing the treatment burden. They mainly focus on the problem of drug taking behavior rather than the patient's attitude to drugs. Drug administration is more important to communicate with doctors, understand the benefits and risks of treatment, and solve the treatment problems of patients. Many factors affecting poor medication compliance mean that only sustained coordinated efforts can ensure the best medication compliance and realize all the benefits of current therapy.

3 System Design

3.1 System Architecture

Figure 1 is the service blueprint of the project, showing the whole service system. The operation process of patients in this service is mainly divided into two parts:

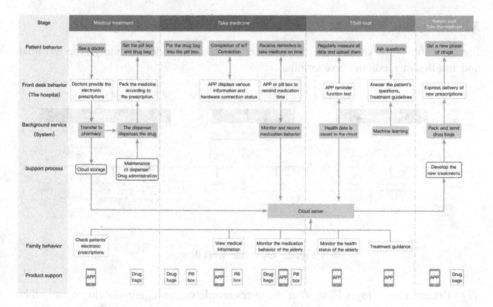

Fig. 1. Medication administration services blueprint.

(1) **The process of seeing a doctor and taking medicine.** First, the user registers in the system with real identity information, and then USES the identity certificate (ID card, medical insurance card, etc.) to register. After consultation, the doctor issues an electronic prescription, which is uploaded to the cloud server and bound with the patient's identity. At the same time, the prescription is transmitted to the pharmacy. According to the prescription information, the pharmacy uses the dispenser to package the single-dose drug package for the patient and connects them according to the order of taking. Finally, the user completes the payment for the medicine. If the smart medicine box is not equipped, the patient can receive the medicine for free. When receiving the medicine, the device ID will be bound with the user ID.

(2) **Daily medication.** First of all, the user will get a single dose of medicine from the hospital package list into the bag, then in the mobile terminal App using the identity information to complete the login, and paired with pill boxes, to implement the pill boxes, mobile phone App, the cloud server synchronization of information (number of prescribing information, drug medication, medication time, taboo, medication history, etc.), at this point, the standby working phase. When it's time to take the medicine, the smart medicine box and the mobile App will remind the user at the same time, and the smart medicine box will monitor and record whether the user takes the medicine. Finally, the system will record the number of remaining packets in the medicine box. When the amount is insufficient, it will ask whether the user needs to supplement. If so, the payment can be made online or through cash on delivery, and the medicine will be delivered to the user's home by express delivery.

3.2   User-Side Workflow

Figure 2 shows the overall operation process of the user-side, including App terminal and intelligent medicine box terminal.

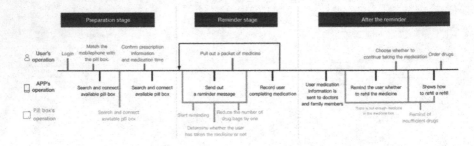

Fig. 2. User-side workflow

(1) **Preparation Stage.** First, after the user completes the registration/login and other operations on the App side, the next step is to pair and connect the smartphone medicine box. At this time, the method guidance for connection will be displayed in the App interface. After the connection is completed, the App and the smart medicine box will load the prescription information of the user from the cloud server.

Next, the App will display the loaded prescription information, and the user can check the information according to his/her own situation. After confirmation, he/she can check the reminder time set by the system automatically. If he/she is not satisfied with the set time, he/she can adjust it within a certain range. When everything is ready, App and smart medicine box will enter the working state and wait for the reminder time.

(2) **Reminder Stage.** When the alarm time set by the system is reached, the phone App and the smart medicine box will send out the alarm at the same time. The

App reminds users by the form of sound and popover. At the same time, the App interface provides the option of "delay taking medicine". Users can choose to take medicine after delay for a period of time (within a certain time range). The smart pill box USES sound and light to alert users.

(3) **Daily phase.** Users can check their medication history, know their medication compliance over a period of time (whether they take the medicine on time), and inform the user that this data will be shared with the attending doctor and their relatives, so as to urge users to take medicine on time according to the doctor's advice.

3.3   The Design of User Terminal Equipment: Smart Pill Boxes

As shown in Fig. 3, as the receiving box of medicine packets, the medicine boxes are made of hard plastic materials with clean color matching, which is more in line with the aesthetics of the elderly. The medicine box focuses on simplicity, pursuing minimalism in both structure and function. Minimize cost based on function implementation. After the elderly patient puts the medicine package into the medicine box, the APP can be connected for use. In this way, the terminal device can achieve all the functions required in the service with the simplest construction and the lowest cost, and provide users with simple and convenient operation experience.

Fig. 3. Hardware design

4   Experiment

This part mainly carries out usability test and evaluation for the drug administration service system. The international standard ISO 9241 defines usability as the effectiveness, efficiency and satisfaction of a specific user when using a product for a specific target in a specific usage scenario [5]. Satisfaction should be considered from a deeper level, and the effectiveness and efficiency of the user segment product evaluation of this topic should be evaluated by observing and recording the cognitive behavior of patients in the use of APP and the functional operation of the medicine box. Satisfaction involves users' subjective evaluation, so it should be collected through users' self-evaluation scale. The user experience scale used here was developed by Schrepp, Hinderks and Thomaschewski [6]. After the user experiences the service design proposed in this topic, the author will ask the user to fill in the user experience scale and collect the results.

4.1 Participators

In this study, the elderly and their families were recruited by random sampling method, and 4 elderly and 2 families were recruited. In order to ensure fairness and diversity, the specific screening conditions for the elderly are as follows: 1. Ranging from 60 to 75 years old; 2. Suffering from chronic diseases requiring long-term medication without other complications, taking medication more than twice a day; 3. Having the ability of listening, speaking, reading and writing; 4. Able to use smart phones.

4.2 Contents of the Evaluation

Before the design evaluation, as preparation for the experiment, the author installed "Daily Health" APP for the mobile phone of the elderly, connected the pill box and designed and packed their drugs according to the single-dose package proposed by the topic. Then let the elderly patients and their families use it for 3 days. After 3 days, questions and usability test results were collected from these patients while performing these tasks.

- Task 1: Use APP to browse the health report and diagnosis and treatment records (treatment plan and diagnosis and treatment information) of the product prototype.
- Task 2: Single-dose packaging and use of drugs for the elderly
- Task 3: Set medication time for the elderly, APP and medicine box remind patients to take medication.
- Task 4: Connect the medicine box for operation. APP and the medicine box will remind the patient to take the medicine together when the time for taking the medicine arrives.
- Task 5: Visualization of Health Plan Data
- Task 6: Family members of the elderly check the health report, diagnosis and treatment records and medication records of the elderly.

4.3 Results of the Evaluation

- Task 1: Use APP to browse the health files and diagnosis and treatment records (treatment plan and diagnosis and treatment information) of the product prototype.

Feedback: From the perspective of content, both elderly patients and their families expressed clear information structure, but doubted the authority and accuracy of the content. In addition, the contents of the health report need to be filled in manually, such as blood pressure value, blood sugar, etc. It is hoped that APP can also be connected with other intelligent blood pressure measuring instruments in the future to automatically fill in data.

Optimization: The content design specification of diagnosis and treatment information shall be formulated by medical experts. It is suggested to add the source after the treatment plan. In the future, the hardware connection of APP can not only connect medicine boxes, but also connect other smart medical equipment to provide more health data recording services.

- Task 2: Single-dose packaging and use of drugs for the elderly

Feedback: All subjects agreed with this single-dose packaging method. If the hospital provides this service, they will find it very convenient. However, some patients may only take 2 pills a day. It feels a bit wasteful to put 2 pills in one package.

Optimization: For those who take only a small amount of medicine, there is no need for single-dose packaging.

- Task 3: Set medication time for the elderly, APP reminds patients to take medication.

Feedback: APP reminds people to take medicine in a way that helps busy old people to remind them to take medicine. An old man said that toast's reminder is a little weak and sometimes not heard. In the active card punching behavior, younger elderly people will enter APP to enter the card punching after taking medicine. However, for some older people, they do not have the consciousness to clock in voluntarily.

Optimization: The current design is to remind the patient to take the medicine once every 5 min when the medicine taking time arrives, and not to remind the patient again until the user clocks in. The button on TOAST prompt frame guides the elderly patients to clock in.

- Task 4: Connect the medicine box for operation. APP and the medicine box will remind the patient to take the medicine together when the time for taking the medicine arrives.

Feedback: As a storage box, the medicine box can really make the medicine storage neater. Most patients said that sometimes the connection status of drug boxes was unstable, which affected the effect of monitoring data.

Optimization: Continue to explore more appropriate connection technologies and methods.

- Task 5: Visualization of Health Plan Data

Feedback: Patient data visualization is simple, but it is hoped that all individual data visualizations can be summarized into one page.

Optimization: The data visualization interface that won't make sense in the future will be integrated into one interface for display.

- Task 6: Family members of the elderly check the health records, diagnosis and treatment records and medication records of the elderly.

Feedback: The family members of the elderly said that the online prescription information is simple and easy to read. Seeing the prescription information remotely can make them know more about the illness of the family members. One patient expressed that he did not want to read only on the APP every time. In the future, medical information can be read through sharing WeChat.

Optimization: In the future design, patients can share the diagnosis and treatment records to WeChat.

Finally, after the evaluation experiment, the user experience usability questionnaire was collected from 6 subjects. The average score of each index of user experience is shown in Table 1.

Table 1. User experience testing result

User experience testing result	
Obstructive/supportive	4.2
Complicated/easy	3.8
Inefficient/efficient	4.2
Confusing/clear	4.3
Boring/exiting	4.3
Not interesting/interesting	5
Not innovative/innovative	5
Usual/leading edge	4.8

The usability test evaluation proves that the service design has certain practical significance. On the one hand, the service design integrates different ways to interfere with medication compliance and user experience strategies for the elderly, which can effectively improve the medication compliance of the elderly, and at the same time optimize the user experience of empty nest elderly patients in medication management.

5 Discussion and Conclusion

This paper defines the user-side products from the perspective of the architecture design and optimization of the whole service system to solve the problems of medication compliance and medication management, instead of designing only from a single product itself. Through the design and practice of medication management service design under the life style of the elderly, it is proved that this service design has certain practical significance. On the one hand, it integrates different ways of intervening medication compliance and user experience strategies for the elderly through service design to improve the medication compliance of the elderly. On the other hand, adjust and optimize the health service system, improve the quality of medical care, and realize the maximization of medical value through accurate treatment. However, due to the limited time, there are still some limitations in the research. I hope that it can be further improved and improved in the future research. In the further study of the influence of customized intervention on drug compliance, the needs of hospital medical staff must also be considered, and the needs of many groups must be explored. In the later stage of product development, interdisciplinary cooperation should be carried out with the artificial intelligence team to enhance the user experience goal.

References

1. Balkrishnan, R., Rajagopalan, R., Camacho, F.T., et al.: Predictors of medication adherence and associated health care costs in an older population with type 2 diabetes mellitus: a longitudinal cohort study. Clin. Ther. **25**(11), 2958–2971 (2003)
2. Lin, E.H., Katon, W., Von Korff, M., et al.: Relationship of depression and diabetes self-care, medication adherence, and preventive care. Diab. Care **27**(9), 2154–2160 (2004)
3. Fischer, M.A., Stedman, M.R., Lii, J., et al.: Primary medication non-adherence: analysis of 195,930 electronic prescriptions. J. Gen. Intern. Med. **25**(4), 284–290 (2010)
4. Insel, K.C., Einstein, G.O., Morrow, D.G., et al.: A multifaceted prospective memory intervention to improve medication adherence: design of a randomized control trial. Contemp. Clin. Trials **34**(1), 45–52 (2013)
5. Pielot, M., Poppinga, B., Heuten, W., Boll, S.: Tacticycle: supporting exploratory bicycle trips. In: Proceedings of the 14th International Conference on Human-Computer Interaction with Mobile Devices and Services, pp. 369–378. ACM (2012)
6. Schrepp, M., Hinderks, A., Thomaschewski, J.: Design and evaluation of a short version of the user experience questionnaire (UEQ-S). IJIMAI **4**(6), 103–108 (2017)

HCI in Business and Society

Affordable Rideshare Service for Female Urban Corporates in Developing Countries: A Case Study in Dhaka, Bangladesh

Nuren Abedin(✉), Kenji Hisazumi, and Ashir Ahmed

ISEE, Kyushu University, Fukuoka, Japan
nuren@f.ait.kyushu-u.ac.jp, nel@slrc.kyushu-u.ac.jp,
ashir@ait.kyushu-u.ac.jp

Abstract. This paper introduces a rideshare model for Small and Medium Enterprises (SMEs) and their employees for their daily commuting needs in emerging cities providing them with staff bus, SME corporate errand service, SME rental car and Holiday rental car services. The model offers a safe, more comfortable and affordable commuting service. We conducted experiment in two phases. In the first phase, we surveyed 315 employees of 20 SMEs located in Grameen Bank Complex about their traveling need and pattern. In the second phase, we designed a pilot from the gathered data and run 2 10-seat cars in two routes for 2 months with 18 participants from those SMEs. We conducted another survey end of the pilot regarding changes in travel experience while using SSW Staff bus service. We have discussed the experiment method and design and demonstrated the findings. We have also discussed affordability aspect of such ride share. SSW staff bus service is slightly expensive than local transports, but cheaper than commercial rideshare services. This service brings many benefits including adding approximately 7.7 h for work and 11.3 h for personal work s month to employees. Participants reported to enter work place with a stable mental condition when they travel by SSW Staff bus. Incidents like robbery, theft, accidents, sexual harassment could significantly be reduced.

Keywords: Rideshare · SMEs · Social adoption · Safe · Affordable

1 Introduction

Demand of mobility is changing with the increasing number of people more actively engaging themselves in economic activities. More women, people with disability and special needs are actively participating in the economic wave. Change in population demography in a city is bringing changes in commuting needs. Public transports in emerging cities like Dhaka, the capital of Bangladesh, are perceived unreliable and not safe due to substandard/poorly maintained vehicles, noise of vehicles, reckless driving etc. [1]. Long waiting time on road, multiple transfers, crowded vehicles and incidents like eve-teasing and harassment on fleet make them inconvenient, unsafe and uncomfortable for the passengers, especially female passengers. According to a study by Bangladesh Rehabilitation Assistance Committee (BRAC), 94% of women using public transportation in Dhaka, Bangladesh have experienced physical and verbal

C. Stephanidis and M. Antona (Eds.): HCII 2019, CCIS 1088, pp. 283–289, 2019.
https://doi.org/10.1007/978-3-030-30712-7_36

sexual harassment while travelling by public transportations [2]. Newly introduced ridesharing services are getting popular but are not affordable to commute to office every day. In our previous study, we introduced a new rideshare model called SSW (Social Services on Wheels) for rural communities [3]. In this paper, we propose a rideshare model for SMEs in emerging cities. Rideshare concept has been popular in a different form without using any demand-driven booking system. We propose to use ICT based rideshare management system for a community (not for an individual). In order to reduce the idle time of the vehicle and increase the revenue to be financially sustainable, multiple services are designed on SSW model. The services considered are: staff bus service, corporate errand service, car rental service for SMEs on weekdays and holiday car rental service for their employees. We carried out a survey on 315 employees in 20 SMEs to understand their mobility needs, attitude towards rideshare services, their commuting pattern including time, cost and distance. Based on their location data, available routes, we designed an experimental environment to run two cars in two different routes with two different sets of passengers. The duration of the pilot was for two months for 18 employees from different SMEs. At the end of the pilot, we surveyed on the passengers to know the mental status, time efficiency, safety issues and their desired fare for this service. The results are discussed in Sects. 4 and 5.

2 Social Services on Wheels (SSW) SME Model

The Social Services on Wheels (SSW) is designed to accommodate SME employees travel need while making it safer, more comfortable and affordable for them. The model is shown in Fig. 1 and the staff bus service pattern is shown in Fig. 2.

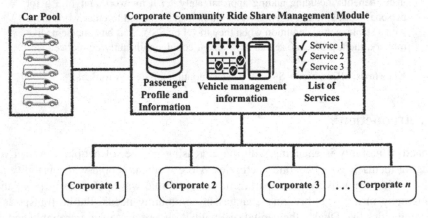

Fig. 1. SSW SME elements

Only providing the staff bus service creates long resource idle time, thus not generating sufficient revenue to sustain. Hence, we need to come up with new service ideas that can be operated during the idle hours. We designed two other services for SME commuting needs. One is a corporate errand shuttle bus service which multiple

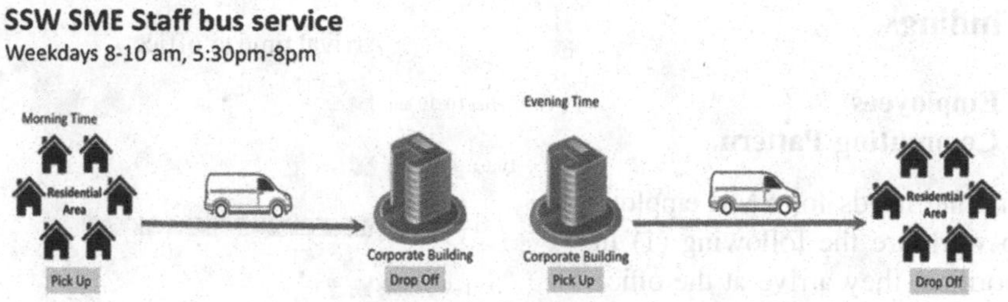

SSW SME Staff bus service
Weekdays 8-10 am, 5:30pm-8pm

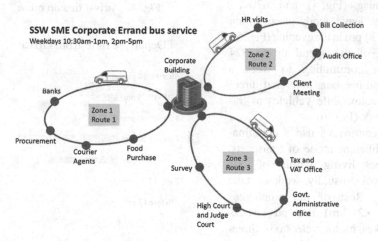

Fig. 2. SSW SME Staff bus service

SMEs can use to travel to the common destinations for completing their routine errand tasks (Fig. 3). Two other services are also designed which are - a rental service for SME companies and employees during holidays and weekends for office or personal work.

Fig. 3. SSW SME corporate errand service

3   Methodology of Experiment

This study was conducted in two phases. In the first phase, Survey-1 was conducted for collecting employees' commuting pattern, mode, expense, and attitude towards using rideshare to work among 315 people from 20 SMEs located in Grameen Bank complex, in Mirpur, Dhaka, Bangladesh. In the second phase, potential routes, passengers and cars were determined based on the information collected. Two 10-seated cars served as staff buses for 18 employee participants; one car for female participants only, and the other car for both male and female participants. Survey-2 was conducted during the pilot regarding impacts of using the Staff bus service on employees work and life.

4 Findings

4.1 Employees Commuting Pattern

Commuting needs for SME employees to work are the following (1) In the morning, they arrive at the office at a fixed time at a fixed place, but need to be picked up from different locations (2) In the evening, they leave from a specified location at almost a specified time but dropped off at different location.

71% of employees arrive their workplace from 9:30 to 10:00 am in the morning (Fig. 4) and 67% of employees leave work place within 5:30 to 6:30 pm in the evening (Fig. 5).

Most of the spend up to $24 USD for commuting to work a month and use bus, taxis and three-wheeler automobile vehicles to travel to work (Fig. 6).

The employees use a combination of different mode of transports. Employees living within of less 3 km (56%), usually walk or take rickshaw. Rest of the employees (>3 km, <21 km) use bus, Rickshaw, bikes, motorcycle, taxis, three-wheeler taxis and other forms of informal transports. Only a few of them use private or office cars.

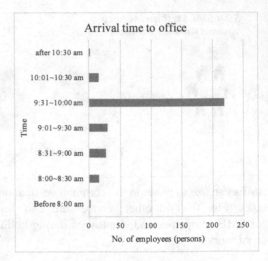

Fig. 4. Arrival time to office

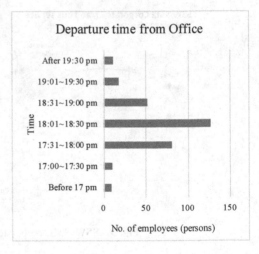

Fig. 5. Departure time from office

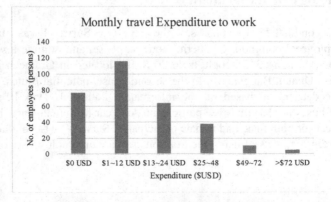

Fig. 6. Monthly travel expenditure to office

33.9% SME employees said that they would like to use rideshare service for commute to work and 59.1% would like to use such ride share for non-work purpose commute.

4.2   Traveling Experience with SSW

From Survey-2, it was found that participants in average reported to have 23 min extra work time and 34 min extra personal time when they traveled by SSW to work (Fig. 7).

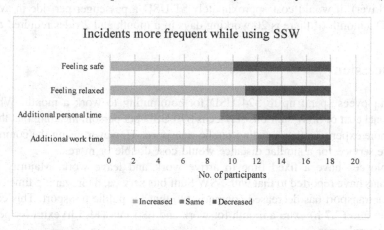

Fig. 7. Incidents more frequent while using SSW Staff bus

Participants were asked about their travel experience by SSW Staff Bus. Participants said the number of unpredicted incidents (such as losing belongings, robbery, theft), unwanted incidents (e.g. reckless driving, crowded vehicle) decreased significantly.

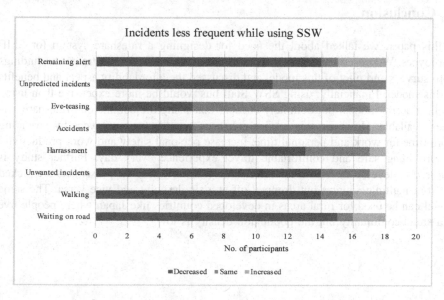

Fig. 8. Incidents less frequent while using SSW Staff bus

Participants reported to remain alert the whole time while using public transports, but this phenomenon significantly decreased while using SSW Staff bus (Fig. 8).

4.3   Operational Cost

From our estimation, it was found that a cost of $354 USD incurs for employing on 10-seated car on one route. If the car has 100% occupancy rate with 9 passengers (1 seat for the driver), it would cost approximately $1 USD a passenger per ride in average, $40 USD a month (if there is 20 working days in a month and 2 rides required a day).

5   Discussion

SME employees spend up to $24 USD for commuting to work a month. Whereas, Operational cost of SSW staff bus service is $40 USD per person, meaning that the staff bus is more expensive than existing public transports. However, using the commercial rideshare service for a similar distance would cost double or more.

Employees have a fixed time to arrive work and leave work. Majority of the participants have reported to that with SSW Staff bus service, their waiting time on road to avail a transport has decreased comparing to that for public transport. This can add up to 460 min (7.7 h) extra a month for work and 680 min (11.3 h) extra for personal work for employees.

We also found that SSW could enhance travel safety by reducing the possibility of accidents, unwanted incidents (robbery), harassment etc. to zero. Participants reported to reach in good mental status when used SSW to work.

6   Conclusion

In this paper, we talked about the need for designing a rideshare system for SME employees. We described SSW SME rideshare model. We demonstrated the findings from surveys and pilot of this model and discussed the affordability aspect and benefits of this model. Financially, using SSW Staff bus would be more expensive than using public transportations, but definitely cheaper that using the commercial rideshare services available. However, this service enhances benefits for employees by providing more time for work and personal time, increase personal safety and work productivity by providing safe and comfortable travel experience every day. Further study is required to develop the best route selection algorithm where the passengers are picked up from multiple sources but dropped off at a single point and vice versa. The same model can be used for rural areas in developed countries like Japan where people live in a small community but the population density is low.

References

1. Abedin, N., Kamau, J., Hossain, M.I., Maruf, R.I., Fukuda, A., Ahmed, A.U.: A case study to design a mobility as a service model for urban female corporates to improve their work performance. In: TENCON 2017 - 2017 IEEE Region 10 Conference, Penang, Malaysia, vol. 2017-December, pp. 1445–1450 (2017). https://doi.org/10.1109/tencon.2017.8228085
2. 94% women victims of sexual harassment in public transport. Article published on BRAC homepage on 25 March 2018. http://www.brac.net/latest-news/item/1142-94-women-victims-of-sexual-harassment-in-public-transport
3. Abedin, N., et al.: Providing safe and affordable transportation to reduce female students dropout: a case study on college girls in rural Bangladesh. In: 2016 IEEE International Conference on Systems, Man, and Cybernetics, SMC 2016 - Conference Proceedings, Budapest, Hungary, pp. 4130–4134 (2017). https://doi.org/10.1109/smc.2016.7844879

HCI Technologies in National S&T Master Plan of Korea

Changtaek Choi[(⊠)]

Korea Institute of S&T Evaluation and Planning, Seoul, South Korea
ctchoi@kistep.re.kr

Abstract. The Korean government establishes a S&T master plan to set the direction of national S&T policy every five years. It also suggests '120 Key Technologies' that need intensive investment and cultivation to create economic and social value at the national level. Technologies in the HCI field are also included as key technologies for improving quality of life and creating new industries. This paper analyzes the characteristics of HCI technologies in the national strategy, technology competitiveness, technology life cycle, etc., and also suggests policies that the government should implement first. The role of the government was classified into four categories considering the market and private capacity of the technology sector. Based on the classification, I introduced customized policy measures such as intensive investment, improvement of regulations, training of manpower. Different strategic directions have been derived depending on the characteristics of the technologies in HCI field. This study can be used as a basis for establishing R&D policy in HCI technology field in the future. It will also help to identify trends and levels of HCI research in Korea.

Keywords: S&T master plan · National strategy · Investment

1 Introduction

The Korean government establishes a 'Science and Technology Basic Plan', which is a mid- to long-term development strategy that sets goals and directions of S&T policy every five years. This is a top-level plan to be used as a basis for promoting S&T policies and R&D projects in each ministry. In addition to the policy tasks, the 'Science and Technology Basic Plan' also presents the '120 Key Technologies' that the government should foster to contribute to the resolution of national issues. These technologies are subject to national level evaluation of technology level and 'R&D survey'. It is also used as a base technology for establishing future growth engines and mid- and long-term investment strategies. 'Key Technologies' are linked to the future technologies of 'Science and Technology Foresight'. From the results of the science and technology foresight that derives future technologies that are expected to appear in the next 25 years, we derive the technologies to be fostered over the next five years.

'Key technologies' are the technology that is important for national investment and fostering with high economic and social value such as contribution to economic growth, job creation, and quality of life. It is selected based on comprehensive

© Springer Nature Switzerland AG 2019
C. Stephanidis and M. Antona (Eds.): HCII 2019, CCIS 1088, pp. 290–295, 2019.
https://doi.org/10.1007/978-3-030-30712-7_37

evaluation of economic and social contribution, technological contribution, techno-logical competitiveness, innovation of technology, and conductivity. They derive '120 Key Technologies' from 11 sub-categories and 43 sub-categories. These are linked to eight tasks, such as fostering innovative growth engines, fostering manufacturing industries and service industries, and creating a comfortable living environment.

Human-Computer Interaction is a field that focuses on effective methods to improve the interaction between computer system and users. Various studies are actively conducted in various disciplines such as computer graphics, design, ergo-nomics, industrial engineering, and psychology (1). In particular, HCI is not only a human-computer interaction, but also a leading factor in a wide range of changes in the academic domain, technology domain, and product·service domain. Therefore, the technologies of HCI field were selected as one of '120 Key Technologies'. Total of 13 HCI technologies are included in the '4th Science and Technology Plan' (2).

These are the categories of ICT·SW, Life science, Mechanical engineering and Construction. In this paper, I examine the HCI technologies included in the key technologies, and analyze their investment trends, research subjects, and R&D types. In addition, technologies have been classified into four categories based on technological competitiveness and industrialization rate that have been secured while selecting key technologies. Policy directions and policy issues to be pursued by the government according to the classification.

2 Approach

The data such as investment trends and type of R&D of 'Key Technologies' are obtained from 'National R&D Survey and Analysis' (3). The key technologies are surveying the status data of investment, subject, and technology characteristics at the research project level every year through national-level R&D survey.

In this study, data on investment amount, type of R&D for each year are analyzed for the results of four years from 2014 to 2017. It was conducted a questionnaire survey to investigate the characteristics of technologies (4). Through this, data on economic and social contribution, technological competitiveness and industrialization rate of key technologies have been obtained and detailed analysis has been carried out. The questionnaires were given to 2181 researchers in Korea (4).

According to the domestic private competitiveness of HCI technologies and the speed of industrialization, four kinds of technologies are classified. The characteristics of the technologies in each category were examined. This led to the policy issues that each technology needed.

3 Results

HCI Technologies in '4th Science and Technology Basic Plan' are presented in of ICT·SW, Life science, Mechanical engineering and Construction. In the field ICT·SW, 'Virtual and mixed reality technologies', 'Intelligent content creation technologies', 'NUI/NUX', and 'Realistic broadcasting and media service technologies' were presented. In particular, 'Intelligent content creation technologies' was first presented in the 4th Science and Technology Basic Plan (Table 1).

Table 1. HCI technologies in '4th Science and Technology Basic Plan'

S&T categories	S&T division	Key technologies
ICT·SW	Contents	Virtual and mixed reality technologies, Intelligent content creation technologies, NUI/NUX, Realistic broadcasting and media service technologies
ICT·SW	Display	User-friendly display technologies
ICT·SW	BigData and AI	Intelligent analysis and application of Bigdata
Life sciences	Bio fusion and convergence	Digital healthcare technologies, Medical robotics
Life sciences	Brain science	Brain signal monitoring and modulation technologies
Life sciences	Medical devices	Technologies for the assistive devices to help with rehabilitation and daily activities
Mechanical engineering	Robotics	Adaptive service robotics, Robotic technologies for rescue and exploration
Construction and transportation	Construction	Smart home technologies

'Smart Home technologies', 'Adaptive service robotics', and 'Robotics technologies for rescue and exploration' were suggested in the fields of Mechanical engineering and Construction. In the field of Life sciences 'Digital healthcare technologies', 'Medical robotics', and 'Technologies for the assistive devices to help with rehabilitation and daily activities' were suggested.

3.1   Investments and Type of R&D of HCI Technologies

In HCI technologies, 'Big Data technologies' is the most invested, and investment is increasing rapidly. On the other hand, HCI part in 'Big Data Technologies' is part of utilizing personal big data and life log data, but it is difficult to grasp the accurate investment amount of these. In second place, investments were made in 'Brain signal monitoring and control technologies' and 'Adaptive robot technologies'. 'Intelligent content creation' and 'Virtual and mixed reality technologies' have also increased investment (Fig. 1).

Experimental development is the largest R&D type, followed by basic research. Recently, in Korea, the government has invested heavily in basic research, which is difficult for the private sector to invest. In the same way, the HCI technologies field shows the increase of basic research and the decrease of development research in 2017 (Fig. 2).

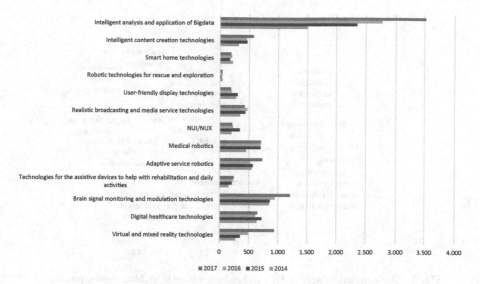

Fig. 1. Investment of HCI technologies (2014–2017), billion won

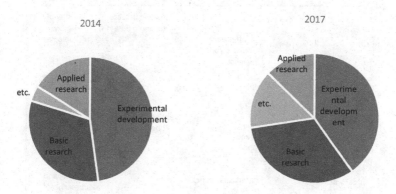

Fig. 2. R&D type of HCI technologies (2014, 2017)

3.2 Technical Characteristics of HCI Technologies

HCI technology competitiveness was highest in 'Smart home' and 'User friendly display technologies'. In the other hands, 'Assistive technology' and 'Medical robot technologies' were the lowest. The competitiveness of the private sector and public technology is in proportion (Figs. 3 and 4).

I distinguished the technologies of HCI in terms of private technology competitiveness and industrial maturity. There are 'User-friendly display', 'Digital healthcare technologies' in the field of high private technology competitiveness and fast industrialization (Type 1). Robot technologies such as 'Service robots' and 'Medical robots' were common in the field (Type 2) where private competitiveness was low and industrial maturity was low. 'Virtual and mixed reality' and 'Realistic broadcasting

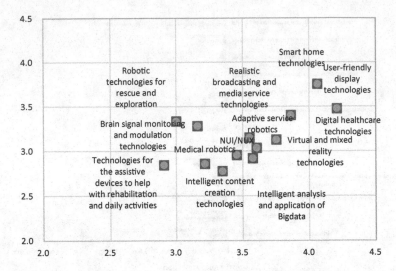

Fig. 3. The competitiveness of HCI technologies (x-axis, public, y-axis, private)

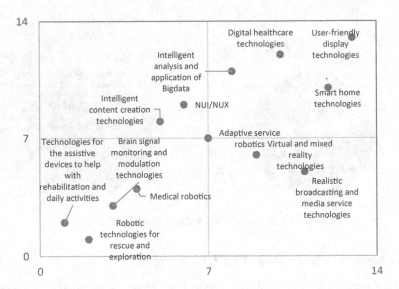

Fig. 4. Type of HCI technologies according to private technology competitiveness (x-axis) and industrial maturity (y-axis)

technologies' had high private competitiveness, but the industrialization rate was slow, so it will take time for the market to form (Type 3).

4 Conclusion

Through the 'National R&D Survey and Analysis' data on the research projects that the government invests annually, I confirmed the investment and R&D type of the HCI technologies for the past four years. Investment in HCI technologies is on the rise. Especially, big data field is increasing.

In terms of private technology competitiveness and industrial maturity, it is necessary to provide other policy support depending on the technology characteristics. In the case of Type 1, which has a rapid technological competitiveness and rapid industrialization, the government needs to play an auxiliary role such as regulation improvement and manpower training so that the government can generate performance in the market rather than R&D investment. On the other hand, in Type 2, where the private technology competitiveness and industrialization rate are all low, the government needs to actively expand R&D investment. Finally, in the case of Type 3, which has high private competitiveness but is not yet rapid in industrialization, it can play a role of forming an initial market such as public purchasing to promote industrialization.

HCI technologies are key technologies for future products and services, and contribute to economic growth and quality of life. Therefore, in this study, the status and characteristics of the HCI technologies covered in the 'Science and Technology Basic Plan' of Korea were examined. Future technology development strategies were examined. In the future, it will be necessary to examine the technology development strategy of a particular HCI technology, and examine the direction of investment in government R&D through analysis of relevant industry status.

References

1. Jenny, P.: Human-Computer Interaction. Addison-Wesely, Boston (1994)
2. 4th Science and Technology Basic Plan (2018)
3. National R&D Survey and Analysis (2018)
4. Study on the development of national strategy technology to establish future promising technology acquisition strategy
5. The 5th Science and Technology Foresight (2017)
6. NTIS.go.kr

Transforming a Specialized Q&A System to a Chatbot System: A Case of a Simplified Taxation in Korea

Jihye Jang[1] and Keeheon Lee[2,3(✉)]

[1] Graduate School of Communication, Yonsei University, Seoul,
Republic of Korea
[2] Underwood International College, Yonsei University, Seoul,
Republic of Korea
keeheon@yonsei.ac.kr
[3] Graduate School of Information, Yonsei University, Seoul, Republic of Korea

Abstract. In this paper, we propose a way to transform traditional Q&As into conversational Q&As for an efficient information retrieval in special knowledge. Special knowledge involves difficult words. It requires users to raise a series of questions and get the answers to them to pinpoint the desired information. And, conversational Q&A is appropriate than the traditional Q&A because it allows a user to narrow down searches in a solution space. To transform a given set of Q&As to conversational Q&A system for special knowledge search, we first explore not only the present traditional Q&A systems and conversational Q&A systems for general knowledge search, but also those for special knowledge search. From this, we induce an appropriate search process in conversational Q&A systems for special knowledge. Secondly, we build an ontology with the help of machine learning to support the navigation in special knowledge. Finally, we give a way to evaluate performance after embedding the ontology on our search process of conversational Q&A. We apply this procedure to the case of Korean simplified taxation in a Korean Q&A system, Naver Jisik-In Q&A. We found that searching through Jisik-In Q&A with ontology has better usability than using Jisik-In Q&A only. Therefore, this study aims to improve the usability of special knowledge search, lower the threshold of special knowledge, and develop special knowledge as general as common knowledge using conversational Q&A based on ontology. However, as the number of user experimented is limited and the classifier for the extracted words from existing Q&A system should be reviewed by tax expert, so the future work is demanded.

Keywords: Transformation · Conversational Q&A · Search behavior · Ontology · Special knowledge

1 Introduction

People retrieve necessary information by sending a specific query term or phrase that becomes a starting point to a search engine to fetch the relevant documents that may contain necessary information. However, it is difficult for users to pick the most

© Springer Nature Switzerland AG 2019
C. Stephanidis and M. Antona (Eds.): HCII 2019, CCIS 1088, pp. 296–308, 2019.
https://doi.org/10.1007/978-3-030-30712-7_38

relevant query term or phrase to the necessary information that users want [1]. On the other hand, a Q&A system where users can participate in raising questions and answering to the questions collectively, narrows down the search scope but has the same problem as the other search engines still. The problem is that the users must send a search term or phrase to the system and get the relevant answers iteratively until users discover necessary information. Even worse, if the search term or phrase is somewhat irrelevant, the users have to perform many iterations of sending possible queries to search engines. When the desired information involves special knowledge rather than general knowledge, the number of iterations tends to get larger, facing unfamiliar words which we cannot imagine. Additionally, Q&A systems are unable to let users narrow down the possible answers iteratively and it results in low satisfaction, low accurate answers, and long time to get a satisfactory answer. To improve user experience on having satisfactory answers to a question in expert domain, it is necessary to have an alternative way to search the desired information, which can simplify the search process, and get the correct answer using easy words.

One alternative is a conversational Q&A system that allows users to nail down solution search space along with a series of queries. Conversational system is a service that can communicate with computer or artificial intelligence in natural language and has an interactive structure the system can ask user first, which is not only user can ask, like chatbot. Since conversational system like chatbot to date have mainly focused on conversations that have been set up during development, conversations with the system are limited [2]. Conversational Q & A is where user can ask questions and get answers in the form of words or phrases in conversation. In particular, as the scope of information retrieval is limited in conversational Q&A system, they may not get the answer easily if they do not enter keywords that chatbots or other conversational system can understand.

In order to overcome the difficulty of this information retrieval and limitations of existing conversational system and Q&A system, we propose conversational Q&A system through chatbot in this study.

Our case is Jisik-In which is Q&A system in Naver which is the largest portal site in Korea and has a search engine. The service that makes Naver become a national portal site is Q&A service called Naver Jisik-In, and up to now, there are 320 million responses on Naver Jisik-In. Jisik-In takes the form of a community forum where the user asks and answers the. To construct the conversational Q&A in this study, we extract, analyze, and classify information and articles in Jisik-In to create an ontology that shows what the user is asking about a particular topic and which words to use for the question.

In this study, we show how to transform expert Q&A system to a chatbot system in case of a simplified taxation in Korea. The simplified taxation was designed to reduce the hassle of tax payment by considering that small businesses do not have the capability for tax affairs or to hire tax experts. Otherwise approximately 35,000 questions about simplified taxation have come up on the dominant expert Q&A system, Jisik-In. In other words, although it has tried to provide convenience by allowing the small business to handle tax tasks itself, there are situations in which it is unavoidable to suffer another inconvenience for this convenience. So, it can be expected that if the required information can be conveniently and easily delivered to small businesses to carry out their own tax affairs, they can reduce the cost and mental burden of taxation of small businesses. Therefore, we aim to design a query response system using a ontology based chatbot for the purpose of improving usability to obtain desired information easily and conveniently in the field of specialization.

2   Literature Review

2.1   Information Search Behavior

First, we need to know what information retrieval procedures users have to search for information. The Information Search Process (ISP) is a structured activity that extracts knowledge and information that enables users to solve problems they may have [3]. From the user's point of view, the information retrieval process is said to be able to integrate with the user's situation to improve the efficiency of solving the problem [4]. To summarize, the search process is a procedure in which users get information efficiently to solve their problems.

Information Search Behavior (ISB) is a set of behaviors that users take to find information, and there are very diverse patterns, but only a few of them are suggested to be used [5]. It is also thought of as a search strategy, which is the act of finding clues about information to find the information that the user wants. And this search behavior in the domain knowledge is different from search behavior in general knowledge [6]. However, rather than being based on the information search behavior of users, the search engines that conduct such information search are more like those that organize information according to keywords, number of views, and so on. Therefore, it is necessary to identify what information people are searching for and what they are most interested in, and to optimize the information search behavior of users based on this information.

2.2   Ontology

Chatbot is a chatting program that makes you feel like you are talking to people and is actively used in areas such as customer service and entertaining service. It also serves as a kind of search engine, the most common way being a keyword-based or optional interactive chatbot that is specialized to expert information. Chatbot is a substitute for a search engine that can shorten searching time and acquire accurate and specific information while simplifying search behaviors in order to look for desired information in the sea of massive information. But owing to the feature of rule-based, chatbot has limitations including knowledge representation, information retrieval and dialogue capabilities which is that it gives to user what it knows only [7].

Ontology is a way to make people understand and read easily with well-defined meanings [8]. Thus, rather than simply being entered programmatically, the language itself is information that people can understand and read. Chatbots are designed to allow people to communicate with artificial intelligence in a natural language. Many chatbots are designed on the basis of ontology, because, to communicate with people, they need to be expressed and typed in the language of the people, which can increase the efficiency of organizing conversations. Recently, it has been proposed to convert unstructured data into an ontology, and a chatbot based on it. It seems to be able to complement the limitations of existing rule-based chatbots. Especially we focused on the conversations about special knowledge.

Ontology in AI community is often regarded as specification of conceptualization [13, 14]. And it is based on the understanding of people about the specification and conceptualization of a specific concept, word or phrase, so that the exact meaning can be derived, and ontology exists for this [15]. In other words, it is necessary to distinguish concepts that are used for special knowledge or terminology depending on how people understand specific concepts in common, and it is the ontology that can connect special knowledge to concepts that people commonly understand. In addition, semantically composed Q&A system could have flexible search environment [26]. Therefore, we propose that conversational Q&A is designed to be based on an ontology that can understand people's common expertise.

2.3   Evaluation for Searching Through Ontology

There have been many evaluations of information search procedures through chatbots or search engines. One study proceeds usability evaluation for Dave and four other chatbots in linguistics. Another study suggests ways to improve the user experience and satisfaction, then to personalize the user by chatbot [27, 28]. In addition, other study suggests a tailored usability theory to evaluate the decision model of ontology [29]. But there has been no evaluation of information retrieval based on ontologies before. Since the ontology can be developed as an interactive Q&A system, it is necessary to continuously evaluate the ontology itself and apply feedback derived from the user to develop it. In this study, ontology will be used for user evaluation because it can affect information retrieval behavior to optimize user information search procedure.

3   Methods

In this study, we first review search behaviors of Q&A based on the present search engines and conversational Q&A based on chat bots in both general and special knowledge. Through a systematic review on the relevant literature and services, we categorized the type of search behavior according to search engine and conversational Q&A for common knowledge and special knowledge. Then, we induce the search behavior that necessary for conversational Q&A on special knowledge. And then, we introduce a method of human and machine collaboration to transform the present Q&A into conversational Q&A on special knowledge. In this method, we build an ontology of special knowledge using accumulated human knowledge and automated relation extraction. We use the traditional category system of the special knowledge as well as an automated semantic relation extraction from the words building the special knowledge based on word2vec. And then, a coder draws a skeleton of an ontology using the traditional category system and adds flesh to the skeleton by mapping important words related semantically to the words in the skeleton. In this study, we apply our method to a popular Korean Q&A system, Naver Jisik-In. We add the ontology to the induced conversational Q&A process to make user search specific parts of special knowledge efficiently and effectively. Lastly, we evaluate our conversational Q&A with an experiment that gives users two search options and compares usability between the two options. The two options are searching special knowledge through Jisik-In only and Jisik-In with the ontology.

3.1   Types of Information Search Behavior

One study examined the time and behavioral moves involving finding knowledge using online methods [5]. In other study, they compared information seeking behavior between experts and non-experts. As a result, there was no difference between general topics and general search engines, but not in professional areas [9]. And commonly, the factors that determine the user's search engine are the reputation of the search engine, the effectiveness, the familiarity with the search engine, or the usability of the interface [22].

In this study, user behavior for information retrieval will be divided into four types. The criteria for classification are divided into the search engine and the conversational Q&A regarding to interface, and also divided into common knowledge and special knowledge regarding to domain of knowledge. Special knowledge is regarded as expert knowledge, which is information about a specific topic that is not universally known to many people [16]. Therefore, expert interpretation or opinion is needed, and this special knowledge is obtained through training, skills, and research [17, 18]. Common knowledge could be regarded as public knowledge and derived from a kind of social consensus. In addition, it is a fundamental concept used in everyday interactions between people [19].

Here, the search engine includes a portal site and a web search, and in particular, a Q & A system belonging to a portal site Naver is also classified as a search engine. Conversational refers to the interaction of a conversation that helps people talking to them, talking like them through text or voice [20]. The role of the conversation here lies in clarifying what the user wants, to help the user [21]. Conversational Q & A refers to ontology-based chatbots proposed in this study.

Type A is a type that searches general knowledge through existing search engine, and searches again to retrieve appropriate terms or add terms. That is a typical narrowing search. It is the most common type of ISB using common search engine (Google, Naver). However, since this method varies from time to time, it would not be guaranteed that finding the same information will yield the same result. One study has suggested that hierarchical term decomposition is considered necessary in search behavior [10]. In other words, it refers to a method of predicting a desired keyword through an upper and lower relationship between terms, and type A may be included to this. One study suggests that user who commonly use yahoo and keyword search, took less time to finish specific task in conducting known-item searches than in unknown-item searches [23]. Simply, imagine googling 'awesome house', comparing to search 'what to write on the contract paper of house'.

Type B is a type of finding special knowledge through a common search engine. One study suggests that finding special knowledge seems to influence finding the appropriate words for people [11]. Therefore, to search for special knowledge, you need to be able to pick out the search words that will produce relevant results for your special knowledge. However, there are also some ironies that need to know jargon to search for special knowledge. For instance, when medical students were looking for data on microbiology, they added concepts and gradually narrowed down the concept to continue specifying the concept [6]. Also, in the most common pattern, M.A students often find information in a way that broadens or specifies the dimension [24]. Following above, academic searching such as looking for appropriate literature in specific domain could be one of type B examples. Or finding a legislation which could be applied to specific case, using search engine of public web of judicial authority would be type B, either.

Type C is a type that finds general knowledge through Q&A chatbot. Nowadays, it mainly focuses on chatbots that provide information on a specific topic. However, as it is about a specific topic, the information that can be found through chatbot is limited, so if you enter the routine term in this way, it could be possible that you will not find the information you want. As the example of type C, SuperAgent which is customer service chatbot of Amazon.com provides product information, customer Q&A [25]. Through Chatbot of SkyScanner, user can do ticket search which is the key features such searching the cheapest ticket.

Type D is a conversational Q & A chatbot based on ontology proposed in this study. It is a type that deals with professional knowledge. Through Naver Jisik-In Q&A system, we propose an ontology composed of extracted words from the most frequently asked questions and answers, then an interactive Q & A based on them. According to this process, conversational Q&A could satisfy what people would ask most about specific knowledge. There are some examples of conversational Q&A system in expert domain. For instance, TEBot has selective type of Q&A system about Big Data, and the questions are like 'How do we compare Kafka to Flume' or 'How do we compare RDBMS to NoSQL Databases'. Law Soup's chatbot has Q&A system about law and the question we can ask could be 'What laws protect free speech?'. 'Do I have rights to content I create and put on the internet?'.

3.2 Ontology Based on Q&A

The search strategy for retrieving and getting information depends on the search method and the search target. In this chapter, we search in the Q&A system from search engine and conversational Q&A system as general knowledge and special knowledge. We can see what processes users take to search and take action, then organize search strategies with search behaviors. Also, in selecting the retrieved information, it is possible to know what information is taken and what information is excluded by users.

We use Naver Jisik-In Q & A system to find out what users want to know about specific special knowledge and what questions they frequently ask. When users post articles on Naver Jisik-In Q & A system, they explain their situation and ask the answerer for the correct answer. Therefore, the situations are different but the same answer is often posted for different questions. That is, there are frequently asked questions by users, and the way to present them to users in the order of frequently asked questions can shorten the user's search behavior.

1. **Data Crawling.** In this study, the purpose of the ontology is to create a Q&A chatbot for special knowledge, so first we had to find out what people are curious about a particular keyword. Therefore, we crawled 10,000 questions and answers with keyword of simple taxation from Naver Jisik and segment them into corpus. Then, remove the stopwords among the collected morphemes and words.

2. **Extracting Keywords.** Then, we extract the top 500 words that appear frequently among the collected corpuses. The purpose of this is to present the question to the user by the important keyword. Also, in order to investigate the connectivity between words, 10 words closest to each of the extracted 500 words were extracted by using Word2Vec. By using Word2vec, it is possible to estimate the distance to all the words related to a specific word in multidimensional rather than to gradually approach the limited words associated with the one-way cognitive and thought processes of human, so the multiple words can be extracted at once. In other words, through associative methods that go beyond human cognitive and thought processes, we derive more relevant words before humans do. As a result, it can play a role of artificial intelligence that progresses the most basic human association process endlessly and multi-dimensionally, but achieves more results faster than humans.

3. **Connecting Keyword.** Then, create a keyword map that categorizes ranges that have been sorted under the tax law. The centralized vocabularies are included in the upper category. And link the tax terms extracted from the tax law with the vocabulary corresponding to the upper category. This creates a kind of small network. In Fig. 1(p.4), the vocabulary in the bold box belongs to the upper category in the tax law, and the contents in the box with the thin line are the main words extracted from the contents of the tax laws regulations and the above process. Here, the main words belong to the most frequently used words, or vocabularies that simultaneously satisfy both the vocabulary words and tax law terms.

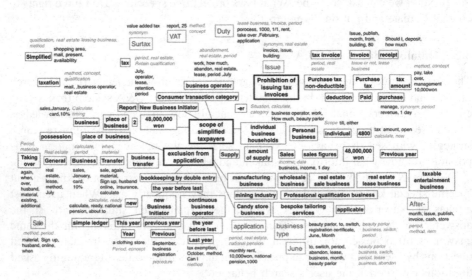

Fig. 1. Ontology

4. **Categorizing corpus.** Once again in this category network, the extracted top 500 terms and the words associated with each term are placed. By determining where each term belongs to on the map, terms would be categorized and sorted to each range. So the map shows the link and status of adjacency between the words.
5. **Identifying corpus.** On this step, the word or corpus which are outside the box in Fig. 1 were classified into 'what', 'how', 'when', 'situation', 'conception', 'type of business', 'analogue'. These words identify what other words mean in the context of questions and answers. For example, 'what' covers what the user is trying to find or say about including 'conversion', 'abandonment', and 'bill'. 'How' indicates the method of the subject in the information that the user wants to know including 'how', 'calculation', 'imposement rate', and 'method'. 'When' suggests whether the time is contained in the information that the user desire, including 'time', 'when' and 'period'. 'analogue' matches words that have a similar meaning to the suggested word including 'revenue – income', 'supply price – sales'. It should be noted here that most of the users do not use revenue and income separately. 'Type of business' is the type of industry in which the user is engaged or the assumption of the type of industry the user might be engaged in according to the information desired, including 'real estate business' and 'hairstyling'. 'Concept' is the type of information the user wants to ask, such as 'application scope', 'issue or not' and 'whether'.

3.3 Evaluation Simulation

Also, for evaluating the usability of conversational Q&A system, it is needed to compare the usability evaluation of the searching special knowledge through Jisik-In only and Jisik-In with the ontology to numerically show the change in the usability actually felt by the users. There are seven indicators in the honeycomb model of Peter Mobile that can be used for usability test [12]. As shown in Table 1, the indicators of honeycomb model are 'useful', 'usable', 'desirable', 'findable', 'accessible', 'credible', and 'valuable'. 'Useful' asks whether to be faster than existing the searching method, 'usable' asks whether to be easy to search for information you want, 'desirable' asks to be willing to use the searching method, 'findable' asks whether to be able to find the desired function, 'accessible' asks whether there is many ways to use such the searching method, 'credible' asks whether to trust the search interface and 'valuable' asks to be satisfied with the searching method. It is necessary to investigate later whether ontology - based chatbots are more efficient than traditional chatbots and provide empirical value to humans.

4 Result

This study investigates the search behavior of ontology based chatbots comparing with the existing search methods such as search engines and existing chatbots. In chatbot which is based on the ontology below, when a user inputs a routine term, professional vocabularies would be suggested which are related to the routine term input first, and when the user selects a professional vocabulary. In summary, when a user enters a

Table 1. Contents of usability test

Indicator	What to ask
Useful	Is it faster than existing search engine?
Usable	Is it easy to search for information you want?
Desirable	Are you willing to use the conversational Q&A based on ontology?
Findable	Is it easy to find the desired function?
Accessible	Is there many ways to use this kind of search method?
Credible	Do you trust the information this searching method gives you?
Valuable	Are you satisfied with the searching process?

routine term, professional vocabularies would be suggested which are related to the routine term input first, and when the user selects a professional vocabulary, secondarily, the selected term is automatically completed. Then questions including the selected terminology are suggested so user can pick one which he/she looks for. We are showing the difference between types of search behavior using search engine and conversational Q&A for common knowledge and special knowledge. Following user's search behavior, we identify and organize what actions the user takes to initiate until ending the search.

4.1 Comparison of ISB According to Types

Type A (search engine for common knowledge) and B (search engine for special knowledge). First, user asks questions and finds the keywords associated with him. Assuming that the word user input is a common term, it is necessary to switch to terminology. Therefore, the search engine is used to look for the keyword to convert it into a legal tax term. You can browse through the search for the appropriate terminology, and use multiple search engines in the process. After obtaining the appropriate terminology, the user input the terminology to search through search engine. Again, we filter and narrow down the information we want to obtain and find the answer we want. In summary, type A follows steps of putting routine word, searching and looking up and down to get common knowledge user wants and type B follows steps of putting routine word, searching for analogue or synonym, converting to terminology, putting as terminology and looking up and down to find special knowledge.

In this process, of course, there may be differences according to the field of knowledge or people, but it is more complicated, time consuming, and it is not easy to obtain the information that you want, even if in the case of the general and common procedure for searching routine knowledge. In other words, productivity and efficiency of search behavior is relatively low. This research suggests chatbot as an alternative to solve the inefficiency of this search behavior.

Type C (conversational Q&A for common knowledge) and Type D (conversational Q&A for special knowledge). In general, the most common search behavior of conversational Q&A can be divided into two types. The first method is a system that can receive an immediate answer by inputting a common term or general sentence. The other is a system to select the category according to the question to be found and to input the appropriate vocabulary to get the answer. In summary, type C follows steps of putting routine word or sentence and looking up and down or, choosing categories, putting routine word and looking up and down to get the information user wants. However, Q&A chatbots so far have not been able to get the answers if the keywords are not included in the dialogs set by the developers of chatbots, or they have questions to ask for chatbots to understand.

Special knowledge conversational chatbot should go through the search behavior in the chatbot with the general knowledge. The search behavior of chatbots for special knowledge search can also be divided into two ways. First, when the user enters a routine term, the user selects an appropriate vocabulary from among the jargon related to the proposed routine term, searches and selects the questions listed in the order frequently asked by the Jisik-In including the terminology. The second is to list the terminology which the user already knows or sentences containing these terms, and if the questions from Jisik-In, including vocabularies input, are presented in order of frequency, the user selects the appropriate questions and obtains immediate answers. In summary, type D follows steps of putting routine word, looking up and down, selecting terminology and looking up and down again or, putting terminology and looking up and down to get special knowledge user wants.

Type B (search engine for special knowledge) and Type D (conversational Q&A for special knowledge). Let us consider the case where the user searches for special knowledge using routine terms only, then compare the case of searching in Jisik-In only and the case of searching in Jisik-In with the presented ontology. If you look at the procedure for retrieving terminology from Jisik-In, you will take a look at the synonyms from searched common terms for the conversion to specialized knowledge after searching. It is possible to divide into 2cases also. The case of finding the proper terminology and the case of failing finding the proper terminology. In the case of finding the terminology, the user searches the terminology again and searches the results retrieved in the terminology. If you could not find it, may use the category settings to narrow down the questions you are looking for and then repeat the process of browsing the results. When Jisik-In is used with an ontology, the terminology associated with the term is presented in order of frequency, and when the terminology is selected, the related questions are presented in order of frequency. The user first looks up frequently searched questions and searches for appropriate information. In summary, user follows steps in order of search behavior of putting routine word, searching for analogue or synonym, converting to terminology, inputting as terminology and looking up and down or putting routine word, searching for synonym, failing to convert to terminology, narrowing down using categories and looking up and down to get special knowledge through Jisik-In only. Also, user who uses Jisik-In with ontology to get special knowledge follows steps of putting routine word, selecting terminology among suggested and looking up and down.

4.2   Ontology of a Part of Simplified Taxation

Overall, Fig. 1 associates keywords belonging to the upper category, such as the scope of simple taxpayer, the scope of simple taxation, and the exemption of simplified taxation, then arranges the corpuses or words associated with the keyword along with the information type. The light-colored vocabulary in the pale thin-line box was inserted into the category network in consideration of its importance, rather than belonging to one category (in one bold or thin box) on the category network. In addition to this ontology, we have also put together all concepts corresponding to simplified taxation in a keyword map. The more detailed the keywords related to simple taxation (the less common legal terms are used), the fewer keywords users have written down on the ontology.

4.3   A Simulation for Evaluation

To evaluate the ontology that has undergone this transformation process, experiments are conducted on 3 subjects. Given the same task, we can compare and evaluate when using Jisik-In combined with ontology and when using only Jisik-In. A simple experiment and user interview was conducted to find special knowledge, using Naver Jisik-In only and Naver Jisik-In with ontology. The usability test was a comparison between the four ISB types described above using 7criterias suggested. Most of the users answered searching through Naver Jisik-In with ontology was more useful, usable, desirable and credible. Especially, some of them told that slight difference between words and selecting word before searching special knowledge always bother them searching in the existing search engines, but, Jisik-In with ontology could solve the problems. and had no trouble finding special knowledge. In addition, it seems that the difficulty of selecting terms was reduced and the desired results come out more often because the routine terms could be viewed in order of frequency to convert to related jargon terms.

5   Conclusion

In this paper, we propose conversational Q&A, which is based on ontology about specialized knowledge domain that can convert the existing Q&A system into chatbot. And we suggest it would shorten the search behavior and re-evaluate the efficiency of information retrieval. Especially conversational Q & A based on ontology is shown to be able to reduce the steps of ISB, which made it more useful, usable, desirable and desirable. It also appears that the difficulty of choosing terms is reduced, and the accuracy is improved because it is easier to search in appropriate terms. We can see the effect that ontology can have on the conversational Q&A system, and the necessity is suggested.

One of the important reasons why ontology based chatbot should be actively utilized in the field of special knowledge lies in the divergence between common term and terminology. Chatbots can solve users' questions through conversations, and conversations are interactive rather than one-sided communication. In other words, the user can inquire about the questions that he/she is curious about and can obtain results with high accuracy. If it is difficult to select the appropriate words to search for special knowledge, the user can ask the user what he/she wants by suggesting similar terminology related to the inputted common term, and then it can make a dialogue that lists and presents questions in order. Therefore, it simplifies the complex search behavior in special knowledge search and enables users to find out what they are interested in through active intervention. These chatbots should be based on the ontology and can be optimized by applying the Q & A system that users have raised their own questions.

5.1 Future Work

However, this study suggests only the specialized Q&A chatbot concept, and there is a limitation in identifying classifier for mapping on the category network. It is necessary to ask for expert about the category of the terms or make specific classifier for simplified taxation. Also, it is necessary to ask usability to much more users to quantize. We show the transformation process to conversational Q&A system, so the number of attendants for usability test is not enough to rationalize the efficiency. It could be next step for this study and would make conversational system more useful.

Acknowledgement. This work has been conducted with the support of the "Design Engineering Postgraduate Schools (N0001436)" program, a R&D project initiated by the Ministry of Trade, Industry and Energy of the Republic of Korea.

References

1. Peterson, R.A., Merino, M.C.: Consumer information search behavior and the internet. Psychol. Mark. **20**(2), 99–121 (2003)
2. Radziwill, N.M., Benton, M.C.: Evaluating quality of chatbots and intelligent conversational agents (2017)
3. Kuhlthau, C.C.: Inside the search process: information seeking from the user's perspective. J. Am. Soc. Inf. Sci. **42**(5), 361–371 (1991)
4. James, R.: Libraries in the mind: how can we see users' perceptions of libraries? J. Librariansh. **15**(1), 19–28 (1983)
5. Kiestra, M.D., Stokmans, M.J.W., Kamphuis, J.: End-users searching the online catalogue: the influence of domain and system knowledge on search patterns. Electron. Libr. **12**(6), 335–343 (1994)
6. Wildemuth, B.M.: The effects of domain knowledge on search tactic formulation. J. Am. Soc. Inform. Sci. Technol. **55**(3), 246–258 (2004)
7. Al-Zubaide, H., Issa, A.A.: Ontbot: ontology based chatbot. In: International Symposium on Innovations in Information and Communications Technology, pp. 7–12. IEEE, November 2011
8. Augello, A., Pilato, G., Vassallo, G., Gaglio, S.: Chatbots as interface to ontologies. In: Gaglio, S., Lo Re, G. (eds.) Advances onto the Internet of Things, pp. 285–299. Springer, Cham (2014). https://doi.org/10.1007/978-3-319-03992-3_20
9. Carmel, E., Crawford, S., Chen, H.: Browsing in hypertext: a cognitive study. IEEE Trans. Syst. Man Cybern. **22**(5), 865–884 (1992)

10. Bhavnani, S.K., Bates, M.J.: Separating the knowledge layers: cognitive analysis of search knowledge through hierarchical goal decompositions. In: ASIST 2002: Proceedings of the 65th ASIST Annual Meeting, Philadelphia, 18–21 November 2002, vol. 39, pp. 204–213 (2002)

11. Vakkari, P.: Subject knowledge, source of terms, and term selection in query expansion: an analytic study. In: Crestani, F., Girolami, M., van Rijsbergen, C.J. (eds.) ECIR 2002. LNCS, vol. 2291, pp. 110–123. Springer, Heidelberg (2002). https://doi.org/10.1007/3-540-45886-7_8

12. User Experience Design. https://semanticstudios.com/user_experience_design/. Accessed 29 Mar 2019

13. Gruber, Thomas R.: A translation approach to portable ontology specifications. Knowl. Acquis. **5**, 199–220 (1993)

14. Gruber, T.R.: Toward principles for the design of ontologies used for knowledge sharing? Int. J. Hum. Comput. Stud. **43**(5–6), 907–928 (1995)

15. Giaretta, P., Guarino, N.: Ontologies and knowledge bases towards a terminological clarification. Towards Very Large Knowl. Bases Knowl. Build. Knowl. Sharing **25**, 32 (1995)

16. Martin, T.G., et al.: Eliciting expert knowledge in conservation science. Conserv. Biol. **26**(1), 29–38 (2012)

17. Armstrong, J.S.: Combining forecasts. In: Armstrong, J.S. (ed.) Principles of Forecasting, pp. 417–439. Springer, Boston (2001). https://doi.org/10.1007/978-0-306-47630-3_19

18. Burgman, M., et al.: Redefining expertise and improving ecological judgment. Conserv. Lett. **4**, 81–87 (2011)

19. Halpern, J.Y., Moses, Y.: Knowledge and common knowledge in a distributed environment. J. ACM (JACM) **37**(3), 549–587 (1990)

20. Radlinski, F., Craswell, N.: A theoretical framework for conversational search. In: Proceedings of the 2017 Conference on Conference Human Information Interaction and Retrieval, pp. 117–126, March 2017

21. Nordlie, R.: "User revealment" – a comparison of initial queries and ensuing question development in online searching and in human reference interactions. In: Proceedings of the ACM SIGIR International Conference on Research and Development in Information Retrieval (SIGIR), pp. 11–18 (1999)

22. Pew Internet and American Life Project. Search Engine Users (2005). Accessed 19 Apr 2019

23. Hsieh-Yee, I.: Research on web search behavior. Libr. Inf. Sci. Res. **23**(2), 167–185 (2001)

24. Heinström, J.: Broad exploration or precise specificity: two basic information seeking patterns among students. J. Am. Soc. Inform. Sci. Technol. **57**(11), 1440–1450 (2006)

25. Cui, L., Huang, S., Wei, F., Tan, C., Duan, C., Zhou, M.: Superagent: a customer service chatbot for e-commerce websites. In: Proceedings of ACL 2017, System Demonstrations, pp. 97–102 (2017)

26. Uren, V., Lei, Y., Lopez, V., Liu, H., Motta, E., Giordanino, M.: The usability of semantic search tools: a review. Knowl. Eng. Rev. **22**(4), 361–377 (2007)

27. Coniam, D.: The linguistic accuracy of chatbots: usability from an ESL perspective. Text Talk **34**(5), 545–567 (2014)

28. Duijst, D.: Can we improve the user experience of chatbots with personalisation. Doctoral dissertation, M.Sc thesis, University of Amsterdam (2017)

29. Casellas, N.: Ontology evaluation through usability measures. In: Meersman, R., Herrero, P., Dillon, T. (eds.) OTM 2009. LNCS, vol. 5872, pp. 594–603. Springer, Heidelberg (2009). https://doi.org/10.1007/978-3-642-05290-3_73

The Relationship Between Video Game Play and Suicide Risk Among Japanese Young Adults

Yoshiki Koga[1]([⊠]) and Daisuke Kawashima[2]

[1] Graduate School of Psychology, Chukyo University, 101-2 Yagotohonmachi,
Showa-ku, Nagoya, Aichi, Japan
y.koga0502ga@gmail.com
[2] School of Psychology, Chukyo University, 101-2 Yagotohonmachi,
Showa-ku, Nagoya, Aichi, Japan

Abstract. The current study aimed to explore the relationships between game playing and suicide risk among Japanese young adults. A sample of 310 players aged 20–39 years were recruited through an Internet research company and completed a questionnaire. The questionnaire contained several items measuring game addiction, violent game play, time spent on games, suicide proneness, perceived burdensomeness, thwarted belongingness, acquired capability for suicide, and demographic variables (including age and gender). The result of correlation analysis revealed that game addiction was associated with suicidality, perceived burdensomeness, thwarted belongingness. However significant correlation between violent game play and suicidality, depression were only for males.

Keywords: Game addiction · Violent games · Suicide

1 Introduction

1.1 Video Game Play and Related Problems in Japan

Video and computer games are widespread in industrialized societies. In Japan, more than 50% of males and females in their teens, twenties and thirties play games regularly [1]. Given this situation, problems related to excessive, compulsive and/or pathological game play (referred to as "game addiction") have received increasing research attention [2, 3].

To address this situation, a number of recent studies of game addiction have been conducted, particularly in Europe and United States, leading to the development of several scales to examine game addiction [4, 5]. Further, previous studies have identified aggression, loneliness, life satisfaction, anxiety, and depression as influential factors related to game addiction [4, 6, 7]. Despite the findings described above, relatively few studies have examined game addiction in Japan. To address this situation, Koga and Kawashima [8] developed a Japanese version of the Game Addiction Scale and explored related variables. However, the number of studies is currently limited.

C. Stephanidis and M. Antona (Eds.): HCII 2019, CCIS 1088, pp. 309–314, 2019.
https://doi.org/10.1007/978-3-030-30712-7_39

1.2 Pathological Game Play and Suicide Risk

Several previous studies have examined the relationship between game play and suicide risk. For example, Ivory, Ivory & Lanier [9] examined various risk factors related to excessive game play among university students, identifying a relationship with suicide risk. Regarding game addiction, Kim, Kim, Lee, Hong, Cho, Fava ...& Jeon [10] indicated that clinical samples of individuals exhibiting addictive game play showed higher rates of suicide ideation, planned suicide, and attempted suicide, compared with the general population.

In addition, recent studies using the interpersonal theory of suicide [11] reported that excessive game play was significantly associated with interpersonal needs [12], and that violent game play was significantly associated with acquired capability for suicide [13, 14]. According to this theory, suicidal ideation is affected by interpersonal needs (perceived burdensomeness and thwarted belongingness), and attempted suicide is derived from acquired capability for suicide (i.e., pain tolerance and fearlessness about death). Overall, excessive and violent game play appears to be related to interpersonal aspects of suicide (i.e., interpersonal needs and acquired capability for suicide), and these factors elevate the risks of suicidal ideation and suicide attempts. However, the number of related studies is relatively small, and the generalizability of the findings described above remains unclear. Furthermore, no previous studies have examined the relationship between game addiction and suicide risk based on this theory. Based on the interpersonal theory of suicide, we assumed that there would be significant associations between game addiction and interpersonal aspects of suicide.

1.3 Aim of the Current Study

The current study aimed to explore the relationship between game play and suicide risk among Japanese young adults.

2 Methods

2.1 Procedure and Participants

A sample of 314 Japanese young adults were recruited from Japanese general public who had registered as potential respondents with an internet research company, in September 2017. Completed questionnaires were received from 314 participants. Four participants provided inconsistent responses, and were excluded from the analysis. Thus, data from 310 participants in their twenties and thirties who played a game at least once in the past month were included in the current study.

All participants provided written informed consent and participated in the study voluntarily. At the end of the survey, information was provided as an available resource for suicide prevention support. This study was part of a larger study of Japanese attitudes toward suicide, and was approved by the Chukyo University Institutional Review Board.

2.2   Questionnaire

Game Addiction: We employed the Game Addiction Scale 7-item version (GAS7) [4, 7] consisting of seven items scored additively, indicating a respondent's experience of game addiction in the 6 months prior to completing the survey. These items were scored on a 5-point Likert scale extending from 1 (never) to 5 (very often). In this study, scale scores ranged from a low score of 7 to a high score of 35 ($M = 11.49$, $SD = 5.11$, Cronbach's $\alpha = .87$). Applying the same cut-off point used in a previous study [4], 12.9% of participants were considered to exhibit problematic game playing.

Game Category and Subjective Violent Content: The participants were asked to report one game category that they spent the most time playing, out of four categories: action (first-person shooter, horror, fighting, and crime/war-themed games); adventure (role-playing games, massively multiplayer online games, and adventure games); simulation (music games, racing, and sports); and education/traditional (puzzles, board games, educational games, and traditional games, such as chess, using a computer or smartphone). In addition, participants were asked to rate the range of violence of the game they spent the most time playing. This item was scored on a 4-point Likert scale ranging from 1 (not at all violent) to 4 (very violent). When asked to report which types of games they spent the most time playing, 10.0% of participants selected "action", 39.7% selected "adventure", 11.0% selected "simulation", and 39.4% selected "educational/traditional".

Time Spent on Games: We measured the number of days per week and the number of hours per day spent playing games. We scored the number of hours spent on games by multiplying the days spent on game playing per week by the hours per day, and the score was used in the current study. The score ranged from a low of 1 h to a high of 98 h ($M = 12.19$, $SD = 13.73$).

Suicide Proneness: This scale was originally developed by Park, Im & Ratcliff [15]. Respondents rated each item on a dichotomous scale of either No (0) or Yes (+1). The sum of responses indicated suicide proneness. A higher score indicated a higher level of suicide proneness. In this study, the scores ranged from 0 to 6, ($M = .70$, $SD = 1.30$, Cronbach's $\alpha = .78$).

Perceived Burdensomeness and Thwarted Belongingness: We employed the Interpersonal Needs Questionnaire (INQ) [16, 17] consisting of 15 items, scored additively, indicating a respondent's recent experience of perceived burdensomeness (six items) and thwarted belongingness (nine items). These items were scored on a 7-point Likert scale extending from 1 (not at all true for me) to 7 (very true for me). In the current study, perceived burdensomeness scores ranged from a low of 6 to a high of 42 ($M = 19.23$, $SD = 9.17$, Cronbach's $\alpha = .96$), and the thwarted belongingness score raged from a low of 9 to a high of 61 ($M = 33.13$, $SD = 10.08$, Cronbach's $\alpha = .88$).

Acquired Capability for Suicide: We employed the Acquired Capability for Suicide Scale (ACSS) [17, 18] consisting of 20 items, scored additively, indicating a respondent's experience regarding the acquired capability for suicide. These items were scored on a 5-point Likert scale ranging from 0 (not at all) to 4 (very true). In the current study, the scale scores ranged from a low of 3 to a high of 72 ($M = 31.40$, $SD = 11.12$, Cronbach's $\alpha = .83$).

Demographic Variables: We obtained information about the participants' gender and age (55.2% were male, 44.8% were female; age: $M = 30.13$ years, $SD = 5.29$ years).

3　Results

We calculated the distribution of game playing for participants of each gender (male and female) and age group (twenties, thirties). A chi-square test revealed no significant differences in the number of game players between gender and age groups (χ^2 [1] $= .024$, $p = .878$, Cramer's $V = .01$). We then performed a 2 (gender) $\times$ 2 (age group) analysis of variance using GAS7 scores and subjective violence as dependent variables. No interaction effects were significant on GAS7 ($F[1, 306] = 2.79$, $p = .10$, $\eta^2 = .01$), and subjective violence ($F[1, 306] = .48$, $p = .490$, $\eta^2 = .00$). Scores for males were higher than those for females (GAS7: $F[1, 306] = 8.48$, $p < .01$, $\eta^2 = .03$, subjective violence: $F[1, 306] = 19.52$, $p < .001$, $\eta^2 = .06$), whereas there were no significant differences depending on age (GAS7: $F[1, 306] = 1.49$, $p = .223$, $\eta^2 = .01$, subjective violence: $F[1, 306] = 1.09$, $p = .30$, $\eta^2 = .00$). Therefore, we analyzed the data separately by gender in the subsequent analyses.

We examined the correlations between variables of game playing such as scores of GAS7 and game category, and other variables separately by gender (Table 1). For males, correlation analysis showed that GAS7 scores were significantly and positively correlated with the action category ($r = .20$), time spent on games ($r = .38$), suicide proneness ($r = .18$), perceived burdensomeness ($r = .31$), and thwarted belongingness ($r = .29$). The action category was significantly and positively correlated with subjective violence ($r = .29$) and suicide proneness ($r = .17$). In addition, there were significant positive correlations between time spent on games and perceived burdensomeness, time spent on games and thwarted belongingness, suicide proneness and perceived burdensomeness, suicide proneness and thwarted belongingness, perceived burdensomeness and thwarted belongingness ($rs = .17$ to .55). For females, correlation analysis revealed that the GAS7 score was significantly and positively correlated with subjective violence ($r = .25$), time spent on games ($r = .37$), suicide proneness ($r = .23$), perceived burdensomeness ($r = .23$), and thwarted belongingness ($r = .37$). The action category was significantly and positively correlated with subjective violence ($r = .22$). Regarding the other variables, there were significant positive correlations between most of the variables ($ps = .17$ to .61), except for the relationships between subjective violence and the others, time spent on games and suicide proneness, and time spent on games and ACSS scores.

Table 1. Correlations between game play, suicide proneness, INQ, ACSS

	(1)	(2)	(3)	(4)	(5)	(6)	(7)	(8)
(1) GAS7	1	.10	.25 **	.37 ***	.23 **	.23 **	.37 ***	.12
(2) Action category	.20 **	1	.22 **	−.03	.00	−.07	−.02	.08
(3) Subjective violent	.14	29 ***	1	.07	.10	.04	.15	.08
(4) Time spent on games	.38 ***	.05	.04	1	.10	.17 *	.18 *	.05
(5) Suicide proneness	.18 *	.17 *	−.01	.04	1	27 ***	23 ***	.19 *
(6) INQ (PB)	31 ***	.12	−.04	.17 *	.19 **	1	.61 ***	.37 ***
(7) INQ (TB)	29 ***	.14	−.10	.17 *	.22 ***	.55 ***	1	.30 ***
(8) ACSS	−.01	.14	.08	−.05	.08	.04	−.02	1

Notes: *** $p < .001$, ** $p < .01$, * $p < .05$

The upper part of this table shows data from female participants, and the lower part shows data from male participants.

Action category (action = + 1, other categories = 0),

PB = perceived burdensomeness, TB = thwarted belongingness

4 Discussion

In the current study, we explored the relationship between game play and suicide risk among Japanese young adults. The correlation analysis indicated significant relationships between game addiction, suicide proneness, similar to the findings of previous studies (e.g.) [7, 9, 10]. However, we did not find any significant correlations between the indexes of violent and excessive game play (such as action game play and excessive hours of game play) and acquired capability for suicide. This pattern of results is inconsistent with those in a previous report by Mitchell et al. [13]. In addition, we found a significant correlation between game addiction and interpersonal needs (i.e., perceived burdensomeness and thwarted belongingness) but found no significant relationships with acquired capability for suicide. We did not find significant associations between indexes of violent game play (i.e., action game play and subjective violence) and interpersonal needs. These results were inconsistent with those of previous reports [13, 14]. Time spent on games was positively correlated with interpersonal needs, in accord with a report by Gauthier et al. [12]. Moreover, we found significant correlations between violent game play and suicide proneness only in male participants.

Although the current findings were suggestive, our study had limitation that it is unclear whether the relationship can be adapted to other populations such as teenagers, clinical samples of individuals with game addiction, and non-Japanese people.

References

1. Computer Entertainment Supplier's Association: General consumer survey report: Game users & non-game users in Japan. CESA, Tokyo (2018)
2. Chiu, S.I., Lee, J.Z., Huang, D.H.: Video game addiction in children and teenagers in Taiwan. Cyberpsychology Behav. Soc. Netw. 7(5), 571–581 (2004)
3. Fisher, S.: Identifying video game addiction in children and adolescents. Addict. Behav. 19(5), 545–553 (1994)
4. Lemmens, J.S., Valkenburg, P.M., Peter, J.: Development and validation of a game addiction scale for adolescents. Media Psychol. 12(1), 77–95 (2009)
5. Brockmyer, J.H., Fox, C.M., Curtiss, K.A., McBroom, E., Burkhart, K.M., Pidruzny, J.N.: The development of the game engagement questionnaire: a measure of engagement in video game-playing. J. Exp. Soc. Psychol. 45(4), 624–634 (2009)
6. Mehroof, M., Griffiths, M.D.: Online gaming addiction: the role of sensation seeking, self-control, neuroticism, aggression, state anxiety, and trait anxiety. Cyberpsychology Behav. Soc. Netw. 13(3), 313–316 (2010)
7. Gaetan, S., Bonnet, A., Brejard, V., Cury, F.: French validation of the 7-item game addiction scale for adolescents. Eur. Rev. Appl. Psychol. Rev. Eur. Psychol. Appl. 64(4), 161–168 (2014)
8. Koga, Y., Kawashima, D.: Development and validation of Japanese version of the game addiction scale for adolescents. Japan. J. Pers. 27(2), 175–177 (2018)
9. Ivory, A.H., Ivory, J.D., Lanier, M.: Video game use as risk exposure, protective incapacitation, or inconsequential activity among university students: comparing approaches in a unique risk environment. J. Media Psychol. Theor. Methods Appl. 29(1), 42–53 (2017)
10. Kim, D.J., et al.: Internet game addiction, depression, and escape from negative emotions in adulthood: a nationwide community sample of Korea. J. Nervous Mental Dis. 205(7), 568–573 (2017)
11. Joiner Jr., T.E., Van Orden, K.A., Witte, T.K., Rudd, M.D.: The Interpersonal Theory of Suicide: Guidance for Working with Suicidal Clients. American Psychological Association, Washington, DC (2009)
12. Gauthier, J.M., et al.: The interpersonal-psychological theory of suicide and exposure to video game violence. J. Soc. Clin. Psychol. 33(6), 512–535 (2014)
13. Mitchell, S.M., Jahn, D.R., Guidry, E.T., Cukrowicz, K.C.: The relationship between video game play and the acquired capability for suicide: an examination of differences by category of video game and gender. Cyberpsychology Behav. Soc. Netw. 18(12), 757–762 (2015)
14. Teismann, T., Fortsch, E., Baumgart, P., Het, S., Michalak, J.: Influence of violent video gaming on determinants of the acquired capability for suicide. Psychiatry Res. 215(1), 217–222 (2014)
15. Park, B.C., Im, J.S., Ratcliff, K.S.: Rising youth suicide and the changing cultural context in South Korea. Crisis J. Crisis Interv. Suicide Prev. 35(2), 102–109 (2014)
16. Van Orden, K.A., Cukrowicz, K.C., Witte, T.K., Joiner, T.E.: Thwarted belongingness and perceived burdensomeness: construct validity and psychometric properties of the interpersonal needs questionnaire. Psychol. Assess. 24(1), 197–215 (2012)
17. Aiba, M., Tachikawa, H., Lebowitz, A.: Development of Japanese version of the Interpersonal Needs Questionnaire (INQ) and the Acquired Capability for Suicide Scale (ACSS). In: 57th Conference of the Japanese Society of Social Psychology, Hyogo, Japan (2016)
18. Ribeiro, J.D., et al.: Fearlessness about death: the psychometric properties and construct validity of the revision to the acquired capability for suicide scale. Psychol. Assess. 26(1), 115–126 (2014)

The Role of Image Sharing and User's Interactions on Social Media to Promote Handloom Fashion Industry

Nilima Haque Ruma[✉], Md. Sultan Mahmood, and Eunyoung Kim

School of Knowledge Science, Japan Advanced Institute of Science
and Technology, Nomi, Japan
{ruma18, sultan, Kim}@jaist.ac.jp

Abstract. Handloom industry has a rich history in Bangladesh and almost all regular clothes used to make in local handloom manufacture. However, these manufacturers have declined due to its obsolete business model. The development of information technology and the rise of social media is playing an important role to overcome various challenges related to the promotion of the handloom Jamdani business. The case analysis of 'Jamdani Ville' revealed that the main factor to the handloom fashion industry is the emergence of internet and communication technology. 'Jamdani Ville' share the products image with the followers; this is the way how they advertise, promote and understand the customers demand by connecting through social media. Image sharing service on social media helping to connect customers, fulfilling the demands of customers, promoting the traditional handloom Jamdani and empowering the handloom Jamdani weavers. This research explores how the image sharing service and the user's interactions in social media contribute to promoting the handloom fashion industry. We conducted a case study with the owner and online customers of Jamdani Ville. To collect data, the study employed a semi-structured interview and questionnaire survey.

Keywords: Fashion industry · Handloom Jamdani · Social media · Entrepreneurs · Jamdani Ville · Bangladesh

1 Introduction

Social media has transformed the world in every aspect, changing the way of communication, breakdown the traditional way of interaction and become a valuable marketing tool for many companies [1–3]. Facebook provides a way for corporations to directly interact and respond to their consumers. Nowadays, customers can get updated information to introduce different kinds of handloom products. Now everything can be done online starting from choosing desirable product and payment. Much online business emerged in Bangladesh that relates to customers in wide range especially in Facebook with a variety of online pages such as Jamdani world, Jamdani Ville, Jamdani Mela, Dhakai Jamdani, Jamdani Museum and so on. 'Jamdani Ville' is one of them, which allow customers to buy their desired product through social media. Nowadays, social media like Facebook has become the primary source for Jamdani

© Springer Nature Switzerland AG 2019
C. Stephanidis and M. Antona (Eds.): HCII 2019, CCIS 1088, pp. 315–322, 2019.
https://doi.org/10.1007/978-3-030-30712-7_40

lovers. However, this is just the beginning of a long journey enabled by disruptive technologies and human-computer interaction. With the introduction of the online business platform, the seeds laid for a new trend in the handloom industry.

The popular platform is Jamdani Ville, founded in 2014. The formation of the company is based on a website and Facebook page where customers can cheek the variety of Jamdani products, communicate with the seller and decide the most appropriate products sitting their home. These kinds of services enabling social interaction between customers and sellers. However, the aim of this research is to investigate how the image sharing service and user's interaction through social media can benefit both entrepreneurs and consumers by reducing the intermediary commissions.

For this purpose, the customer's perception and the reaction have been analyzed. To attain the study objectives, we conducted a case study of the social media-based entrepreneurs in Bangladesh. For the case study, we have selected 'Jamdani Ville' considering the reputation, experiences in working with the handloom fashion industry and many online customers. 'Jamdani Ville' is one of the successful business models supported by technology that enables to connect so many customers globally. So far, Jamdani Ville reached 240,336 followers on Facebook. These statistics show the rapid expansion of handloom Jamdani and hence affect the traditional business model of the handloom industry [4].

This study investigates on how the social media-based entrepreneurs contributing to expanding the handloom fashion industry. We have conducted a qualitative case study that supposed to use an inductive approach rather than the deductive reasoning of testing hypotheses or theories [5]. We have collected data from company owner, 45 Jamdani weavers and 10 online customers. We purposively selected 05 master weavers and randomly selected 40 artisans and helpers. On the other hand, we purposively selected 10 customers who experience online shopping from Jamdani Ville at least two times or more. To conduct the interview, we designed three sets of semi-structured interview questionnaires: one for Jamdani Ville owner, one for the Jamdani weavers and another for Jamdani Ville customers. The result motivated me to develop a model by which we explained how to the handloom fashion industry expanding through social media marketing and benefiting both handloom entrepreneurs and customers.

2   Literature Review

Currently, the handloom industry is facing many problems and barriers to getting raw material, proper marketing facilities, and sales network. Most of the weavers making backdated products because they are not much known about the current market trend [6]. Mostly, the handloom products reach the ultimate customers through three inter-mediary groups namely merchant, wholesaler and retailers. However, the traditional supply chain management of handloom Jamdani is no more effective to reach the customers easily. To expand the handloom Jamdani it is very necessary to minimize the gap between the handloom Jamdani weavers and the customers.

However, electronic commerce, known as e-commerce by which we can perform buying, selling, transferring or exchanging products or services over the internet and other computer networks. In Bangladesh, the e-commerce industry is growing very rapidly. Many retailers and small-scale entrepreneurs are now creating their personal websites. Some retailers are only operating their business over the Internet, mainly Facebook commerce that is known as F-commerce. The widespread of ICTs moving the global business community towards Business-to-Business e-commerce [7]. The Internet is the potential tool with many features to create a completely new industry. The internet strongly embraces all level such as businesses, individuals, government, and entrepreneurs. Now, every country using the internet in every sector and in most of the company.

Moreover, Social media interaction is fundamentally changing communication between brands and customers. Social media is dedicated to community-based input, interaction, content sharing and collaboration as the collective of online communications channels. Facebook, twitter, google+, Wikipedia, LinkedIn, and Pinterest are some well-known examples of social media. More recently, Facebook is most popular social networking website that allows the users to create profiles, uploads photos and video, send messages and keep in touch with friends, family, and colleagues around the world. Statistics show that comparing any other website internet users spend more time on Facebook than any other website in the United States [8]. Bangladeshi marketers are using Facebook as a powerful medium of business since 2010. Small-scale entrepreneurs and corporate houses are practicing this social media business remarkably. As of 2013, there are over 130 different stores in Bangladesh whose main existence on Facebook. Majority of these businesses belong to online boutiques, music, books, play station games, etc. [9].

3   Case Study of Jamdani Ville

The case analysis of 'Jamdani Ville' revealed that the main factor to expand the handloom apparel industry is the emergence of internet and communication technology. Social media marketing is a powerful way for the business of all sizes that is very helpful for small-scale enterprises to promote the specific brand and reach a good number of customers. Jamdani Ville started social media business to spread the fame of handloom.

Jamdani worldwide. Jamdani Ville is playing an intermediary role between customers and handloom weavers to co-create value as shown in Fig. 1. In order to explain how the handloom Jamdani industry is expanding globally through the user's interaction, this research draws upon the role of image sharing service on social media. This study found that 'Jamdani Ville' investing money to the handloom Jamdani community to produce quality Jamdani sari. On the other hand, 'Jamdani Ville' share the product image with the followers; this is the way to advertise, promote and understand the customers demand by connecting through social media. Image sharing service on social media helping to connect customers, fulfilling the demands of customers, promoting the traditional handloom Jamdani and empowering the handloom Jamdani weavers.

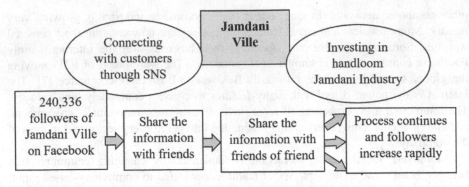

Fig. 1. Value co-creation process of Jamdani Ville

3.1 Facebook Page Analysis of Jamdani Ville

The Facebook page of Jamdani Ville consists of several features that allow customers to find the appropriate products and some other information like business policies, contact information, and products information. See Fig. 2.

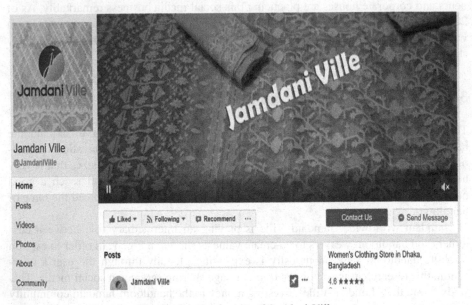

Fig. 2. Facebook page of Jamdani Ville

The mission of Jamdani Ville is to spread the great heritage Jamdani and its fame all over the world. To order Jamdani Sari, customers are requested to send the code number of the Sari, which they like to purchase. Most of the cases, the price of products is mentioned but in case of exclusive Sari, the price is hidden, and customers are requested to know the price by inbox inquiries. Thus, customer can get detailed information about every product from the Facebook post. They clearly mention the product materials, color combination and the price most of the cases. Figure 3 shows the Facebook post of the Jamdani Ville with product details.

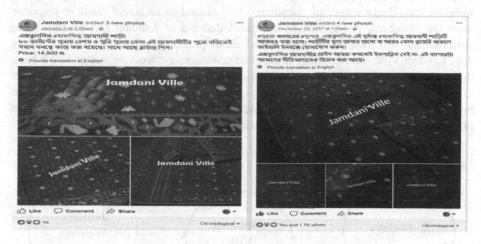

Fig. 3. Facebook post of Jamdani Ville

When customers buy the products, they willingly confess their review on the products and services as well. The reviews from the customers play an important role to validate the quality of Jamdani products, services, promotion of the cultural heritage Jamdani as well as the reputation of Jamdani Ville. These kinds of review help in building trust between customers and entrepreneurs. Here are the examples of customers review:

> "The jamdani I bought from the page is very soft. I liked it. **It's of premium quality**. Thanks. Hope **to buy more** in the future". (Customer A, Female).
> "Are there any ways that I can give them 100 on 5? I don't want to rate them by stars. Trust me they are way beyond that! **Excellent collection,** they do not compromise their **quality,** and the owner is an angel. l has never met her, but she is such a sweet **genuine gentle and an honest lady.** I ordered a saree for my mom to gift her on Eid festival, the owner was sick, bedridden for some days. But still, she made it sure that I get the saree for my mom on time! And I got the saree as I wanted. **Incredible! Excellent customer service.** They are doing a great job. They're producing **export quality jamdani.** It shows their **patriotism** as well. I'd love to shop from them more and more in the future. My best wishes always" (Customer B, Female).
> "I like the **prompt communications** from 'Jamdani Ville'. I'm an overseas customer but I'm getting my deliveries at my local contacts **without any delays.** Also, I like the cotton Jamdanis of your collection. **Price may be a little high, but I don't mind if the product satisfies me.** Look forward to getting the more beautiful product for my cotton Jamdani collection. Thank you Iffat Sharmin, thank you Jamdani Ville". (Customer C, Female).

3.2 The Strategies of Jamdani Ville to Reach the Customers

'Jamdani Ville' started to introduce the Jamdani sari and the way of weaving Jamdani sari with their customers. They believe that more the people will know about the process of Jamdani weaving and the life of Jamdani weavers, more the people will realize the value of Jamdani products. However, the customers are fully satisfied with the quality of Jamdani sari and now they have knowledge about the creator's hard labor invested to produce appealing Jamdani products and the reason behind the high price of Jamdani sari. Every action of 'Jamdani Ville' started to receive a positive response from the customers and gained an increased demand of Jamdani sari globally. The customer has full trust in 'Jamdani Ville' about product quality and services. Every day, Jamdani Ville receives many orders and consequently, weavers started to get back the work speed instead of passing lazy days. Nowadays, weavers spend a very busy day to deliver a lot of Jamdani sari to the customers. Here, "Jamdani Ville" playing an intermediary role between customers and handloom weavers. 'Jamdani Ville' is a platform to bridge the gap between Jamdani lover and Jamdani weavers. See Fig. 4.

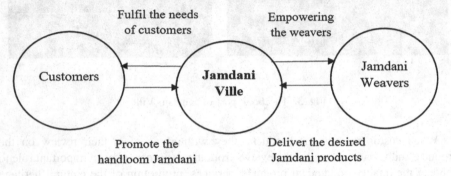

Fig. 4. Bridging the gap between customers and weavers

3.3   The Engagement of Customers with Handloom Jamdani

The case analysis of 'Jamdani Ville' shows that there are 240,336 followers who are getting every update related to new Jamdani products and get to know about the story of handloom Jamdani weavers. Customers are highly satisfied with the quality and price of handloom Jamdani. So far, customers did not complain that the price is high because they are now conscious of the hard labor of the poor weavers. Even, some customers pay more than the actual price and request to the Jamdani Ville to give that extra money to the poor family of Jamdani community. The customers are very happy with the services provided by 'Jamdani Ville' and they have full trust in 'Jamdani Ville'. This is the big achievement of 'Jamdani Ville' to gain the trust of customers where most of the online shops fail to gain trust. To collect data, this study purposively selected 10 customers who experienced online shopping from Jamdani Ville at least two times or more. To conduct the interview, semi-structured interview questionnaires were designed and sent to the selected customers through Facebook messenger. After getting the response from customers, the analysis shows that customers are satisfied with the Jamdani products and services of 'Jamdani Ville'. 60% of respondents are highly satisfied, 40% are satisfied and none of them are dissatisfied.

3.4   Image Sharing and Users Interaction in the Social Media for Handloom Fashion Industry

Social media interaction is literally changing the pattern of communication between brands and customers. Comparing to corporate-sponsored communication through traditional promotional activities, image sharing in social media attracts consumers more to gain trustworthy information. Social media play a key role in the brand's success in the luxury sectors [10]. However, the previous study described luxury brands' social media marketing as combining five dimensions: entertainment, interaction, trendiness, customization, and word of mouth (WOM). Our study simply focuses on two dimensions, one is image sharing and another is users interaction to promote the handloom fashion industry. In a broader sense, image sharing and users interaction do not limit to selling and buying but includes entertainment, trendiness, customization, and word of mouth (WOM) [11]. Our study findings reveal that the interaction not only held between the business (Jamdani Ville) to the consumer but also consumer to consumer. For example, 'Jamdani Ville' connecting the consumer through image sharing on Facebook. On the other side, the consumer also connecting with another consumer through sharing their online shopping experience with friends, family and the review section of 'Jamdani Ville's Facebook page which include comments, opinions, sentiments and most importantly branding of the handloom Jamdani. Researchers defined this consumer to consumer interaction as word of mouth (WOM) and suggested to use of this WOM on social media from three perspectives: opinion seeking, opinion giving, and opinion passing [12]. Consumers with a high level of opinion seeking behavior tend to search for information and advice from other consumers when making a purchase decision. Consumers with a high level of opinion-giving behavior also called opinion leaders to have a significant influence on consumers' attitudes and behaviors. Moreover, offline interaction is inevitable between 'Jamdani Ville' and handloom Jamdani weavers to promote handloom Jamdani industry. Users interaction helping to understand the market trend and customers preference about the design of handloom Jamdani. Overall, image sharing on Facebook page and different user's interaction playing a major role to promote handloom fashion industry globally.

4   Conclusion

The 'Jamdani Ville' is the main driving force who started a Facebook-based online business in 2014 with the aim to expand handloom Jamdani. Gradually, 'Jamdani Ville' was able to reach almost 3 million customers on the Facebook page. Jamdani Ville has built a strong connection between poor Jamdani weavers and potential customers over the world using social media like Facebook. The review of Jamdani Ville revealed that customers are satisfied with Jamdani products and the need for products increasing day by day. Weavers are working day to night to fulfill the increasing demand of customers. These all become possible because of the incredible role of social media on image sharing and users interactions.

Acknowledgments. This study was partially funded by the Japan Advanced Institute of Science and Technology (JAIST), Japan.

References

1. Peruta, A., Ryan, W., Acquavella, G.: Organizational approaches to social media branding: comparing brand Facebook pages and websites. In: International Conference on Communication, Media, Technology, and Design (ICCMTD), pp. 286–291, May 2012. http://scholar.google.com/scholar?hl=en&btnG=Search&q=intitle:No+Title#0
2. Labrecque, L.I., Markos, E., Milne, G.R.: Online personal branding: processes, challenges, and implications. J. Interact. Mark. **25**(1), 37–50 (2011). https://doi.org/10.1016/j.intmar.2010.09.002
3. Zhou, L., Wang, T.: Social media: a new vehicle for city marketing in China. Cities **37**, 27–32 (2014). https://doi.org/10.1016/j.cities.2013.11.006
4. https://www.facebook.com/JamdaniVille/. Accessed 12 June 2019
5. Williams, C.: Research method. J. Bus. Econ. Res. **5**(3), 67 (2007)
6. Goswami, R., Jain, R.: Strategy for sustainable development of handloom industry. Glob. J. Finan. Manag. **6**(2), 93–98 (2014)
7. Mohiuddin, Md.: Overview of e-commerce in Bangladesh. IOSR J. Bus. Manag. (IOSR-JBM) **16**(7), 01–06 (2014)
8. Imene, K.: Social media define the era in digital media. Int. J. Humanit. Soc. Sci. Invention **6**(6), 01–03 (2017)
9. Zabeen, M., Ara, H., Sarwae, N.: F-commerce in Bangladesh: "Venit, Vidit, Vieit". IOSR J. Humanit. Soc. Sci. **17**(5), 01–08 (2013)
10. Godey, B., et al.: Social media marketing efforts of luxury brands: influence on brand equity and consumer behavior. J. Bus. Res. **69**(12), 5833–5841 (2016). https://doi.org/10.1016/j.jbusres.2016.04.181
11. Kim, A.J., Ko, E.: Do social media marketing activities enhance customer equity? An empirical study of luxury fashion brand. J. Bus. Res. **65**, 1480–1486 (2012)
12. Chu, S.C., Kim, Y.: Determinants of consumer engagement in electronic Word-of-Mouth (eWOM) in social networking sites. Int. J. Advert. **30**(1), 47–75 (2011)

For Our Cities

Sense, Behavior and Design

Nelson Jose Urssi[✉]

Centro Universitário Senac, Sao Paulo, Brazil
nelson.jurssi@sp.senac.br

Abstract. This article presents the research developed by the Metacity project, belonging to the UrbeLab group in the Research Program of the Senac University Center, during the year of 2018. The scope of the project includes the development of data and information mappings that seek to identify people experience the city of São Paulo in their daily activities. In the first stage, the researchers used graphic, digital, personal and urban forms of cartography to collect ethnographic, subjective, equipment and infrastructures and language data, sketches, spreadsheets, designs, models and prototypes). The content will be analyzed and qualified through three-dimensional models, date-visualizations and infographics to compose a digital and interactive platform. The aim of the researchers is to propose a reflection on our habits and behaviors in the city center of São Paulo, Brazil, starting from the social, infrastructural, economic, architectural and technological scenarios to developing proposals for redesigning our life.

Keywords: City · Territory · Infrastructure · Systems · Flows

1 Introduction

Cities around the world have evolved unevenly, under pressure from diverse, critical and emerging industrial societies. Today our cities present a post-industrial reality in a daily life full of uncertainties of liquid and fast characteristics. The adoption of new media embodied in our daily activities materialized information at all times and in all places. According to MacKenzie and Wajcman (apud Sykes 2013, 281), technology as place includes three qualities to be explored: patterns of human activities, sets of objects, and human knowledge. Cities give physics to this technology-place dichotomy and, even with their weaknesses and qualities, allow this reflection from the physical and urban point of view as well as digital and informational. Thus, we chose the city of São Paulo, the largest metropolis in South America, as an urban environment of great complexity and object for explorations of such urban experiences.

Urban computing, embedded, ubiquitous and mobile, transformed our daily life and forms of knowledge. Learning has become a ubiquitous action to everyday life. So, it's natural to see people engrossed in their particular digital world, the movement of their fingers sliding across the screen of the smartphone, eyes drifting, and the mind migrating from one subject to another researching or reading something on social

C. Stephanidis and M. Antona (Eds.): HCII 2019, CCIS 1088, pp. 323–328, 2019.
https://doi.org/10.1007/978-3-030-30712-7_41

networks or interacting with people, facts and places. Connected full-time, they navigate through momentary and private environments constantly updated by connections over wireless networks. When they take their eyes off the screen, they emerge from their particular cocoon, witnessing a new daily life. Information and communication technologies (ICT) have broadened the way we understand this environment by continuously generating data across all our activities. Thus, technologies have shaped our destiny and the urban environment is our laboratory of the future.

2   The Research

The research project selected a fragment of the urban territory of the city of São Paulo as an object of study in which the researched elements are being applied through data surveys, constructions of narratives, juxtaposition of flows and infrastructures. This metropolitan territory, the center of the city, was chosen and delimited as a field of experimentation by the recurrence in which public power, organized society and users new demands and proposals for their occupation are launched, bringing the need for different looks for on-site understanding and intervention.

The research seeks to understand the urbanity of the city center of São Paulo. Here the expression Urbanity is understood as the quality of experience of the urban space - private and public - and the availability of services. The idea is to identify experiences and qualify the urban fabric so that we can propose efficient and effective projects for the city. The research began with an understanding of the city's different construction moments - the past, the present and indications of future transformation - to the reflections for each of these times, applying the surveyed elements through the understanding of the city. This involvement with urban reality will link the theoretical reflections typical of academic research with practical, empirical and applied research in future spatial and projective propositions, both architectural and urban.

The Metacity project, belonging to the UrbeLab group: infrastructures, systems and flows of the city formed by PHD professors Valeria Fialho, Ricardo Silva, Marcelo Suzuki and Nelson Urssi, had as students researchers from the bachelor's degrees in Design, Architecture and Urbanism, all participants in the Scientific Initiation Program of the Senac University Center. In 2018, the project raised and organized sets of data on the transformations that occurred in this territory assuming the premises: how it was, how it is and how it will be transformed during the actions and proposals undertaken by society. The research is guided by the urban condition of our existence. Its main objective is to reveal and to explain the processes of transformation of the central territory of the city of São Paulo cataloging and organizing data that will subsidize the identification of demands. The region is constantly changing with regard to the forms of urban mobility, real estate, social and cultural relations, in the identification and proposition of other possible forms of human interaction and urban intervention. To do this, we initially used bibliographic databases, data and information from government portals, the mapping of geolocated services applications (geoapps), questionnaires and interviews directed to users in the region. This diversity of research grants required new forms of urban representation and indicated that traditional maps are no longer adequate to observe the city in all complexity.

3   Hypercartographies

Our day-to-day has become denser and more complex by the use of app services we carry on our cell phones. We create and provide data about ourselves and relate it to local information by constructing a multi-level cartography of reading and exploration. Sensing and mapping technologies extend this amount of data and how we conceive the information by profoundly modifying how we communicate and interact with the city. Sensing the urban fabric is an important tool to better understand our world by organizing, visualizing and articulating our daily activities. The city's fixed and mobile sensors provide for the construction of a much more pluralistic urban environment and as such it is available to develop new ways of using the city.

The urban structures keep all the necessary information so that we can attend to the questions that are presented, they are places of action and reflection of its own original design added to the bigdata generated continuously. Mobile devices make this condition so that people become individual sensors in the urban space and thus provide other looks for where we live. In this urban environment, where geographic and temporal referentials are relativized, space and information construct our urbanity. Through this new cartography, what we call hypercartography, the reading of the urban fabric provides meaningful physical interaction that presents itself as a fragmented and amalgamated space for the flows, full of meaning and information.

The central metropolitan territory was chosen and delimited as a field of experimentation by the recurrence in which are launched, by the public power, organized society and users, new demands and proposals for their occupation that bring the need for different looks for understanding and intervention in the local. The netnographic investigations are the great explorations of the process that add us tools of observation, analysis and reflection in fundamental approaches of projects for the community. The term Netnography (Kozinets 2010) is defined in this research as the field research process of an ethnographic nature within a digital environment. We use the mapping of data from geolocated applications installed on mobile devices - smartphones and tablets - and urban sensors to design information that qualifies the city of São Paulo, its culture and daily use.

Initial surveys of ethnographic, subjective, equipment, and infrastructure data begin to compose the platform. The interpretation of these data is contributing to the identification of existing and changing uses, preferences and habits of the residents of the region. The project has been systematizing the various action scenarios and possible co-creation tools and solutions. The information identified as primordial for the research, showed the city as we experienced it, from the use of urban space by the individualities of its users (Fig. 1).

4   Metacity

In the last 20 years, the use of urban technologies has permeated our lives, causing changes in habits and new ways of living. The idea of a city as a place of daily activities permeated by information has altered what we know about the urban nature of our lives. We participate in the process of building a society that values the diversity

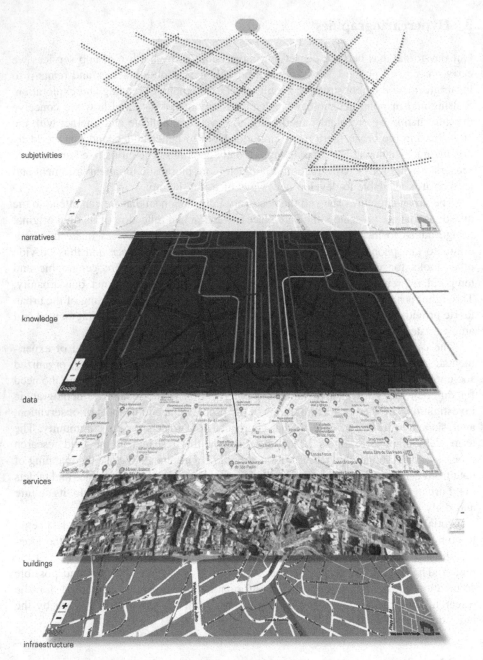

subjetivities

narratives

knowledge

data

services

buildings

infraestructure

Fig. 1. Mapping the urban environment through our daily activities.

and multiculturality that each new technology advances to multiple forms of interaction, languages and social structures. If we take advantage of the historical, aesthetic and social experience of the Moderno with the understanding of the contemporary individual and his desires, designers will be prepared to play a fundamental role in the conception of cities.

Social design or human-centered design gives the dimension of needs to a city in search of balance. The design with greater human focus finds in the exploratory, participative and collaborative performance a social projective process. This challenge represents a chance for design to help define opportunities and shape future experiences in cities. An important possibility for us to understand every detail in the formation of committed agents with consistent design processes to solve the complex systems of the contemporary city. The objective is to facilitate decision-making with collective participation and collaboration in urban actions using theoretical tools and urban technologies in the human activities in the city. This challenge represents a chance for design to help define opportunities for action and shape future experiences in cities.

The idea of Metacity incorporates the city as a propositional environment of diversified daily realities, as a space in perpetual process of multiplication and expansion of its layers of meaning. Metacity is the environment of projective and metaprojective explorations that uses as a source the urban life abundant of data and permeated by the information. It is the city whose physicality is increased by the flow of information provided by the intense technological evolution.

Metacity is what we imagine for our cities in the near future. An urban space, continuous and interlaced with information, new materials and projected forms, reflection and design exercise for an urban informational ecosystem, whose object is the space permeated by the data, shared at every moment and political action. It is the opportunity for artists, designers, architects and engineers to imagine a daily life that is enlarged and responsive to the needs of the population. Metacity as our second nature is a complex urban process in full structuring and development. The city with these conditions is an endless environment where places, languages and expressions, fruit of the use of space at different levels and needs. It presents itself as the sum of individual and plural dimensions, a complex experience constantly updated by the use where people interact with space by becoming active, participatory and collaborative agents.

The understanding of the central territory of the city of São Paulo allows for reflection on issues pertaining to the nature of the project and the development of new possibilities for the project and innovation professional in a culturally diverse and complex society. For the next phase of the research, we will use a physical model of the chosen territory in scale 1: 500 for insertion of samples of content in audiovisual format through augmented reality. The information inserted in the platform will be made public and accessible contributing to future researches and propositions of the studied area.

References

Beiguelman, G., La Ferla, J.: Nomadismos tecnológicos. Editora Senac, São Paulo (2011)
Bourriaud, N.: Radicante – por uma estética da globalização. Martins Fontes, São Paulo (2011)
Kozinets, R.V.: Netnography. Doing Ethnographic Research Online. Sage Publications, Los Angeles (2010)

Lidwell, W., Holden, K., Butler, J.: Universal Principles of Design. Rockport Publishers Inc., Beverly (2003)

Mayer-Schönberger, V.: Big Data: Como Extrair Volume, Variedade, Velocidade e Valor da Avalanche de Informação Cotidiana. Elsevier, Rio de Janeiro (2013)

Meirelles, I.: Design for Information: An Introduction to the Histories, Theories, and Best Practices Behind Effective Information Visualizations. Rockport Publishers, Beverly (2013)

Offenhuber, D., Ratti, C.: Decoding the city. Urbanism in the age of big data. Birkhäuser, Basel (2014)

Preece, J., Rogers, Y., Sharp, H.: Design de interação: Além da interação homem-computador. Bookman, Porto Alegre (2007)

Silva, R.: Elogios à inutilidade: a incorporação do Trapeiro como possibilidade de apropriação e leitura da Cidade e sua alteridade urbana. Tese (Doutorado em Arquitetura e Urbanismo) Universidade Presbiteriana Mackenzie, São Paulo (2017)

Sykes, A.K. (org.): O campo ampliado da arquitetura: Antologia teórica 1993–2009, pp. 135–142. Editora Cosac Naify, São Paulo (2013)

Thackara, J.: In the Bubble: Designing Complex Systems. MIT Press, Cambridge (2005)

Urssi, N.J.: Metacidade: design, bigdata e urbanidade. Tese (Doutorado em Design e Arquitetura) Faculdade de Arquitetura e Urbanismo da Universidade de São Paulo, São Paulo (2017)

Design Driven Innovation for Sustainability: An Analysis of 7 Cases

Jing Wang[✉]

TONGJI University College of Design and Innovation, 281 Fuxin Road, Shanghai, China
Wangjing7733@tongji.edu.cn

Abstract. The current consumption and production pattern is unsustainable. How to make sustainable economy possible requires an influencing agent to promote. With the multi-stakeholder participation, design enhanced as a powerful driving force for the sustainable transformation and improving people's well-being.

Based on the literature review and 7 case studies, including ecosystem restoration camp, 100-mile food movement, world widely organic farms, collaborative chronic care network, participatory ground water management project, Chinese ancient cosmetics restoration project and a flax project, this paper aims to explore the role of design in promoting sustainable changes with an attempt to complete the theory of social innovation design.

"Design-driven innovation" taking the understanding of the evolution process of the social culture and put forward the new perspectives in regard to the persistence of the new vision. The design-driven innovation is the result of the research process of the social action network, which need to be achieved with joint efforts of the actors ranging from the institutions, enterprises, non-profit organizations, citizens, associations. This is conducted with special emphasis placed on stimulating the bottom-up actions to enable the sustainable economic model to become the mainstream.

Keywords: Design driven innovation · Sustainability · Cases study

1 Introduction

In 1992, the United Nations Conference on Environment and Development (UNCED) clearly put forward to change current consumption and production patterns. Schumacher E.F. questioned about the worthiness of yearning for the goal of the Western economy in his book "Small is Beautiful", by criticizing the use of economic growth as the standard for measuring the national progress. Since 2000, The concept of "Anthropocene" put forward by Paul J. Crutzen has made more and more people realize that human activities have in fact a tremendous impact on the Earth, which exceed even the limits of what the ecosystem itself can regulate. The economic growth requires that the stock of natural capital could be taken into consideration in the political decision-making process [1]. The central task facing mankind today is to find a sustainable alternative to complete the social transformation. It is really a hard work and the barriers

C. Stephanidis and M. Antona (Eds.): HCII 2019, CCIS 1088, pp. 329–342, 2019.
https://doi.org/10.1007/978-3-030-30712-7_42

are as follows: the deep-ingrained social awareness, the existing socio-economic system, the social infrastructure and the technological processes which have limited us strictly on the existing track, putting a curb on the sustainable alternatives. According to Schumpeter, the existing development model depends on creatively destroyed, thus stimulating and create an inlet for introducing and developing a brand-new model.

2   Three Dimensions of Sustainability

It was realized that there cannot be an overarching all-encompassing specific sustainability target to strive for [2, 3]. Sustainability is neither the state of the system nor is it a target to be achieved. Sustainability is an ideal to the system which inter-relates different aspects of economy, environment and society.

2.1   Environment Dimension: People, Planet and Profit

The origin of Sustainable Economy and its ideas can be traced back to Kenneth E Boulding, an American scholar, who put forward the concept of coming spaceship earth economics in 1969. He mentioned that human beings are just like on a small spaceship in the vast space. Sooner or later, the disorderly growth of population and economy will exhaust the limited resources in the ship, and the waste discharged during production and consumption will eventually lead to the pollution of the spacecraft. The concept of sustainability introduced the natural capital as a new constant into the accounting of development cost, this modification takes both efficiency and fairness into consideration [4].

Most climate change policies focus on long-term choices, such as the introduction of new low-carbon energy technology and the establishment of total carbon emissions control and trading systems. While the academia has introduced new tools from some more specific ways, such as "ecological footprint", "carbon emissions" and "community marketing" [5–7], with attention to the impact of human beings on the environment from more specific aspects in terms of life behavior. For example, ecological footprint [5] visualizes the impact of resources needed by households, communities, regions and countries on the environment. Dietz [6] started with carbon emissions from family behavior to assess the plasticity of 17 kinds of family behaviors. He suggested that the policy should focus on family action and citizen action from the macro level.

2.2   Social Dimension: Well-Being and Welfare

Jackson [67] analyzed originally the relevance of the relationship between human development and economic growth, pointing out that human development and well-being do not depend exclusively on the economic growth, and holding that we should get rid of the obsession with economic growth, and that the concept of human well-being needs to be replaced by a new philosophical concept [8].

Sustainability, as a concept of the future, is defined as the environment, public health, social justice, and other options available for human beings and the biosphere [9]. It is also identified as a system-related human value [10] that improves the quality of human life within the affordability of ecosystems [11].

The well-being of the developed countries has long been successfully decoupled from their economic growth, emphasizing other factors such as time well-being and autonomy than consumption. For example, the United States advocates "Recycling Your Time" to reduce the working hours, and achieve sustainability without any special emphasis on sustainable consumption. In addition, the discussion of well-being can also help people realize the limitations of material consumption on the promotion of human well-being.

Non-material factors are equally important for human well-being, such as: Security, Attribution, Social Cohesion, Equity and Social Relations [12]. Layard [68] emphasized the importance of fair distribution of wealth to happiness, Veenhoven [69] argued that autonomy is more important than distributive justice. In general, the better society is the more fair one described by Wilkinson and Pickett [70].

2.3   Economy Dimension: Reciprocity and Solidarity Relations

The assessment of another dimension of sustainability involves the economic dimension. After all, the solution of the social problems depends on the economic development. And this index of assessment does not lie in the growth of GDP, much less in the use of money to measure the value of people.

Reciprocity, as a social mechanism, has a close connection to people's daily life. When reciprocity finds economic expression to provide goods and services, the socio economy emerges [13]. Reciprocal economy utilizes virtue ethics, expands economic business, such as micro-credit, mobilizes local social networks, and creates opportunities for the poor [14], For example, Time Bank, employed as a community currency, rewards people for their work in the community [15].

The ecologists have been fully aware of the interconnectedness of life networks with their overall environment and provides us with theoretical tools to extend these relationships to the social systems and identify their common organizational patterns as the self-organizing networks [3]. The close cooperative partnership is established in the network platform with wide participation of multi-stakeholders (enterprises, universities, scientific research institutions, financial institutions). The economic subject interact with each other interdependently, and constantly carrying out the sharing of knowledge, value exchange, information transmission, and capital flow through material, energy, and financial institutions. The continuous transmission and circulation of information will execute self-regulation and feedback, thus maintaining the continuous existence and the evolution of the system, realizing the restructuring of the innovative elements, promoting more the new economic models, and completing the transformation of the sustainable development.

3   Design Driven Innovation

MIT Sloan Management Review describes innovation as the path to the next industrial revolution [71]. According to the analysis of global national competitiveness, our economy will face a major transformation from efficiency-driven to innovation-driven [72], which means the innovation-driven economy [73]. Social innovation serves as a prerequisite for sustainable economy [74], innovation cluster will be an important tool for national competitiveness [75].

3.1 Design and Social Responsibility

The idea that designing and building the physical environment carries social and ethical responsibilities is not new, but since the building boom of the early 21st century and subsequent market crash, there has been a growing discussion of socially responsible design. Socially responsible design goes by a number of names (including Design Activism, Public Interest Design, Human-Centered Design, Social Impact Design, Social Design) and has not been formally defined, but it is generally characterized by attitudes that value justice, equality, participation, sharing, sustainability, and practices that intentionally engage social issues and recognize the consequences of decisions and actions.

3.2 Design as Approaches

Eco Design. Eco design is a product-based management system merging environment aspects into product development [16]. It used to be accepted by the electrical, electronics and domestic appliance sector. The challenge for eco-product developer is to provide a benefit to the customer at the lowest environmental cost [17]. It requires radical and creative thinking to reduce environmental impacts by a factor of between four and 20 times. Eu regulation on ecolabelling and energy labelling and a Dutch government Ecodesign programme aimed at Small and medium-sized enterprise [18].

Green Design. When we talk about a green product or service which include design for remanufacturing, design disassembly and for recycling [19]. Many green design studies have focused on complete disassembly of an end-of-life product to recover valuable components [20].

Cradle to Cradle Design. Cradle-to cradle design present an alternative design and production concept to the strategies of zero emission and eco-efficiency [21]. The concept of eco-effectiveness proposes to enable materials maintain their status as resources and accumulate intelligence over time and generates a synergistic relationship between ecological and economic systems. This closing resource loops strategy inspired business model for a circular economy [22]. Circular economy is a concept promoted by the EU [23]. While the current and traditional linear extract-produce-use-dump material and energy flow model of the modern economic system is unsustainable, Circular economy provides the economic system with an alternative flow model, one that is cyclical [24]. The ultimate goal of promoting CE is the decoupling of environmental pressure from economic growth [25].

Product-Service System Design. The product service (PSS) is described in the framework of the new type of stakeholder relationships and partnerships, producing a new convergence of economic interests and a potential concomitant systemic resources optimization [26].

Design for the Base of the Pyramid (BoP). More recently scholars have explored the importance of social innovation and social entrepreneurship in the context of BoP [27]. One of the promising approaches to tackle the wicked problem of poverty is business development combined with poverty alleviation [28]. With a particular emphasis on bottom-up approaches and on an active role for users as co-creators [29].

Design for Social Innovation. Design have mainly been part of the social and economic problems that we have to face. Social innovation is defined as "a new idea that works in meeting social goals" [30]. Especially when we found the wellbeing and ways of living is not sustainable, new conceptual and methodological tools need to be develop to exploring how to imagine and build a sustainable future [31]. Democratic innovation is an original look at the political future of democracy, exploring the latest ideas aimed at renewing popular power [32]. Democratic innovation practice with the original vision of participatory design, which is democratized through easy access to production tools and lead-users as the new experts driving innovation [33].

Design for System Innovation and Transitions. Design has expanded from product-centric focus towards large scale system level changes [34]. The idea of multilevel dynamic which is called Multilevel perspective (MLP) [35] play a crucial role in connection. System innovations and transitions central to understanding the mutually reinforcing transformation of structure and patterns action [36].

Observing the design approaches evolution that contribute to the economy, society and environment and make a rough statistical analysis based on the relevant literature numbers, it is found that the emerging system innovation and transformation design has great potential to development (Fig. 1).

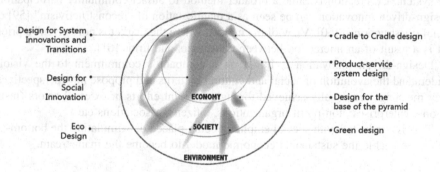

Fig. 1. Seven design driven approaches for system innovation and transitions

3.3 Design as Meaning Strategy

Norman and Verganti questioned the feasibility of user-centered design methods in promoting radical innovation [37]. Design-driven innovation, as a radical innovation, changes the rules of competition by using a meaning strategy [38]. The concept of "design is making sense of" originally proposed by Krippendorff [39–41], Meaning originates from the interaction between a person and an Artifact, whose form follows its meaning rather than its function. Sensemaking process is associated with the belief system, Organizations use information to construct meaning, create knowledge and make decisions [42, 43].

The classical debate between function and form (functionalism and rationalism) mislead the understanding of forms as the beauty of the product's appearance and style. Beside the functional value, the emotional and symbolic value of the product-meaning - is the real important issue. Meaning proposes a value system to the user as a personality and identity that transcends formal style [44].

The concept of "meaningful interaction" (MI) was put forward by WG DE Medeiros who discussed three key ideas in current design: semantics, emotion and interaction. From the perspective of product semantics, He explored the understanding behavior of users in interactive behavior and stimulated people's emotion based on the whole interactive process [45]. Meaning, as the main conceptual building block of design-driven innovation, brings forward interpretative qualities and understanding that for radical change one needs to actively interact with the network of stakeholders in an ongoing discourse and meaning co-generation [46]. Innovation as the process of new value co-creation and resource recombination through meaningful value proposition Value co-creation and resource reorganization through meaningful value proposition [47, 48].

3.4   Design as an Actor Network Process

Design-Driven Innovation as a Networked Research Process, Spans widely outside the boundaries of the films, Co-create with several other actors [49–58]. The process of interaction transformed the way of power distribution and activated more innovators in the system. Co-creation became a broader method to attract community participation. Design-driven innovation can be seen as a manifestation of "reconstructivism" [59] or social-constructionist [60]. View of the market, where the market is not "given" a priori but is a result of an interaction between consumers and firms [61].

Design-driven innovation is based on a company's commitment to the vision. Understand the evolution of social and cultural patterns and propose new perspectives. New meanings are usually achieved through the joint efforts of external actors (institutions, enterprises, non-profit organizations, citizens, associations etc.).

This is conducted with special emphasis being placed on stimulating the bottom-up actions to enable the sustainable economic model to become the mainstream.

4   Case Studies

Small, local and spontaneous practice of social innovation emerging on a global scale provide us with valuable insights. Social actors including institutions, businesses, nonprofits, citizens, associations cooperate with each other demonstrated that, it is possible to explore the alternatives beyond the mainstream model. They created a new production system which rooted in local and connected with the global network.

4.1 Permaculture

The health of ecosystem is related to the well-being of human beings. The natural ecosystem provides products and services that support human survival and economic development. However, we used to dividing human and nature into two parts and ignoring that we are actually a whole. Permaculture is a series of system-centered design principles which simulate and directly utilize the patterns and elastic characteristics of natural ecosystems. Being used in regenerative agriculture, ecological restoration, community ecology, organizational design and other fields, it gradually develops into a sustainable design agriculture dominated by citizens and becomes a popular global network and a global social movement (Permaculture Movement). The culture of Permaculture design is a philosophy of cooperation with nature. It interacts with nature through long-term observation instead of regarding it as a resource pool of human.

The Ecological Restoration Cooperative includes a broad community of researchers, landscape designers, farmers, gardeners, engineers and many other professionals. People from more than 70 countries have joined the Cooperative as founding members including many of the top Permaculture designers and trainers in the world (Fig. 2).

Fig. 2. Ecosystem restoration camp.

4.2 100-Mile Food Movement

Another case is a 100-mile food movement which encourages people to eat only foods grown or produced within 100 miles away from home to gain insight into the source of food. Since the food does not need to be transported over long distance, it greatly reduced carbon footprint of individual. The 100-mile food movement aims to learn about the local agricultural communities, to maintain close ties with local farmers and to choose a sustainable diet, no matter in the farmer's market, attending CSA or meeting regularly with food cooperatives, so as to cause people's transition from a global food system to a more local thinking.

Locally produced foods are perceived by some consumers to provide important societal, environmental, and personal benefits (Fig. 3).

Fig. 3. Search for local food sites through website

4.3 World Wide Organic Farms (WWOOF)

The Law of Thermodynamics indicates that the closed system will gradually decay into chaos and tend to be maximum entropy. However, life systems are "open" and they constantly utilize external energy and maintain a stable low-entropy state away from thermodynamic equilibrium[1]. Open innovation, expressed in one sentence, is to purposefully use knowledge inflow and outflow to accelerate internal innovation and expand external market. WWOOF, an organic farm of global network and a network community open to the world with global thinking and local action (Think global - Act local). The Global Network Alliance not only focuses on the profound value of local wisdom and traditional knowledge, but also keeps a positive attitude to external changes. It lists organic farms, ranches and huts through its website and invites volunteers to help them work together in exchange for food and accommodation. WWOOF attracts 100,000 new members each year, bringing together 14,000 farms in more than 50 countries. Such travel platforms and farm projects are emerging, reflecting new life relationships, new stories of reciprocity and connections (Fig. 4).

Fig. 4. The organic farms spread in different countries

4.4 Collaborative Chronic Care Network

Collaborative chronic care network is a non-profit hospital, research center and innovative laboratory. It is also a learning-based social production system that gathers patients, medical staff and researchers to work together. It aims to reform the IBD system of chronic disease care. It provides an accessible and interactive learning database to create a more reliable medical service system of chronic gastrointestinal diseases for children and their families. Through an open source framework for data

---

[1] Schrodinger, E. What is Life? Dublin Institute for Advanced Studies: Dublin, 1943.

sharing, it overcomes the obstacles of intellectual property rights, privacy, medical legal liability and so on. It allows patients to upload data, which means mobile phones become a sensor for disease tracking. At the same time, it enhancing the education for patients and help raise questions and improve communication. The nursing teams with family members involved seek the best nursing methods through transparent cooperation, so as to provide the best results for children (Fig. 5).

Fig. 5. Collaborative chronic care network for children

4.5 Participatory Groundwater Management Project

Take the Participatory Groundwater Management Project in Andhra Pradesh, India as an example: Due to the scarcity of water resources, illegal drilling can not be prevented. With no effective management obtained, more than 600 villages take the local waters as common resources to manage. Groundwater can be quantified and managed through data collectors of splay mark units (monitor daily rainfall, water level, outflow of wellbore, daily stream flow) to enable communities and stakeholders to monitor and manage groundwater as a public resource itself (Fig. 6).

Fig. 6. Participatory groundwater management

4.6 Ancient Chinese Cosmetics Restoration Project

The modern lady imbued in the consumerist culture are inevitably tired of the industrial aesthetics of "crystal texture". They have a Utopia space in the imagination of distant time and space from themselves. A young entrepreneur, Wang Yi Fan deductive people's ideal space makes it into a vivid story.

When she was young, She has always been obsessed with "Yanzhi" and "Meidai" which is the makeup suite used by Chinese ancient women. Drawing inspiration from Chinese ancient paintings, books and museums, she has already systematically restored 32 kinds of ancient women's cosmetics from Qin dynasty (213BC) to Qing dynasty (1644–1912). Her passion for traditional Chinese culture in the forms of stories infected a large number of fans who all hope that Chinese traditional culture can be well inherited.

These restoration cosmetics abstracted from pure natural plant, such as soybeans, madder root as a pure natural way of skin care without any chemicals. However, in contrast to functional improvements, the semantic and emotional meanings that the packaging deliver are more thought-provoking (Fig. 7).

Fig. 7. Restoration of Chinese ancient cosmetics by Young entrepreneur wang yi fan

4.7   A Flax Project

Sustainable economic is not driven by users' needs, but by companies' persistence in vision, and possible implications of new products. Companies need to understand the evolution of social and cultural patterns, propose new perspectives and meanings, understand and predict new meanings of products.

Christien Meindertsma, a Dutch designer, has launched a very interesting project and named it: A Flax Project. It aims to produce local products with reasonable price, scalability and environmental protection while exploring new production processes. Recording the production process is an important part of the flax project. Christien cooperated with film maker Roel van Tour to record all the steps of flax production. The film shows different scenes of flax producers, processors and users, such as seed sowing, spinning in Hungary, horses eating flax chaff in flax village and flax dust that used for providing energy for bio-fermentation (Fig. 8).

Fig. 8. Flax material products exhibition

5   Discussion and Concluding Remarks

The role of design evolved from products design, product service system design to collaborative organization transition design. Design-driven innovation processing a self-presentation stage for human and non-human beings. The problem is how to create a common problem situation to coordinate all participants [62]. Cultural material is involved in the design process which is based on participation, communication, and negotiation.

Participatory design thinks that design has a voice in the design process, and tends to develop effective project participation strategies for the resource-disadvantaged groups. And in a broader sense, engaging in design involves people expressing themselves creatively and engaging in meaningful activities.

Design-driven social innovation is not required to completely change social and cultural patterns, but to observe these social phenomena from a broader perspective, and influence it in a long term. It is driven by the enterprise's vision for possible product languages and breakthrough meanings in the future [38].

User participation is very beneficial to the innovation process [33, 62–64], Especially for radical innovation [65, 66].

In general, a supporting social innovation context such as legal protections, open media and network is vital to accelerating the social innovation process.

But we think a lot of ideas fail not because of inherent flaws, but because of the lack of sufficient mechanisms for them expand to scale. it requires good innovative businesses driven by technology support, public subsidies, private investment, venture capital, market competition, adapting to market conditions.

References

1. Costanza, R., d'Arge, R., De Groot, R., et al.: The value of the world's ecosystem services and natural capital. Nature **387**(6630), 253 (1997)
2. McElroy, M.W., Jorna, R.J., van Engelen, J.: Sustainability quotients and the social footprint. Corp. Soc. Responsib. Environ. Manag. **15**(4), 223–234 (2008)
3. Hjorth, P., Bagheri, A.: Navigating towards sustainable development: a system dynamics approach. Futures **38**(1), 74–92 (2006)
4. Turner, R.K., Pearce, D.W.: The ethical foundations of sustainable economic development. International Institute for Environment and Development (1990)
5. Wackernagel, M., Rees, W.: Our ecological footprint: reducing human impact on the earth, vol. 9. New Society Publishers (1998)
6. Dietz, T., Gardner, G.T., Gilligan, J., et al.: Household actions can provide a behavioral wedge to rapidly reduce US carbon emissions. Proc. Nat. Acad. Sci. **106**(44), 18452–18456 (2009)
7. Mckenzie-Mohr, D.: New ways to promote proenvironmental behavior: promoting sustainable behavior: an introduction to community-based social marketing. J. Soc. Issues **56**(3), 543–554 (2000)
8. Victor, P.A.: Managing Without Growth: Slower by Design, Not Disaster. Edward Elgar Publishing, Cheltenham (2008)
9. Dobson, A.: Fairness and futurity: essays on environmental sustainability and social justice (1999)
10. Davis, J., Lin, P., Borning, A., et al.: Simulations for urban planning: designing for human values. IEEE Comput. **39**(9), 66–72 (2006)
11. Young, T.: Caring for the earth: a strategy for sustainable living, vol. 352 (1991)
12. Scitovsky, T.: The joyless economy: the psychology of human satisfaction. Oxford University Press on Demand (1992)

13. Restakis, J.: Defining the social economy-the BC context (2006). Northern Ontario, Manitoba, and Saskatchewan Social Economy Regional Node
14. Khavul, S.: Microfinance: creating opportunities for the poor? Acad. Manag. Perspect. **24**(3), 58–72 (2010)
15. Seyfang, G.: Time banks: rewarding community self-help in the inner city? Community Dev. J. **39**(1), 62–71 (2004)
16. Donnelly, K., Beckett-Furnell, Z., Traeger, S., et al.: Eco-design implemented through a product-based environmental management system. J. Cleaner Prod. **14**(15–16), 1357–1367 (2006)
17. Luttropp, C., Lagerstedt, J.: EcoDesign and The Ten Golden Rules: generic advice for merging environmental aspects into product development. J. Cleaner Prod. **14**(15–16), 1396–1408 (2006)
18. Brower, C., Mallory, R., Ohlman, Z.: Experimental Eco-Design. RotoVision, Brighton (2009)
19. Tseng, M.-L., Tan, R.R., Siriban-Manalang, A.B.: Sustainable consumption and production for Asia: sustainability through green design and practice. J. Cleaner Prod. **40**, 1–5 (2013)
20. Shi, H., Peng, S.Z., Liu, Y., et al.: Barriers to the implementation of cleaner production in Chinese SMEs: government, industry and expert stakeholders' perspectives. J. Cleaner Prod. **16**(7), 842–852 (2008)
21. Braungart, M., McDonough, W., Bollinger, A.: Cradle-to-cradle design: creating healthy emissions–a strategy for eco-effective product and system design. J. Cleaner Prod. **15**(13–14), 1337–1348 (2007)
22. Bocken, N.M.P., de Pauw, I., Bakker, C., et al.: Product design and business model strategies for a circular economy. J. Ind. Prod. Eng. **33**(5), 308–320 (2016)
23. Gregson, N., Crang, M., Fuller, S., et al.: Interrogating the circular economy: the moral economy of resource recovery in the EU. Econ. Soc. **44**(2), 218–243 (2015)
24. Korhonen, J., Honkasalo, A., Seppälä, J.: Circular economy: the concept and its limitations. Ecol. Econ. **143**, 37–46 (2018)
25. Ghisellini, P., Cialani, C., Ulgiati, S.: A review on circular economy: the expected transition to a balanced interplay of environmental and economic systems. J. Cleaner Prod. **114**, 11–32 (2016)
26. Manzini, E., Vezzoli, C.: A strategic design approach to develop sustainable product service systems: examples taken from the 'environmentally friendly innovation' Italian prize. J. Cleaner Prod. **11**(8), 851–857 (2003)
27. Bitzer, V., Hamann, R.: The business of social and environmental innovation. In: Bitzer, V., Hamann, R., Hall, M., Griffin-EL, E.W. (eds.) The Business of Social and Environmental Innovation, pp. 3–24. Springer, Cham (2015). https://doi.org/10.1007/978-3-319-04051-6_1
28. Jagtap, S., Larsson, A.: Design of product service systems at the base of the pyramid. In: Chakrabarti, A., Prakash, R. (eds.) ICoRD 2013. LNME, pp. 581–592. Springer, New Delhi (2013). https://doi.org/10.1007/978-81-322-1050-4_46
29. Chakrabarti, R., Mason, K.: Designing better markets for people at the bottom of the pyramid: bottom-up market design. In: Concerned Markets: Economic Ordering for Multiple Values, pp. 153–177. Edward Elgar Publishing, Cheltenham (2014)
30. Manzini, E.: Making things happen: social innovation and design. Des. Issues **30**(1), 57–66 (2014)
31. Manzini, E.: Design research for sustainable social innovation. In: Michel, R. (ed.) Design Research Now, pp. 233–245. Springer, Heidelberg (2007). https://doi.org/10.1007/978-3-7643-8472-2_14
32. Saward, M.: Democratic Innovation: Deliberation, Representation and Association. Routledge, London (2003)

33. Björgvinsson, E., Ehn, P., Hillgren, P.-A.: Participatory design and democratizing innovation. In: Proceedings of the 11th Biennial Participatory Design Conference, pp. 41–50. ACM (2010)

34. Ceschin, F., Gaziulusoy, I.: Evolution of design for sustainability: from product design to design for system innovations and transitions. Des. Stud. **47**, 118–163 (2016)

35. Kemp, R., Schot, J., Hoogma, R.: Regime shifts to sustainability through processes of niche formation: the approach of strategic niche management. Technol. Anal. Strat. Manag. **10**(2), 175–198 (1998)

36. Grin, J.: The multilevel perspective and design of system innovations. In: Managing the Transition to Renewable Energy: Theory and Practice from Local, Regional and Macro Perspectives, pp. 47–80. Edward Elgar Publishing, Northampton (2008)

37. Norman, D.A., Verganti, R.: Incremental and radical innovation: design research vs. technology and meaning change. Des. Issues **30**(1), 78–96 (2014)

38. Verganti, R.: Design Driven Innovation: Changing the Rules of Competition by Radically Innovating What Things Mean. Harvard Business Press, Brighton (2009)

39. Krippendorff, K.: On the essential contexts of artifacts or on the proposition that "design is making sense (of things)". Des. Issues **5**(2), 9–39 (1989)

40. Krippendorff, K.: Product semantics: a triangulation and four design theories (1989)

41. Krippendorff, K.: The Semantic Turn: A New Foundation for Design. CRC Press, Boca Raton (2005)

42. Weick, K.E.: Sensemaking in Organizations, vol. 3. Sage, Thousand Oaks (1995)

43. Choo, C.W.: The knowing organization: how organizations use information to construct meaning, create knowledge and make decisions. Int. J. Inf. Manag. **16**(5), 329–340 (1996)

44. Verganti, R.: Design as brokering of languages: innovation strategies in Italian firms. Des. Manag. J. (Former Ser.) **14**(3), 34–42 (2003)

45. de Medeiros, W.G.: Meaningful interaction with products. Des. Issues **30**(3), 16–28 (2014)

46. Korper, A.K., Holmlid, S., Lia, L.: Bridging design-driven and service innovation: consonance and dissonance of meaning and value. In: ServDes 2018. Proceedings of the ServDes 2018 Conference on Service Design Proof of Concept, 18–20 June, Milano, Italy, no. 150, pp. 1130–1143. Linköping University Electronic Press (2018)

47. Lusch, R.F., Nambisan, S.: Service innovation: a service-dominant logic perspective. MIS Q. **39**(1), 155–175 (2015)

48. Fyrberg-Yngfalk, A., Cova, B., Pace, S., et al.: Control and power in online consumer tribes: the role of confessions. In: Consumer Culture Theory, pp. 325–350. Emerald Group Publishing Limited (2014)

49. Heskett, J.L.: Service Breakthroughs. Simon and Schuster, New York (1990)

50. Margolin, V., Buchanan, R.: The Idea of Design. MIT press, Cambridge (1995)

51. Cooper, R., Press, M.: The Design Agenda: A Guide to Successful Design Management. Wiley, Hoboken (1995)

52. Petrowski, H.: Invention by Design. Harvard University Press, Cambridge (1996)

53. Friedman, K.: Theory construction in design research: criteria: approaches, and methods. Des. Stud. **24**(6), 507–522 (2003)

54. Lloyd, P., Snelders, D.: What was Philippe Starck thinking of? Des. Stud. **24**(3), 237–253 (2003)

55. Bayazit, N.: Investigating design: a review of forty years of design research. Des. Issues **20**(1), 16–29 (2004)

56. Norman, D.A.: Emotional Design: Why We Love (or Hate) Everyday Things. Basic Civitas Books, New York (2004)

57. Mazé, R., Redström, J.: Form and the computational object. Digit. Creativity **16**(1), 7–18 (2005)

58. Karjalainen, T.-M.: Strategic design language: transforming brand identity into product design elements. In: 10th International Product Development Management Conference, June, pp. 10–11. Citeseer (2003)
59. Chan Kim, W., Mauborgne, R.: Value innovation: The strategic logic of high growth. Harvard Bus. Rev. **82**(7–8), 172–180 (2004)
60. Prahalad, C.K., Ramaswamy, V.: Co-opting customer competence. Harvard Bus. Rev. **78**(1), 79–90 (2000)
61. Verganti, R.: Design, meanings, and radical innovation: a metamodel and a research agenda. J. Prod. Innov. Manag. **25**(5), 436–456 (2008)
62. Ehn, P.: Participation in design things. In: 2008 Proceedings of the Tenth Anniversary Conference on Participatory Design, pp. 92–101. Indiana University (2008)
63. Björk, J., Magnusson, M.: Where do good innovation ideas come from? Exploring the influence of network connectivity on innovation idea quality. J. Prod. Innov. Manag. **26**(6), 662–670 (2009)
64. Von Hippel, E.: Lead users: a source of novel product concepts. Manag. Sci. **32**(7), 791–805 (1986)
65. Lettl, C.: User involvement competence for radical innovation. J. Eng. Technol. Manag. **24** (1–2), 53–75 (2007)
66. Björgvinsson, E., Ehn, P., Hillgren, P.-A.: Agonistic participatory design: working with marginalised social movements. CoDesign **8**(2–3), 127–144 (2012)
67. Jackson, T.: Prosperity without growth: Economics for a finite planet, Routledge (2009)
68. Layard, R.: Rethinking public economics: the implications of rivalry and habit. Econ. Happiness **1**(1), 147–170 (2005). Oxford University Press, Oxford
69. Veenhoven, R.: Healthy happiness: effects of happiness on physical health and the consequences for preventive health care. J. Happiness Stud. **9**(3), 449–469 (2008). Springer
70. Wilkinson, R., Pickett, K.: The spirit level. Why equality is better for everyone (2010)
71. Senge, P.M., Carstedt, G., Porter, P.L.: Next industrial revolution. MIT Sloan Manag. Rev. **42**(2), 24–38 (2001)
72. Vares, H., Parvandi, Y., Ghasemi, R., et al.: Transition from an efficiency-driven economy to innovation-driven: a secondary analysis of countries global competitiveness. Eur. J. Econ. Finan. Adm. Sci. **31**, 124–132 (2011)
73. Kuznetsova, N.P.: Economic growth in the large and small-scale economies and the role of resources in the conversion of energy-oriented to innovation-driven economy. Ekonomika/Economics, 88 (2009)
74. Pot, F., Dhondt, S., Oeij, P.: Social innovation of work and employment. 见: Challenge social innovation, Springer, 261–274 (2012)
75. Meng, H.-C.: Innovation cluster as the national competitiveness tool in the innovation driven economy. Int. J. Foresight Innov. Policy **2**(1), 104–116 (2005). Inderscience Publishers

The Trend of Governmental Investment on HCI-Related Research to Solve Social Problem in Korea

Seung-Kyu Yi[✉]

Center for Social Innovation Policy, Korea Institute of S&T Evaluation
and Planning (KISTEP), Seoul, South Korea
skyist@kistep.re.kr

Abstract. As both the demand for quality of life and the speed of social change are increasing, solving structural problems of society is becoming important. In particular, as not only the proportion of technological drivers in many social changes increases, but also searching for solutions using advanced science and technology is being actively discussed, the interaction between technology and human/society is become important research object for social problem. The purpose of this paper is to show the importance and main characteristics of HCI in Korean governmental research investment, especially relations to solving social problems. The R&D budget of FY2009, 2013, and 2017 were analyzed, and some characteristics are analyzed in terms of different indices, such as research and experimental development stages, the type of research-conducting agent, and the socio-economic purpose in view of social problem solving. In this study, HCI related categories were carefully selected using Korea's standard science and technology classification system. These empirical analysis will provide practical implications for the role of HCI technology in the policy for solving social problems.

Keywords: Korea · Government R&D · HCI · Social problem · S&T classification system

1   Introduction

Importance of Human Computer Interaction (HCI) related research is growing not only in a technical point of view but also in a social point of view. As shown in the case of the digital transition and the 4th industrial revolution, the proportion of technology drivers in recent social change is increasing, and it is actively discussed to secure measures to cope with social change using advanced science and technology. "Human" and "computer" are no longer far apart, and convergence research linking the two fields is actively under way. Looking at trends in HCI-related research in Korea's government R&D, which has the highest ratio of R&D budget/GDP in the world, helps to predict what HCI-related research can play in terms of social change and solving social problems. It will also provide implications for establishing R&D policies related to HCI for the future.

© Springer Nature Switzerland AG 2019
C. Stephanidis and M. Antona (Eds.): HCII 2019, CCIS 1088, pp. 343–348, 2019.
https://doi.org/10.1007/978-3-030-30712-7_43

2 Approach

In order to analysis the trend of HCI-related research in Korea's governmental R&D, HCI-related research subjects were extracted from the data of 'Governmental R&D Survey and Analysis in 2009, 2013 and 2017'. 2009 and 2013 were chosed as starting point and 2nd point of analysis because HCI-related research is convergence research between Human and Computer and 'The basic plan for the development of convergence technologies ('09–'13)' started in 2009 and ended in 2013. The third analysing point is 2017, the fifth year from 2013, which was choosed to compare the first five-year period and 2nd five-year period. According to the Korea governmental R&D surveys and analysis data, there are 39,565 research subjects in 2009, 50,865 in 2013, and 61,280 in 2017. Using Korea's national standard classification system for science and technology, we have identified which of these tasks is related to HCI, including 33 sectors, 369 sectors, and 2,899. Nine categories were selected, seven categories are associated with "Human", and two categories for "Computer". HCI-related research subject is simultaneously classified into both one of the "Human"-related categories and one of the "Computer"-related categories (Table 1).

Table 1. HCI related categories from the Korean national standard classification system on S&T

	Field	Category
Human	H. Humanities	HA. History/Archeology
		HB. Philosophy/Religion
		HC. Linguistics
		HD. Literature
		HE. Culture/Arts/Sports
	O. Human Science and Technologies	OA. Brain Sciences
		OB. Cognitive/Emotion & Sensibility Sciences
Computer	E. Engineering	ED. Electricity and Electronics
		EE. Information/Communication

To analysis trend of HCI-related research, the characteristics of HCI-related subjects in 2009, 2013 and 2017 were analysis. Then the recent trends of HCI research was analyzed by comparing change of characteristics of the first 5-year period 2009–2013 and the second 5-year period 2013–2017. The analyzed characteristics are the rate of increase of research fund, the subject proportion by R&D stage, the subject proportion by 6T sector, and the type of research institute (player). In particular, economic and social purpose of research was analyzed to examined how HCI-related research can be related to social problem solving. The table below summarizes the relevant indicators and their contents (Table 2).

Table 2. List of indices analyzed

View	Index	Contents
Importance	R&D Spending	Expenditure/Number of Subjects
Technological Maturity	R&D Stage	Basic research/Applied research/Experimental development
Actor	Type of research-conducting agent	University/Industry/GRI; Government Related Institute
Technological field	Classification in terms of 6 kinds of technologies (6T)	IT (information)/BT (biology)/NT (nano)/ CT (culture)/ET (environment)/ST (space)
Purpose	Socio-economic objective	13 categories in Public sector (Social objective) and 20 categories in industry (Economic objective)

3   Results

3.1   Importance in Governmental R&D: R&D Spending

The result of comparing analysis shows that research in HCI categories increased more than 5.6 times faster than entire government R&D during recent five-year period. Especially this growth rate is higher than 4.7 times of previous five-year period. This means importance of HCI is growing in government R&D and technologies in the future (Table 3).

Table 3. Comparing R&D spending on HCI categories (2009–2013 vs 2013–2017)

(USD, Million $)*	2009	2013	2017	CAGR(%) 2009–2013	CAGR(%) 2013–2017
R&D in HCI categories	6.5	23.3	47.6	**37.6%**	**19.6%**
Government R&D	10,978.1	14,956.9	17,148.5	**8.0%**	**3.5%**

*adapted annual average exchange rate in 2017 year (Korea Won (KW) to U.S. Dollar (USD))

3.2   Characteristics of R&D

The result of comparison analysis in terms of R&D stage shows that the proportion of the basic research subject in the last five-year period is still the highest at 66.1%, but fell 4.3% from previous five-year period. Experimental development is the second proportion at 16.1%, increased by 2.2% than the previous five-year period. Applied research is the lowest proportion except "other" at 11.3%, decreased by 2.7% than previous period. These results suggest that some of the researches started in the previous period have progressed to the commercialization phase or that the researches for practical use in the short term have increased recently (Table 4).

Table 4. Comparing proportion of HCI-related research subjects by R&D stage (2009–2013 vs 2013–2017)

R&D stage	2009	2013	2017	Increase/Decrease 2009–2013	Increase/Decrease 2013–2017
Basic research	40.9%	70.4%	66.1%	29.5% ↑	4.3% ↓
Applied research	34.1%	13.9%	11.3%	20.2% ↓	2.7% ↓
Experimental development	25.0%	13.9%	16.1%	11.1% ↓	2.2% ↑
Other	–	1.8%	6.5%	1.8% ↑	4.7% ↑

The result of comparison analysis in terms of actor shows that the proportion of the research subject by university in the last five-year period is still the highest at 74.8%, especially increased 29.6% from previous five-year period. On the other hand, the proportion of the research by GRI decreased to the 6.5%. These results mean university became overwhelming player in governmental HCI research project, and the role of GRI was greatly reduced (Table 5).

Table 5. Comparing research-conducting agent of R&D on HCI categories (2009–2013 vs 2013–2017)

Conducting agent	2009	2013	2017	Increase/Decrease 2009–2013	Increase/Decrease 2013–2017
University	70.1%	43.2%	74.8%	**26.9% ↓**	**29.6% ↑**
GRI	22.1%	19.0%	6.5%	**3.1% ↓**	**12.5% ↓**
Industry	5.7%	16.7%	15.6%	**11.0% ↑**	**1.1% ↓**
Other	2.1%	21.0%	3.0%	**18.9% ↑**	**18.0% ↓**

The result of comparison analysis in terms of technological field, namely 6T, shows that research in field of IT (Information tech.) is still most active area and CT (Culture tech.) field is the second active in HCI research. There was no significant change in the proportion of all 6 fields (Table 6).

Table 6. Comparing technological field of R&D on HCI categories (2009–2013 vs 2013–2017)

6T	2009	2013	2017	Increase/Decrease 2009–2013	Increase/Decrease 2013–2017
BT	11.4%	10.2%	13.9%	**1.2% ↓**	**3.7% ↑**
IT	65.9%f	54.6%	51.3%	**11.3% ↓**	**3.3% ↓**
NT	–	1.9%	3.9%	**1.9% ↑**	**2.0% ↑**
CT	18.2%	27.8%	27.4%	**9.6% ↑**	**0.4% ↓**
ET, ST	–		0.4%	–	**0.4% ↑**
Other	4.5%	5.6%	3.0%	**1.1% ↑**	**2.6% ↓**

The result of comparison analysis in terms of research purpose shows that the proportion of the research for public purpose in last five-year period (2013–2017) increased slightly by 3.8% compared to previous five-year period (2009–2013). Among public purpose research, the proportion of the research for "Health" was the highest at 11.3%, increased the most by 6.9% compared than the previous five-year period. Also the proportion of the research for "Education" was increased by 3.4%, that for "Political and social systems, structures and process" was increased by 3.7% for last five-year period. On the other hand, the proportion of "Culture, recreation, religion and mass media" research has disappeared. These results suggest that HCI research has more public purpose than industrial application, and it means that the proportion of research for solving social problems is increasing. This is supported by the fact that the proportion of the research for health, education, security, and social system, which are the main areas of social problems, have increased over the past five years compared to previous five-year period (Table 7).

Table 7. Comparing socio-economic purpose of R&D on HCI categories (2009–2013 vs 2013–2017)

Socio-economic objective of R&D	2009	2013	2017	Increase/Decrease 2009–2013	Increase/Decrease 2013–2017
Exploration and exploitation of the Earth	–	–		–	–
Environment	–	–			–
Exploration and exploitation of space	–	–			–
Transport, telecommunication and other infrastructures	–	0.9	1.7%	0.9% ↑	0.8% ↑
Energy	–	–			–
Health	13.6	4.6	11.3%	9.0% ↓	6.9% ↑
Agriculture	4.5	–	0.4%	4.5% ↓	0.4% ↑
Education	–	0.9	4.3%	0.9% ↑	3.4%↑
Culture, recreation, religion and mass media	4.5	6.5		2.0% ↑	6.5% ↓
Political and social systems, structures and processes	–	3.7	7.4%	3.7% ↑	3.7% ↑
General advancement of knowledge	11.4	5.6	7.4%	5.8% ↓	1.8% ↑
Defense	–	–	1.4%	–	1.4% ↑
Other public purpose	2.3	12.0	3.0%	9.7% ↑	9.0% ↓
Sum of public purpose	*36.3%*	*34.2%*	*37.0%*	*2.1%*	*3.8% ↑*
Industrial production and technology	63.7	63.0	63.0%	0.7% ↓	0.0%
Other industrial purpose	–	2.8		2.8% ↑	2.8% ↓
Sum of industrial purpose	*63.7*	*65.8*	*63.0*	*2.1%*	*2.8% ↓*

4   Conclusion

The change in scale of HCI related research has increased HCI's importance in Korea's national research and development and will strengthen HCI's role in future. It also provides implications for the further promotion of policies. Considering the high growth rate of the scale of HCI research funds, it becomes clear that HCI's relative importance to Korea's national research and development will increase rapidly. Especially relative ratio of basic research as well as new and complex research carried out by universities as well as industries has been high or increased. This means that the base of research systems have been strengthen and that it is very probably that HCI research will consistently be expanded. As a consequence, policies that efficiently create and spread research outcomes have become essential. This further means that the CT area among 6T has gained great relative importance among the characteristics of the main technological field. As regards the economic and social objectives of research, this study showed that the objectives of the public sector as well as the industrial sector are becoming more and more diversified. These changes demonstrate that there's a possibility for HCI to become widely used in society which farther means that it is important to establish a legal framework, and introduce policies to develop the infrastructure that is needed for such a development. Last but not least, from an industrial perspective it is necessary to persistently work on the needed system and monitor the environmental changes of industries that have emerged as main fields of application.

References

1. National S&T Commission, Governmental R&D survey and analysis in FY2009 (written in Korean), October 2010
2. The Ministry of Science, ICT and Future Planning, Governmental R&D survey and analysis in FY2013, August 2014
3. The Ministry of Science and ICT, Governmental R&D survey and analysis in FY2017 (written in Korean), August 2018
4. National Science and Technology Information Service. http://www.ntis.go.kr

Big Data, Machine Learning and Visual Analytics

Graph-Based Format for Modeling Multimodal Annotations in Virtual Reality by Means of VAnnotatoR

Giuseppe Abrami[✉], Alexander Mehler, and Christian Spiekermann

Texttechnology Lab, Goethe University Frankfurt, Frankfurt, Germany
abrami@em.uni-frankfurt.de

Abstract. Projects in the field of *Natural Language Processing* (NLP), the *Digital Humanities* (DH) and related disciplines dealing with machine learning of complex relationships between data objects need annotations to obtain sufficiently rich training and test sets. The visualization of such data sets and their underlying *Human Computer Interaction* (HCI) are perennial problems of computer science. However, despite some success stories, the clarity of information presentation and the flexibility of the annotation process may decrease with the complexity of the underlying data objects and their relationships. In order to face this problem, the so-called VANNOTATOR was developed, as a flexible annotation tool using 3D glasses and augmented reality devices, which enables annotation and visualization in three-dimensional virtual environments. In addition, multimodal objects are annotated and visualized within a graph-based approach.

Keywords: Annotation · Virtual Reality · VAnnotatoR · Image analysis · Digital Humanities

1 Introduction

Projects in the field of *Natural Language Processing* (NLP), the *Digital Humanities* (DH) and related disciplines dealing with machine learning of complex relationships between data objects need annotations to obtain sufficiently rich training and test sets. The visualization of such data sets and their underlying *Human Computer Interaction* (HCI) are perennial problems of computer science. In any event, visualizing annotations is an old topic, and various projects (e.g. [10,11,17,22]) have experimented with mostly 2D models thereby achieving considerable success. Despite these success stories, one can nevertheless observe that the clarity of information presentation and the flexibility of the annotation process decrease with the complexity of the underlying data objects and their relations. In order to overcome these pitfalls, the interface of annotation tools needs to be developed considerably: It must leave behind the narrow tracks of 2D graph-like visualizations that make annotations confusing as soon as a certain

© Springer Nature Switzerland AG 2019
C. Stephanidis and M. Antona (Eds.): HCII 2019, CCIS 1088, pp. 351–358, 2019.
https://doi.org/10.1007/978-3-030-30712-7_44

number of annotation units and their relations is exceeded. And it must become much more interactive by ideally exploiting the full bandwidth of human multimodal information processing to map objects and their network relations. In recent years, technological progress in HCI has largely focused on the development of 3D interfaces, if performance and flexibility optimization is ignored. However, the implementation of 3D interfaces in the field of manual annotations of information objects is still pending. Therefore, one can state that interfaces of current annotation tools are still a barrier for new forms of visualization and interaction with information objects.

In order to overcome these barrier and to implement intuitive annotation methods, the so-called VANNOTATOR [20] was developed. It uses state-of-the-art technologies of *Virtual Reality* (VR) and *Augmented Reality* (AR) to address the interface problem. VANNOTATOR (VAR) is not the only annotator or visualizer in VR (e.g. [6,21]) but differs from other projects in terms of its flexible data model and the collaborative parallel use that it enables in AR.

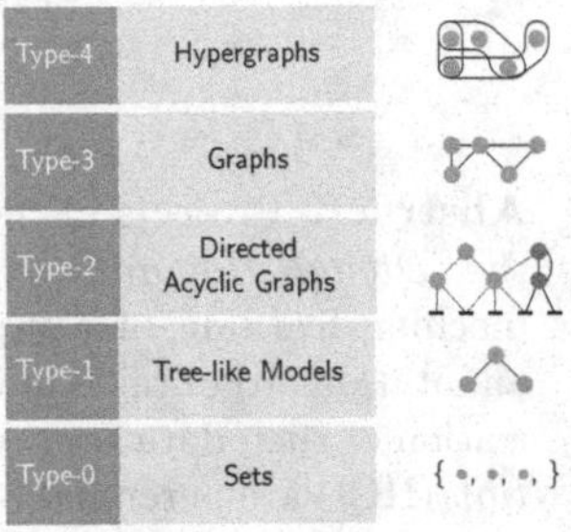

Fig. 1. Graph structures which can be annotated and visualized by means of VAR.

This paper will exemplify the annotation of instances of the graph-like structures (as enumerated by Fig. 1) by means of VAR. Furthermore, it will describe the capabilities of VAR regarding the implicit, inferential annotation of object relations. This will be done by example of text-image and text-image-building relations where the buildings are animated as walk-on-able artifacts.

2   Related Work

In addition to the projects already mentioned, annotation in a three-dimensional virtual environment is the subject of various disciplines and research, in which only a few are actually used. A simple annotation tool in virtual environments such as [5,6,8,10] allows the annotation of objects with texts or voice recordings. This may not sound like much at first glance, but it is an essential point in virtual annotation tools. Since entering text without a keyboard is a challenge in itself, there are already innovative solutions available [7]. At the same time there are also annotation systems in the medical [19] and educational field [18]. This work focuses on the aspect of the interface and the implicit annotation of multimodal objects. As far as known, there is still no solution for three-dimensional virtual environments in this context. With VAR that gap will be closed.

3   Technology

The annotation of multimodal (e.g. textual and pictorial data) data is associated with various requirements. In order to meet these requirements, VAR utilizes a graph-based annotation model that covers a wide range of types of information objects as enumerated in Fig. 2. The data structure used by VAR to let users generate examples of this sort is UIMA [9], a data format commonly used in NLP. UIMA enables the creation of flexible annotation schemes, while numerous automatic annotators exist for pre-processing text resources that generate UIMA-compliant documents (e.g. Hemati et al. [11]).

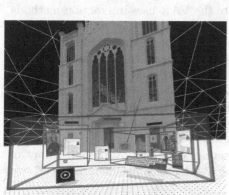

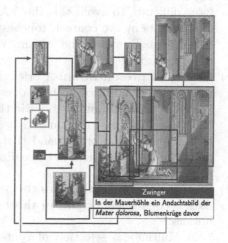

Fig. 2. An overview of a section of multimodal information units (video, audio, geo coordinates, images, 3D models, URLs (visualized as virtual browser windows)), their relations (lines) and their hierarchical encapsulation (large boxes) with VAR. Please note that all 3D objects can also be modeled and entered as independent rooms as well as set in relation to discourse referents in the same virtual environment. In the background the 3D model of the former main synagogue in Frankfurt, which was destroyed during the Nazi regime, is shown. The model was created during a student practical training course [14]. This data is taken from the Stolperwege project [15].

Fig. 3. Illustration [12] of a scene from Goethe's Faust. Based on the stage instructions on Faust I - Vers 3587 ff., ("In der Mauerhöhle ein Andachtsbild der Mater dolorosa, Blumenkrüge davor" Translation: *In the wall cave, a devotional picture of Mater dolorosa, flower jugs in front of it*), the picture was illustrated according to the artist's imagination. The lines show the segmentation of individual image sections for a more detailed description. The arrows connect the individual text passages with the respective described contents. In this example, individual segments were created recursively from the main image (the example is kept simple for clarity).

To enable the database-oriented processing of such documents, VAR utilizes the *UIMA Database Interface* [2]. In order to enable the annotation of multimodal networks, the following properties are required for VAR's interface:

(a) **Flexibility:** Some applications have to annotate strictly according to a scheme, and others are very flexible. In both cases, however, it is essential that both situations are addressed by the interface. For this purpose, VAR visualizes all relationships and objects based on the classes available in the underlying data model. This allows to limit or extend the annotation capabilities by modifying the data model.

(b) **Intuitive Handling:** In order to enable the usability of an interface, its usage must be simple. However, the use of 3D glasses and the corresponding controllers or other input devices makes this requirement considerably more difficult. To avoid this the VAR combines the possibilities of selecting elements by eye contact, touches by the corresponding controllers or by data gloves. To reduce the learning rate the VAR uses interaction methods borrowed from real life.

(c) **Clarity of presentation:** A brief view on complex graph structures shows that their visualization usually does not contribute to clarity. In order to keep the clarity, the annotations in the VAR are displayed in different ways. This means on the one hand that nodes can be grouped, expanded and hidden and on the other hand that edges can be equipped with different detail levels. In addition, in three dimensional environments this is the most complex component.

(d) **Simple data entry:** Besides the presentation of annotations, the input of data is equally important. In this case VAR basically differs between two options:

  – Multimodal selection of content in VR using virtual browsers and RESOURCES2CITY [13]. The first enables the selection of various contents (text, videos, audio, images) from a virtual browser into the virtual environment (Fig. 2). The second allows the selection of resources on the local system by visualizing the folder structure as a traversable city with buildings for the files.

  – The text input is done via the virtual keyboard which also supports speech to text.

VAR is completely controlled by the virtual hands, which can be used via VR controller or data gloves. These allow the user to interact with the environment and create various objects at any location. As visualized in Fig. 2, a collection of different multimodal objects were created in the virtual environment. Besides the possibility to load the different data types into the virtual environment, they can also be modified, linked or used for further actions. The latter means in VAR that texts and images can be segmented (cf. Fig. 4) and text or image elements from browsers can be selected. Furthermore, all objects can be linked (lines) and grouped (boxes). In order to link objects with each other,

Table 1. Extract of the spatial relationships within an image.

Orientation
in
partOf
inFrontOf
behindOf
aboveOf
belowOf
rightOf
leftOf

a line must be drawn between objects using the *virtual finger*, which can subsequently be attributed. In addition, objects can be grouped hierarchically by creating nodes in which different amounts of objects can be assigned (Fig. 2). At the same time, the editability of the group can be switched on and off to prevent the objects in the grouping from being accidentally ungrouped. The annotations described previously are explicit, in the sense that an object is actively related to another object. There are also implicit annotations, which annotate objects based on spatial relationships. These relationships are established by the annotation process itself and create a meta-annotation, which in this case can only be effective through the three-dimensional annotation environment, since in this case depth perception can be used. As exemplified in Fig. 5, the spatial positions of the previously segmented images are related to each other. Here, the relationship "Orientation:*inFronOf*" is implicitly annotated by the visual positioning of a segment in front of another segment. It is performed by comparing the relative positions of the individual segments on the original image with each other to determine the spatial relationship. In the case of incorrect classifications, these annotations can be adjusted through movement. In addition, all spatial relationships, taken from [4], (see Table 1), which can be annotated more than once (e.g. Object **A** is *inFrontOf* and *aboveOf* **B**). Furthermore, the distinction whether an object is a *in* another or is placed in *frontOf* it is determined by perspective implicit annotation (cf. Figs. 4, 5). Notice that this functionality is currently only implemented in the VR version of VAR. Moreover, this option can be disabled so that an annotator does not accidentally change the implicit annotation of elements when moving them. By default, however, this is enabled.

4   Annotation Scenario

To illustrate the advantages of a 3D tool as exemplified by VAR, we consider a scenario of multimodal annotation taken from the "Faust" [1] project and start with annotating in a 2D fashion. Figure 3 illustrates several content elements of an image and an accompanying text that are linked with each other to manifest, for example, part-whole and intermedial relations. In [3] we described several annotation layers that need to be related in such an annotation scenario. Figure 3 exemplifies an outline of them by using a graph

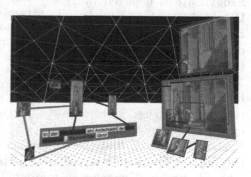

Fig. 4. Similar task as annotated in Fig. 3 in the virtual environment of the VAR.

layout in which information objects are linked as vertices by means of colored arcs. Obviously, network-like representations, as shown in this example, quickly become unclear, so that object connections become hardly distinguishable. Any additional annotation (regarding, for example, dependency relations among tokens in the embedded text, positional relations (e.g. *inFrontOf*) of pictorial objects or ontological relations (`Mater dolorosa` *is a* "devotional picture") would render this representation even more unclear. In order to circumvent this problem of *decreasing representational clarity as a result of increasing annotational depth*, VAR uses a 3D representation format that can be manipulated in a multimodal manner: explicitly and implicitly. As illustrated in Fig. 4, VAR generates the same relations as the so called *OWLnotator* [3]. The difference to *OWLnotator* and comparable tools is in the used data model as well as in the 3D visualization and placement of annotations. As mentioned, VAR enables implicit perspective annotations through movements and actions performed by its users. Figure 5 shows this by considering the same annotation scenario as Fig. 3.

The information units in the text to be annotated are represented as discourse referents (cubes) [16,20]. Discourse referents (DR) are conceptual representations of objects as subjects of statements, attributions etc. within a semiotic aggregate (i.e. a text or an image). Starting from a text, visual depictions of DRs (cubes) are connected with the corresponding tokens manifesting them. In the scenario depicted by Fig. 5, `Mauerhöhle` is depicted by the DR M, `Blumenkrüge` by B and the `Andachtsbild` by A. `Mater dolorosa` is a multi-word token that is represented by the DR D. The annotations of Fig. 5 have been created by means of simple controller-based gestures, as explained in Section Technology.

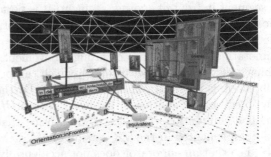

Fig. 5. Extended annotation of Fig. 4. The segmented images are arranged in perspective and their content is related to each other (e.g. pink segment). The segments are related with discourse referents (blue box "Gretchen" as literary person) or get any attributes defined by the existing data model. There are relations between discourse referents (all objects in the VR implicitly become discourse referents) which can be related together (purple line) as a hyper edge to another object (e.g. red line). Implicit relations (green dotted line) can be visualized as well as groupings (DR D). (Color figure online)

It should be noted that the annotation of object relations is partly done by the implicit positioning of virtual objects within the VAR's 3D environment. The relationship `Blumenkrüge` *inFrontOf* `Mater Dolorosa` was annotated, for example, by placing the corresponding representations within the VR. In this way, we take profit from a *fourth dimension* in which perspective topological arrangements of annotation objects are explored to annotated them. From this perspective, it is a relatively small step towards motion-controlled annotations as by-products of the annotator's movements in space. Figure 5 additionally demonstrates the visualization of a subgraph of Type 4 (red line in conjunction with red arrow) (for these types see Fig. 1) and of an implicit, inferential annotation (green dotted arrow): since the `Blumenkrüge` are in *inFrontOf* the

Mauerhöhle and the Mater dolorosa is *in* the Mauerhöhle, the Blumenkrüge are also *inFrontOf* of the Mater dolorosa. Though annotations can be positioned at any desirable location in VR, the format underlying VAR is limited with respect to the amount of information that can be displayed and processed in a graph-like manner. However, moving within such a space allows annotators for freely changing their perspective with respect to focal annotation objects and to use a wider bandwidth of multimodal information processing to manipulate them.

5   Conclusion

In this paper we presented VAR as a tool for graph-based annotations of multimodal objects. Through the use of 3D glasses, this tool enables an immersion of common and complex annotation processes. For this, a scenario for multimodal annotation of image segments was presented in comparison to the 2-dimensional annotation tool *OWLnotator* in which the three-dimensional annotation environment provides considerable advantages. These advantages become evident when not only the representation of multimodal information units is explored, but also the possibility of implicit annotation through the movement of the annotators. Although the graphical representation of complex correlations can still be extensible, a considerable complexity can be represented with the previous implementation. For this reason, the next development steps will include the implementation of a graph algorithm to automatically position the elements of a graph and the automatic analysis of images. It is also important to identify the scope to which the principle of implicit annotation of relations among objects can be used and implemented in augmented reality. Anyway, the development and exploration of annotation and visualization methods in three-dimensional virtual environments has just begun.

References

1. Abrami, G., Freiberg, M., Warner, P.: Managing and annotating historical multimodal corpora with the eHumanities desktop - an outline of the current state of the LOEWE project Illustrations of Goethe's Faust. In: Historical Corpora, pp. 353–363 (2015)
2. Abrami, G., Mehler, A.: A UIMA database interface for managing NLP-related text annotations. In: 2018 Proceedings of LREC, LREC 2018, 7–12 May, Miyazaki, Japan (2018)
3. Abrami, G., Mehler, A., Pravida, D.: Fusing text and image data with the help of the OWLnotator. In: Yamamoto, S. (ed.) HIMI 2015. LNCS, vol. 9172, pp. 261–272. Springer, Cham (2015). https://doi.org/10.1007/978-3-319-20612-7_25
4. Bateman, J.A., et al.: A linguistic ontology of space for natural language processing. Artif. Intell. **174**(14), 1027–1071 (2010)
5. Bowman, D.A., Hodges, L.F., Bolter, J.: The virtual venue: user-computer interaction in information-rich virtual environments. Presence **7**(5), 478–493 (1998)

6. Brown, R.A.: Conceptual modelling in 3D virtual worlds for process communication. In: 2010 Proceedings of APCCM, APCCM 2010, Brisbane, Australia, pp. 25–32. Australian Computer Society Inc. (2010)

7. Dudley, J.D., Vertanen, K., Kristensson, P.O.: Fast and precise touch-based text entry for head-mounted augmented reality with variable occlusion. ACM Trans. Comput.-Hum. Interact. **25**(6), 30:1–30:40 (2018)

8. Gabbard, J.L.: A taxonomy of usability characteristics in virtual environments. Ph.D. thesis, Virginia Tech (1997)

9. Götz, T., Suhre, O.: Design and implementation of the UIMA Common Analysis System. IBM Syst. J. **43**(3), 476–489 (2004)

10. Harmon, R., et al.: The virtual annotation system. In: 1996 Proceedings of the IEEE Virtual Reality Annual International Symposium, pp. 239–245. IEEE (1996)

11. Hemati, W., Uslu, T., Mehler, A.: TextImager: a distributed UIMA-based system for NLP. In: Proceedings of the COLING 2016 System Demonstrations. Federated Conference on Computer Science and Information Systems, Osaka, Japan (2016)

12. Frankfurter Goethe-Haus/Freies Deutsches Hochstift. Gretchen vor der Mater dolorosa (2015). https://hessen.museum-digital.de/index.php?t=objekt& oges=2058&navlang=de

13. Kett , A., et al.: Resources2City Explorer: a system for generating interactive walkable virtual cities out of file systems. In: Proceedings of the UIST 2018, Berlin, Germany (2018)

14. Kühn, V., et al.: Digital reconstruction of the former main synagogue in Frankfurt. Result of a student practical course Ubiquitious Texttechnologies in summer term 2018 (2018)

15. Mehler, A., et al.: Stolperwege: an app for a digital public history of the holocaust. In: Proceedings of the 28th ACM Conference on Hypertext and Social Media, HT 2017, Prague, Czech Republic, pp. 319–320. ACM (2017)

16. Mehler, A., et al.: VAnnotatoR: a framework for generating multimodal hypertexts. In: Proceedings of HT 2018, Baltimore, Maryland. ACM (2018)

17. Mehler, A., et al.: Wikidition: automatic lexiconization and linkication of text corpora. Inf. Technol. **58**, 70–79 (2016)

18. Renner, P., Pfeiffer, T.: Evaluation of attention guiding techniques for augmented reality-based assistance in picking and assembly tasks. In: Proceedings of the 22nd International Conference on Intelligent User Interfaces Companion, IUI 2017 Companion, Limassol, Cyprus, pp. 89–92. ACM (2017)

19. Saalfeld, P., Glaßer, S., Preim, B.: 3D user interfaces for interactive annotation of vascular structures. In: Mensch und Computer 2015-Proceedings (2015)

20. Spiekermann, C., Abrami, G., Mehler, A.: VAnnotatoR: a gesture-driven annotation framework for linguistic and multimodal annotation. In: Proceedings of the AREA Workshop, AREA, Miyazaki, Japan (2018)

21. Teo, T., et al.: Data fragment: virtual reality for viewing and querying large image sets. In: 2017 IEEE Virtual Reality, January, pp. 327–328 (2017)

22. Zhao, J., et al.: Annotation graphs: a graph-based visualization for meta-analysis of data based on user-authored annotations. IEEE Trans. Vis. Comput. Graph. **23**(1), 261–270 (2017)

An Online Comment Assistant for a Better Comment Experience

Ju Yeon Choi[1], Younah Kang[1,2], and Keeheon Lee[2,3(✉)]

[1] Graduate School of Communication, Yonsei University,
Seoul, Republic of Korea
{juyeonchoi, yakang}@yonsei.ac.kr
[2] Underwood International College, Yonsei University,
Seoul, Republic of Korea
keeheon@yonsei.ac.kr
[3] Graduate School of Information, Yonsei University, Seoul, Republic of Korea

Abstract. In this study, we examined online news comment activities that are used as a key means of public opinion and interaction in modern society. We extracted keywords in comments using big data and sorted them according to frequency. Through this process, a chatbot was designed to check the ranking and contents of comments based on keywords represent the most important issues in the comment population and search for classified comments according to keywords before users read the news. Through experiments using this chatbot, we compared and analyzed the nature of the comments in the existing comment system and the characteristics of the system experience. Results shows that the chatbot designed in this study can provide more information than existing comment presentation systems, search for comments by type, and check more information than articles. In addition, assessing the nature of the existing comments reduced the number of sensational, non-slang-oriented comments.

Keywords: Data-driven user experience · Chatbot · Comment analysis · Comment curation

1 Introduction

The value and role of news has been newly defined as online news comment activity has emerged as a key communication tool. In addition, comments from online news provide technical differentiation that allows participation of users and interaction between media and users. Accordingly, online news comment activities have become a system for users to express and share their opinions freely. Online news comment activities are often mentioned as a subject of social controversy, such as the problem of representation due to biased comment participation or the problem of distortion and manipulation of public opinion in the comment list. With a small number of comments taking up a higher share of participation, debate has persisted that the current online news comment structure creates more distortions and monopolies than the traditional media [1]. In particular, the ranking and empathy of comments are considered to be significant factors in accepting comments. Best-ranking comments are often perceived

© Springer Nature Switzerland AG 2019
C. Stephanidis and M. Antona (Eds.): HCII 2019, CCIS 1088, pp. 359–368, 2019.
https://doi.org/10.1007/978-3-030-30712-7_45

as the main public opinion, and many of these comments also have significant control over the user's claims. Furthermore, research is also being conducted on the impact of order of comments, due to phenomena such as more acceptance of top-level comments, even if the order is reversed [2].

Online news usage remains fairly high, and comment sections play a major role as an active public opinion community and venue for dialogue and empathy [3]. As an alternative means of political participation, comments are as much a means of news acceptance as articles [4], and comment activities are often used as a source of confidence in the opinion and allow users to support their opinions, gather their opinions, and make and verify critical comparisons [3]. In addition, the more people who do not trust mainstream media, the more people who actively use comments, disseminate and share news [5], and are used as the main means of grasping public opinion.

In this study, we examined online news comment activities, which are used as a key means of public opinion and interaction in modern society, despite ongoing controversies and problems. We extracted keywords in the comments using big data and sorted them according to frequency. Through this process, a chatbot was designed to check the ranking and contents of comments based on keywords reflecting the most important issues in the comment population and search for classified comments according to keywords before users read the news. Through experiments using this chatbot, we compared and analyzed the nature of the comments in the existing comment system and the characteristics of the chatbot system experience. Results show that chatbots designed in this study can provide more information than existing comment presentation systems, search for comments by type, and check more information than articles. In addition, assessing the nature of the existing comments reduced the number of sensational, non-slang-oriented comments.

2 Literature Review

Prior studies have identified the characteristics and effects of online comments using data analysis techniques and statistical tools. Lee et al. [6] proposed a method for analyzing the quality of comments using the characteristics of comments and setting their weight. Daegun [7] also quantitatively analyzed the distribution of emotions by categorizing the emotions expressed in comments by news category. Similarly, Han et al. [8] constructed and applied a machine learning-based emotional analysis model based on data from four emotions: pleasure, sadness, anger, and disgust. In addition to emotion-based analysis and classification work, studies have analyzed the typical characteristics of comments through visualization work. Lee et al. [9] proposed a system that would statistically analyze postings and comments from a Forum AGORA web blog and cluster them based on similarities, then visualized the system clustering results and showed them in a screen view. Lee et al. [9] classified a large number of comments and visualized them through the TRIB system to search for comments that correspond to specific content and display the entire comment section.

Second, in the field of human–computer interface, studies have been conducted on the impact of user interface (UI) design on users in terms of user experience and interaction. Faridani et al. [10] presented an interface named Opinion Spac. This interface visualizes comments on a two-dimensional plane using dots based on similarity of user opinions. Comments were highlighted by deliberative polling, dimensionality reduction, and collaborative filtering [10]. Madden [11] categorized types of comments by analyzing 66,637 user comments on YouTube videos. Classification schema of the system include information, advice, impression, opinion, response, etc. Sung et al. [12], using visualization techniques of ToPIN and ThemeRiver, presented a novel visualization method to analyze and categorize the topics and content types of users' time-anchored comments. Types consisted of general conversation, question, opinion, complaint, and compliment.

Most of the previous research on comment data was based on emotional analysis. In addition, the research was focused on UI improvement using visualization based on a better understanding of user experience. These studies did not solve the problems of bias and representation issues in existing commenting systems based on the content analysis of comments. To solve this problem, this study attempted to analyze new comments based on frequency analysis of comment keywords and implemented them in a chatbot system. Based on frequency analysis, the chatbot system provided the main topic of the current issue based on rankings and provided classified comments according to each keyword. By doing so, the system measured the characteristics of the comments and method and degree of changes in the system experience compared to the existing list-type comment system. Specifically, the impact on user interaction, public opinion acceptance, recognition of problems among comments, information and usability changes, and links to articles were discussed. As a result, this study showed significant differences in information quality, public opinion search function, association with the text, and changes in the characteristics of the comments.

3 Design of Comment Chatbot

3.1 Data Analysis

Data Collection. The subject of the data was an article on Naver News. Naver offers ranking of the most commented-on article by date through its function of article comment rankings. Five articles and 20,000 accompanying comments were collected. Specifically, the highest-ranking articles and comments were selected and collected on June 9, 2019, regardless of political, economic and social aspects, and the second-highest ranking articles and comments were also selected if the same topic was ranked the highest in the list. Data collection was conducted through crawling. The detailed collection process was completed through the BeautifulSoup library, and the web crawling Python code used to collect comment saved them on a specific date in a text file when the news article and the comment URL were entered.

Data Refinement. KoNLPy is open-source software and is released under a license: GPL v3 or above (http://gnu.org/licenses/gpl.html) [13]. KoNLPy is software for Korean language processing with the Python programming language [14]. The morphological analysis package provided by KoNLPy includes Hannanum, Kkma, Komoran, Mecab, and Twitter Class. This study used Kkma Class, which provides more detailed analysis [15]. Specifically, Kkma packages of KONlpy Plugin were utilized. Pos package was used for processing and filtering in the unit of morpheme. Only NNG information, which means nouns, was extracted, and nouns were sorted by frequency. Based on this, the five most frequent nouns were derived.

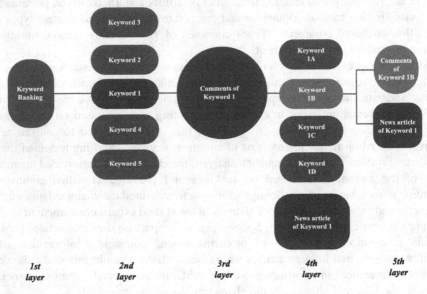

Fig. 1. Structure of the chatbot

3.2 Interface Design

Chatbot Structure. A keyword-based comment chatbot system was designed to complement the existing online comments' limitations [16]. It is designed to check five keywords derived according to the frequency of each comment. The chatbot consisted of five layers, as shown in Fig. 1. First, a speech bubble showed the current ranking of issue keywords with a welcome message. Through this speech bubble, the most frequently mentioned topics in the comments can be identified on a real-time basis, and the numbers and arrows on the right side of the control at the same time as the ranking of the topics presented the frequency of the comments and the trend in rankings among the respective topics. The trend (up or down) was not based on actual data but was applied randomly. At the second layer, the five most controversial topics were presented in a quick-reply button format. Each button was accompanied by the keyword and its frequency. On the third layer, users could check the contents of comments containing the topic by clicking on the button. On the fourth layer, four new keywords associated with the topic selected in the third layer were presented in button format, along with a button linking to the original article. Clicking a keyword button at the fourth layer led to the fifth layer, which was designed to read related comments or check the original article using the link button.

Fig. 2. Ranking of the comment keywords

Fig. 3. Corresponding comments for keyword

Fig. 4. News link for each comment

Chatbot User Flow When accessing the chatbot, users first check the speech bubble for real-time issues as shown in Fig. 2. This allows users to check the current comment keyword ranking and trends based on real-time data. After checking the overall distribution and status, users select the keyword that they are most interested in by clicking the button. Then, as shown in Fig. 3, users read the comments that appeared according to the keyword of choice. If users want to continue to check the comments of keywords associated with the initial keyword, they can click the "linked keyword" button at the bottom of the screen. Finally, if users want to check the original article of the comment by browsing all the comments and related keywords, they can click the "Link button to the original article," as shown in Fig. 4. If users don't want to read an article, they can search for and access different kinds of keywords from the beginning through the "Back" or "Home" buttons.

4 Method

An experiment was conducted with 30 graduate students and office workers in their 20s and 30s living in Seoul and Incheon. The experiment was conducted with a presurvey after using a traditional comment system and a postsurvey and postinterview after using the chatbot system. It lasted 20–30 min in a remote, mobile-enabled environment. Before starting the experiment, participants received a brief introduction about the purpose and method of the experiment. The experiment consisted of two parts. In the first part, participants used Naver News to read comments and articles, then completed the presurvey based on the existing online news comment interface. In the second part, participants used the chatbot designed through this study to perform the subscription and news subscription tasks of the comments and then completed postsurvey questions.

A brief interview was conducted after the two tests. The survey items consisted of 22 questions, each of which was designed by screening and reconfiguring the questions from prior research [1, 17–20]. The questionnaires were designed to measure the nature of the comments, nature of the comment system, and motivation for reading comments. These factors were classified into categories of informality, likelihood of critical reading, relaxation, fun or excitement, problems with comments, convenience, potential of public opinion search, and relevance to the text. The survey was used to measure two systems.

5   Results

Table 1. Results of students' t-tests for categorized survey questions

	F	p	t	n	p	M diff
Problems of comments	1.820	.183	3.345	58	.001	0.744
Explore opinions	1.082	.302	−2.811	58	.007	−0.622

The three questions categorized as **"explore opinions"** through the operational definition of variables—"Comment is effective in identifying other people's interests"; "Comment is effective in recognizing other people's perspectives"; and "Comment is effective in checking comments by type"—showed a statistically significant difference with a probability of less than .05 compared to the existing Naver comment system ($p = .007$, $t = -2.811$, μx-$\mu y = -0.622$). Postinterviews showed some users felt that the ability to "explore opinions" was effective. They mentioned that people's overall interests are well summarized and implicitly presented because keywords were listed in order of frequency. In addition, participants noted that because the content of the comments could be checked, it was easier to understand people's opinions according to keywords. "It was efficient since I could check people's interests just by using the ranking of the keyword" (P18). Some participants said it was efficient to not only see at a glance what is being discussed, but also to understand the generalities of the comments without the articles. "It was great to see what was being discussed at a glance, and even though I didn't know the content of the article, I could get a good overview of what was being said" (P23).

The three questions categorized as "Problems of comments" through the operational definition of variables—"The comment in the chatbot is sensational"; "Chatbot's comments are vulgar"; "Chatbot's comments are unreliable"—showed a significant difference ($p = .001$, $t = 3.345$, μx-$\mu y = 0.744$) between presurvey and postsurvey. Postinterviews also showed that many users were satisfied with the refined expressions. "I was pleased to see the comments that were to be selected or filtered" (P15). Keywords were organized based on the topic nouns, and the comments could be refined during the classification process (Table 1).

Table 2. Results of students' *t*-tests for each survey question

	t	*n*	*p*	*M diff*
Comments are effective in getting new information	−3.053	58	.003	−0.800
The comments are effective in checking the comments by type.	2.616	58	.011	0.700
The system shows more information than the article	3.063	58	.003	0.800
Chatbot's comments are unreliable	2.920	58	.005	0.733
The system is effective in checking comments by type	−4.480	48	<.001	−1.367
The comments give us more information than the articles.	−2.155	58	.035	−0.567

Before the operational definition of variables, the analysis results indicated six items showed statistically significant values: "Comments are effective in getting new information" ($p = .003$, t = -3.053, μx-μy = -0.800); "The comments are effective in checking the comments by type" ($p < .001$, $t = -4.480$, μx-μy = -1.370); and "The system shows more information than the article" ($p = .003$, $t = 3.063$, μx-μy = 0.800). Postinterviews also showed a statistically significant difference in responses to "The system is effective in checking comments by type." Users could select a specific keyword to check comments together, and the process of navigating other keywords associated with an initial keyword allowed users to check different kinds of comments effectively. Users said that just as readers might look at headlines first and select an article on a topic they want to see, this system also provides a selective reading experience in that users can choose what to read depending on the topic. "I felt as if I was looking at the headlines. The comments chatbot was designed like reading the comments according to the title of interest" (P19). Therefore, users said that the effectiveness of the chatbot is maximized if the user is interested in a particular topic and has any questions regarding the topic. Positive responses to the item "Chatbot's comments are effective in getting new information" were also shown in a postinterview session. A group of users who had a pattern of obtaining information through comments before reading an article responded that it was beneficial to check the comments to learn more about the content of the article without reading it. The item "The comment give us more information than the articles" also showed a statistically significant difference, with the possibility of obtaining information that is difficult to obtain from the articles also mentioned. "In the case of political articles, I tend to understand them by looking at people's explanations since it is too hard to understand the article, but in this system it made me understand them well since I read the comments about political articles beforehand in this system" (P23) (Table 2).

6 Discussion

The chatbot-type comment presentation method used in this study has been confirmed to provide more information, search for comments by type, check more comments than articles, and filter out suggestive, non-slang-oriented comments. In addition to these findings, additional discussion points were found on how issue keywords were presented, relationships of comments to articles, comment-filtering algorithms, and chatbot systems.

First, although the survey analysis did not reveal any significant differences, postinterviews showed varying assessments of comments and the relevance of articles. Many users responded that accessing the comments before reading news would create interest in the article and also have the effect of helping readers become interested in articles in which they were not previously interested. "Like the movie Thumbnail, it seems to draw interest in the article" (P28). But the comment-oriented chatbot system showed that interest in the story was reduced by concentrating most of the focus to the comments. Also, it was pointed out that the negative attributes of the comments themselves caused articles to be rejected or deemed biased even before it was read. Furthermore, the characteristics of the comments, which tended to lean toward specific opinions, can create disadvantages that make articles appear biased to one side when users read comments before reading the article.

Second, disbelief and concern over the involvement of the algorithm in the comment system also emerged. Users were curious about how keywords were represented and filtered, whereas others said that the current algorithm-based comment recommendation system was not reliable because it was more likely to be manipulated than the previous comment system. In addition, the recommended algorithm-based comments also raised the question of the effect of highlighting the comments that appear at the top and front. This has confirmed the need to think about how to place comments in a neutral and fair way, and the limitations of the list format in the existing system have not been fully overcome by the chatbot system.

Furthermore, there were also various usability evaluations of new search methods and UI configurations in the chatbot system. First, users were familiar with the speech balloons in the chatbot program, which were comfortable and easier to read than conventional systems. Users were interested in how they were implemented through buttons and said it was convenient that comments could be collected in Kakao Talk. However, users also asserted that system was more cumbersome and limited in terms of the absolute amount of comments. There was also feedback on how information was provided in the chatbot. The chatbot's introduction message consisted of text and emoticons, providing only simple information, and thus, it did not transmit information well and was not intuitive compared to the information provided by the website. In addition, users who were familiar with empathy ranking assessed that the comments presented on the chatbot did not discriminate between right or wrong, and that the current method of providing information did not meet the needs of users who read comments to explore the general perspective of most people.

7   Conclusion

In this study, real-time issue-keyword rankings of comments were derived using the number of nouns in comments. Through this method, a chatbot was designed to check the distribution and content of comments by searching each classified comment according to issue keywords. The chatbot designed in this study provides more information than existing comment presentation systems, searches comments by type, checks more comments than articles, and reduces sensational, non-slang-oriented comments that have emerged as problems with existing comment systems. However, in addition to the nature of the comments and the experience of the chatbot system, which were the initial goals of this study, various opinions on the issue keyword presentation method, article association, filtering algorithm, and chatbot system were presented. Therefore, the need for more specific and controlled research was confirmed. Subsequent studies will investigate the user experience based on the filtering criteria of comments and identify the effects of each filtering algorithm incorporated into an interactive interface. Specifically, we plan to refine the filtering criteria for all comments to design the comments algorithm based on frequency and distribution, recommendation, and emotion. These factors will be measured first using traditional comment systems and then in the chatbot system to determine how the interface effects information filtering. In addition, the comment chatbot in this study has limitations related to data-mining technology and the proper way of accessing news articles. Some respondents said that the level of credibility of the keywords was somewhat lower because they provided comments based on keyword-oriented frequency, and extracted keywords were less representative because the categories of comments presented according to keywords were too broad. Because this chatbot system is based on the frequency of keyword-based comments, not many types of keywords were provided and representation of each keyword was lacking; therefore, the content scope of the comment categories was too large. In addition, the comment-oriented system design method was considered somewhat inconvenient in terms of how news articles were presented. Participants indicated that the comments, without knowing the headlines, were not understandable immediately, and that it was difficult to understand what the comments were trying say just by showing through a chatbot. Therefore, future research should incorporate more advanced natural language-processing technologies and reorganize the UI regarding how comments and articles are connected.

Acknowledgements. This work was conducted with the support of the Design Engineering Postgraduate Schools (N0001436) program, an R&D project initiated by the Ministry of Trade, Industry and Energy of the Republic of Korea.

References

1. Lee, C., Lee, H.: The pattern of portal news use among portal users and their recognition of portal as a press. Korean J. Commun. Inf. **46**, 177–211 (2009)
2. Pan, B.: In Google we trust: users' decisions on rank, position, and relevance. J. Comput. Mediat. Commun. **12**, 801–823 (2007)
3. Na, E.K., Lee, G.H., Kim, H.S.: Social implication of reading/writing online comments (replies) in representative democracy: Internet news comments (replies), political trust, media trust, and political knowledge. Korean J. Journal. Commun. Stud. **53**, 109–132 (2009)
4. Kang, J.-W., Kim, S.-J.: A study on the effect of comments posted under Internet news articles: in consideration of the degree of involvement in issues and whether or not opinions are in Accord. Korean. Journal. Commun. Stud. **56**, 143–166 (2012)

5. Rojas, H.: "Corrective" actions in the public sphere: how perceptions of media and media effects shape political behaviors. Int. J. Public Opin. Res. **22**, 343–363 (2010)
6. Lee, K., Kim, J., Seo, H., Rhyu, K.: Feature weighting for opinion classification of comments on news articles. J. Korean Soc. Mar. Eng. **34**, 871–879 (2010)
7. Daegun, Y.: Development of an emotion-based analytics tool for characterizing online news, comments, and users. In: Proceedings of the Symposium of the Korean Institute of Communications and Information Sciences, pp. 851–852 (2018)
8. Han, J., Kim, W., Han, K.: Development of a multi-emotional model for online news comments and its application. In: HCI Korea 2018, pp. 893–897 (2018)
9. Lee, Y., Ji, J., Woo, G., Cho, H.: Analysis and visualization for comment messages of internet posts. J. Korea Contents Assoc. **9**, 45–56 (2009)
10. Faridani, S., Bitton, E., Ryokai, K., Goldberg, K.: Opinion space: a scalable tool for browsing online comments. In: Proceedings of the SIGCHI Conference on Human Factors in Computing Systems, pp. 1175–1184 (2010)
11. Madden, A., Ruthven, I., McMenemy, D.: A classification scheme for content analyses of YouTube video comments. J. Doc. **69**, 693–714 (2013)
12. Sung, C., Huang, X., Shen, Y., Cherng, F., Li, W., Wang, H.: ToPIN: a visual analysis tool for time-anchored comments in online educational videos. In: Proceedings of the 2016 CHI Conference Extended Abstracts on Human Factors in Computing Systems, pp. 2185–2191 (2016)
13. Park, K.Y., Lee, Y., Kim, S.: Deciphering monetary policy board minutes through text mining approach: the case of Korea. Bank of Korea White Paper (2019)
14. Park, E.J., Cho, S.Z.: KoNLPy: Korean natural language processing in Python. In: Proceedings of the 26th Human & Cognitive Language Technology, pp. 133–136 (2014)
15. Song, H.J., et al.: A web service for evaluating the level of speech in Korean. Appl. Sci. **9**, 594 (2019)
16. Kim, J.W., Jo, H.I., Lee, B.G.: Analyzing the characteristics of online news best comments. J. Dig. Contents Soc. **19**, 1489–1497 (2018)
17. Kim, J.K., Kim, D.H.: Motivation of reading and writing internet reply and satisfaction of college student internet reply users. J. Cybercommun. Acad. Soc. **25**, 5–47 (2008)
18. Kim, C.: Uses and effects of interactive satisfaction in online news replies. J. Commun. Sci. **9**, 5–44 (2009)
19. Ahn, J., Park, K.: A study on the comparison press dot coms with portal sites: related news, hyperlink, and reply of the internet media. J. Commun. Sci. **7**, 335–372 (2007)
20. Kim, K.: Gatekeeping of mobile portal news' influence on using news in the perspective of journalism. Korean. J. Commun. Stud. **6**, 117–144 (2016)

Visual Exploration of Topic Controversy in Online Conversations

Enamul Hoque[⊠] and Esha Abid

York University, Toronto, ON, Canada
enamulh@yorku.ca, itsea@my.yorku.ca

Abstract. Online conversations are often quite long with a lot of comments. Readers of these conversations may be interested in understanding how controversial the discussion is and how the differences of opinions arise for different topics. In this work, we are combining natural language processing with information visualization to support readers in exploring disagreements in online conversations. We present an initial prototype and discuss the possible directions for future work.

Keywords: Visual analytics · Social media · Online conversations · Natural language processing

1 Introduction

With the proliferation of social media, there has been an exponential growth of asynchronous online conversations. An online conversation in forums such as Reddit, Slashdot and Digg may start with a news article link, question or opinion and later generate a long thread with hundreds of comments [7]. Readers may become interested in understanding how disagreements arise in such conversations and how differences of opinions arise and evolve for different controversial topics [2].

In this ongoing work, we focus on supporting the exploration of topic controversy in a casual online conversation between users. To this end, we combine natural language processing (NLP) with information visualization techniques. On the side of NLP, we first apply a topic modeling technique that automatically clusters the sentences within a conversation into multiple topic segments and then assigns a keyphrase to describe what a given topic is about [10]. We then perform sentiment analysis and disagreement detection to discover how different comments react to a given topic [2].

We have been designing interactive visualization techniques with an aim to support users in exploring the results of these NLP methods to better understand the topic controversy in an online conversation. The goal is to help the user in getting a quick overview of the controversial topics and then drilling down to the detailed comments that trigger controversy. In this paper, we present visualization techniques for exploring controversial topics and then discuss the possible directions for future work.

© Springer Nature Switzerland AG 2019
C. Stephanidis and M. Antona (Eds.): HCII 2019, CCIS 1088, pp. 369–373, 2019.
https://doi.org/10.1007/978-3-030-30712-7_46

2   Related Work

Recently, visual analysis of topics and opinions in social media conversations has received a lot of attention [11,12,14,17]. Some early works aimed to identify and visualize the primary themes or topical clusters within conversations [4, 15]. TIARA system applies an enhanced Latent Dirichlet Allocation (LDA)-based topic modeling technique, which automatically derives a set of topics to summarize a collection of documents and their content evolution over time [16]. Each layer in the graphical representation represents a topic, where the keywords of each topic are distributed along time. From the height of each topic and its content distributed over time, the user can see the topic evolution.

To support users explore sentiment in a large collection of tweets, Twit-Info [14] displays proportion of positive and negative tweets using pie charts in real-time. OpinionFlow [17] combines Sankey graph with tailored density maps to provide visualizations to analyze opinion diffusion for different topics in social media. Visualizations for opinion analysis is also examined in blogs, forums and multi-party conversations [3,5,7]. For example, ConVis [7,8] facilitated multi-faceted exploration of a blog conversation based on topics, authors, and sentiment using stacked bar charts. MultiConVis further extended this interface for exploring topics for a set of conversations [9]. ConToVi [5] visualizes speakers dynamics with regard to different topics in conversations like political debates using animations using radial visualization. It also displayed speaker's behavior using categories like sentiment, politeness, and eloquence.

While there have been some significant work on exploring topics and opinions in online conversations, visualizing the disagreements between participants for controversial topics have rarely been examined. Yee et al. [18] organize a discussion by creating a tree layout, where the parent comment is placed on top as a text block, while the space below the parent node is divided between supporting and opposing statements. ConsiderIt [13] builds a pro-con list from participants and shows a bar chart to augment personal deliberation to help users identify common ground from diverse opinions. Opinion Space [6] is a tool for browsing online opinions which combines ideas from deliberative polling, dimensionality reduction and collaborative filtering using a scatter plot visualization. Pol.is is another tool focusing on organizing the comments by the percentage of agreements based on a combination of machine learning and information visualization methods [1]. However, none of these works focus on automatically extracting topics and visualizing topic controversy.

3   Visual Exploration of Topic Controversy

In order to design our visual interface, we analyze the possible tasks that the user wants to perform while exploring topic controversy. For example, the user may be interested in knowing how controversial was the conversation. Were there substantial differences in opinion? Why are people supporting/opposing an opinion? To help the user in answering these questions, the visual interface should show the topics as well as their controversy scores. The interface should also encode the sentiment score for each comment so that the reader knows how disagreements happen between participants for a topic.

In order to extract the important information from conversations, we first apply a topic modeling technique [10] that clusters the sentences from a conversation into thematically coherent clusters. It then extracts keyphrases from each cluster that describe that topic cluster. We then apply a classification method that determines how controversial each topic is [2]. After applying the NLP techniques for extracting information, we have designed an initial visualization prototype (shown in Fig. 1). The visualization follows an overview + detail approach, where the overview shows all the topics in a conversation and the amount of disagreements among participants for each topic. The detail view shows all the comments of a conversation in a scrollable list view. In the overview, the topics are arranged vertically, where each row shows a topic along with its controversy score. It also arranges the comments for each topic as circles along the x-axis where x-axis represents time, so that the reader get a sense of how the sentiment evolve over time in the discussion.

We have designed a set of interactions for filtering and sorting topics as well as drilling down to individual comments in a conversation. For example, the user can select a topic from the visual overview and then drill down to a specific subset of comments interests in the detailed view. The user can also sort topics based on controversy score or the number of comments belonging to each topic. Together, these interactions are designed to help users to quickly browse through topics and to understand disagreements that arise between participants.

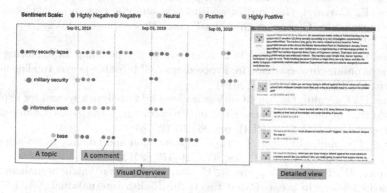

Fig. 1. An initial prototype for exploring topic controversy. The visual overview in the left shows the topics and how controversial they are along with positive/negative comments while the detail view shows the list of comments.

4   Conclusions and Future Work

In this ongoing work, we are designing visual interfaces for exploring controversial topics in online conversations. Our immediate plan is to iteratively refine the prototype and carry out user studies to evaluate the potential efficacy of our visualization approach. We would also like to apply more advanced NLP methods such as stance detection and emotion analysis [19]. Finally, we would like to improve the visual encodings and interaction techniques to address scalability issues. In particular, we would like to explore different layouts where more comments can be arranged without occlusion as well as interactive techniques to gradually zoom into the timeline.

References

1. Pol.is. https://pol.is/gov (2019)
2. Allen, K., Carenini, G., Ng, R.T.: Detecting disagreement in conversations using pseudo-monologic rhetorical structure. In: Proceedings of the Empirical Methods on Natural Language Processing (EMNLP) (2014)
3. Annett, M., Kondrak, G.: A comparison of sentiment analysis techniques: polarizing movie blogs. In: Bergler, S. (ed.) AI 2008. LNCS (LNAI), vol. 5032, pp. 25–35. Springer, Heidelberg (2008). https://doi.org/10.1007/978-3-540-68825-9_3
4. Dave, K., Wattenberg, M., Muller, M.: Flash forums and forumReader: navigating a new kind of large-scale online discussion. In: Proceedings of the ACM Conference on Computer-Supported Cooperative Work (CSCW), pp. 232–241 (2004)
5. El-Assady, M., Gold, V., Acevedo, C., Collins, C., Keim, D.: ConToVi: multi-party conversation exploration using topic-space views. In: Computer Graphics Forum, vol. 35, pp. 431–440. Wiley Online Library (2016)
6. Faridani, S., Bitton, E., Ryokai, K., Goldberg, K.: Opinion space: a scalable tool for browsing online comments. In: Proceedings of the ACM Conference on Human Factors in Computing Systems (CHI), pp. 1175–1184 (2010)
7. Hoque, E., Carenini, G.: ConVis: a visual text analytic system for exploring blog conversations. In: Computer Graphics Forum (Proceedings EuroVis), vol. 33, no. 3, pp. 221–230 (2014)
8. Hoque, E., Carenini, G.: ConVisIT: interactive topic modeling for exploring asynchronous online conversations. In: Proceedings ACM Conference on Intelligent User Interfaces (IUI), pp. 169–180 (2015)
9. Hoque, E., Carenini, G.: MultiConVis: a visual text analytics system for exploring a collection of online conversations. In: Proceedings of the ACM Conference on Intelligent User Interfaces (IUI), pp. 96–107 (2016)
10. Joty, S., Carenini, G., Ng, R.T.: Topic segmentation and labeling in asynchronous conversations. J. Artif. Intell. Res. 47, 521–573 (2013)
11. Kempter, R., Sintsova, V., Musat, C., Pu, P.: EmotionWatch: visualizing fine-grained emotions in event-related tweets. In: Eighth International AAAI Conference on Weblogs and Social Media (2014)
12. Kontopoulos, E., Berberidis, C., Dergiades, T., Bassiliades, N.: Ontology-based sentiment analysis of Twitter posts. Expert Syst. Appl. 40(10), 4065–4074 (2013)
13. Kriplean, T., Morgan, J., Freelon, D., Borning, A., Bennett, L.: Supporting reflective public thought with ConsiderIt. In: Proceedings of the ACM 2012 Conference on Computer Supported Cooperative Work, CSCW 2012, pp. 265–274 (2012)
14. Marcus, A., Bernstein, M.S., Badar, O., Karger, D.R., Madden, S., Miller, R.C.: TwitInfo: aggregating and visualizing microblogs for event exploration. In: Proceedings of the ACM Conference on Human Factors in Computing Systems (CHI), pp. 227–236 (2011)

15. Sack, W.: Conversation map: an interface for very-large-scale conversations. J. Manag. Inf. Syst. **17**(3), 73–92 (2000)
16. Wei, F., et al.: TIARA: a visual exploratory text analytic system. In: Proceedings ACM Conference on Knowledge Discovery and Data Mining, pp. 153–162 (2010)
17. Wu, Y., Liu, S., Yan, K., Liu, M., Wu, F.: OpinionFlow: visual analysis of opinion diffusion on social media. IEEE Trans. Vis. Comput. Graph. (Proc. VAST) **20**(12), 1763–1772 (2014)
18. Yee, K.P., Hearst, M.: Content-centered discussion mapping. Online Deliberation 2005/DIAC-2005 (2005)
19. Zhang, L., Wang, S., Liu, B.: Deep learning for sentiment analysis: a survey. Wiley Interdisc. Rev.: Data Min. Knowl. Discov. **8**(4), e1253 (2018)

AR-VIS: Augmented Reality Interactive Visualization Environment for Exploring Dynamic Scientific Data

Hannah Hyejin Kum-Biocca[1]($\boxtimes$), Hyomin Kim[2], Frank Biocca[3], and Yeonhee Cho[4]

[1] School of Art and Design, College of Architecture & Design, New Jersey Institute and Technology, Newark, NJ, USA
hyejin.kum-biocca@NJIT.edu
[2] Physics Department, New Jersey Institute and Technology, Newark, NJ, USA
Hyomin.kim@NJIT.edu
[3] Department of Informatics, Ying Wu College of Computing, New Jersey Institute and Technology, Newark, NJ, USA
biocca@NJIT.edu
[4] Teaching, Learning, and Leadership Division, The University of Pennsylvania, Philadelphia, PA, USA
yeonhee@gse.upenn.edu

Abstract. The AR Vis project is a general-purpose interactive data visualization platform for collaborative interaction with scientific data. The platform is designed for augmented reality displays of data supporting multi-user interaction and simulations. Methods developed include a procedural pipeline for data culling, modeling, visualization, and porting to multiuser augmented reality.

A prototype interactive visualization application demonstrates the system via visualization and simulation of magnetic fields. The magnetic field visualizations are attached to physical objects or embedded in the environment. The invisible magnetic fields are transformed into tangible models of nano and geospatial scales magnetic phenomena accessible to a user's full body (embodied) interaction.

The project seeks to make a significant contribution to scientific visualization. Extending beyond the cognitive impact of traditional scientific visualization, the goal of the AR Vis platform is to additionally leverage human perception and spatial cognition and make data patterns tangible, manipulable and more accessible. In supporting augmented information cognition in scientists and learners, AR Vis design supports data discovery and learning.

The prototype implementation uses physics data modeling of the invisible and largely intangible forces of magnetism across different scales. The project yields both a prototype platform and develops a data visualization pipeline. Both demonstrate a substantial and concrete implementation and demonstration of AR Vis techniques.

Keywords: Augmented reality · Magnetic fields · Interactive visualization · Scientific data

C. Stephanidis and M. Antona (Eds.): HCII 2019, CCIS 1088, pp. 374–380, 2019.
https://doi.org/10.1007/978-3-030-30712-7_47

1 Introduction

The visualization of scientific data and large network data have been evolving with the arrival of computer graphic techniques. Most recently key developments have involved the ability to process large amounts of data and render them in new and different graphical formats. The array of information remains primarily constrained to 2D dimensional projection (e.g., Tableau) or 2D renderings of 3-dimensional arrays.

Data visualizations are used to access the powers of human cognition. Data visualizations leverage the powerful capacities of human spatial, object, and color perception to detect patterns, trends, and anomalies in physical forms.

The introduction of virtual reality and especially augmented reality has enabled scientists, data analysts, and the general public to interact with scientific and big data visualizations in more intuitive ways. Augmented reality and virtual reality array data in a simulated physical space around the body. In this way, the leverage all of the visualization capabilities of traditional visualization but are further augmented by human spatial cognition and tangible, full body, physically interaction with the data. Virtual and augmented reality array the data around the body and engage in body-centric spatial awareness to detect patterns and comprehend scale and relationships. Full body interaction with data visualizations enables users given them new ways to engage, alter, and "interrogate" the data.

1.1 Visualizing Unseen Phenomena at Various Scales: Magnetic Fields

Magnetic fields are largely invisible phenomena exerting effects in the world. Magnetic fields are pervasive and can be modeled at different scales from the nanoscales to larger geospatial scales such as the interaction of sun and the earth's magnetic fields. Magnetic fields lend themselves to the possibility of visualization at different scales including the superimposing on the real-world objects, the magnification of smaller scale magnetism, and the visualization of large scale early magnetism at an experiential scale of the body. In the project we start the interactive visualization of Environmentally Mapped View; these interactive visualizations view data mapped directly at one-to-one scale on physical objects or the surrounding environment.

2 Specific Objectives

The specific objectives are:

- Develop a general-purpose interactive data visualization platform.
- Visualize, simulate, and overlay natural physical processes on physical objects and natural spaces.
- Develop and demonstrate the approach via the visualization of magnetic and electromagnetic phenomena.
- Transform visualization to body-centric, tangible, and interactive scientific visualization
- Visualize and simulate magnetic fields at different scales.

- Support improved understanding of physical phenomena for scientific data exploration and education.

3   Methods and Procedures

3.1   Overview

Our development of a graphics and interactive design pipeline for the creation of interactive visualizations of time-based and environmental phenomena rendered in the physical environment to an embedded 3D observer. The procedure for body-centered, tangible experience using a multi-user augmented reality environment we call AR Vis.

3.2   Data Sources

We are building a general-purpose platform and a set of procedures for interactive visualization suited to display spatial and environmental data varying over time and different scales. For the prototype study, we demonstrate the visualization using magnetic data from the Center for Solar-Terrestrial Research at NJIT.

Magnetic Field Data: From the Inviable to the Tangible. At the beginning of project work, magnetic field data that are used for the study of solar and terrestrial sciences are visualized (Fig. 1).

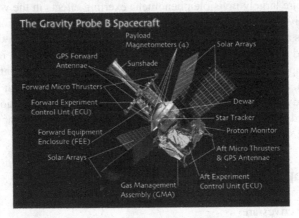

Fig. 1. Space magnetometer collecting terrestrial data at different Scales (Source: NASA)

They are typically acquired by the instrument called "magnetometer" that measures the background (ambient) or time-varying component(s) of magnetic fields. It has a wide range of applications and is one of the widely utilized instruments for geospace research. There are a number of science magnetometers in operation in ground-based observatories and aboard spacecraft.

Magnetic field data sets are publicly available either online (e.g., NASA) or upon request. They are provided in the text-based ASCII format or Common Data Format (CDF) which contains the three-axis components (vector) or scalar (absolute) values to represent magnetic fields around the Earth.

The Earth's magnetic fields are never constant, being disturbed by various sources. One of them is the continuous flow of charged particles from the Sun called "solar wind." Thus, monitoring the Earth's magnetic fields provide critical information about the environment between the Sun and Earth.

A member of this project, Dr. Kim at NJIT Center for Solar-Terrestrial Research (CSTR), is currently in charge of the operation of magnetometers in the polar regions in both hemispheres including Canada, Norway, Greenland, and Antarctica and has extensive experiences in analyzing data from the magnetometers. We are also participating in a satellite program run by NASA.

Here, we visualize such data sets from the various magnetometers and thus to provide the general public with more tangible experience with the unseen forces that surround us.

Data Mining, Reduction, and Culling. Data mining and culling extract spatial and time-varying components. Data sets are modified and formatted to support 3D visualization tools.

3.3   Visualization and Interactive Simulation Model Building

The magnetic field visualization prototype was created in Unity and the scripts were written in C#. The Microsoft Mixed Reality ToolKit was used to implement the Hololens functionality of the Unity Project.

The Mixed Reality ToolKit was necessary for the project because it allows Unity projects to be directly built onto the Hololens. It also contains scripts and prefabs which allows for a Hololens scene to be setup easily. For example, the Mixed Reality Tool Kit Parent Prefab was used to represent the Hololens' in the scene. In addition, the prefab contained scripts and other objects attached to it that help with gazing and head position. There are also other prefabs in the Mixed Reality Toolkit that help with input and other essential things needed for a Hololens' project.

The grid was created using two geometry shaders. The shader language used was Cg, which is a variant of HLSL. A series of vertices are passed to the GPU, the first geometry shader draws a cube at each of these points, while the second geometry shader draws lines connecting neighboring points. In addition, a script calculates the distance between the magnetic object in the scene and the player, as well as the distance between the player and each vertex. The sum of these calculations is adjusted by a manually tweaked value and applied to the vertices' positions to make them move rapidly or slowly. The number is also used to determine the color of the grid vertices (Fig. 2).

Fig. 2. Environment sensors and optical displays within the augmented reality platform to be integrated into AR Vis interactive visualizations. (Source: AR_Vis interactive Visualization)

Platform Porting and Interactivity. The interactive visualizations and simulations are ported for interaction in an NJIT multiuser environment using Hololens and hardware. Hololens is an augmented reality system using optic see-though HMD for blending virtual objects into the physical environment. We begin with the networked dual-use platform (Fig. 3).

Our visualizations Micro Software, Hololens's application framework. We are able to support multiple spatial computing and visualization experiences to run at the same time.

Fig. 3. AR Vis interactive visualization platform using Hololens augmented reality head-mounted displays. (Source: Science & Art Exhibition at CoAD Library, NJIT)

Multi-observer Environment. Because users and scientists often interact with data in teams, the interactive simulations design for two or more observers of the environment. Both are able to simultaneously view shared visualization. Models are shared across devices in real time (Fig. 4).

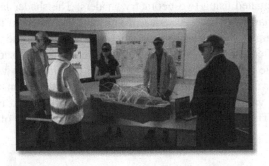

Fig. 4. Example of field data rendered for multi-user augmented reality interaction. (Source: MS web.)

Augmented Reality Views. The platform yields visualizations at different views using augmented reality. The current prototype supports the visualization of body-centered magnetic fields. Users are instrumented with a magnetometer and move through a real-time dynamic visualization of the magnetic fields in the room or space around their body. Actions include selection or even physical motion modify the data or support interaction.

The platform envisions different types of augmented reality views of magnetic data described below and include an object or environmentally mapped views and observer or "Gods eye" views of very large planetary scale static or real-time magnetic field activity.

Environmentally Mapped View	
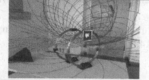	These interactive visualizations view data mapped directly at one-to-one scale on physical objects or the surrounding environment.
Body center views	
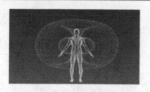	These interactions visualization map data at different scales directly around the body of the user to engage embodied cognition and tangible interaction.
Observer "God's eye" views	
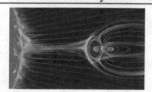	Phenomena at a smaller or larger scale (e.g., solar-terrestrial data modify to support a 'god's eye' interaction with interactive simulation so that the data appear tangible and physical.

4 Future Plans

This project supports the development of a prototype and development pipeline for an augmented reality, visualization interface.

Preliminary user studies examine the usability, interactivity, of the interactive visualization. Learning and discovery outcomes are also be assessed by comparing the spatial augmented reality visualizations to traditional visualizations of the same data.

The multi-user system will be generalizable to the visualization and augmentation of other information including for example architectural and structural visualization, embedded visualization of urban and physical environments, electrical grid and infrastructure visualization, medical patient data visualization, big data visualizations, radiation, and environment mapping.

Acknowledgments. This project partly founding by the 2018–2019 Faculty Seed grant from NJIT.

References

1. Bhagat, K.K., Liou, W.-K., Michael Spector, J., Chang, C.-Y.: To use augmented reality or not in formative assessment: a comparative study. Interact. Learn. Environ., 1–11 (2018)
2. Neumann, U., You, S., Hu, J., Jiang, B., Sebe, I.O.: Visualizing reality in an augmented virtual environment. Presence: Teleoperators Virtual Environ. **13**(2), 222–233 (2004). https://doi.org/10.1162/1054746041382366
3. Olshannikova, E., Ometov, A., Koucheryavy, Y., Olsson, T.: Visualizing big data with augmented and virtual reality: challenges and research agenda. J. Big Data **2**(1), 22 (2015). https://doi.org/10.1186/s40537-015-0031-2
4. Patterson, R.E., et al.: A human cognition framework for information visualization. Comput. Graph. **42**, 42–58 (2014). https://doi.org/10.1016/j.cag.2014.03.002

Interactive Recommendation Model for Optimizing Data Visualization

Jaeyong Lee, Daehee Park$^{(\boxtimes)}$, and Scott Song

Samsung Electronics, Seoul, Republic of Korea
{jae-yong.lee, daehee0.park, sangkon.song}@samsung.com

Abstract. The study describes a Guideline Model that allows users who want to visualize Data to generate visualizations that are tailored to their tasks and purposes as intended. Data analysis is widely used in the research design process, depending on the recent environment in which the importance of data is gaining attention, but it is not easy for users to freely design and visualize data in a cognitively optimized form. Through this study, we reviewed all of the data visualization studies published in InfoVis, and developed nine key elements for Data Visualization UX by analyzing in depth 59 of the findings that could be used in the Guideline design. We intend to innovate the Data Visualization UX by building the Guideline created through this process into an interactive recommendation interface that makes it easier and more accurate for users to understand. This was developed from a prior study called Voyager system.

Keywords: Data visualization · Guideline · Interactive recommendation

1 Introduction

Visualizing multi-dimensional data is regarded as a difficult task for novice users, especially, expressing as a cognitively optimized form. There are several reasons for that, the first reason indicates that most novice users feel it is difficult to crease a dataset for data visualization. Second, novice users could not find out or determine the effective visual effects which to be applied [1]. Above issues have been discussed several years in the field of data visualization, thus, many researchers conducted various studies to solve above issues and to help novice users their data visualization.

2 Related Work

Wongsuphasawat et al. [2] developed a kind of data visualization system, which called "Voyager". It is supporting exploratory visual analysis method by using the Vega specification. In addition, the system recommends several options in both data field selection and visual encoding [2, 3]. Hence, users are able to visualize their data effectively with using the system, in which recommends data fields and visual encoding. In addition, the users could understand the trend of the data easily, so they can catch up insight well from the data.

© Springer Nature Switzerland AG 2019
C. Stephanidis and M. Antona (Eds.): HCII 2019, CCIS 1088, pp. 381–385, 2019.
https://doi.org/10.1007/978-3-030-30712-7_48

However, in order to use the system provided by Wongsuphasawat et al. [2], the users who use the system are asked to have higher levels of comprehension of data visualization. Furthermore, several problems are still remaining. First, the users could not recognize how each option of the system influences on the effectiveness of data visualization. Second, the users could not perceive the potential problems of data visualization provided by the system in the aspect of cognitive engineering. Finally, the users could not know which part needs to be supplemented in the data visualization to choose the best decision making. In order to overcome above issues, we developed a system including the Interactive Guide Model that recommends how to optimize data visualization so that it helps users can choose proper decision. With this perspective, we try to stare at what kinds of knowledge users need to convey in visualizing data and how such knowledge should be communicated, and finally, we study how these systems can contribute to make the best decision on data visualization.

3   Multi-dimensional Data Visualization Guideline

In the initial stage, we conducted a work domain analysis to define components of visualization recommendation model. The results of work domain analysis described that a systematic visualization guide defined as rule-based that is required for the data visualization general principle [4]. To develop general visualization principle guidelines, we analyzed the papers published at the InfoVis conference, which is considered to be the most influential in the field of data visualization. Total 684 papers published during the period (1995–2017) have been analyzed, then 59 (8.6%) papers regarded as relevant papers to our purposes. Thus, chosen papers have been discussed in order to be used as fundamental visualization guidelines [5, 6]. These papers presented guidelines using keywords such as, consideration, design, framework, guideline, guidance, implication, lessons learned and taxonomy. The results of the study have been investigated into 9 categories, which could be divided into 3 groups according to each step in the process of data visualization to the user (Table 1).

Table 1. Visualization guidelines classified into 3 groups, 9 categories

Group	Category	Description
Design composition	Color	How to use colors effectively
	Text	How to visualize characters effectively
	Animation	How to show information through dynamic movement of component
Visualization technique	Chart	Guidelines for visualization charts
	Multiple views	Layout method for various visualizations charts
	Application	Visualization techniques optimized for specific domains
Cognitive model	Perception	The way humans accept visual information
	Cognition	How to understand perceived information
	Memorability	How to remember perceived information

We have organized the contents into 3 types of templates so that users who will use this guide can understand more easily and clearly what our findings are intended to convey (Fig. 1).

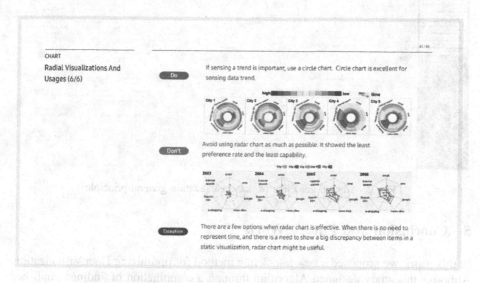

Fig. 1. Sample guideline of data visualization general principle

4 Interactive Recommendation Model for Data Visualization

We concentrated on "Data Operation" and "Visual Encoding" among 4 steps of the data visualization process suggested by Munzner in order to communicate the organized data visualization guidelines to users most effectively [7]. In addition, we added an interactive guide panel to the right of the existing Voyager System (Fig. 2). In that panel, the optimal tips for visualizing their data will be presented to the users. In the case of cognitive problems might be occurring, the system suggests several problems through pop-up style and the system also describes the reasons of problems and corresponding solutions to help users to know how to improve it. Through this process, although the users do not have a deep knowledge of the data visualization, they are given three detailed information to the user so that they can optimize their visualizations as intended. Firstly, the system suggests the advantage or disadvantages of choosing each option. Secondly, the system presents the preview of choosing each option. Lastly, the system provides an animated transition that indicates which components are changed from the current visualization to be an improved visualization. Particularly, Heer and Robertson insisted that animated transition could influence significantly on the users' understanding of the difference between AS-IS and TO-BE [8].

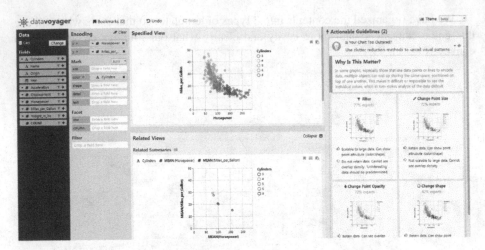

Fig. 2. Sample guideline of data visualization general principle

5 Conclusion and Future Work

In this paper, we proposed a new interaction method for optimizing Data Visualization. Although this study designed Algorithm through a combination of findings published in InfoVis, It could also further develop into user data-driven data visualization by analyzing results of user's data visualization and creating algorithms. Finally, from a user's perspective, we will continue to work on these studies that they will be able to quantitatively and qualitative evaluate how well they can design their desired Data visualizations to further explore the highly complex elements that make up the Data Visualization UX.

References

1. Sadiku, M.N., Shadare, A.E., Musa, S.M., Akujuobi, C.M.: Data visualization. Int. J. Eng. Res. Adv. Technol. (IJERAT) **2**(12), 11–16 (2016)
2. Wongsuphasawat, K., Moritz, D., Anand, A., Mackinlay, J., Howe, B., Heer, J.: Voyager: exploratory analysis via faceted browsing of visualization recommendations. IEEE Trans. Vis. Comput. Graph. **1**, 1 (2016)
3. Wongsuphasawat, K., et al.: Voyager 2: augmenting visual analysis with partial view specifications. In: Proceedings of the 2017 CHI Conference on Human Factors in Computing Systems, pp. 2648–2659. ACM, May 2017
4. Naikar, N., Hopcroft, R., Moylan, A.: Work domain analysis: theoretical concepts and methodology (No. DSTO-TR-1665). Defence Science and Technology Organisation Victoria (Australia) Air Operations Div. (2005)
5. Ellis, G., Dix, A.: A taxonomy of clutter reduction for information visualisation. IEEE Trans. Vis. Comput. Graph. **13**(6), 1216–1223 (2007)
6. Grammel, L., Tory, M., Storey, M.A.: How information visualization novices construct visualizations. IEEE Trans. Vis. Comput. Graph. **16**(6), 943–952 (2010)

7. Munzner, T.: A nested process model for visualization design and validation. IEEE Trans. Vis. Comput. Graph. **6**, 921–928 (2009)
8. Heer, J., Robertson, G.: Animated transitions in statistical data graphics. IEEE Trans. Vis. Comput. Graph. **13**(6), 1240–1247 (2007)

Data Collection and Image Processing Tool for Face Recognition

Francimar Rodrigues Maciel, Sergio Cleger Tamayo, Aasim Khurshid[✉],
and Pauliana Caetano Caetano Martins

SIDIA Instituto de Ciência e Tecnologia, Manaus, Brazil
{francimar.maciel,sergio.tamayo,aasim.khurshid,
pauliana.caetano}@sidia.com
https://www.sidia.org.br/en/home/

Abstract. Many biometric systems are being used to identify transactions and increase security levels. These systems analyze the different registers that can recognize a person, for example, fingerprint, face, voice, and iris. Face recognition systems are widely studied for security, surveillance applications, transaction, and general services. The accuracy of these systems depends mainly on two closely related factors, quality data and machine learning techniques used. In this paper, we present a data collection and image analysis tool for face recognition with evolved parameters (ergonomic and visual) setting. The proposed tool is capable of collecting face data with various poses while making the user interaction intuitive and comfortable. The details of the different stages of study, along with discussions, is presented based on results extracted from 79 users.

Keywords: Data collection · Face recognition ·
Robust face data collection

1 Introduction

Many biometric systems have been proposed in the literature to allow access to secure systems [1,2]. These biometric systems include fingerprint recognition, face recognition, voice recognition, iris recognition, and palm recognition [1,3]. Face recognition is one of the most studied biometric systems [4]. In the security and surveillance applications, a high recognition rate is mandatory.

Recently, machine learning algorithms have produced high accuracy in face recognition systems [5]. Machine learning algorithms have two building blocks, which are: data and the algorithm. However, machine learning based face recognition methods requires a large number of labeled samples which are expensive and time consuming to collect. The performance of these methods often improves with the amount and quality of the available data.

There are two possibilities to obtain a large amount of data, i.e., Collection of face data from users, and data augmentation from limited available data.

C. Stephanidis and M. Antona (Eds.): HCII 2019, CCIS 1088, pp. 386–392, 2019.
https://doi.org/10.1007/978-3-030-30712-7_49

Masi et al. [6] discussed the need of collecting huge numbers of face images for effective face recognition, and proposed an augmentation method to enrich the existing dataset by introducing face appearance variations for pose, shape, and expression. The methods of "one-to-many augmentation" can mitigate the challenges of data collection, and they can be used to increment the datasets [7]. They are categorized into four classes: data augmentation, 3D model, CNN model, and GAN model.

- **Data augmentation:** Data augmentation methods consist of photometric and geometric transformations. Transforms include a range of operations from the field of image manipulation, such as shifts, flips and zooms [7];
- **3D model:** To enrich the diversity of training data, different generic 3D models are used for rendering to augment faces;
- **CNN model:** Rather than reconstructing 3D models from a 2D image and projecting it back into 2D images of different poses, CNN models can generate 2D images directly;
- **GAN model:** Generative Adversarial Network (GAN) is also used for image augmentation, which combines prior knowledge of the face data distribution (pose and identity perception loss). Wang et al. [8] compared traditional transformation methods with GANs to the problem of data augmentation in image classification.

The specific data augmentation techniques used for a training dataset must be chosen carefully considering the context of the training dataset and knowledge of the problem domain. Besides, it can be useful to experiment with data augmentation methods in isolation and test to see if they result in a measurable improvement to model performance, perhaps with a small prototype dataset, model, and training. These techniques are robust but can be computationally intensive.

On the other hand, collecting real-world face database is expensive and time-consuming. However, real-world collected data provide better contextual meaning and allows the classifier to learn efficiently. For this reason, a data collection tool can help improve classification accuracy, especially for small and secure systems. In this paper, we propose a data collection and image processing tool that can be used to collect data for facial recognition. Our proposed tool is evaluated and updated from the feedback of users in three stages. Importantly, this tool allows for capturing 96 facial pose variations while making user-interaction with the system pleasant. Rest of the paper is organized as follows: Sect. 2 describes the stages considered in the data collection process and the main visual and ergonomic parameters. Next, the evolution of the developed tool is presented in detail in Sect. 3, followed by the user evaluation in Sect. 4. The conclusions and future research lines are placed in Sect. 5.

2   Data Collection Process

The user image capturing process may take a few seconds from image acquisition to processing and then subsequent use by recognition system. Some aspects may affect depending on the task that will be performed, for example, distance with which it was taken to photo and capture angle. Different studies recognize a necessary number of photos (approximately 30) but do not define the values of visual and geometric parameters present in the interaction with users [4,6,7]. Based on this analysis, a data collection tool that is composed of several visual and ergonomic parameters with minimal interaction is proposed that should be evaluated with users for parameters adjusting in any recognition system.

The following parameters are considered in each iteration:

- **Participants height:** This aspect was considered to determine the height of camera from ground for final data collection;
- **Camera height:** The current height of the camera from ground level;
- **Camera angle:** The current angle of camera with respect to horizontal axis;
- **Capture stages:** The stages of user's image capture process;
- **Yaw angle:** The maximal horizontal rotation of the head by users;
- **Pitch angle:** The maximal vertical rotation of the head by users;
- **Number of images:** The number of face images captured per user;
- **Discarded faces:** The average number of discarded faces per user;
- **Average capture Time:** The average capture time per user;
- **Worst capture Time:** The worst capture time per user.

Mennesson et al. [9] showed that the degree of head yaw rotation is very important for the task of face detection (e.g $\pm 15°$). The authors further commented about how the number of detected faces decreases to zero with a Gaussian decay when user pose is far from the frontal face. Evidently that the maximum of detected frontal faces is obtained with a yaw angle near zero degree (a frontal face).

Visual and ergonomic concepts were studied to facilitate data collection. During the process, three major challenges need to be addressed:

1. To guide the user naturally considering comfort while moving his head;
2. Considering that most of the users are not familiar with face recognition technology, an efficient visual language is necessary to give instructions, when something is not going well;
3. Identify external factors that can influence the quality of experience while using Face Recognition.

The first step was searching parameters that could be used to mediate the human-technology communication. In this regard, three aspects of user interface were observed [10,11]:

1. Physical aspects (operating with a device as a physical object);
2. Handling aspects (the logical structure of interaction with the interface);
3. Subject-object-directed aspects (the mapping of objects "in the computers" with the objects in the real world).

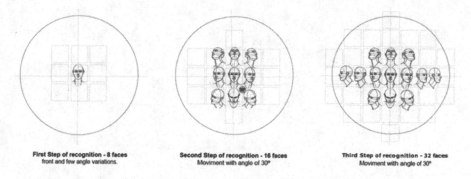

First Step of recognition - 8 faces
front and few angle variations.

Second Step of recognition - 16 faces
Moviment with angle of 30°

Third Step of recognition - 32 faces
Moviment with angle of 30°

Fig. 1. Second stage - rectangular matrix.

3   Image Processing Tool

In the first stage, users start from a frontal position and perform yaw and pitch movements of the face responding to the text indications received from the device.

In the second stage, the registration process was divided into three steps for a total of 56 faces as shown in Fig. 1. The principal problem in this stage was that the interface didn't provide comfort and freedom for users. The users commented that the process was slow and the matrix interface was artificial and they needed mechanic movements.

In the third stage, the register was divided into two steps for a total of 96 faces. As you can see in Fig. 2 the initial steps of the previous stage were merged. In order to improve the human-computer interaction, after testing with the user, we detected improvement points that were implemented in this phase, for example:

- Facilitate the movements of the head at the capture time;
- To reduce time and effort to capture faces;
- Increase the amount of captured faces.

The strategy tested at this stage showed one critical result. A significant number of users failed to turn their face in the 30° for yaw and pitch angles. This leads to a result that the during the test phase, these angles are not expected to go beyond this limit.

The fourth stage was divided into two steps. The registered number of faces is set to 96, but changes are made in user interaction. In the first step, the register was divided into four quadrants where eight images were taken with 5° of head variation in each quadrant. In the second step, we divide into eight pieces where four photos were captured per quadrant, with a maximum head variation of 15°.

This last strategy provided a more intuitive and comfortable interaction, because by reducing the head angle movement, and the capture time, we promoted more natural movement for the user.

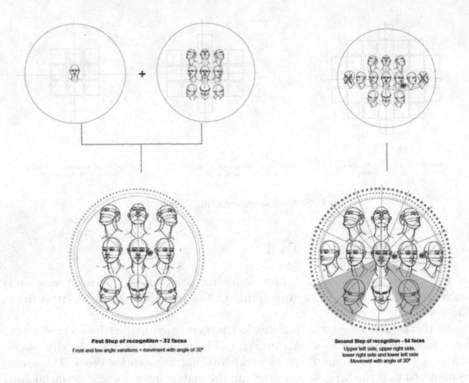

Fig. 2. Third stage - pie chart.

4 Users Evaluation

The experiment took place in an environment with controlled lighting conditions, where participants were tested individually with an average time of 3 min per user. A total of 79 users served as participants for this experiment. Their ages ranged from 21 to 45 years.

Table 1 shows experimental evaluation and the parameter settings. Based on the parameters from the state-of-the-art in face recognition [7], the initial parameters for the first Proof of Concept (PoC) were established. To cover all possible face poses and shapes, n numbers of images are captured ($n = 96$, in current experiments).

About ergonomic parameters, the feedback in all stages allowed to adjust these parameters, such as camera height and camera angle. The camera height is changed to 131 cm in the second stage and 140 cm in the last stage, in response to user discomfort in the experiments. The camera angle was only increased in the last stage for usability reasons. Another interesting element was to capture the rotations (yaw, pitch, and roll) in an angle greater than 15°, a situation that made the user lose control and attention. This difficulty was removed by making improvements in the design (Fig. 3).

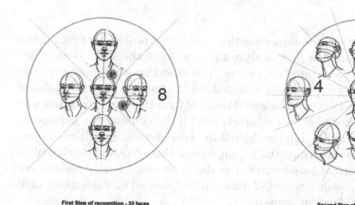

First Step of recognition - 32 faces   Second Step of recognition - 64 faces

Fig. 3. Fourth stage.

Table 1. Parameter settings.

	First stage	Second stage	Third stage	Fourth stage
Participants	25	40	7	7
Shorter (cm)	161	150	155	160
Taller (cm)	180	187	179	170
Camera height	140	131	131	140
Camera angle	60	60	60	70
Capture stages	3	1	2	2
Yaw angle	≤ 30	≤ 30	≤ 15	≤ 15
Pitch angle	–	≤ 20	≤ 15	≤ 15
Face by User	30–35	56	96	96
Discarded faces (%)	–	10	–	–
Average capture Time	150 s	180 s	180 s	120 s
Worst capture Time	2 min	5 min	3 min	3 min

Among the functionality parameters, two steps were achieved in the final stage to complete the register, being insufficient and very ambitious to achieve it in one stage, and considered as excessive more than two stages. The different parameters adjustments allowed reducing the average registration time to two minutes, with the variance of one minute, highlighting as an acceptable time of user interaction.

The proposed changes meet the requirements from development and design teams. In the future, we intend to improve the communication when the user is not doing the correct head movements.

5   Conclusions

In this method, we propose a data collection and image processing tool for face recognition applications. We first analyze the process of the facial data collection and explains the data collection phases. The most important geometric and visual parameters are discussed and analyzed. In the final stage of the data collection tool, those parameters are selected that conform the system requirements and also allows a comfortable user interaction with the system. The parameters and their adjustments, although considered in other studies, show their importance in specific people and contexts. In conclusion, this system allows to collect facial data with important poses covered in the most user friendly manner and that in addition, high quality collected data can be obtained for subsequent tasks of face recognition in different scenarios.

Acknowledgment. The authors would like to thank the support provided by SIDIA Instituto de Ciência e Tecnologia and teams. The authors also like to thank the users, who helped create the system by providing useful feedback during the process.

References

1. Blasco, J., Chen, T.M., Tapiador, J., Peris-Lopez, P.: A survey of wearable biometric recognition systems. ACM Comput. Surv. **49**(3), 43:1–43:35 (2016)
2. Ratha, N.K., Connell, J.H., Bolle, R.M.: Enhancing security and privacy in biometrics-based authentication systems. IBM Syst. J. **40**(3), 614–634 (2001)
3. Delac, K., Grgic, M.: A survey of biometric recognition methods. In: 46th International Symposium on Electronics, Zadar, Croatia, pp. 184–193 (2004)
4. Özdil, A., Özbilen, M.M.: A survey on comparison of face recognition algorithms. In: 2014 IEEE 8th International Conference on Application of Information and Communication Technologies (AICT), pp. 1–3, October 2014
5. Prihasto, B., et al.: A survey of deep face recognition in the wild. In: 2016 International Conference on Orange Technologies (ICOT), pp. 76–79, December 2016
6. Masi, I., Tran, A.T., Leksut, J.T., Hassner, T., Medioni, G.G.: Do we really need to collect millions of faces for effective face recognition? CoRR abs/1603.07057 (2016)
7. Wang, M., Deng, W.: Deep face recognition: a survey. CoRR abs/1804.06655 (2018)
8. Perez, L., Wang, J.: The effectiveness of data augmentation in image classification using deep learning. CoRR abs/1712.04621 (2017)
9. Mennesson, J., Dahmane, A., Danisman, T., Bilasco, I.M.: Head yaw estimation using frontal face detector, pp. 517–524, January 2016
10. Bødker, S.: A human activity approach to user interfaces. Hum.-Comput. Interact. **4**(3), 171–195 (1989)
11. Kaptelinin, V., Nardi, B.A.: Acting with Technology: Activity Theory and Interaction Design. MIT Press, Cambridge (2009)

A Model for the Interpretation of Data from an ECU by Means of OBD Devices

Jefferson A. Sánchez(✉), Juan F. Valencia, and Maria L. Villegas

Universidad Del Quindío, Armenia Q., Colombia
jefferson_909690@hotmail.com

Abstract. The creation of a model for the interpretation and transformation of data from the computer of automobiles (ECU) will serve on a large scale to the automotive sector. The main objective of this work is to facilitate the understanding of the data provided by the ECU of automobiles, through a model composed of five phases (Connection, loading, interpretation, loading and visualization). The model has usability criteria. Each phase is comprised of the most convenient processes for the context, seeking to reduce complexity and inefficiency. Finally, with the application of the proposed model in mobile applications or desktop software, a person can perform an automotive "Diagnostic" with or without mechanical knowledge, will be able to understand and interpret the information provided and will have certainty about the mechanical state of the revised automobile.

Keywords: Automotive diagnostic · Data interpretation · Model · On board diagnostic

1 Introduction

As of the year 1998 all cars are manufactured with an integrated computer denoted as ECU. The ECU (Electronic Control Unit) is the unit in charge of receiving all the information collected from the vehicle by means of different capturers and probes, analyzes and processes this information and controls the different ignition and injection organisms [1]. Taking into account the above, one could know the mechanical status of the vehicles manufactured at a date after 1998 by simply connecting to the ECU and interpreting the data that it provides.

Currently there are different applications that allow to visualize the data generated by the ECU, by means of an OBD II device; but with the great difficulty that it is not easy for a natural person to understand the information that is shown there, being then not very useful to make diagnoses of the vehicles. It is thus seen that there is no method available to interpret the data from the ECU so that any natural person can understand them. It is necessary then, the creation of a model for the interpretation of the data coming from the ECU through an OBD device that allows to make the connection with the ECU via Bluetooth or Wifi. Because each automaker has its own ECU, the OBD II system uses several types of protocols, where each has its own communication speed and voltage levels [2]. With the aforementioned model, any person with or without

© Springer Nature Switzerland AG 2019
C. Stephanidis and M. Antona (Eds.): HCII 2019, CCIS 1088, pp. 393–410, 2019.
https://doi.org/10.1007/978-3-030-30712-7_50

mechanical knowledge could perform a "Diagnostic" to your vehicle and know efficiently the mechanical state of the car.

The proposed model is comprised of five phases (connection, initial load, interpretation, final load and visualization), the latter built with criteria such as usability. The word Usability in its most precise interpretation is: ease and simplicity of use of an article or object [3]. Criteria such as metaphors will also be used. A metaphor is defined as the translation of the straight sense of a voice to another figurative, by virtue of a tacit comparison; that is, making sense of an object through comparison [4]. Other criteria from the area of HCI (human-computer interaction) will be used in order to provide a perspective as understandable as possible.

2 Proposed Model

2.1 Characteristics of the Model

In the development of this work, it is the data interpretation model, the main component. The model that is available that is applicable to existing software in the field and in that order of ideas, can also be a considerable basis for the creation of future applications of the context in question. Thus, the main characteristics that the model must supply are:

1. The ability to be able to program in an object-oriented language (be sequential).
2. Improve aspects of usability in the application.
3. Increase the understandability of the information that the application throws.

Starting from the previous characteristics taken from the objectives of the work, we arrive at a graphic representation of the model (See Fig. 1).

In each of the phases of the model a specific procedure is done, same as described below.

2.2 Phase 1

The 5 communication protocols of the OBDII devices with their internal variations, work as follows [5]:

- SAE J1850 PWM: Used exclusively by vehicles manufactured and belonging to Ford. This protocol uses differential signals and has a transfer speed of up to 41.6 Kbps and its feeds to the diagnostic connector are: Pin 5 - Earth, Pin 16 - Battery voltage, Pin 2 - Data 1 and Pin 10 - Data 2.
- SAE J1850 VPW: This protocol is used almost exclusively by General Motors (GM) and Chrysler vehicles since 2000. Its power supplies to the diagnostic connector are: Pin 5 - Earth, Pin 16 - Battery voltage and Pin 2 - Data.
- ISO 9141-2: Used by Chrysler until 1999 and some models after 2000, BMW, Mercedes Benz, Porsche and some other European and Asian brands. Its feeds are: Pin 5 - Earth, Pin 16 - Battery voltage and Pin 7 - Data.

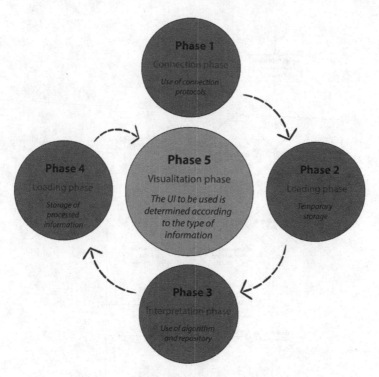

Fig. 1. Graphical representation of the data interpretation model

- ISO 14230-4 (KWP2000): It is the protocol of the European standard EOBD and is very common in vehicles from 2003 on brands such as Renault, Peugeot, etc. Its feeds to the diagnostic connector are: Pin 5 - Earth, Pin 16 - Battery voltage, Pin 7 - Data 1 and Pin 15 - Data 2.
- CAN (ISO 11898/15765): The CAN protocol for the diagnostic bus began in use in 2003 in some models of brands such as Ford, Chrysler, GM, among others. Since 2008, its implantation has been mandatory in American vehicles. Its feeds are: Pin 5 - Earth, Pin 16 - Battery voltage, Pin 6 - High data and Pin 14 - Low data.

For a Bluetooth or Wi-Fi interface, it is necessary prior to the data transfer with the OBDII device, a pairing through the Bluetooth or Wifi service provided by the mobile device. In the case of a Bluetooth OBDII device, for pairing, it is necessary to have a connection pin that asks the device to connect to it. There are three pins that are normally used: 0000, 1111 or 1234.

Once the previous connection to the data transmission is made, an algorithm is proposed for the automatic selection of the protocol to be used, according to the reception of pins; said algorithm is shown in Fig. 2.

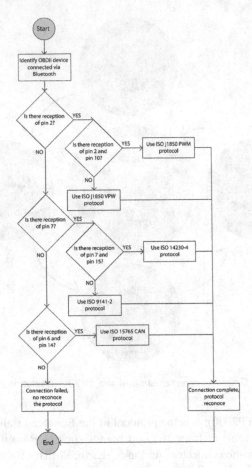

Fig. 2. Selection protocol algorithm

2.3 Phase 2

Due to the ease provided by data structures such as Lists, since in their declaration it is not necessary to determine their total dimension; allowing adding a variable amount of data. It is proposed the use of a List for the storage of the errors reported by the ECU, since there may be zero or many errors that arise in the diagnosis. Figure 3 shows the list that is proposed and how it would be the location of the errors that are received.

It should be noted that only the error code should be saved, no other portion of the text should be there, which does not hinder the subsequent data crossing process of Phase 4.

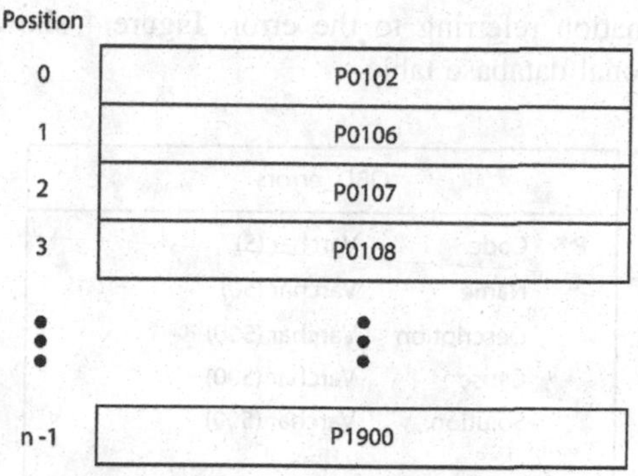

Position

0	P0102
1	P0106
2	P0107
3	P0108
⋮	⋮
n-1	P1900

Fig. 3. List for temporary storage of errors

2.4   Phase 3

In this intermediate phase, it is available, as a result of a research and data collection work; a repository of the errors that an ECU can generate. Which has a complete interpretation of the errors, going from a technical and unknown language, to a natural one that is understandable to a person like that who does not possess mechanical knowledge. In Table 1 you can see a position of the repository and how is its structure.

Table 1. Error information repository

Code	Description	Cause	Solution
P0102 - Low input of the mass air flow circuit (MAF - Mass Air Flow)	The Air Mass Flow Sensor (MAF) is mounted on the air intake duct of the vehicle's engine...	When the error code P0102 OBDII is established, it may be due to: There may be intake air leaks. Mass Air Flow (MAF) sensor cables or connectors may be shorted, rubbing with some other component causing a poor electrical connection ...	The steps to solve the diagnostic code P0102 OBD2 are: Performs an inspection of all cables and respective connectors related to the Air Mass Flow Sensor (MAF) ...
...	...	...	...
P1900 - intermittent failure of output shaft speed sensor circuit	The speed sensor signal from the output shaft to the PCM is irregular or interrupted	Fault code P0723 OBD2 is established by the following: Harness connector not seated correctly. Harness intermittently short-circuited, or open. Harness connector damaged. OSS sensor damaged or not installed correctly	The steps to solve the DTC code P0723 OBDII are: Check harness and connector integrity. Verify the correct installation of the OSS sensor

The end of this phase comprises a small and simple algorithm that compares the error codes present in the List of Phase 2 with those provided by the repository. You must compare the fields in the List with the primary keys of the error table and thus extract all the information referring to the error. Figure 4 shows the format of the repository, in a relational database table.

OBD_errors	
P* Code	Varchar (5)
Name	Varchar (50)
Description	Varchar (500)
Cause	Varchar (500)
Solution	Varchar (500)
OBD_errors_PK(Code)	

Fig. 4. Repository relational database format

2.5 Phase 4

In this section, the final assembly of the information is done to finally be shown to the user. We can say that the data structures provide a technical knowledge to choose the best and most efficient way to organize our data for the solution of problems commonly used in programming [6]. In the specific case that is addressed in this paper, a temporary data structure is necessary, since each time the vehicle is diagnosed the procedure is repeated; that provides the characteristics and functionalities of a structure type Key/Value. It is understood that the keys or keys, are going to be the error codes.

Starting from the above, the use of maps for this phase is proposed, since they are structures that have all the key/value structure of the one being spoken and in languages such as java, certain methods are provided for easy administration. Then in Fig. 5 the map that is proposed with its structure is illustrated.

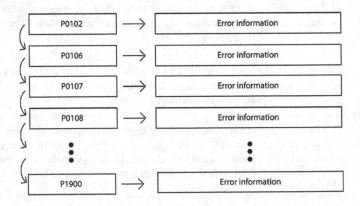

Fig. 5. Processed information map

As it is clearly seen in the previous map, for each error an object is related to what was called "error information", which is made up of several attributes. Figure 6 shows in detail the composition of the object in question with its restrictions of attributes and methods (private or public).

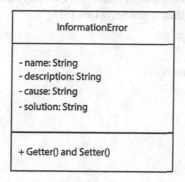

Fig. 6. Information object diagram

2.6 Phase 5

In the last phase of the model, a study is made based on the Roadmap methodology shown in Fig. 7. This results in an information architecture, a theme (colors and combinations) and a type (visual architecture) of Graphic interface; on which the visual design of the entire application is made, in order to increase characteristics such as usability in the process, with respect to existing designs.

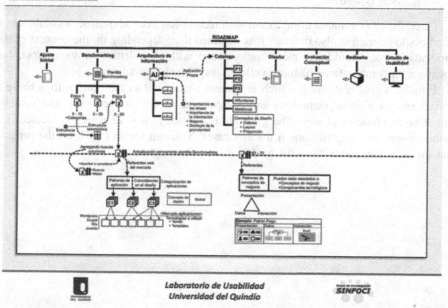

Fig. 7. Roadmap for the development and design of graphic interfaces. Formulated under the research of the SINFOCI research group of the University of Quindío [7].

After the development of the benchmarking mentioned in the methodology, the following information architecture is reached, which is the most elementary and appropriate architecture; taking into account that end users are people who do not know mechanics and may be in their vehicles when using it.

- Connection
  - Interface
  - Connection type (protocol)
- Diagnosis
  - State
  - Error codes
  - Report
- Settings
  - Language
  - Version
- Vehicle specifications
  - Model
  - Brand
  - Mileage
  - Cylinder capacity
  - Gas
- Graphics (if it is required to show data graphically)
  - Boards
  - GPS
  - performance
  - Records (speed)

Once the most suitable information architecture has been identified, a combination of colors to be used is also defined. It is assumed that, depending on the context of the application, you should use clear backgrounds with dark letters or vice versa, but always with combinations of blue, yellow, gray, black and white.

Finally, a grid is defined, which is a mesh that is left to the bottom to achieve a design and location of metaphors and components in the most orderly, and visually attractive and functional way. The grid that is defined is 7×12 which is located in a mobile phone mockup (IPhone 6 for this case). You can see in Fig. 8 all the process that includes the design from the grid.

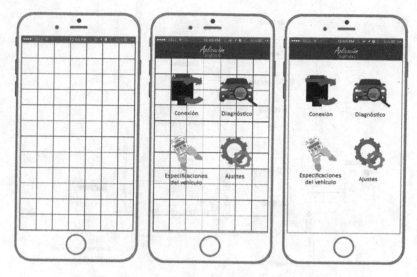

Fig. 8. Design process based on themes and grid

The rest of interfaces and the navigation map of the application can be seen in Figs. 9 and 10 respectively.

Fig. 9. Application interfaces

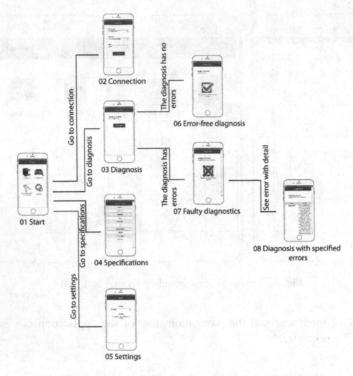

Fig. 10. Application navigation

Validation of Interfaces

To verify that the proposed design meets good usability standards, some tests are done in the usability laboratory of the Quindío University; where a set of users are taken, they are assigned some tasks to develop and at the end they are asked some questions about their experience in the interaction with the application. The above is in order to determine which components have design problems and in which specific aspects they are failing, in order to redesign them.

The study of 11 indicators that qualify, in a first instance, the development that the user had in the test. A minimum value of 80% of "Yes" responses from users is defined in an indicator, to accept it; as long as this is a positive indicator for the design. Thus, if the value is less than 80%, it must be submitted to redesign. In the opposite case, if an indicator is negative for the design and more than 20% of the answers to it in the tests were "Yes", it must be submitted to redesign. Table 2 shows the collection of all the results obtained by the users in the test around the proposed indicators.

Table 2. Context of the indicators statistics

Project name: model for the interpretation of data of an ECU by means of OBD devices		Number of users: 8			
Indicator	Valor	Users that DO apply the indicator		Users that do NOT apply the indicator	
		Number	%	Number	%
Indicator 1: The user manages the correct meaning of metaphors	Positive	7	87,5	1	12,5
Indicator 2: The user easily identifies the connection icon	Positive	7	87,5	1	12,5
Indicator 3: The user easily identifies the settings icon	Positive	8	100	0	0
Indicator 4: The user gives many clicks on the application	Negative	1	12,5	7	87,5
Indicator 5: The user clicks on each of the fields assigned to him	Positive	7	87,5	1	12,5
Indicator 6: The user clicks on the field to perform diagnostics	Positive	7	87,5	1	12,5
Indicator 7: The user makes the connection	Positive	8	100	0	0
Indicator 8: The user identifies how to choose the protocol to use	Positive	4	**50**	4	50
Indicator 9: The user identifies the generated error code	Positive	6	**75**	2	25
Indicator 10: The user identifies the error that the application shows	Positive	5	**62,5**	3	37,5
Indicator 11: The user clearly identifies the connection PIN	Positive	3	**37,5**	5	62,5

Thus, it is clearly identified that indicators 8, 9, 10 and 11 are below the acceptance threshold, indicating that a redesign of the aspects of the application that intervene in these indicators is needed.

Now, we proceed with the analysis of the tasks and the questions of the test. Three tasks were determined to be performed during the test, which would be evaluated by the user in binary form (1 when the task was successful and 0 otherwise). The tasks that were arranged are:

- Task 1: Connect with the OBDII device in bluetooth mode.
- Task 2: Determine the correct number of errors displayed by the ECU.
- Task 3: Identify the causes of the first error shown.

The results of the users regarding the tasks, can be seen in Fig. 11.

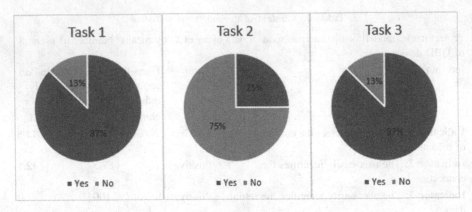

Fig. 11. Percentage of completion per task

It is seen that task 2 could not be carried out by a large portion of the users, assuming that the aspects that are involved need to be redesigned.

On the other hand, after the test, 2 questions were asked which allowed the user to give their opinion on important aspects of the design. The questions were:

1. What did you expect to find in the connection interface?
2. What do you think about the explanatory text about the errors?

The responses of the users, discretized and collected, can be seen in Fig. 12.

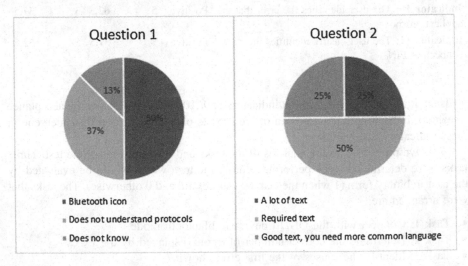

Fig. 12. Percentage of answers per question

Redesign

According to the results of the tests, it is then determined that the design of the interfaces that relate to the aspects of:

1. Use a metaphor for the use of Bluetooth.
2. Make transparent the protocol to use (increase the level of abstraction).
3. Clearly identify the connection PIN.
4. Identify the generated error code.
5. Text segmentation (Do not see too much text in a single interface).
6. Determine the correct number of errors displayed by the ECU.

It is thus evidenced that the connection interface is the one related to the aspects of redesign 1, 2 and 3; and aspects from 4 onwards, with the diagnostic interface. The new design of the connection interface, where it is also decided to implement a more telling feedback (Positive or negative); next to the new design of the diagnostic interface with its segmentation and the new interface for displaying the details of the error, they are shown in Figs. 13 and 14 respectively.

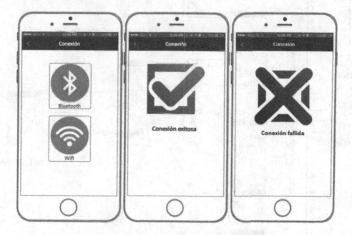

Fig. 13. Redesigned connection interfaces

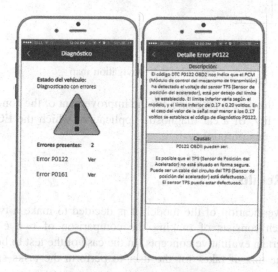

Fig. 14. Redesigned diagnostic interfaces

The new navigation map that resulted from the redesign is shown in Fig. 15.

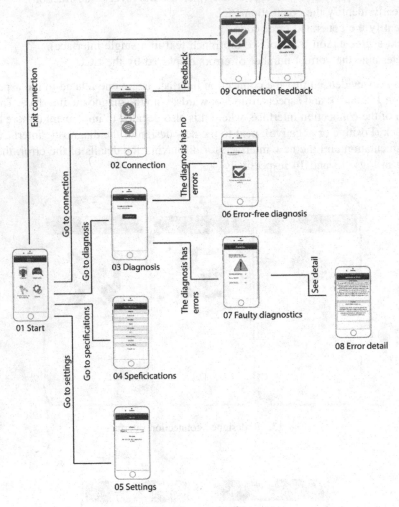

Fig. 15. New navigation map

This concludes the model proposed for the improvement of the concepts of usability and data intelligibility, of a car diagnostic application, which the ECU uses through OBDII devices for this purpose.

3 Test and Results

To make a final verification of the model, it is decided to make a type of test called "Test A/B", which consists of making the comparison of two elements by their qualification in certain evaluative concepts. In the case of the test to be developed, it is decided to use the time it takes for the user to perform the tasks specified, such as comparative metrics; since, when measuring this time, concepts such as the cognitive load on the user, veracity of the metaphors, clarity of navigation, proportion of elements, among others, can be analyzed.

It was taken as the evaluation model "A" to which was evaluated in the beginning with eye-trackers. The tasks to develop are the same that were formulated for the test with eye-trackers, as well as the profile of the users, so that there was no advantage in any of the tests. It should be noted that in the redesign the results of the test with eye-trackers were taken into account, since it was important to take into account the user's focus and verify that the user's attention was focused on the elements that were desired. The tasks that were evaluated were:

- Task 1: Connect with the OBDII device in bluetooth mode.
- Task 2: Determine the correct number of errors displayed by the ECU.
- Task 3: Identify the causes of the first error shown.

After making the data collection of the test, we arrive at Table 3, which contains the average of times and percentage of approval for tasks. This table shows the data in a comparative way.

Table 3. Test A/B results

Test A/B	Test – Model A (Initial)		Test – Model B (Redesign)	
	Average time (seconds)	Approved (%)	Average time (seconds)	Approved (%)
Task 1	48,50	70	8,90	100
Task 2	42,00	20	12,93	100
Task 3	83,99	70	31,80	80

The graphs of Figs. 16 and 17 show the comparison in terms of the evaluation aspects between both designs.

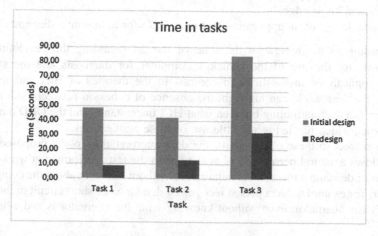

Fig. 16. Comparison of interaction time per task

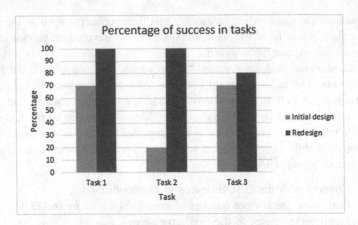

Fig. 17. Comparison of percentage of completion per task

It can be seen then, that the reduction in the execution time is approx. 81.65% in task 1, 69.21% in task 2 and 62.14% in task 3. This indicates that the cognitive effort the user had to make to understand the way in which he had to develop the task, because he only had to intuit the way to do it, no help of any kind was allowed. The design of the metaphors and the proportion in terms of the components was adequate, the user did not need to make a significant visual effort to locate the elements and understand their function. The improvement in terms of the general usability of the application can be seen in the second graph, where an increase of 30%, 80% and 10% can be seen, in successful completion of tasks 1, 2 and 3 respectively.

The contribution made in the present thesis of formulation of a model for the interpretation of data of an ECU by means of OBD devices, can be given in aspects related to:

1. HCI in the context of automotive diagnostic applications.
2. Language of an application of the mechanical context, oriented to people without mechanical knowledge.
3. Interface design of an application that uses ECU for automotive diagnostics.

According to the review of the state of the art regarding the development of applications for the use of the vehicle's computer for diagnosis and the study of existing applications in the field, in contrast to the theories of HCI and the tools available for their work, can highlight the absence of cohesion between both entities, also, there is a deep uprooting between what HCI understands and the OBD diagnostic applications, which has led to the little use of these applications.

With respect to these observations, the data interpretation model proposed in this thesis, allows a natural person and as evidenced in the tests performed at work, would be able to understand a mechanical failure even without knowing about the components of the car; for example, that a person recognizes that he has a short circuit in the circuit that feeds the alternator, even without knowing what the alternator is and what is the circuit that feeds it. With this information, a person could easily go to their trusted mechanic and solve the problem in a very short time, since the time spent on the revision to find the fault is suppressed; in the same way it mitigates the risk of wasting money on unnecessary arrangements or that were not the cause of the failure.

The contributions can then be discretized in the following way.

Theoretical Contributions

- Concepts of usability: The fact of studying all the interaction and the key points of interest of a user when using a mechanical diagnostic application, provides a theoretical basis of concepts that had not previously been identified, nor worked in this type of Applications; allowing, after this work, to have a base of concepts that as a minimum should be taken into account in this type of development that promotes the investigation of more concepts that may be considered useful.
- Internal structuring model: The model allows a structuring of how the operation of an application of the field should be internally, improving both the data, the efficiency in the operation and its design, as well as a more important aspect at the business level, such as it is the acceptance in the market, because a very good product is useless, if it is not sold.

Technological Contributions

- Interface design: The interfaces that were designed in this work provide a certified and evaluated template, know how the graphic components should be and their distribution within the interface according to the segmentation of the screen.

4 Conclusions

In summary, of the finished work; a model has been developed that allows transforming the data provided by the computer of a vehicle, from a very technical language to a natural language. All the errors of the Data Sheet of the ECU computers have been compiled and a complete translation and interpretation has been made. A set of graphic interfaces has been designed with high levels of usability that serve as a template for the development of an automotive diagnostic application through the ECU. An information architecture has been consolidated for an automotive diagnostic application, based on field benchmarking.

Acknowledgements. First of all, we thank God for allowing us to carry out this work and equip ourselves with the capacities and ideas necessary to develop it. Special thanks to the director of this thesis, the PhD. Maria Lili Villegas and the SINFOCI research group of the University of Quindío for opening the doors and lending us the necessary equipment to carry out the usability tests.

References

1. Amaya, S., Villareal, A.: Investigación de la influencia del uso del software dedicado en la reprogramación en red para el mapeo de la ECU programable en el motor Peugeot 407. Universidad de las Fuerzas Armadas ESPE Extensión Latacunga, Latacunga (2017)
2. Landín, M., Arlén, C., Valverde Jimenez, U.Y.: Scanner Automotriz Interfaz PC (2010)
3. Matos, R.: La Usabilidad Como Factor De Calidad De Páginas Web (2013)
4. RAE: Diccionario de la Real Academia de la Lengua Española. RAE, Madrid (2014)
5. Sanchez, J.: Simulador de una ECU y diagnóstico mediante una CAN y OBD-II. Politécnica de Cuenca, Cuenca (2017)
6. Liza Ávila, C.: Estructura de Datos con C ++. Fondo Editorial UPN, Lima (2013)
7. Giraldo, W., Villegas, M.L., Collazos, C.: Incorporación de HCI: Modelo de Ecosistema, Eje Cafetero. In: GRIHO-AIPO (ed.) CHIJOTE 2018 – II JOrnada de Trabajo sobre Enseñanza de HCI, Palma de Mallorca, p. 69 (2018)
8. Sommeville, I.: Ingeniería del Software. Pearson Education, London (2005)
9. Norman, D.: The Design of Everyday Things. Basic Books, New York (2013)
10. Naur, P., Randall, B.: Software Engineering: A Report on a Conference Sponsored by the NATO. In: NATO (1969)
11. Martínez Orge, J.L.: Modelos de HCI basados en interfaces multitáctil para dispositivos móviles
12. Grijalva, M., Alfredo, D., Cholota, V, Fernando, D.: Diseño y construcción de un modulo interface con la ECU para el control de operación de las RPM del motor (2009)
13. Marcos, M.-C.: HCI (human computer interaction): concepto y desarrollo. El Prof. la Inf. **10**, 4–16 (2001)
14. Liang, S., Strahler, A.H.: Calculation of the angular radiance distribution for a coupled atmosphere and canopy. IEEE Trans. Geosci. Remote Sens. **31**(2), 491–502 (1993)
15. Hewett, T., et al.: ACM SIGCHI Curricula for Human-Computer Interaction (1992)
16. García Hoyas, V.L.: Un desarrollo Android para el control de dispositivos acoplados a un automóvil (2015)
17. Dimaté Cáceres, J.M., González Castillo, P.M.: Diseño de una interfaz gráfica en Labview para el diagnostico de vehículos por medio de OBD2 (2010)
18. Anchapaxi Socasi, A.R.: Recolección de datos del sistema OBD II de un automóvil usando un dispositivo Android (2016)
19. Adler, P., Winograd, T.: Usability: Turning Technologies into Tools. Oxford University Press, New York (1992)
20. Acevedo, J.: El transporte como soporte al desarrollo de Colombia. Una visión al 2040. Universidad de los Andes, Bogotá (2009)

User Studies

Index of Difficulty Measurement for Handedness with Biometric Authentication

Kathleen Brush[(⊠)], Nabil El Achraoui, Jennifer Boyd, Jacob Johnson, Randy Chepenik, Tarik McLean, Sadida Siddiqui, Aditee Verma, John Sheridan, Avery Leider, and Charles C. Tappert

Seidenberg School of Computer Science and Information Systems, Pace University, Pleasantville, NY 10570, USA
{kb31851p,ne91668n,jb91235n,jj7373n2,rc71331n,tm00333p,ss05380p,av11813n, js58363p,aleider,ctappert}@pace.edu

Abstract. This study attempts to identify the variance between right- and left-handed users when utilizing touch screen devices. Three experiments were created in Flutter to gather data and identify the differences in functionality by left- and right-handed users on touch screen devices. These experiments focused on speed and accuracy while also using mirrored images. Experiment one focused on Fitts' law while two and three focused on steering law. This paper focuses primarily on the Fitts' law experiment. The collected data were analyzed and visualizations created to provide insight into whether these biometric experiments prove or disprove the existence of deficiencies in touch screen devices for left-handed users. Data was collected from the native touchscreen and timing features for each participant. A preliminary visual analysis of the data indicates a significant variance between right- and left-handed users, but a machine learning analysis is necessary to verify this hypothesis definitively.

Keywords: Human-computer interaction · Fitts' law · Steering law · Flutter · Firebase authentication · Biometrics

1 Introduction

1.1 Background

Touchscreen technology interfaces may have inadvertently been designed to favor right-handed users. The right-handed favored design reaches across all interfaces, including computers, tablets, mobile phones, gaming consoles, and other user interactive machines. Settings can be adjusted on mouse buttons to reverse the controls for left-handed users, however the hand and extended forearm get in the way of displayed content on touchscreens as the fingers replace the mouse cursor control. Typing and keyboard use does not have the same right-handed bias. Interestingly enough, an individual typing with both hands in the conventional

C. Stephanidis and M. Antona (Eds.): HCII 2019, CCIS 1088, pp. 413–423, 2019.
https://doi.org/10.1007/978-3-030-30712-7_51

manner on standard 'qwerty' keyboard can type in the neighborhood of 3400 words with solely the left hand, whereas only 450 words are typed solely with the right hand. There are many theories on skills and adaptability of left-handed users ability to use a right-handed tool easier than a right-handed individual's ability to use a tool built for left-handed individuals. However, there is very little public awareness of left-handed accessibility issue and accommodation in UX/UI and HCI, human computer interaction.

Fitts' law calculates the time to click a point on the screen as a function of the distance traveled and width of the target. It is used in HCI to design UI/UX of mobile apps. Using time, distance, and width the difficulty coefficient can be calculated. In the following formula, the variables MT, A, and W represent movement time, moving range, and the breadth of the target, respectively [1].

$$MT = a + b \cdot log_2(\frac{A}{W})$$

Index of Difficulty, is also called the difficulty coefficient and is represented by ID [1].

$$ID = log_2(\frac{A}{W})$$

Fitts' law predicts movement from one location to another [1]. It has been concluded in an experimental study of right handed users that the screen quadrant measured most difficult to access should be avoided when designing touchscreen apps [2]. However, if one is using the left hand, that display area may not be difficult to access. This research, based on the study by Zhang, et al., includes both right-handed and left-handed participants performing the experiment using each hand in succession. Hypothesis one is that there will be a symmetric, or mirror difference for right and left-handed subjects. Steering Law, derived from Fitts' Law, is used to calculate accuracy while swiping across a mobile device. This law is a predictive model of subject movement that describes the time required to navigate or steer through a tunnel. Below is the mathematical equation where A = length of tunnel, and W = width [3]. Figure 1 illustrates this concept:

$$IDs = A/W$$

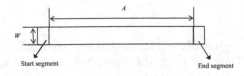

Fig. 1. Steering law [3]

Based on Inkpen's research, any application requiring on-screen input (i.e., Left-Handed Scrolling 105 hyperlinks, buttons, text entry forms, context menus, etc.) should make the placement of their input widget dynamic based on handedness [4]. For example, it is common for applications to left align their drop-down menu or sub-menus. This works well for readability as English is read left to right but is inefficient given right-handedness. Left-handed users receive the benefit of not having to reach across the screen to select the drop-down bar, where right-handed users have to occlude their screen to make the interaction.

1.2 Objectives

The purpose of this work was to gain additional insight and data on the responsiveness of self-identified left and right-handed individuals using a mobile application developed in Flutter.

To that end, this research study set out to accomplish the following:

– Develop a biometrics application to measure the variance between right- and left-handed users using Flutter, supporting both Android and iOS mobile devices.
– Record data for right handed users, left handed users, right handers using their left hand, and left handers using their right hand.
– Create a database using Firebase to perform data analytics and summarization of variance on the data that was collected from the experiments.
– Calculate the Index of Difficulty using Fitts' law and steering law formulas with consideration of the movement time, as well as the direction of hand movement.
– Use machine learning to test for any significant authentication biometrics.

2 Literature Review

Although keystroke analysis lacks the amount of studies compared to other biometric modalities, it is one that demands our attention. The first reference to the conceptualization of keystroke analysis dates to Spillane's research in 1975 [5]. At first, studies proved that keystroke dynamics work well when enough data is acquired to create the model of a user. Now, the same can be done without demanding a plethora of data from the user. Studies on keystroke analysis all attempt to provide a powerful yet economical authentication method.

In a study that exemplifies this, a novel keystroke biometric system for long-text input was developed and evaluated for user identification and authentication applications. The system consisted of a Java applet that collected raw keystroke data, a feature extractor, and pattern classifiers that made the final decision in authentication. Data was collected from over 100 participants to investigate two input modes (copy and free-text) and two keyboard types (desktop and laptop). This study used 239 feature measurements to characterize a typist's key-press duration times, transition times between keys, the percentage in the use of non-letter keys and mouse clicks, and typing speed. By varying between the two input modes as independent variables, the distinctiveness of keystroke patterns can be determined. The data yielded four quadrants: desktop copy, laptop copy, desktop free text, and laptop free text. These are the four ideal conditions. It was determined that accuracy was greater under these four conditions, however, it decreased as the population size increased. Longitudinal studies were also incorporated to study the accuracy of identification and authentication over time. Results showed that only about 300 keystrokes were needed for sufficient accuracy for various applications. Therefore, it reduces the text input requirement to less than half of that used in the experiments. An equal error rate (EER) value was obtained in the authentication study under ideal conditions. Ultimately, the study found that keystroke biometrics is useful for identification and authentication applications, if two or more enrollment samples are available and if the same type of keyboard is used to produce both the enrollment and questioned samples [6].

In yet another study that exemplifies keystroke analysis as an economical tool and how it can be integrated into existing computer security systems with minimal alteration and user intervention, the majority of the keystroke dynamics research works from the last three decades are summarized and analyzed [6]. The advantages of implementing keystroke analysis are undeniable. Understanding the history of keystroke dynamics can help researchers further their studies in the appropriate direction (Fig. 2).

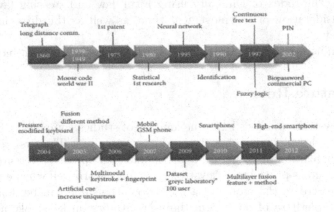

Fig. 2. A timeline on the overview of keystroke research work evolution

3   Methodology

3.1   Flutter

To design the experiments for this study, a new application development software, Flutter was used. Flutter 1.0 was released in 2018 and is being used by over 250K developers and counting. Flutter is an efficient way to build applications for both iOS and Android devices. Most application development software options in the past require a developer to create their app in either iOS or Android. The Apple iOS SDK, or Software Development Kit, was released in 2008, and the Android DSK in 2009. These kits were based on different languages, and require that a developer understand both languages to properly code an app. Flutter takes a different approach. Unlike its predecessors that required a bridge to communicate between the native language and the application, Flutter uses a "compiled" programming language called Dart, that removes the requirement for the bridge between the native code and the application code. By removing the bridge, apps run faster, and require a programmer to only learn Dart, rather than both iOS and Android programming languages. Another key feature of Flutter that makes it a significant improvement from other development kits is the way it manages widgets. Widgets need to be fast, customizable, and have an appealing look and feel. Flutter provides its own widgets which allows for quick development of attractive, fast widgets within applications. More specifically, Flutter was chosen because it is open source, it creates cross platform apps and it has hot reload, meaning as soon as we make any change in the code, it gets reflected on the simulator. It uses Material Design which is the design language and it gives very aesthetic and distinctive look to the UI (Fig. 3).

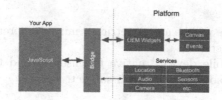

Fig. 3. App development with bridge

3.2 Firebase

Data and analytics from the Flutter app are tracked through the back-end database system, Firebase, for the experiments. With the data points gathered, the team was able to determine if there were deficiencies present for left handed users during the experiments. Firebase allows for device data to be gathered on multiple platforms such as IOS and Android in which the flutter application is deployed. Firebase also runs its own analytics on app and platform usage as well as performance of the flutter application. After data is collected, Firebase provides a dashboard view to characterize and analyze the data. The dashboard for this project is shown below (Fig. 4).

In addition to the dashboard, there are specific graphical breakdowns of the data available.

Fig. 4. Firebase dashboard

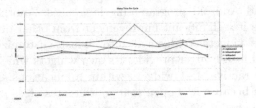

Fig. 5. Firebase dashboard

4 Hypotheses

Hypothesis One: There will be a symmetric, or mirror difference for right-handed and left-handed subjects.
Hypothesis Two: Mobile devices' native touchscreen and timing features will yield authentication biometrics for each subject.

5 Experiment One

The experiments have been designed to test and document whether there is a significant difference in response times to user interfaces and applications based on the individual's dominant hand. In this study, time was recorded in microseconds. Recorded fields include a main object called data that has all data of users. Then there is a user object for each participant having the name they entered in the experiment's opening screen. Inside the user object there are two handednesstype objects (generated dynamically based on leftdominant hand or rightdominant hand user). For right hand dominant people, the handedness objects are: righthanded, left handnondominant. For left hand dominant people, the handedness objects are: lefthanded, righthandnondonimant.

We based our first experiment on Zhang, et al's paper [2]. After these data points were collected, we analyzed each category by dominant hand to see if there was a difference between speed and accuracy results for right and left, as well as the non-dominant hand. Fitts' law calculates the time to click a point on the screen as a function of the distance traveled and width of the target. While there were eight target points, only one target point appeared on screen at a time per click test, in addition to the source point. These eight click tests around the dial comprised one cycle test. The experiment consists of eight cycle tests. Then, the subject repeated the cycle tests with their non-dominant hand.

In experiment one, the distance from the source button to the target button A is 250 pixels. The width of the target button W is 60 pixels. Therefore, as Zhang calculated, the difficulty coefficient for each angle is ID = 1.43 [2]. Zhang et al. conclude that the screen quadrant measured most difficult to access by Fitts' Law should be avoided when designing touchscreen apps [2]. When handedness is taken into account, that quadrant of the display screen will differ, respectively, for left and right-handed users.

The experiment tested how long it took a person to touch the center target, and then a point on the dial. They then touched the center again and the next placement on the dial. The user went around the dial, each time clicking in the center before clicking on the next target (Fig. 6).

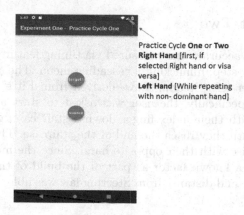

Fig. 6. Practice screen

This experiment was conducted with all subjects using the same Android device. They were presented with a screen that asked them to identify their stronger hand. The identification of an individual is based on their preference, and self-identification, rather than a scientific assessment of their skill and ability to perform with one hand or the other [7].

The experiment tested how long it took a person to touch the center source button and then click a target point on the dial. The click tests continued from source to target in each of eight target placements on the dial. This test was conducted through eight test cycles, and the results were recorded. The user was then asked to perform the same cycles using their other hand. Again, the times were recorded and assessed. These results were entered into the Firebase database, and stored as part of the overall experiment data (Fig. 7).

Fig. 7. Experiment one

6   Experiment Two

In Experiment Two accuracy was measured via timing features and touchscreen features with a stair step, mimicking a cascading menu. The stair traveled from upper right to lower left. Steering Law, derived from Fitts' Law was used to calculate results. Specifically, the user was asked to start at the upper right corner and trace with their index finger down a stair case, going down, right, down, right, etc, until they reach the end of the staircase. They are then asked to repeat the exercise with their opposite hand. Since the measurement points between stairs was a known factor as part of the build of the application, the data related to time and distance from Steering law was able to be collected and analyzed (Fig. 8).

Fig. 8. Staircase data point measurement

7   Experiment Three

The third experiment aimed to see if the hand obstructed the display screen. The user was asked to click on a image and then swipe to another image. They were then asked to swipe back in the opposite direction. As with Experiment two, the user was asked to perform the same task with the opposite hand. The image was flipped symmetrically and the user performed the same test in reverse with both hands. All of the results were collected and put in the Firebase database for further analysis. The implementation was not adequate to produce meaningful data. Therefore, this experiment will constitute future work.

8   Preliminary Data

Preliminary data completed on both Experiment One and Experiment Two show trends in favor of both right handed and left-handed individuals. Experiment One shows the right-handed users were more effective with their dominant and non-dominant hands as opposed to left handed users who were slower with both dominant and non-dominant hands. The overall trend for Experiment One when comparing all users both dominant right and dominant left using their right hand showed a flat trend in favor of using your right hand while using a device as opposed to your left hand, as depicted in Fig. 5, the dashboard image.

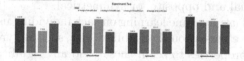

Fig. 9. Experiment two user data

Experiment Two favored right-handed individuals as the trend shows right handed individuals on average had a lower time differential. Right-handed individuals were also better using their non-dominant hand in this experiment than left-handed individuals using their non-dominant hand. Figure 9 shows the mean values of time difference for each of the four categories: left-handed, left non-dominant, right-handed, right nondominant.

9   Conclusions

The study's programmers have successfully built two working experiments from end to end on the Android platform. Preliminary data stored on the Firebase platform was retrieved and placed into visuals for the two working experiments. Preliminary data shows that touchscreen devices have deficiencies for left-handed users. This raises more questions. The focal point now moves towards further analysis, additional data collection, and further development and alterations to the three experiments. As future alterations to the experiments are made they will focus on more challenging operations for both right-handed and left-handed users. By measuring the variance between right- and left-handers, data patterns may emerge that provide reasonable biometric authentication. That hypothesis remains inconclusive.

10 Future Considerations

There are several opportunities to continue these experiments and the associated research. Extending experiment two to include a mirror image, and fixing experiment three will provide a more complete data picture to the user experience.

For experiment one, the visualization could be randomized so that the test data does not include any learned behavior relating to expectation of what target to click next. It is possible that clicking on targets presented in a circle, the speed could be impacted by the fact that the user gets accustomed to the process and is faster not due to handedness, but instead as a result of the learned behavior of where the next click will be. Randomizing the targets would eliminate any potential learning from the order of the targets.

Additionally, designing the mirror images for experiments two and three would provide data collection of dominant hand - original image, non-dominant hand - original image, dominant hand - mirror image, and non-dominant hand - mirror image. These four data points would ensure that the measurements from steering law are equal and opposite, or symmetrical.

Future work will use machine learning on each individual user's data collected via the built-in native sensors on the mobile device, such as gyroscope, accelerometer, and pressure properties to see if these yield any significant authenticating biometrics. While preliminary visual analysis of the data indicates a significant variance between right- and left-handed users, a machine learning analysis is necessary to verify this hypothesis definitively.

References

1. IDF Instructor, Fitts's Law: The Importance of Size and Distance in UI Design (2016). https://www.interaction-design.org/literature/topics/fitts-law/
2. Zhang, C., Li, X., Gao, F., Zhou, F., Xu, L.: An experimental research on the directivity of Fitts' law in human-computer interaction. In: 2015 IEEE International Conference on Progress in Informatics and Computing (PIC), pp. 226–229, December 2015
3. Zhou, X.: How does the subjective operational biases hit the steering law. In: IEEE International Conference on Computer Science and Automation Engineering (CSAE), pp. 654–658 (2012)
4. Inkpen, K., et al.: Left-handed scrolling for pen-based devices. Int. J. Hum. Comput. Interact. 21, 91–108 (2006)
5. Spillane, R.: Keyboard apparatus for personal identification. IBM Tech. Disclosure Bull. 17, 3346 (1975)

6. Teh, P.S., Teoh, A., Yue, S.: A survey of keystroke dynamics biometrics. Sci. World J. **2013**, 408280 (2013)
7. Adamo, D.E., Taufiq, A.: Establishing hand preference: why does it matter? Hand N.Y. **2011**, 408280 (2011)

Is Tourist Markovian Under Asymmetric Information?

Karim Elia Fraoua$^{(\boxtimes)}$ and Sylvain Michelin$^{(\boxtimes)}$

Université Paris-Est Marne-La-Vallée, Equipe Dispositifs d'Information
et de Communication à l'Ere Numérique (DICEN IDF), Conservatoire National
des Arts et Métiers, Université Paris-Nanterre, EA 7339, Champs-sur-Marne, France
{karim.fraoua, sylvain.michelin}@u-pem.fr

Abstract. This work presents a new way to formalize the serendipity in a tourism experience through an application. Tourist discovers rarely a new site during his trip other than the sites defined by some classical way (travel agency, website…). In this paper we analyze tourism behavior as a DPM Markovian process associated with a reward component.

Keywords: Markov process · Tourist behavior · Recommendation system

1 Introduction

Our main idea is how to improve our application on which we have already indicated the major functions [1] and how it can help or play the role of a guide to better accompany a tourist in a city, how to improve his experience and especially to maximize it. If the role of a guide is undeniable, a tourist should have a guide during his stay, but the financial aspect can't be avoided in his point of view. Some tourists have an access to this privilege or use a guide for a group, but what's about a single tourist not in a group? In this paper we discuss these aspects, particularly the customer experience and the new expectations of customers, which are more and more demanding in terms of experience. Due to the large numbers of dedicated connected tools (video, wiki…), tourists can nowadays find any information on any activity site with a simple click on the web.

So we have to offer an application with a high quality human-machine interface to offer users a very rich experience. That guides our application and our research perspectives in this field is how to assist, help or influence the way tourists prepare or organize their trip introducing a dimension of positive surprise, in leading tourists up to new sites during their normal trajectory, and the appropriate term seems to be the serendipity.

This could be solved through the application we develop, which integrate expectations of customers, an SEO of all the official sites that are sought by visitors, museums, monuments, places,…. In this context of information overabundance, the search for specific contents assumes first a goal well-defined before potential unexpected discoveries avoiding to choice trivial approaches such as the most widespread solutions, the best ranked solutions, the best ranked sites by Tripadvisor, …

C. Stephanidis and M. Antona (Eds.): HCII 2019, CCIS 1088, pp. 424–433, 2019.
https://doi.org/10.1007/978-3-030-30712-7_52

Like in the digital tools and traditional approaches, we have also integrated the use of traditional guides first in advance reservation model [2]. However, we have also integrated a new innovation, linking up with guides available at the last minute. A navigation map shows not only the location of the recommended points of interest, but also the position of the close guides with whom it is possible to communicate. This new feature is very useful and would be linked to a very handy interface essential for a decision-making point of view. Indeed, we have planned that the tourist can have access both to the guide card and rates which can be modulated according to the time of day. Various other parameters should be included by the guide in his card, its's allow us to calculate a rate according to an algorithm.

From the perspective of this challenge, we it is possible to improve our tool even more in a time optimization approach. Indeed, it turns out that the tourist can walk randomly in the city without real prospect and that he can discover places by chance, what we previously call the serendipity [3]. This random walk can be analyzed as a Markovian approach [4]. So, the question that arises here is to understand which kinds of actions an agent can take during his journey, where he is in asymmetric information, and where he does not necessary know if the action will lead him to interesting site or not. In general, we consider that the tourist is quite deterministic in his choices and that he takes into account the known places and indications in the tourist brochures as entry fee,... [5]. The places that are not listed by these tools are inaccessible for him and a mediator is necessary to discover these places. It's the role devoted in general to the guide who is an expert of the city and knowing it generally better than its own inhabitants.

Fundamentally, the action which leads an agent to take a decision could be treated as of MDP Markovian process [6]. In a previous work, we analyzed how the knowledge of places via a new interface taking into account the nature of the tourist, allowed him to improve his tourist experience [1, 2]. In the present work, we suppose that the tourist walks around the city without having the application in front of him and without any information about the site that can located around him, and we will show here how the application can interact with the tourist in a discreet way to indicate which would be interesting to visit according to the user's tastes. This recommendation process can be analyzed in two ways.

First of all, information we treat can be classify in three types: explicit, implicit or inferred [7]. The first is the information given by the application without taking into account the position of the tourist like information in classical tourist guides that indexes all the tourist sites by city or by district. In the second case, the information is implicit, i.e. it depends on the position of the tourist and may depend on his tastes so that our recommendations are "in line" with his expectations, and therefore impact his experience. Finally, inferred information implies that this information is obtained using datamining and exploration methods through datamining.

The main problem consists in challenging the agent according to his own indications or his tastes and to analyze the causes that would lead him to act. So the complexity comes from knowing if the tourist would visit these sites or not, and as a consequence, it will be necessary to calculate if this detour is interesting or not? This choice can be modeled by Markovian process: the position at the instant t cannot be planned in its trajectory that is we can estimate that it does not depend on the moment t − 1. Indeed, only the closest past is taken into account to determine the probabilities of going to this new state. In this case, the agent has "deviated" from his main trajectory found by himself in this new trajectory only under the effect of the application. We can suppose that this agent will act under a state of uncertainty. Under these assumptions, several models can allow us to analyze the behavior of the agent, as the prospect theory [8] resulting from the game theory but each leading systematically to the concept of risk reduction [9]. So, the behavior of the agent requires an understanding of the behavior of agents in situations of risk and uncertainty.

The expected utility theory (EUT) helps to understand the behavior of the agent [10]. We will return to these aspects in a subsequent evolution. We seek here to confine to modeling the serendipity that often leads the tourist to beautiful discoveries and thus to experience a positive experience during his visit.

The second approach consists in analyzing the history of the places visited by the tourist to suggest new places according to a system of recommendation [11]. Indeed, our application has been defined to work either via the application itself, or via mediators such as guides and consequently all the sites of the application are referenced according to different attributes we will discuss after.

The Markov process provides a simple tool for modeling a particular class of discrete states. Our goal is to define the result of an action on an agent in information asymmetry and to allow this agent (a tourist) to discover a new site, which will become an ideal positive experience. In this approach, the consumer has a behavior based on a classical reward decision process. However, the agent may decide that this result is risky or uncertain. Each task being linked to a necessary amount of resources, the agent will apply a minimal loss strategy. For instance, indicating a site which is on the path of the tourist consumes resources (transport, time,…) and the agent has to arbitrate between maximizing the gain or minimizing the regret according to Savage.

One of the main interests of the application is to propose a place that maximizes the gain. This so-called serendipity feature, allows accompanying the tourist during his visit of the city.

2   The Customer Experience and Tourist Expectations

The customer experience is a major factor in the choice of the customer before his move but also after his experience in a testimony process. He enjoys narrate his visit but also be able to testify of his experience with other future tourists to eventually guide their choice. Some sites have created value around this testimony and become extremely important tools in the decision making of tourists. We quote the most major as Tripadvisor, Yelp…

Nowadays a common behavior is to consider a trip pleasant only if the experience is very strong [12] The use of reviews is very important in the choice of destinations but also sites to visit [13]. Two main problems are underlying, the price which is the fundamental element but also the time of the visit. For instance, many tourists coming to France, realize once on Paris that it is almost impossible to visit the Palace of

Versailles and the Louvre on a single day because the time queuing is never indicated on the brochure. Despite the quality of the visit and the cultural wealth of content, tourists leave with regrets. We observe the same phenomena each time the waiting time is not observed or integrated.

An analog behavior appears when a tourist that has a random walk without a specific goal discovers afterwards that he had missed a site that could have interested him. It is for instance the case, when a tourist comes directly back to he's residence place. In this case, the application could offer an interesting positive alternative based on criteria such as notoriety, recommendation or simply because the tourist has filled personal interest areas on the application. For example, a colleague is currently preparing a route on Saint Jacques and we can find elements little or not present in tourist guides and seem to be of great interest to those who prepare the pilgrimage of Saint Jacques de Compostele [14].

In summary, a positive tourism experience is harder to be achieved today than in the past because it's almost like a consuming process. Experience becomes a kind of capital of knowledge, of emotions, which one can experiment, and transform at each new discovery. On this basis, it must be a tool capable of meeting unnecessary needs so that the tourist can marvel but also that his circuit is planned so as not to waste time in unnecessary visits [15].

3   Serendipity and the Markov Process

Serendipity is the sudden discovery of new objects of interest. In this paragraph, we first describe the Markov process before explaining our approach from the perspective of serendipity. Markov decision processes (MDP) are defined as controlled stochastic processes satisfying the Markov property, assigning rewards to state transitions [16].

Let's define a MPD as a quintuplets (S, A, T, p, r) where:

- S is the space of states achievable by the process;
- A is the space of the actions a_i that control the dynamics of the state;
- T is the space of time t;
- p() are the probabilities of transition between two successive states;
- r() is the reward function related to the transitions between the two states.

The following figure shows a short classical example of a MDP in the form of an influence diagram. At each instant t of T, the action a_t is applied in the current state s_t, influencing the process in its transition to the state s_{t+1}.

In our model, each state corresponds to a site susceptible to be visited by the tourist. The reward r_t between two states is directly linked to a tourist serendipity evaluation during this transition.

The reward r_t can be either positive or negative, positive r_t values can be considered as gains and negative values as costs. We see then, that if the visit does not like him then he will express a regret of having lost time or money if this action has a price (displacement, visit, ...).

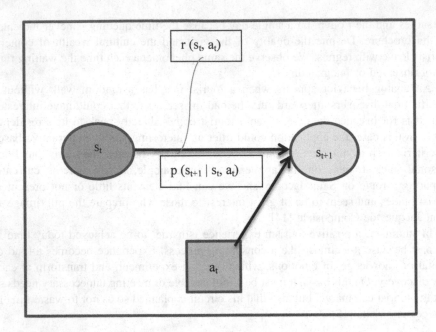

Let's introduce the question of history. Indeed, the agent's action does not depend on its history but on its position at time t. A Markov chain is a sequence of random variables whose probability of each element depends only on the previous one. That is, that a Markov chain (a particular instance of Markov process) describes the transition of a set of states from an entity at time t into a set of states at time t + 1. Technically, Markov chains are described as processes with discrete time steps and are often used to model the evolution of an agent system, within a stochastic environment. We call policy (denoted π), or strategy, the procedure followed by the agent to choose at each moment the action (a) to execute.

The main problem consists in defining an efficient model for analyzing the transition from a current state s_t, to the state s_{t+1}.

In any case, we consider the final state is still interesting from the experience point of view, either it is recommended in different guides…, or, based on our historical analysis, we consider that the site corresponds to a real wish of the tourist. In any case, we have the same main goal: improving the tourist experience.

In a classical analyzing process, and if we consider a unique possibility associated to a positive reward, the choice depends only on the initial states of the tourist: fatigue, money available, children…. If we only consider the gradient, the positive variation of rewards, this approach seems to be too static and leads to cost calculus too simple, not efficient because of a non-objective evaluation of the reached state due to the personal perception of each tourist. Under these assumptions, the Markovian model consists in considering the incertitude of the reward and as a consequence the possible accessible states and gains, independent of the possibilities we can propose.

More precisely, the Kripke's model [17] seems to be a pertinent analogy. He introduces the notion of "possible worlds": each agent should a specific vision of the real world. This personal vision of the real world is not necessary the same reality for another agent and an agent can consider another world as possible or practicable. For this, a relation of indistinguishability is introduced for each agent. If we consider N agents, we can define N accessibility relations labelled by the agent name [18].

In this approach we consider that if an agent does not know something, he knowns that he does not known. We consider also that agents reason and perfectly evaluate all facts. But evidently this creates an incertitude notion and as a consequence we can associate a probability of realization. Under these assumptions, we can speak of markovian model.

So our goal is either leading the agent in an information state (our application should contribute to this approach by using wiki, testimonies...), or consider that he has not the time to integrate all these information and that he will develop his personal analysis from his own beliefs, his own experience for a personal reward.

We must distinguish two situations depending on deterministic or non-deterministic approaches. Either we build a policy that can encourage the action to be performed and simply define a probability distribution according to which this action that will be selected, or build and offer a policy based on the history h_t of the process.

In the first classical approach, one can predict if the tourist knows where to go, namely to a site already registered in his program or a site whose proximity we will reveal. The policy depends only on the initial state S_t, and therefore in this case $\pi_t (s_t)$ or $\pi_t (h_t)$ since the action is already known by the tourist. The application allows the tourist, before or during his trip, to register all the sites he want to visit with possibly a priority and during his walk, these sites will appear on the application and therefore encourage him to visit them in an optimum path and the algorithm is easier to put in place. This form of serendipity will be both pleasant and objective because the tourist will visit all sites suggested.

On the other hand, in the random case, we base our approach as well on the preferences of the users but also on the known recommendations on the sites and we will then propose them to the agent. This purely random approach will depend on several factors, mainly the question of reward, and in this case $\pi_t (a, s_t)$ or $\pi_t (a, h_t)$ represents the probability of selecting a. It is this action that we must suggest to the tourist in order to offer him to choose or not according to his strategy of rewards. This central point of reward is described in the next paragraph. We therefore understand that if the tourist follows a path without a specific objective or even if he must return to his accommodation place, we can offer him a place to visit, of course taking into account the time of the composition of the constraints of the visitor (alone, as a couple, with children depending their ages, language, taste, history, ...).

The main question is what action we have to establish in order that the agent feels positively this action in terms of serendipity and what kind of reward can he claim. In this context, let us observe the different types of risks and rewards that are observed, especially that for the agent is placed in an uncertain future.

4 Reward Concept and Main Models

Beyond the information we have provided to the agent, we are not sure that the choice is obvious. It turns out that the agent does not know the experience he will draw from this visit. Remember that the sites we will promote are not listed in classic guides but come from our own resources, either from local residents or tourists themselves. This system of recommendation remains to be developed on the basis of data that we will have collected as and when. For that, let's take an example to better situate the problem. Indeed, our tool will only be efficient if it takes into account the profile of the agent and his beliefs. Imagine these three scenarios, where the agent is in an initial state that is the continuation of his path or the visit of a place unknown to him but that we have suggested. Take the example of a tourist who must make a decision among three possible situations (Fig. 1).

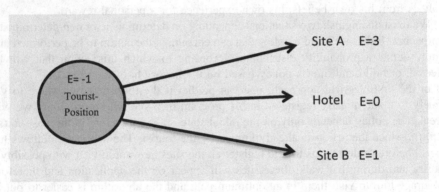

Fig. 1. Different situations of reward in terms of experience (3 for site A, 0 for hotel, 1 for site B): the result is the satisfaction gain after the visit.

Consider that the tourist is in a state where he considers that his experience is equal to -1, because he does not take advantage of his trip as he wishes and that can encourage him to return to his hotel and that this choice leads to an experience without any gain. Two other possibilities can increase his reward but the tourist is clearly in an incertitude situation.

	Initial state	Final state
Situation 1	-1	**3**
Situation 2	-1	**0**
Situation 3	-1	**1**

Let us first define the different possible rewards $r(s_t, a_t)$ according to the profile of the agents before transposing them in the case of an tourist incentive. There is a complexity inherent to the agents themselves. It's depending on their own history of past choices, on their culture and their beliefs, if the tourist is alone or accompanied with children or no, on their age... The path to perform it can be a constraint even if the suggested idea can be interesting. Different behaviors are well-known in the literature [19].

4.1 Optipmist Criterion

In this behavior, the tourist selects the best final state possible. We maximize the gain; so that the best choice is the first situation (visit site A) with a gain of 3 which is the rate allocated to the site. We can consider that the experience of the tourist regarding to his expectation about his experience [20].

4.2 Wald's Criterion

In this criterium, the behavior of the tourist is more regret driven than gain driven. It is a classical MaxMin strategy, the decision consists in minimizing the regret. In this case, the best choice is situation 2, that is the initial choice (come back to the hotel), the tourist being afraid to express regret [20].

4.3 Laplace's Criterion

In this reward model, the agent maximizes an average regret. This criterIon supposes that the agent considers that the states are equiprobable.

Situation 1 leads to a gain of: $(-1 + 3)/2 = 1$
Situation 2 leads to a gain of: $(-1 - 0)/2 = -0,5$
Situation 3 leads to a gain of: $(-1 + 1)/0 = 0$

The best choice is situation 1.

4.4 Hurwicz's Criterium

In the Hurcwicz's approach, we ponder the gain by a coefficient α which is applied to the strategy. The more strong regret is pondered by the α coefficient while the lowest is pondered by $(\alpha - 1)$ [21].

For example, with $\alpha = 0,6$ (optmistic approach) we obtain:

Situation 1 the gain is: $-1 * 0.4 + 3 * 0.6 = 1,4$
Situation 2 the gain is: $-1 * 0.4 + 0 * 0.6 = -0.4$
Situation 3 the gain is: $-1 * 0.4 + 1 * 0.6 = 0,2$

The best choice is situation 1 in this situation.

4.5 Savage's Criterium

In this situation, and for each state of nature, one seeks the strongest regret. We will obtain the matrix of regrets on the basis of a calculation for each decision in each state of nature, the regret that is to say the difference between the strongest regret retained and the expected regret [21] (Table 1).

Savage advises to choose the strategy that makes minimum regret possible. We then take the decision that minimizes the maximum regret and therefore we try to minimize the shortfall. It is based on the gain matrix, and it holds for each state of nature the decision the one that ensures the best gain and it subtracts from each column the other gains made.

Table 1. Matrix of regrets

Regret value for each situation
MAX – VALUE i.e. 3 – V
3 – 3 = 0
3 – 0 = 3
3 – 1 = 2

The best decision is therefore 1 where the minimum is 0 because the tourist must choose a destination and cannot stay on the spot. Of course the choice of the agent will be influenced moreover by the cost of the visit which we will suggest to him. If the activity is free, it can have a big influence on its choice.

5   Conclusion

In conclusion of this work, we present a serendipity approach of a tourist behavior views from the angle of Markov's decision-making model. It leads to an improvement of the tourist's overall experience. Having knowledge of his profile and his tastes, we can even optimize his experience and even beyond these proposals, predict his future actions when he visits a city. This predictive approach must be refined through real data collection and thus optimize the cost of the visit through specific commercial offers but also by working more on mobility which will become a major issue during a trip, especially because of a large variety of constraints (increasingly restricted visiting time…).

References

1. Fraoua, K.E.: Tourist information in asymmetric situation, a new way to enhance a tourist experience. In: 99th IASTEM International Conference, Tokyo, Japan, 29 December 2017 (2017)
2. Fraoua, K.E., Michelin, S.: Interface for a better tourist experience, Bayesian approach and cox-jaynes support. In: Stephanidis, C. (ed.) HCI 2018. CCIS, vol. 850, pp. 40–45. Springer, Cham (2018). https://doi.org/10.1007/978-3-319-92270-6_6
3. Cary, S.H.: The tourist moment. Ann. Tourism Res. **31**(1), 61–77 (2004)
4. Xia, J.C., Zeephongsekul, P., Arrowsmith, C.: Modelling spatio-temporal movement of tourists using finite Markov chains. Math. Comput. Simul. **79**(5), 1544–1553 (2009)
5. Choi, A.S., Ritchie, B.W., Papandrea, F., Bennett, J.: Economic valuation of cultural heritage sites: a choice modeling approach. Tour. Manag. **31**(2), 213–220 (2010)

6. Puterman, M.L.: Markov decision processes. Handb. Oper. Res. Manag. Sci. **2**, 331–434 (1990)
7. Gavalas, D., Konstantopoulos, C., Mastakas, K., Pantziou, G.: Mobile recommender systems in tourism. J. Netw. Comput. Appl. **39**, 319–333 (2014)
8. Tversky, A., Kahneman, D.: Advances in prospect theory: cumulative representation of uncertainty. J. Risk Uncertain. **5**(4), 297–323 (1992)
9. Slovic, P., Fischhoff, B., Lichtenstein, S.: Behavioral decision theory perspectives on risk and safety. Acta Physiol. **56**(1–3), 183–203 (1984)
10. Edwards, W.: The theory of decision making. Psychol. Bull. **51**(4), 380 (1954)
11. Garcia, I., Sebastia, L., Onaindia, E., Guzman, C.: A group recommender system for tourist activities. In: Di Noia, T., Buccafurri, F. (eds.) EC-Web 2009. LNCS, vol. 5692, pp. 26–37. Springer, Heidelberg (2009). https://doi.org/10.1007/978-3-642-03964-5_4
12. Uriely, N.: The tourist experience: conceptual developments. Ann. Tourism Res. **32**(1), 199–216 (2005)
13. Gretzel, U., Yoo, K.H.: Use and impact of online travel reviews. Inf. Commun. Technol. Tourism **2008**, 35–46 (2008)
14. Bourret, C.: Personal wok (2019)
15. Sharpley, R., Stone, P.: The habit of tourism: experiences and their ontological meaning Graham K. Henning. In: Contemporary Tourist Experience, pp. 41–53. Routledge (2014)
16. Puterman, M.L.: Markov Decision Processes: Discrete Stochastic Dynamic Programming. Wiley, Hoboken (2014)
17. Tiu, A.: Introduction to logic (1998)
18. van der Hoek, M.: Epistemic Logic for Computer Science and Artificial Intelligence (1995)
19. Lee, T.H.: A structural model to examine how destination image, attitude, and motivation affect the future behavior of tourists. Leisure Sci. **31**(3), 215–236 (2009)
20. Sharma, J.K.: Business statistics. Pearson Education India (2007)
21. Zaraté, P., Belaud, J.P., Camilleri, G.: (eds.) Collaborative Decision Making: Perspectives and Challenges, vol. 176. IOS Press (2008)

Robot Sociality in Human-Robot Team Interactions

Kevin Liaw$^{(\boxtimes)}$, Simon Driver, and Marlena R. Fraune

New Mexico State University, Las Cruces, NM, USA
{kliaw, sjdriver, mfraune}@nmsu.edu

Abstract. Robots are entering everyday life (e.g., TUG medical robots, Roomba vacuum cleaners) to help improve quality of life. Research shows that humans collaborate more effectively with social robots than with nonsocial robots, but does this mean that humans trust social robots more than nonsocial robots? In this study, we examined how robots' social appearance and behavior (mechanomorphic vs. anthropomorphic) affected how trustworthy participants felt the robots were. Participants played a game in teams of two humans and two robots against similarly-composed opposing teams. After the game, participants rated how much they trusted their robotic teammates. Overall, people trusted anthropomorphic robots slightly more. In general, people had intermediate levels of trust for robots and felt low levels of uneasy around them. Therefore, future designs of robots should be more anthropomorphic and social to increase trust ratings.

Keywords: Trust · Mechanomorphic · NAO · iRobot · Anthropomorphic · Security · Respect · Unease

1 Introduction

Humans and robots are becoming more interconnected and are interacting with each other more. Designing robots for humans to be comfortable with is vital for increasing willingness to interact with them. Previous studies have shown that people responded positively to a robot that displayed human-like behavioral characteristics, in contrast to a purely functional design [4].

In this study, we compared human trust of anthropomorphic (NAO) versus mechanomorphic (iRobot) designed robots during a collaborative game. This study examines differences in trust of the two types of robots. We expect that humans will be more trusting towards anthropomorphic robots.

2 Background

2.1 Anthropomorphic Robot (NAO)

From year to year, robots are becoming more anthropomorphic and human reactions with them become more similar to human interactions [1]. For example, when they are

© Springer Nature Switzerland AG 2019
C. Stephanidis and M. Antona (Eds.): HCII 2019, CCIS 1088, pp. 434–440, 2019.
https://doi.org/10.1007/978-3-030-30712-7_53

with another human, humans showed "desirable traits" with an anthropomorphic robots even though they knew the subject was a robot [1]. That is, humans show respect towards anthropomorphic robots, treating them as if they were another human.

Similarly, the more anthropomorphic robots are, the more humans trust them. Some robots are designed to mimic many human-like traits to the extent that they are nearly indistinguishable (visibly) from humans. These robots fall into the "uncanny valley" [7]. First described by Mori, "uncanny valley" elaborates the effect that high levels of robot's anthropomorphism that humans highly distrust them [7]. Humans typically find robots increasingly likeable and trustworthy as robot's humanness increases until they reach a breaking point, at which point, the robots uncannily similar/dissimilar to humans, and humans lose trust is lost. A balance must be found between mechanomorphic- and anthropomorphic-appearing robots to build trust. We decided to pick an anthropomorphic robot (NAO) that would obviously be identified as robot and would not cause the uncanny valley effect but is more anthropomorphic than a mechanomorphic iRobot (Fig. 1).

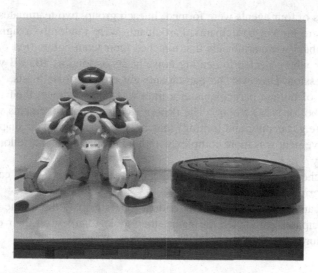

Fig. 1. NAO Robot (anthropomorphic) on the left and iRobot (mechanomorphic) on the right

3 Security/Respect/Unease

Security, Respect, and Unease are the three measures we use to measure trust. Research shows that humans feel higher trust ratings in technologies (e.g. websites and Social networking) when humans feel more secure [4]. In human-human relationships, respect strongly relates to trust [9]. Unease or anxiety indicates a lack of lack of trust [6]. Since these three feelings are heavily related to trust, we chose these three emotions as our measures.

We seek to examine trust during actual human-robot interaction. In our experiment, humans and robots collaborate to win a game in which the human participants must rely on and trust the robots. We study if people trust anthropomorphic or mechanomorphic robots more during actual interaction. We identified (above) several markers for trust, and analyze them below separately. We expect people to trust anthropomorphic robots more than mechanomorphic robots. Therefore, we expect higher ratings in respect and security and lower rating in unease for anthropomorphic compared to mechanomorphic robots.

4   Methods

We examined how humans' trust compares when working with mechanomorphic versus anthropomorphic robotic teammates. Our procedure was taken from previous research on human-robot teaming [5].

4.1   Procedure

1. Two groups of four agents were formed. In each group, two teammates were robots and two were human participants. Participants were randomly assigned to teams. Team members wore armbands that matched their team colors (red or blue).
2. Participants who objected to hearing noise blasts as loud as 105 dB were excused from the session. However, no participants objected to noise blasts.
3. One group of human participants at a time was taken to meet their robotic teammates (iRobot or NAO Robot). The iRobot's designated movements were made to be simple (e.g. beeping and turning) match its mechanomorphic shape. The NAO robot's movement was more complex with human speech (e.g. "Hello, how are you doing today?").
4. The researcher explained the rules of the game teams played against each other (see Game Description section).
5. All participants were directed to individual rooms to play the online game.
6. After participants completed the game, they took a survey on their emotions and other measures (see Measures section).

4.2   Game Description

Participants played a price-guessing game that was programmed using Eclipse. A computer screen displayed an item (e.g. couch, watch), and participants guessed the price of the item. They were told that teammates' answers were averaged for a final answer. This created teams in which the members were interdependent, and the player was required to trust his/her teammates. The team that came the closest to the correct price on a given round won that round, and one member of the winning team would be "randomly selected" to assign noise blasts to all eight players (including themselves) before the next round. The noise blasts choices were ranged from 80db to 120db in intervals of 5 db (e.g. 80, 85, 90, etc.). Each value of noise blast assigned was designated uniquely to that player: if a player gave one person a noise blast of 80, then the player couldn't assign another player a blast of 80 that turn. The experiment included twenty rounds of the guessing game. For each round, participants would be shown the average guess for each team, the actual price, which team won, and if they were the player who would select the volume of noise blasts for this round.

In reality, the game was rigged such that participants actually played on their own, with other players' responses simulated. Participants won approximately 50% of the time and were "randomly assigned" to give noise blasts four times during the main rounds and once in the final round.

4.3   Measures

Participants were asked to report their emotions (e.g., security, trust, respect) in a post-game survey. They rated emotions on a scale from 1 (strongly disagree) to 7 (strongly agree). The study included measures of other emotions [2], perceived sociality of the robots [3], and more, but these measures exceed the scope of this paper and will not be described further.

5   Results

Survey results were analyzed in JASP. *P*-values of less than .05 were considered significant differences.

5.1   Security

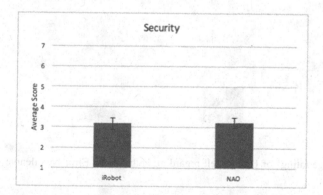

Fig. 2. Average ratings of security felt regarding both robots. Error bars denote standard error

Overall people did not feel very secure to be around the two robots with average response of around 3. There was no significant difference between the two robots (t(*106*) = −0.179, p = 0.890; Fig. 2).

5.2 Respect

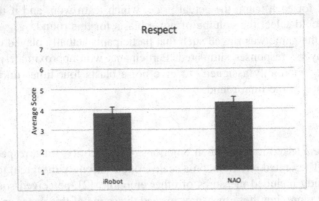

Fig. 3. Average ratings of respect felt regarding both robots. Error bars denote standard error

Most people felt moderate levels of respect towards the two robots. Again, There was no significant difference between the two robots ($t(106) = -1.253$, $p = 0.213$; Fig. 3).

5.3 Unease

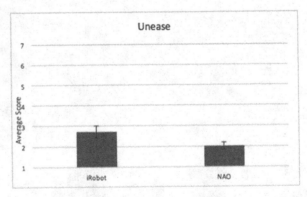

Fig. 4. Average ratings of Unease felt regarding both robots. Error bars denote standard error

There was a very low unease score for the robots. There was a statistically significant difference between conditions; participants indicated more unease around iRobots than NAO robots. ($t(106) = 2.112$, $p = .037$; Fig. 4).

6 Discussion

The main purpose of this study was to analyze how much humans trust robots when working together. In this study, we found partial support for our hypothesis that people would trust anthropomorphic robots more than mechanomorphic robots. We discuss this in more depth below.

- **Security and Respect**: The difference in security and respect ratings of the anthropomorphic and mechanomorphic robots was not significant. Ratings security were below neutral, indicating that participants did not feel very secure with the robots. The result could be caused by the limited time participants and robots had to interact with each other.
- **Unease**: Participants were significantly more uneasy of iRobots than Nao robots, supporting our hypothesis. It may be that mechanomorphic characteristics more strongly affect negative than positive emotions.

Overall, the results only partially support the hypothesis that people trust anthropomorphic more than mechanomorphic robots.

7 Limitations and Future Directions

All participants were students at NMSU, typically aged between 18–23 years old. The age range is significant because these age groups tend to be more familiar with technology than older age groups and may have less trouble adjusting to working with robots than older age groups [8].

Even though our results indicate that there is little to no difference between mechanomorphic and anthropomorphic robots, further research could be conducted on the subject. Different anthropomorphic and mechanomorphic robots might be used to see if the same results appear in comparing different robots. For example, if the two robots were human-size, how would that affect trust? Would humans be more trusting to human-size robots because they are more anthropomorphic because of their size? The opposite effect may occur, were humans are less trusting because the robots have reached "uncanny valley" territory.

Because mechanomorphic and anthropomorphic received relatively similar trust ratings, future studies could revise our experiment to more specific settings. For example, would anthropomorphic or mechanomorphic robots be more trustworthy when working with medical staff in hospitals? Also, multiple other human emotions can be measured to find the degree of trust humans feel (e.g. fear, dismay, happiness, etc.). Since the only significant difference found was in unease (a negative emotion), a further experiment, studying only negative emotions, could lead to more significant differences between anthropomorphic and mechanomorphic robots.

8 Conclusion

In this study, we examined participants in a competitive group setting in which humans had to rely upon robots for success. We then analyzed how much participants trusted the mechanomorphic robot (iRobot) and the anthropomorphic robot (NAO). The two positive measures (respect and security) yielded no statistical difference between anthropomorphic and mechanomorphic robots, but were rated relatively low for the robots overall. The unease factor showed, however, that humans felt more uneasy around mechanomorphic than anthropomorphic robots. This provides partial support to the idea that, humans trusted anthropomorphic robots slightly more than mechanomorphic robots. Overall, humans responded somewhat positively towards robots that exhibited anthropomorphic behavior.

Acknowledgement. We thank all participants of the study for playing the game and completing the survey. We thank our peers Tyler Chatterton, Rocio Guzman, and Tammy Tsai for conducting the study with us.

References

1. Billings, D.R., Schaefer, K.E., Chen, J.Y., Hancock, P.A.: Human-robot interaction: developing trust in robots. In: Proceedings of the Seventh Annual ACM/IEEE International Conference on Human-Robot Interaction, pp. 109–110. ACM, March 2012
2. Cottrell, C.A., Neuberg, S.L.: Different emotional reactions to different groups: a sociofunctional threat-based approach to "prejudice". J. Pers. Soc. Psychol. **88**(5), 770 (2005). Interprofessional Care **22**(2), 133–147
3. Kozak, M.N., Marsh, A.A., Wegner, D.M.: What do I think you're doing? Action identification and mind attribution. J. Pers. Soc. Psychol. **90**(4), 543 (2006)
4. Flavián, C., Guinalíu, M.: Consumer trust, perceived security and privacy policy: three basic elements of loyalty to a web site. Ind. Manag. Data Syst. **106**(5), 601–620 (2006)
5. Fraune, M.R., Šabanović, S., Smith, E.R.: Teammates first: favoring ingroup robots over outgroup humans. In: 2017 26th IEEE International Symposium on Robot and Human Interactive Communication (RO-MAN), pp. 1432–1437. IEEE, August 2017
6. Fraune, M.R., Sherrin, S., Sabanović, S., Smith, E.R.: Rabble of robots effects: number and type of robots modulates attitudes, emotions, and stereotypes. In: Proceedings of the Tenth Annual ACM/IEEE International Conference on Human-Robot Interaction, pp. 109–116. ACM, March 2015
7. Mori, M.: The uncanny valley. Energy **7**(4), 33–35 (1970)
8. Morris, M.G., Venkatesh, V.: Age differences in technology adoption decisions: implications for a changing work force. Pers. Psychol. **53**(2), 375–403 (2000)
9. Pullon, S.: Competence, respect and trust: key features of successful interprofessional nurse-doctor relationships. J. Interprof. Care **22**(2), 133–147 (2008)

An Agent-Based Approach for Cleanup Problem: Analysis of Human-Like Behavior

Nobuhito Manome[1,2]([⊠]), Shuji Shinohara[2], Kouta Suzuki[1,2], and Shunji Mitsuyoshi[2]

[1] SoftBank Robotics Corp., Tokyo, Japan
manome@bioeng.t.u-tokyo.ac.jp
[2] Graduate School of Engineering, The University of Tokyo, Tokyo, Japan

Abstract. Neural networks for solving complex tasks need not have a structure similar to a brain. From the macro perspective, it is meaningful to utilize a neural network that has the functions of an organism in order to grasp the intelligence of organisms. We focused on the fact that memory, for-getting, and the various information perception functions of humans can be represented by a self-organizing map (SOM), and we considered a SOM-based agent that autonomously changes its behavior while observing the behavior of others, like a human. In this study, we conducted a multi-agent simulation using the SOM-based agent on a cleanup problem consisting of a chain of tasks of picking up and disposing of garbage routinely carried out by humans, and verified the human-like behavior observed in the agents. Consequently, we confirmed that the comparatively optimal behavior of agents is derived and their human-like cooperative and altruistic behavior emerges when they mildly observe others.

Keywords: Agent-based modeling · Emulation · Self-organizing maps

1 Introduction

When performing tasks, humans take measures to ensure that they are the best for accomplishing the task. However, in an environment where conditions change from one moment to another, they explore the optimal means of conducting the task at that point in time while maintaining constant awareness of the environment. In particular, when humans perform a task in a group, they observe and refer to the behavior of others and consider the optimal approach.

In recent years, studies have been actively conducted on neural networks for solving complex tasks [1–3]. Studies have also been conducted on constructing computational models by imitating the neuron and synapse structures of organisms [4–6]. However, neural networks for solving complex tasks do not necessarily have the same structure as the brain. To grasp the intelligence of organisms, it is meaningful to utilize a neural network that has the function of an organism.

Self-organizing maps (SOMs) are a type of artificial neural network (ANN) [7]. SOMs were invented by Kohonen and are mainly used in the field of data mining [8–10]. SOMs have negative characteristics from the perspective of data mining, as their storage capacity is limited and they forget learned contents, and studies to improve

© Springer Nature Switzerland AG 2019
C. Stephanidis and M. Antona (Eds.): HCII 2019, CCIS 1088, pp. 441–448, 2019.
https://doi.org/10.1007/978-3-030-30712-7_54

them are being conducted [11, 12]. Moreover, SOMs have human-like properties such as perception, memory, and forgetting of information in a finite storage capacity, and they have been used to elucidate the information processing principles of the brain [13].

We focused on the fact that memory, forgetting, and the various information perception functions of humans can be represented by an SOM, and we considered an SOM-based agent that to autonomously change its behavior while observing the behavior of others, like a human. In this study, we conduct a multi-agent simulation using an SOM-based agent on a cleanup problem consisting of a chain of tasks of picking up and disposing of garbage routinely carried out by humans, to verify the human-like behavior observed in the agents.

2   Materials and Methods

2.1   Cleanup Problem

The cleanup problem comprises a plurality of agents that aim to place garbage existing on a field into a garbage can. The agents in this problem need to perform the chain of tasks of picking-up and disposing of garbage. Moreover, as the task progresses, the garbage on the field decreases and the environment changes, making it difficult to derive the optimum behavior for the problem.

The field is a two-dimensional grid space of size $N \times N$ with the outer frame of the lattice as a wall, and N_a agents, N_g pieces of garbage, and N_{gc} garbage cans arranged in the cells. Figure 1 shows an example of a field of size 10×10, with the number of agents $N_a = 2$, the number of pieces of garbage $N_g = 10$, and the number of garbage cans $N_{gc} = 1$.

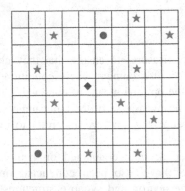

Fig. 1. Example of a cleanup problem field

2.2   SOM

SOMs are ANNs that perform unsupervised learning. The SOM consists of two layers: the input layer and the competitive layer. The competitive layer of the SOM is divided into a square lattice, with nodes arranged in each cell. In addition, each node has a vector of the same size as the number of dimensions of observation data, called a weight. The purpose of the SOM is to map a high-dimensional observation data set onto the low-dimensional space of the competitive layer. The SOM learning algorithm is shown below.

Step 1. Give the initial value $\mathbf{y}_k(0)$ to the weight of each node. Subsequently, let the learning number be $t = 1$.
Step 2. Select one data point $\mathbf{x}$ from the data set as the input vector.
Step 3. Determine the best matching unit c with the closest weight to the input vector $\mathbf{x}$ according to the following equation:

$$c = \operatorname{argmin}_k \|\mathbf{x} - \mathbf{y}_k(t-1)\|^2 \tag{1}$$

Step 4. Update the weight of each node according to the following equation:

$$\mathbf{y}_k(t) = \mathbf{y}_k(t-1) + \alpha h_{ck}\{\mathbf{x} - \mathbf{y}_k(t-1)\} \tag{2}$$

At this time, α is called the learning rate and is given as a constant. Furthermore, $h_{ck}(t)$ is called the neighbor function and is given by the following equation:

$$h_{ck} = \exp(-d_{ck}^2/2\sigma^2) \tag{3}$$

In this case, d_{ck} is the Euclidean distance between the best matching unit c and the neighbor node k. σ is called the neighborhood radius and is given as a constant. Subsequently, the learning number is made $t = t + 1$ and the process returns to Step 2 and is repeated.

2.3 SOM-Based Agents

SOM-based agents are such that, when an agent finds another agent that is performing better than itself at its target task, it observes the status and behavior of the other agent at that time, and learns the status and behavior pair based on the SOM. The SOM-based agent algorithm is shown below.

Step 1. Configure the SOM for the agent.
Step 2. Give an arbitrary initial value $\mathbf{y}_k(0)$ as the weight of each node of the SOM of the agent. Subsequently, let time $t = 1$.
Step 3. At time t, the agent observes another agent. At this time, the agent judges whether the other agent is performing better than itself at the target task.
Step 4. If the other agent is performing better, the agent observes the state and action pair $\mathbf{x} = (s_1, \cdots, s_i, a_1, \cdots a_j)$ of the other agent at that time as an input vector, and updates the weight $\mathbf{y}_k(t)$ of each node of its own SOM by Eq. (1) through Eq. (3). At this time, $\mathbf{x}$ is composed of i kinds of states $\mathbf{s} = (s_1, \cdots, s_i)$, and j kinds of actions $\mathbf{a} = (a_1, \cdots, a_j)$, where each element of state $\mathbf{s}$ is a real number, and each element of

action **a** is a binary value 0 or 1, which indicates whether the action is being performed. If the other agent is performing worse, let $\mathbf{y}_k(t) = \mathbf{y}_k(t-1)$.

By repeating these observation processes, agents autonomously learn the state and action pair at that time. Moreover, owing to the characteristics of the SOM learning, the agents gradually forget the learned state and action. Subsequently, the agent decides the action based on its own SOM according to the target task, and performs the task.

2.4 SOM-Based Agents in Cleanup Problem

The SOM-based agents in the cleanup problem decide whether to take the action of going to dispose of garbage according to their own status, adopting the action to go and pick up garbage as the basic behavior. At this time, each agent has an initial rule of "going to dispose of garbage when holding M or more pieces of garbage." In addition, the weight $\mathbf{y}_k$ of each node of the SOM of each agent is composed of a two-dimensional vector indicating whether to take the action of going to dispose of garbage and the number of pieces of garbage held, and the initial value of the weight of each node at time $t = 0$, $\mathbf{y}_k(0)$, is given by the following equation according to the initial rule:

$$\mathbf{y}_k(0) = (M, 1) \tag{4}$$

The agents behave according to the following process.

Step 1. The agent recognizes the position of garbage, agents, and walls within a radius R centered on the agent itself at time t.

Step 2. The agent decides an action based on its own rule. At this time, the agent decides on the action of going to pick up garbage when holding less than M pieces of garbage, and going to dispose of garbage when holding M or more pieces of garbage.

Step 3. Based on the recognized state and determined action, the agent outputs one of the following operations: advancing to one square out of the surrounding eight squares, picking up garbage, or disposing of garbage. However, each agent outputs an operation simultaneously, and it is not possible for two agents to pass each other or exist in the same cell. In addition, an agent cannot move to cells where garbage exists, the cell where the garbage can exists, or the wall. In the case the agent takes the action of picking up garbage, it picks up garbage when there is garbage next to it, or moves one cell in the direction of garbage when there is garbage in the field of vision of the agent but no garbage next to it. Moreover, when there is no garbage in its field of vision, the agent advances one cell in the direction of travel and searches for garbage. At this time, when unable to proceed in the direction of travel owing to an obstacle etc., the agent changes its direction of travel and advances one cell. If the agent takes the action of disposing of garbage, it discards all garbage held into the garbage can and sets the number of pieces of garbage held to 0 when there is a garbage can next to it. If there is no garbage can next to the agent, it moves one cell toward the garbage can. However, if the number of pieces of garbage held by the agent has not reached the maximum number M_{max} and there is garbage next to the agent, it picks up the garbage. At this time, when unable to proceed in the direction of travel owing to an obstacle etc., the agent changes its direction of travel and advances one cell.

Step 4. The agent updates the weight of each node of its own SOM based on the recognized state. If another agent in the field of vision of the agent disposes of more garbage than the agent, the agent observes the number of pieces of garbage held by the other agent s and a binary value a indicating whether the action of going to dispose of garbage is taken and considers them as a 2-dimensional vector $\mathbf{x} = (s, a)$. At this time, let a be 1 in the case of taking the action of going to dispose of garbage, and 0 in the case of not doing so. Thus, the agent updates the weight of each node with the observed two-dimensional vector $\mathbf{x}$ as the input vector of its own SOM, using Eq. (1) to Eq. (3). Let $\mathbf{y}_k(t) = \mathbf{y}_k(t-1)$ when another agent existing in the field of vision does not dispose of more garbage than the agent itself.

Step 5. The agent updates M for its own rule according to the following equation:

$$\mathbf{y}_k(t) = (s_k, a_k) \tag{5}$$

$$M = \sum_{k=1}^{N_{neuron}} \frac{s_k \times a_k}{\sum_{l=1}^{N_{neuron}} a_l} \tag{6}$$

At this time, N_{neuron} is the number of nodes of the SOM. Subsequently, the process returns to Step 1 with time $t = t + 1$.

2.5   Experimental Methods

In this study, we perform a multi-agent simulation using the SOM-based agent in a cleanup problem and confirm its behavior.

Simulations were performed 1,000 times, each up to 2,000 steps with learning rates of $\alpha = 0.00, \alpha = 0.01, \alpha = 0.10,$ and $\alpha = 0.50$ for the SOM of the agents. In the simulations, the unit time in which the agents act is called a step, and the average value of the number of pieces of garbage disposed of by the agents is used as the evaluation index.

Let the field be a two-dimensional grid space of size 50×50, with the number of agents $N_a = 5$, the number of pieces of garbage $N_g = 300$, and the number of garbage cans $N_{gc} = 1$. Figure 2 shows an example of the initial field arrangement. The initial arrangement of agents, garbage, and garbage cans in the field is determined by a random number for each simulation. Let the agents have a field of view $R = 5$, the maximum number of pieces of garbage held $M_{max} = 10$, and let M for the initial rule be $M = 1, 2, 3, 4, 5$. Let the SOM competition layer of SOM be of size 10×10 and a non-torus type square lattice, and let the neighborhood radius be $\sigma = 5$.

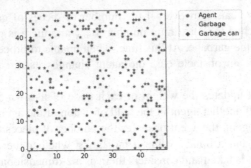

Fig. 2. Example of the initial arrangement of the field in a simulation

3 Results

Here, we describe the results of the simulation. Figures 3, 4, 5 and 6 show the transitions in the average number of pieces of garbage disposed of by each agent in the cases of agent learning rates $\alpha = 0.00, \alpha = 0.01, \alpha = 0.10,$ and $\alpha = 0.50$. Figure 7 shows the transition of the average number of pieces of garbage disposed of by all agents at each learning rate.

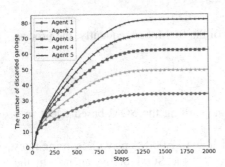

Fig. 3. Transition in the average number of pieces of garbage disposed ($\alpha = 0.00$)

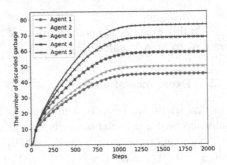

Fig. 4. Transition in the average number of pieces of garbage disposed ($\alpha = 0.01$)

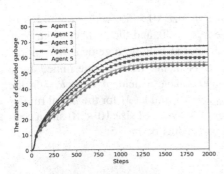

Fig. 5. Transition in the average number of pieces of garbage disposed ($\alpha = 0.10$)

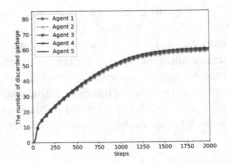

Fig. 6. Transition in the average number of pieces of garbage disposed ($\alpha = 0.50$)

4 Discussion

It can be observed from Fig. 3 that there is a difference in the number of pieces of garbage disposed of by each agent with $\alpha = 0.00$. Moreover, as shown in Fig. 6, the number of pieces of garbage disposed of by each agent is approximately the same in every step for agents with $\alpha = 0.50$. From Figs. 3, 4, 5 and 6, these results show that the agents that observe others develop cooperative behavior in contrast to agents that do not observe others.

Regarding agents with $\alpha = 0.00$, Fig. 3 shows that the agent that disposed of the most garbage at step 2,000 disposed of approximately 80 pieces of garbage. Regarding agents with $\alpha = 0.50$, Fig. 6 shows that the agent that disposed of the most garbage at step 2,000 disposed of approximately 60 pieces. From Figs. 3, 4, 5 and 6, these results show that, from the viewpoint of disposing of the most garbage, the agents that observe others dispose of fewer pieces of garbage than the agents that do not observe others. Notably, while agents observe others for the purpose of disposing of more garbage, the number of pieces of garbage disposed of is reduced by the act of observing others. Moreover, regarding agents with $\alpha = 0.00$, Fig. 3 shows that the agent that disposed of the lowest amount garbage at step 2,000 disposed of approximately 30 pieces. Regarding agents with $\alpha = 0.50$, Fig. 6 shows that the agent that disposed of the lowest amount garbage at step 2,000 disposed of approximately 60 pieces. In other words, if we refer to the number of times garbage is disposed of as the result of each agent, these results show that, while agents that do not observe others experience phenomena like a monopoly of results, agents that observe others develop the altruistic behavior of sharing outcomes with others.

From Fig. 7, it can be observed that the agents dispose of more garbage at an earlier stage in the case of $\alpha = 0.01$. This result shows that the optimal behavior in the cleanup problem of disposing of more garbage at an earlier stage is derived when the agents mildly observe others.

From the above results, it was confirmed that the comparatively optimal behavior of agents is derived and their human-like cooperative and altruistic behavior emerges when they mildly observe others in the cleanup problem.

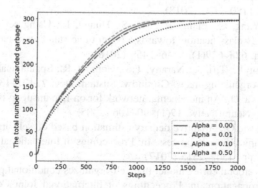

Fig. 7. Transition in the average number of pieces of garbage disposed of by all agents in the cases $\alpha = 0.00, \alpha = 0.01, \alpha = 0.10,$ and $\alpha = 0.50$.

5   Conclusion

In this study, we conducted a multi-agent simulation of a cleanup problem using an SOM-based agent that autonomously changes its behavior while observing others, and confirmed its behavior. Consequently, we confirmed that the comparatively optimal behavior of agents is derived and their human-like cooperative and altruistic behavior emerges when they mildly observe others.

In future, we will focus on the detailed behavior of the agent, and examine whether certain behavior patterns and role sharing etc. can be observed in the group.

References

1. Krizhevsky, A., Sutskever, I., Hinton, G.: ImageNet classification with deep convolutional neural networks. In: Advances in Neural Information Processing Systems 25, pp. 1097–1105 (2012)
2. Zeiler, M.D., Fergus, R.: Visualizing and understanding convolutional networks. In: Fleet, D., Pajdla, T., Schiele, B., Tuytelaars, T. (eds.) ECCV 2014. LNCS, vol. 8689, pp. 818–833. Springer, Cham (2014). https://doi.org/10.1007/978-3-319-10590-1_53
3. Kheradpisheh, S.R., Ganjtabesh, M., Thorpe, S.J.: STDP-based spiking deep convolutional neural networks for object recognition. Neural Netw. 99, 56–67 (2018)
4. Li, X., Chen, Q., Xue, F.: Biological modelling of a computational spiking neural network with neuronal avalanches. Philos. Trans. R. Soc. A Math. Phys. Eng. Sci. 375(2096), 20160286 (2017)
5. Ambroise, M., et al.: Biomimetic neural network for modifying biological dynamics during hybrid experiments. Artif. Life Robot. 22(3), 398–403 (2017)
6. Badhwar, R., Bagler, G.: Robust sigmoidal control response of *C. elegans* neuronal network. In: Polkowski, L., Yao, Y., Artiemjew, P., Ciucci, D., Liu, D., Ślęzak, D., Zielosko, B. (eds.) IJCRS 2017. LNCS (LNAI), vol. 10314, pp. 393–402. Springer, Cham (2017). https://doi.org/10.1007/978-3-319-60840-2_29
7. Kohonen, T.: Self-organizing Maps. Springer, Heidelberg (1995). https://doi.org/10.1007/978-3-642-97610-0
8. Li, Z., Bagan, H., Yamagata, Y.: Analysis of spatiotemporal land cover changes in Inner Mongolia using self-organizing map neural network and grid cells method. Sci. Total Environ. 636(15), 1180–1191 (2018)
9. Li, T., Sun, G., Yang, C., Liang, K., Ma, S., Huang, L.: Using self-organizing map for coastal water quality classification: towards a better understanding of patterns and processes. Sci. Total Environ. 628–629(1), 1446–1459 (2018)
10. Belkhiri, L., Mouni, L., Tiri, A., Narany, T.S., Nouibet, R.: Spatial analysis of groundwater quality using self-organizing maps. Groundw. Sustain. Dev. 7, 121–132 (2018)
11. Furao, S., Hasegawa, O.: An incremental network for on-line unsupervised classification and topology learning. Neural Netw. 19(1), 90–106 (2005)
12. Wang, X., Hasegawa, O.: Adaptive density estimation based on self-organizing incremental neural network using Gaussian process. In: Proceedings of International Joint Conference on Neural Networks, pp. 4309–4315 (2017)
13. Ichisugi, Y.: The cerebral cortex model that self-organizes conditional probability tables and executes belief propagation. In: Proceedings of International Joint Conference on Neural Networks, pp. 1065–1070 (2007)

Analysis of Drivers Information Requirements for Adaptive Cruise Control (ACC) Functions

Jungchul Park[(✉)]

Korea National University of Transportation, Chungju 27469, South Korea
jcpark@ut.ac.kr

Abstract. The purpose of this study is to analyze the information requirements of the driver in using the Adaptive Cruise Control (ACC). The ACC is one of the most important function of the recently developing Advanced Driver Assistance Systems (ADAS). The ergonomic design of the ADAS display is crucial for the safe use of the ACC. That is, the system should be able to visualize and present the necessary information to the driver in a suitable form and in a timely manner. This requires an analysis of the information requirements that drivers need before considering ergonomic visualization options. In this study, the information requirements of the driver using the ACC were identified and converted into variables. Then, the availability of the information and relations between the variables were determined. First, we derived the information needed by the driver from the hierarchical task analysis and expert interview, and translated them into variables. Using the classification proposed in the literature, the derived variables were classified into five types according to availability. The relations between the variables were investigated. The information requirements from this study can be used as basic data to improve the display design of ACC and to propose a new visualization concept. In addition, it is expected that the variables that are not currently measured or inferred in the present system can be used for improving the system by adding sensors and improving the performance of the inference system in the future.

Keywords: Adaptive Cruise Control · Information requirements · Advanced Driver Assistance Systems

1 Introduction

Adaptive cruise control (ACC) is one of the most important functions of the recently developing Advanced Driver Assistance Systems (ADAS). The ergonomic design of the ADAS display is crucial for the safe use of the ACC. That is, the system should be able to visualize and present the necessary information to the driver in a suitable form and in a timely manner (Stanton and Young 2005). This requires an analysis of the information requirements that drivers need before considering ergonomic visualization options.

This study aims to analyze the information requirements of the driver in using the Adaptive Cruise Control (ACC). The information needed by the driver is derived from

C. Stephanidis and M. Antona (Eds.): HCII 2019, CCIS 1088, pp. 449–452, 2019.
https://doi.org/10.1007/978-3-030-30712-7_55

hierarchical task analysis and expert interview, and is translated into variables. Then, the availability of the information and relations between the variables are determined.

2 Task Analysis

A hierarchical task analysis (Annett et al. 1971) was conducted on ACC users' tasks. A hierarchy model of driving tasks (Michon 1985) was adopted, and an existing task analysis results on typical driving tasks (Walker et al. 2015) was employed as a basis for expansion to ACC tasks. Common ACC tasks were extracted from user manuals of four different car manufacturers. Three operational tasks, i.e., 'Control vehicle speed', 'Decrease vehicle speed', and 'Follow other vehicle' were modified from the existing task analysis results. In addition, three new tasks, i.e., 'Perform control authority transition' (strategic), 'Take over after the cancellation of the ACC' (tactical), and 'Control the ACC' (operational) were added to the existing one. Figure 1 show an example of the task analysis result for 'Control the ACC' task.

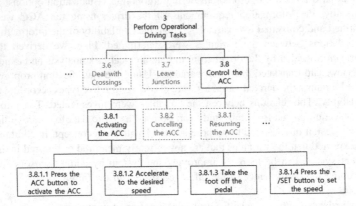

Fig. 1. An example of hierarchical task analysis for an ACC activation task.

3 Identifying the Variables and Their Relations

In order to gain insight into how the ACC system works, an expert interview was conducted with an ACC system engineer. Based on the results of the task analysis and expert interview, the information requirements of the ACC users were identified and expressed as variables. Adapting the classification proposed by Moradi-Nadimian (2002), the derived variables were classified into the following five types according to availability: (1) information obtained directly from the vehicle such as speed, acceleration, steering, etc.; (2) information from external sensors such as camera, radar, and GPS; (3) variables calculated from (1) and (2); (4) variables that are not currently measured; (5) variables that are predetermined. Table 1 shows the variables and their notations classified by the availability of the information.

Table 1. The availability of the variables.

Availability category	Variables	Notations
(1) Information obtained directly from the vehicle	Current speed	v
	Manual acceleration	a_{manual}
	Manual deceleration	b_{manual}
(2) Information from external sensors	Current gap	s
	Speed of the lead vehicle	v_x, v_y
(3) Variables calculated from (1) and (2)	Acceleration of the lead vehicle	a_x, a_y
	Effective desired minimum gap	s^*
	ACC acceleration	a_{acc}
(4) Variables that are not currently measured	Information of the cut-in vehicle	
	Information of the pedestrian	
(5) Variables that are predetermined	Desired speed	v_0
	Safe time gap	T
	Maximum acceleration	a_{max}
	Desired deceleration	$b_{desired}$
	Jam distance	s_0

Some of the variables are single variables, each of which has its own significance, while the others are multiple variables, which can be expressed through the relation between two or more variables. For the multiple variables, the causal and functional relations between the variables can be expressed as mathematical equations. The following two key equations were derived from a study on ACC design (Kesting et al. 2008).

$$a_{acc} = a_{max} \times (1 - v/v_0 - s^*/s) \tag{1}$$

$$s^* = s_0 + v \times T \tag{2}$$

The Eq. (1) describes that the acceleration by the ACC, proportional to maximum acceleration, is determined by the ratio of the current and the desired speed. However, it is also affected by the ratio of the current and the desired distance from the lead vehicle. The Eq. (2) shows how the desired distance is determined by the minimum jam distance (set by the driver), the current speed of the user vehicle, and safe time gap.

Some of the variables in Table 1 are displayed on the vehicle instrument panels and ADAS displays, but the other variables and their relations are not. They can be considered to be included in future displays to enhance users' understanding of the system and the awareness of the situation.

4 Conclusion

This study analyzed the information requirements from hierarchical task analysis and expert interview. The information was defined as variables and their availability and the relations between them were identified. The information requirements from this study can be used as basic data to improve the display design of ACC and to propose a new visualization concept. It is also expected that the variables that are not currently measured or inferred in the present system can be used for improving the system with the addition of sensors and improvement in the performance of the inference system in the future.

Acknowledgements. This research was supported by Basic Science Research Program through the National Research Foundation of Korea (NRF) funded by the Ministry of Education (NRF-2016R1D1A1B03933470).

References

Annett, J., Duncan, K.D., Stammers, R.B., Gray, M.J.: Task Analysis. Department of Employment Training Information Paper 6. HSMO, London (1971)

Kesting, A., Treiber, M., Schönhof, M., Helbing, D.: Adaptive cruise control design for active congestion avoidance. Transp. Res. Part C **16**, 668–683 (2008)

Michon, J.A.: A critical view of driver behavior models: what do we know, what should we do? In: Evans, L., Schwing, R.C. (eds.) Human Behavior and Traffic Safety, pp. 485–520. Plenum Press, New York (1985)

Moradi-Nadimian, R., Griffiths, S.A., Burns, C.M.: Ecological interface design in aviation domains: work domain analysis and instrumentation availability on the Harvard aircraft. In: Proceedings of the 46th Annual Meeting of the Human Factors and Ergonomics Society, pp. 116–120 (2002)

Stanton, N.A., Young, M.S.: Driver behavior with adaptive cruise control. Ergonomics **15**(48), 1294–1313 (2005)

Walker, G.H., Stanton, N.A., Salmon, P.M.: Human Factors in Automotive Engineering and Technology. Ashgate, Farnham (2015)

Passenger Experience Revisited: In Commercial Aircraft Cabin Design and Operations' Sights

Xinye Zhong[✉] and Ting Han

Shanghai Jiao Tong University, Shanghai, People's Republic of China
{Judy_zhongxy, hanting}@sjtu.edu.cn

Abstract. In recent years, Communication and transportation are more frequent owing to globalization. Civil aviation transportation are experiencing rapid growth. However, the competition among airways are getting more fierce and complicated, traditional operation methods are faced with challenges. The definition of passenger experience isn't simple, which not only contains user comfort, but also contains passenger psychology, balance of value and comfort, and service etc. This study revisits passenger experience in the views of human needs, cabin design and operations. By collecting and summarizing research results, builds the passenger experience model in cabin design and operations' sights.

Keywords: Passenger experience · Passenger comfort · Cabin design · Passenger segmentation · Commercial aircraft operation · Passenger experience model

1 Introduction

Owing to the rapid growth of civil aviation transportation around the world, an increasing number of people tend to choose aircraft to travel. However, this potential market isn't always a good sign to airways, the demands of passengers are also changing rapidly, which could be more diversified and difficult to handle. The competition among airways are getting more fierce and complicated, traditional operation methods are faced with challenges. Spending as much as possible to upgrade passengers comfort during flight might no longer be a totally right direction when designers and operators making decisions, they have to weigh on passenger needs and costs, even satisfy "mean" but "tough" clients. Oancea [1] finds that in recent years many airlines seem to restore profitability to focus on economy class, traditional first class somehow have lost their attractiveness to the market, then set the opinion that the operations of first class should be redefined to attract clients.

Passenger experience could be one of the essential issues for people to choose airlines. In the past several years, the concept of Dream liner from Boeing (Fig. 1) has been paid great attention by the public around the world. Although it can be likely regarded as an advertise strategy, it still paid off in the new series of Boeing products and forecasts a tendency of upgrading passenger experience throughout the whole civil aviation industry. Moreover, as the internet technology and related market are

© Springer Nature Switzerland AG 2019
C. Stephanidis and M. Antona (Eds.): HCII 2019, CCIS 1088, pp. 453–462, 2019.
https://doi.org/10.1007/978-3-030-30712-7_56

becoming more widespread and mature, more online services can be provided on board, passenger experience during air travel could be completely different.

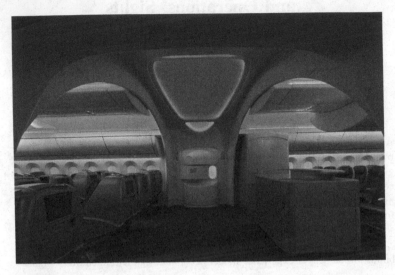

Fig. 1. Boeing's concept of Dream Liner (Source: http://teague.com/work/a-job)

Upgrading passenger experience is ambitious and meaningful, however, this issue is also faced with new challenges. Modern life mode and communication among cultures somehow influence diversity of passenger demands and passenger's preservation of comfort. Nowadays, people are not that easily satisfied with previous cabin facilities and services, and they tend to care more about individual choices and costs at the same time; Meanwhile, as more and more passengers from different backgrounds choose air travel, demands might be harder to satisfy, misunderstanding also exists.

The target population are also changing rapidly. In China, the development of aviation transportation is highly supported, many cities and towns are having their new airports and commercial air commuting systems, which will give more travel opportunity to located people in a short future. In the meantime, many new passengers who aren't quite familiar with air travel may be harder to enjoy the trip during the flight. According to Wang and Li [2], passengers who experienced a lot in air travel are more likely to stay calm during the flight or even come across unusual situations, which means passengers who lack of air travel experience are more likely to be trapped with negative emotions. On the other hand, in foreign countries, the U.S., for example, Cho and Min [3] found that passenger characteristics has significantly changed in 10 years (2005–2015) by examining longitudinal changes of passengers with low-cost carriers (LCCs) and legacy carriers (or non-LCCs).

We explain a brief life cycle of a product and how passenger experience related to it (Fig. 2). Even as complicated as commercial aircraft project, the process is still similar. Developing an aircraft would experience several steps like concept design, detailed design, manufacturing, sales, operation, and finally obsolete after decades or even longer. During this process, it would be modified many times according to feedback from sales and customers. If the value of user experience needs to be improved, everyone should notice it's a challenge of combining different systems.

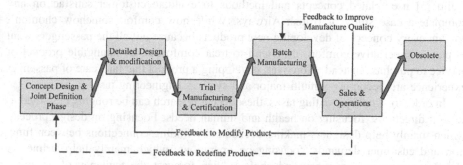

Fig. 2. A brief life cycle of a product - commercial aircraft

2 Passenger Experience

Consideration of passenger experience should be assimilated into aircraft's life cycle in order to make the product greater. Customer's feedback of experience on board easily influences sales and operations. If operation methods couldn't solve problems well, the negative feedback may push airlines and OEMs (original equipment manufacturer) to modify cabin design and facilities. In order to treat customer more effectively, customized refitting service which helps airlines to put their own needs into reality is another way (Fig. 3).

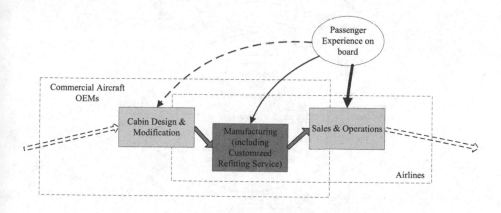

Fig. 3. Passenger experience related to commercial aircraft's life cycle

Passenger experience isn't a new field, some researchers define issues relate to passenger experience as comfort. Passenger comfort on board has been discussed over decades. It's widely known that passenger comfort should be taken seriously because a lower rating can make passengers not want to fly again. And now the research of passenger experience, i.e. passenger comfort, has benefited a lot in improving air transportation industry. Budd, Warren and Bell [4] give passenger health advice after a study of promoting passenger comfort and wellbeing during the flight; Nicolini and Salini [5] use related concepts and methods to evaluate customer satisfaction and complete a case study of British Airways. While now comfort somehow chouldn't contain every concern of developing new products because not all the passengers want to pursue superlative comfort, they tend to treat comfort as an intangible product or service to purchase instead. Moreover, developing a product that take care of passenger experience are becoming a multi-major and systems engineering task.

In order to simplify existing tasks, these recent research can be roughly classified as several directions: focusing on health and human needs; Focusing on design process, which mainly help designers making decisions by finding connections between function and customer demands; focusing on operations, which mainly help airlines to observe passengers' reactions and choices, then forecast the tendency of air transportation market.

2.1   Factors Related to Human Needs

Recent study of passenger needs contains knowledge of medical science, psychology, social science, culture and etc. Although this is a cross-over issue, researchers are creating models to identify and explain it. For example, Patel and D'Cruz [6] suggest that passenger comfort contains internal factors and external factors, and create a new model of aircraft passengers' comfort by collecting and summarizing recent research results (Fig. 4).

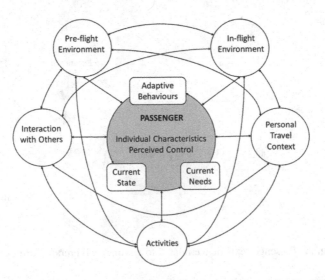

Fig. 4. Model of key factors which influence aircraft passengers' comfort (Source: [6])

On the other hand, increasing kinds of design focus on children, mom with enfants, elder or disabled people. Barrier-free design also can be seen on new series of commercial aircrafts.

In the meantime, several specific situations are also put under the spotlight, negative symptoms like dizzy, tinnitus, negative emotions like irritability, anxiety, etc. Lindseth [7] claimed that flight anxiety of student pilots were identified, while Li, Li, Wang et al. [8] observe the situation of passengers flight anxiety are also exist by collecting and analyzing more than 2500 questionnaires. Ren and Tang [9] examined group emergency events especially air-passengers who come across delays become irritable and even influence others to escalate the situation, in order to prevent or at least reduce negative impacts like the serious social and economic losses and even casualties.

2.2   Factors Related to Product Functions and Operations

Finding factors related to products means finding customer demands and product design and engineering, which would be a gap in practical application. Ahmadpour, Robert, Lindgaard [10] create a comfort model of passengers' emotions in the base of the emotion model by Ortony, Clore, and Collins (OCC), which connect cabin design factors with human fundamental needs (Fig. 5). In this case, they are searching links between demands and design process.

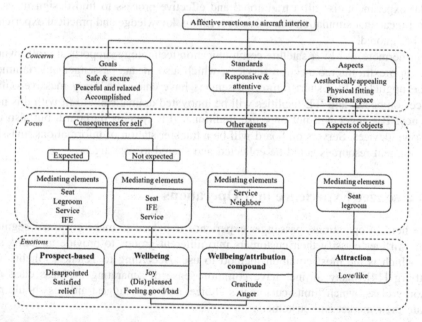

Fig. 5. The cognitive structure of passengers' emotions in relation to comfort, illustrating the appraisal patterns of passengers' affective reactions to the aircraft interior during the flight (adopting and revising the cognitive structure of emotions by Ortony, Clore, and Collins, 1988). (Source: [10])

3 Passenger Experience and Cabin Design

In passenger experience related to cabin design process, designers from different majors are getting together to complete a design project. According to the results above, cabin design process can be roughly concluded as these factors below:

- Seats
- Cabin Configuration & fundamental facilities
- Environment control
- IFE(In-flight entertainment) facilities
- Aesthetic design
- ...

There are many methods to cope with these factors. For example, In design related to ergonomics, Vink, Bazley, Kamp, Blok [11] find that some design factors such as legroom, seat, personal space are clearly related to passenger comfort; Furthermore, recently there are many programs to simulate real situation, such as JACK, RAMSIS and etc., could help designer improve design quality.

In cabin configuration, Delcea, Cotfas, Crăciun and Molanescu [12] simulate several different boarding methods to find out the most effective method; In design related to environment, Pang, Li, Bai, Liu, Zhou, Yao [13] simulate airflow feature of different cabin structures and find relatively reasonable design. Moreover, new simulation tools can be used to improve design effectiveness, but making real shape model to take experiments is still a traditional and effective process to find design flaws. It doesn't mean that simulation can solve everything, knowledge and practical experience can't be ignored.

Furthermore, Wi-Fi & satellite communication technology supports aircraft owners to develop extra interconnection services, which also means passenger entertainment can be upgraded. In a short future, passengers have chance to enjoy massive online services on board, and IFE facilities will be innovated dramatically to fit with this new tendency. Passenger will not only use traditional IFE systems on board, but also use their own devices. Servers on board will be a transfer station of informations, massive entertainment resources could be collected and shared to passengers.

4 Passenger Experience and Operations

In the field of operations, passenger experience is helped to make customer segmentation. Airlines classify their customers into different groups to provide targeting service, which is the most common method to use. According to Teichert, Shehu, von Wartburg [14], many airlines have common sense of separating business class and economy class, which limits customer's choice, and they suggest airlines should reevaluate their market and customers.

In recent years, an powerful support of defining customers' needs is using big data analysis. For example, Gong, Pu, Zhang, Wu [15] uses the K-means clustering method to analyze passenger segmentation, and finally bring out targeting service packages. Those packages can be consisted by giving passenger different services, entertainment devices, more luggage rooms, or more extra food or drinks, etc. Nowadays, although it's common for airlines to take focus on passenger value, the research still shows the tendency of caring more about passenger experience, which shows modern passengers tend to be keen on choosing what they want, and airlines can also benefit from this mode. Many airlines use strategies like selling seats which have more legroom, selling luggage room through extra payment, etc. As internet technology available to use, more online services and new forms of online activities could be improved, which would be more attractive and valuable to young people.

According to the results above, operation process can be roughly concluded as these factors below:

- Service
- Commodity (Food, Drinks…) supplies
- Personal/organized entertainment activities
- Extended Service based on Facilities
- …

Meanwhile, in design and marketing fields, there are researchers use customer portrait, Application of Scenario, etc., to verify customer demands and the strategy of products. Liu, Jiang, Li [16] define customer demands by designing and simulating an almost real scene of customer using target products. This kind of method can more or less be seen in some commercial aircraft passenger studies, but still has lots of unknown areas to be explored.

5 A New Model of Passenger Experience

In the sight of a life cycle of commercial aircraft, connection between cabin design and operations need to be determined for improving passenger experience. We combine these points above to recreate a model of passenger experience (Fig. 6).

This model depicts the relationship among passenger experience on board, cabin design and operations, in which user-centric idea is conveyed. We classify passenger experience as physical needs and mental needs, by corresponding those points to design factors and operation factors, revisit the definition of passenger experience.

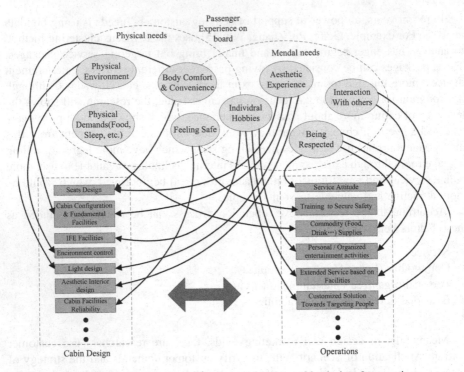

Fig. 6. Model of passenger experience related to cabin design & operations

6   Conclusions

Passenger experience of commercial aircraft could be a long-time issue to be discussed. In this study we review the previous fundamental research which may be related to passenger experience, some research defined experience as passenger comfort. In the previous years, researchers has observed a lot of valuable results, and several kinds of comfort models have been built.

Then we explain the brief life cycle of a product and how passenger experience related to it. In this study we noticed that if the value of user experience needs to be improved, definitely it's an issue of combining different systems. In this case, we try to take a look at passenger experience issue by two sights: cabin design and operations.

The first step is to take focus on human fundamental needs. Several researchers use questionnaire and comfort model to define passenger comfort, while some other researchers use physical and psychological methods to find potential needs. These results contribute to the fundamental definition of passenger experience.

The second step is to find the relationship between human needs and design methods, which is the design sight. In cabin design, researchers and designers use different tools to make their products more comfortable and attractive. Several new tools are used to assist design process, such as environment simulation, 3D human body modeling, which may help designers more ergonomic design works. As the feedback turns out to be clear and convincible, designers are forced to think more effective design to improve functions or fill flaws.

The third step is to observe how the design performs in operations, which is the operations sight. Airways use big data to forecast passengers needs and how they perform. In this case, Passenger segmentation methods are considered, researchers analyse thousands of passengers to find out similarities and diversities. In recent years, increasing amount of research results show that passengers tend to care more about their personnalites, experiences and value than previous times, young passengers are more sensitive to costs so that they tend to choose less comfortable but cheap travels, etc. Passenger value is also a strength point to be mentioned, operators should weigh on balance. Nowadays, airways put more attention to improving their corporation images. Stylized and targeting cabin design could be more helpful to create a good image in passenger's minds and also comfort passengers. Meanwhile, passenger experience and demands are influencing cabin design, operation costs, customer value, in-flight services, potential incomes, etc. Which means both designers and operators should focus on the same issue to weigh on passenger comfort and restrictions.

Finally, we combine these points above to recreate a model of passenger experience, in which cabin design and operations are taken into consideration.

Although the new model has been created, we know that there are so many research results that still not be included in this study. This direction has a lot of unknown area which need to take long time to study further. The gap between design and operations of passenger experience still remains, and we notice that there's unknown knowledge which needs to explore.

References

1. Oancea, O.: Challenges of pricing luxury in commercial aviation–will first class disappear? J. Revenue Pricing Manag. **17**(4), 296–300 (2018)
2. 王悦颐, 李敬强: 基于SCSQ和STAI的航空旅客旅行中出现的焦虑问题研究. 职业与健康 **32**(22), 3083–3087 (2016)
3. Cho, W., Min, D.-J.: Longitudinal examination of passenger characteristics among airline types. J. Air Transp. Manag. **72**, 11–19 (2018)
4. Budd, L., Warren, A.P., Bell, M.: Promoting passenger comfort and wellbeing in the air: an examination of the in-fight health advice provided by international airlines. J. Air Transp. Manag. **17**(5), 320–322 (2011)
5. Nicolini, G., Salini, S.: Customer satisfaction in the airline industry: the case of british airways. Qual. Reliab. Eng. Int. **22**, 581–589 (2006)
6. Patel, H., D'Cruz, M.: Passenger-centric factors influencing the experience of aircraft comfort. Transp. Rev. **38**(2), 252–269 (2018)
7. Lindseth, P.D.: Flight anxiety: predictors and implications for learning. J. Aviat./Aerosp. Educ. Res. **4**(3), 5 (1994)
8. 李敬强, et al.: 航空旅客焦虑情绪特征调查与分析. 中国公共卫生 1–4 (2018)
9. 任新惠, 唐诗琦: 基于情绪感染测量的群体性事件形成机理. 安全与环境学报 **18**(03), 1059–1064 (2018)

10. Ahmadpour, N., Robert, J.-M., Lindgaard, G.: Exploring the cognitive structure of aircraft passengers' emotions in relation to their comfort experience. In: International Conference on Kansei Engineering and Emotion Research, pp. 387–394 (2014)

11. Vink, P., Bazley, C., Kamp, I., Blok, M.: Appl. Ergon. **43**, 354–359 (2012)

12. Delcea, C., Cotfas, L.-A., Crăciun, L., Molanescu, A.G.: Are seat and aisle interferences affecting the overall airplane boarding time? An agent-based approach. Sustainability **10**, 4217 (2018). https://doi.org/10.3390/su10114217

13. Pang, L., et al.: Optimization of air distribution mode coupled interior design for civil aircraft cabin. Build. Environ. **134**, 131–145 (2018)

14. Teichert, T., Shehu, E., von Wartburg, I.: Customer segmentation revisited: the case of the airline industry. Transp. Res. Part A **42**, 227–242 (2006)

15. 刘兰兰, et al.: 情境故事法在产品设计开发中的应用. 包装工程(12), 233–235 (2007)

16. 龚婷, et al.: 基于K-means的航空旅客聚类研究. 价值工程 **37**(35), 52–54 (2018)

Author Index

Printed in the United States
By Bookmasters